Give Me the Money and I'll Shoot

Finance Your Factual TV/Film Project

methuen | drama

Bloomsbury Publishing Plc

1 3 5 7 9 10 8 6 4 2

First published in 2012

Bloomsbury Publishing Plc
50 Bedford Square
London WC1B 3DP
www.bloomsbury.com

Copyright © Nicola Lees 2012

Available in the USA from Bloomsbury Academic & Professional,
175 Fifth Avenue/3rd Floor, New York, NY 10010.
www.BloomsburyAcademicUSA.com

A CIP catalogue record for this book is available from the British Library

ISBN: 978 1 408 13296 8

Typeset by Margaret Brain
Printed in the UK by MPG Books Ltd, Bodmin, Cornwall

Give Me the Money and I'll Shoot

Finance Your Factual TV/Film Project

Nicola Lees

methuen | drama

Contents

PART I: The Idea

PART II: The Funding

PART III: The Reality

Acknowledgments

Thank you to everyone on both sides of the Atlantic who helped me research and write this book: S. J. Cohen, Peter Hamilton and Fernanda Rossi, who encouraged me through the early stages; Kate Kinninmont at Women in Film and Television, London for her ongoing support; Charlie Phillips at Sheffield Doc/Fest and Ian Wyatt at the Indie Training Fund for their help with research and contacts; Danielle Butler, Uli Hesse, Charlotte Fisher and Claudia Sermbezis for their constructive reader feedback and Tatiana Bacchus and Fanta Jarjussey for being my Twitter cheerleaders. A special thank you goes to the TVMole subscribers who responded so enthusiastically to a call for case studies. I'm especially grateful to those who generously allowed me to reprint their proposals: Dan Edelstyn for *How to Re-Establish a Vodka Empire*; Kat Mansoor for *Here's Johnny*, Hilary Durman for *Donor Unknown* and Jilann Spitzmiller and Hank Rogerson for *Shakespeare Behind Bars*. I'm also indebted to Bucy McDonald and Jeremy Neech for their creative input to the cover. Huge thanks are due to everyone who so candidly shared their experiences and insights with me so that I may share them with you. And finally, thank you to Blondie and Mumford & Sons for providing the soundtrack.

Disclaimer

The information and resources included in this book are designed to illustrate the wide range of funding options open to you as a TV producer or independent filmmaker and to help you identify the most appropriate funding partners for you and your project. The list of resources is by no means comprehensive and inclusion implies neither endorsement nor recommendation. Due diligence should be exercised when considering any source of financial agreement. There are many complex rules and regulations relating to film and TV finance, which are different in every country and subject to change, so before entering into any contract you are strongly advised to consult an experienced entertainment lawyer or business affairs executive who can advise you on your specific situation.

Copyright

I don't care where the money comes from, as long as it's not drug money!

—John Landis, Director

Introduction
(and a word of warning)

> *Most documentary filmmakers are polygamous—they marry more than one funder. They have to in order to get the film made.*
>
> —Prenup.org

Inside Job, an Oscar-winning documentary that investigates the cause of the global financial crash, was released in 2010—the year I began researching this book. The events outlined in the documentary, and the resulting global recession, brought a period of enormous change to the TV and documentary industry and, since I started writing, a number of events have further affected, directly or indirectly, the funding of film and television projects. In the UK alone, the British government has become a coalition; product placement is now legal on TV; the UK Film Council has been axed and the Screen Agencies restructured; Teachers TV Channel folded (but teachers rallied to download and save 4,000 videos); a new documentary Enterprise Investment Scheme has launched; Rupert Murdoch staged a takeover bid for BSkyB (thwarted by a phone-hacking scandal); *Big Brother* was canceled after a decade on Channel 4 and resurrected on Channel 5 (after the channel was bought by Richard Desmond, a tabloid newspaper magnate); the first 3D TV programs were transmitted; umpteen commissioning editors changed jobs (some to commissioning roles at different channels, some to go back into production and one to set up her own technology start-up); Channel 4 and Channel 5 introduced advertiser-funded-only slots in their schedules; Sheffield Doc/Fest launched a Crowdfunding Pitch; and as I write this I can see a plume of smoke over north London close to where rioting looters burned down a warehouse and destroyed the entire DVD stock of several independent documentary distributors, including Dogwoof, Peccadillo, Arrow and New Wave. Elsewhere, a deadly earthquake destroyed Canterbury Television in Christchurch, New Zealand; the Icelandic volcano Eyjafjallajökull grounded flights bound for the Cannes Film Festival; a tsunami destroyed part of Japan and caused a run on tape stock; and the USA's credit rating was downgraded.

Amid this global chaos and increased competition from hundreds of new channels, TV and documentary budgets have shrunk considerably. It's been reported that TV producers currently have to cover broadcaster funding shortfalls of 5–60 percent and 85 percent of producers think that the gap in their budgets is going to get worse. I gave this book the title *Give Me Money and I'll Shoot* partly because it amused me, but also because it seemed to appropriately express the frustration felt by the growing number of TV producers and independent filmmakers who are desperately trying to get someone to fund their project before they lose access to their story or have to remortgage their house. I started out with the intention of writing an accessible directory to the various types of funding available to TV producers and independent filmmakers, but as the funding landscape continues to change so rapidly, it is impossible to write a definitive guide. Therefore what I've done instead is to identify the key types of funders in Europe, North America and beyond and analyze their motivation for funding TV programs and films. Once you know and understand what a certain *type* of funder is looking for, you can plan an effective funding strategy that will work for you and your film wherever you are in the world and regardless of whether the specific funding organizations mentioned are still in existence by the time you read this book. What you will learn is that in order to secure funding you need to work out not what you want from a funder, but what a funder wants from *you*.

To successfully pitch ideas you have to be part trend-spotter, part copywriter and part market researcher. To fund your project you have to be all of those things plus a grant writer, negotiator, campaigner, internet marketing expert, and even onscreen talent (more of this in the Crowdfunding chapter). To help you, I've distilled advice from more than forty advertising executives, online marketing gurus, grant writers, multi-award-winning producers and entertainment lawyers. I also share what I've learned from working in factual TV production and development for more than a decade, during which time I've successfully pitched lifestyle formats and science and history documentaries to network and cable channels in the UK and USA. Many of those programs couldn't have been made without co-production money, product placement, prop placement, foundation grants or crowdfunding.

However, for you to be truly successful in your future fundraising efforts, this book must be read in conjunction with some real-world activity. All commissioning, and therefore funding, is dependent on personal relationships. If you don't have an existing relationship with someone who has the means to fund your project it is much more difficult, if not impossible, to get them to part with their cash. Start nurturing relationships with the people you might need to approach for funding long before you actually need to ask for money, whether they be commissioning editors, distributors, or that wealthy uncle you haven't spoken to for years.

While researching this book, I unearthed some fascinating funding stories that variously involved a punk rock icon turned Grail hunter, a Russian oil baron, a Ukrainian vodka factory, an Alaskan fishing village and a film made by advertising executives but funded entirely by Twitter. What all these stories taught me is that there is no blueprint for funding a TV program, and that there are as many ways to fund a film as there are films. However, by the end of the book you will have an overview of all the different kinds of funding available to you, and understand the pros and cons of each.

We'll explore ten different sorts of funding, from the traditional TV channel commission to more complex finance deals involving distributors and investors, through to the traditional mainstays of the independent filmmaker, film funds and grants. We'll also look at emerging models such as advertiser funded programming and crowdfunding. As we move through the different chapters I'll introduce you to each type of funder, offer some pitching tips and, where appropriate, give you examples of written applications.

This book is not designed to help you locate specific funders, like *The Directory of Grant Making Trusts* might; nor is it attempting to guide you through the legal labyrinth of contract negotiations or the finer points of distribution agreements like Mark Litwak's *Deal Making in the Film and Television Industry*. Rather, this book does what few of these specialist texts do: it explains *how* to make an application for funding; what to write in your proposal and how to adapt and tweak your application to appeal to different kinds of funders, from TV executives to internet-surfing strangers. At the end of each chapter there is a list of useful resources such as books, directories and websites where you can explore each source of funding in more detail.

If you are considering setting up an international treaty co-production for the first time, or are thinking of approaching an angel investor—or entering into any other sort of contract or agreement—I strongly urge you to consult a specialist in the field to advise you on your specific circumstances, for I am no entertainment lawyer or business affairs expert.

The book is arranged into three parts:

- **Part I: The Idea**—How to prepare your idea and proposal so you are optimally prepared to pitch to funders
- **Part II: The Funding**—An overview of ten different sorts of funders, starting with those most suited to TV series and established filmmakers, and ending with those funding methods more suitable for independent filmmakers and those making their first film. A glossary or 'Jargon Busting' section appears towards the end of each chapter
- **Part III: The Reality**—Buyers of all kinds explain what they are looking for in a proposal and producers share their funding war stories

I hope this book will help clarify some of the complexity around funding and give you the inspiration to capitalize on the inherent chaos. However, before we continue, I should warn you: an unexpected consequence of researching and writing this book is that I've become the funder of several films. This was not planned and I take no responsibility should you too be sucked into donating, investing, volunteering or otherwise supporting a project that catches your eye while visiting suggested websites.

Give Me the Money and I'll Shoot! is proud to have supported:

Via the filmmaker's website	USD	GBP
1 Second Film—one-second animation	$10.50	
Age of Stupid—feature documentary		£50
Foreign Letters—fiction feature	$100	
How to Re-Establish a Vodka Empire—feature documentary		£50
Lemonade: Detroit—feature documentary	$24	
Strange Powers: Stephin Merritt and the Magnetic Fields—feature documentary	$30	
The Red Robin—fiction feature	$25	
Via IndieGoGo		
Married and Counting—feature documentary	$30	
Still Dreaming—feature documentary	$25	
Via Kickstarter		
Dying to Do Letterman—Oscar campaign for feature documentary	$25	
Porches—documentary TV series	$50	
(the crowdfunding campaign was unsuccessful on this occasion)		

$319.50 + £100

PART I:
The Idea

Getting Ready

> ❝ *Not all stories are ready to be told.*
>
> —Cheryl A. Clarke (grant writer)

As you are reading this book, I assume you already have a TV show or documentary that you want to pitch to funders. Resist the temptation to skip straight to the funding chapters because no matter how many broadcasters, brands, grant-making foundations or distributors you approach, if you can't fully articulate your idea in a way that a potential funder can understand, they won't give you money.

According to Hot Docs Forum and Market Director Elizabeth Radshaw, who has seen hundreds of filmmakers pitch to funders, the most successful pitches are those in which "the filmmaker has decided what they want to achieve before they even open their mouth: they know what their goals are and they know exactly who they are pitching to, what their pitchee has at stake. They have really thought about their audience and they realize that the funder is not just buying into the pitch they are about to give but they are buying into the individual, the company that stands behind them." Having all of that worked out before you step up to pitch gives you an immediate advantage in an extremely competitive marketplace. In fact, Elizabeth goes so far as to say that a filmmaker's actual pitch doesn't matter: "It's the preparation they do up ahead by asking themselves why are they making this film? Why are they doing it now? Why are *they* doing it? Who is their audience and why should the audience care? With that knowledge they can just tell their story; they don't have to say, 'This is why the audience should care'—it will just come up, and when they get those hard questions they will have the answer."

Another reason to thoroughly develop your idea is that you will be less susceptible to being swayed from your vision as you seek funding. Tom Ziessen, Public Engagement Advisor at the Wellcome Trust in London, will sometimes make suggestions to filmmakers who are applying for grants. "We might say, 'This doesn't work for us but if you did it like this, it would.' But I think the danger is that you are pushing someone to make something that isn't really their vision, and this is true of any money, I guess. As a filmmaker, you want to make sure you don't take any money that will mean that you have to change your project."

So before we meet the funders, we should take some time to explore whether your idea is actually *ready* to pitch and build the foundation of a great funding strategy. The work starts long before you even pick up a camera; it involves developing the idea into a workable proposal, constructing a compelling pitch, calculating a realistic budget and schedule, and planning a funding strategy. Skimp on any of these steps and you put your project at risk; by examining your idea from all angles at inception, and at regular intervals throughout the development process, you can spot and remedy any weaknesses. You'll also be better able to target funders that are a good match for your material, achieve a better hit rate and be able to concentrate your energy on making your film rather than perpetually chasing funding.

There isn't space to fully explain how to develop an idea into a commercially viable (by which I mean fundable) TV program or documentary idea; instead I'll give you a list of key elements to consider that will help you get your idea pitch ready. (The companion to this book, *Greenlit: Developing Factual/Reality TV Ideas from Concept to Pitch*, gives a more in-depth step-by-step guide to the whole development process—from originating ideas, developing the format, attaching talent and running a pitch meeting—and explains how the international TV industry works.) I've spent more than a decade developing and pitching science, history and lifestyle TV programs to a range of network and cable channels in the UK and USA. I've also interviewed dozens of international channel executives and asked them what they like, and more importantly, don't like in a pitch. The questions that follow are commonly asked by commissioning executives and other funders and often poorly answered by filmmakers.

What's the Story?

The key to any pitch, and any film or TV project, is the story. One of commissioning editors' biggest irritations (after program makers who proudly exclaim, "Oh, I don't watch TV!") is reading proposals that outline at great length the importance of raising awareness of climate change or human rights abuses, or listening to program makers who describe their detailed research without mentioning what the actual *story* is. The buyer needs to understand the "who," "what," "where," "why," "when," and "how" of the film, the beginning, middle, and end of the narrative, alongside a description of locations, characters or scenes that allows the buyer to "see" in their mind's eye what the audience would see.

The most successful documentaries (commercially and critically), such as *Man on Wire*, or *Touching the Void*, *The Cove* and *Senna*, all have a strong narrative, with a clear beginning, middle and end, and heroic/charismatic characters who embark on some kind of physical or emotional journey full of real jeopardy. It's no accident that these same elements are found in successful Hollywood films.

On the other hand, and to their disadvantage, issue-driven films tend to have a narrative driven by the subject rather than strong and compelling characters. Writing in *The Times* newspaper, journalist Kevin Maher noted that, "eco-documentaries ... are being made by impassioned experts who are devoted to their cause, but are mostly lacking in all but the most rudimentary movie-making skills ... and push us closer to the day when all documentaries will feature angry people telling us we're all going to die." Deferred real world jeopardy (the bees are dying, the ice is melting   we're all doomed) doesn't make for such a good night out at the movies. "At the end of the day, we the audience are coming for drama, for illumination, to be moved and entertained. To shame us for being in more fortunate situations than others is not a filmmaker's job," wrote film critic Shlomo Porath, in *Writing in Midnightcast*, but "many documentaries pretend that we'll become better people if we're sufficiently shocked and depressed." And spare a thought for the poor buyers who travel the globe looking for films to acquire: "Every day you watch 7–10 documentaries mainly dealing with the sadness and misfortunes of the world. You feel physical exhaustion in your body. You become dizzy, confused, even worried," wrote Steffen Moestrup, a Danish journalist of his experience at the Thessaloniki Documentary Festival. If you really care about raising awareness of an issue beyond its existing supporters, I urge you to find a compelling story to tell, and let the issue inform rather than drive the narrative.

Many beginner filmmakers baulk at having to write down or describe their narrative, because the story "hasn't happened yet." Although TV commissioning editors and other film funders fully understand that the film will evolve during filming and post-production, they need to have enough information about the story to make a decision about whether it is a film on which they want to spend thousands of dollars. It's perfectly acceptable to end your proposal with a question if you don't know the outcome, for example, "After months of searching, how will Abigail react when she comes face-to-face with the woman who abandoned her at birth?"

Why Does Your Story Deserve to Be Told Now?

Just because *you* think a story deserves to be told doesn't mean that funders will. Commissioners and other buyers need a reason to fund your project—either because the subject of your film is something they are passionate about, because it's a topical subject that has currency in the current market, because you have a newsworthy angle on a familiar story or a unique format that taps into the zeitgeist, or because your proposal fulfills some other unspoken need, such as a scheduling problem.

In my very first pitch, a one-off documentary for BBC4/TLC, I had a very compelling reason to tell the story. *The Guinea Pig Club* was the story of a group of World War II pilots who had been shot down and were terribly disfigured by facial burns. While undergoing years of plastic surgery, they formed a drinking club and, through good times and bad, the fraternity lasted for sixty years. Every year they held a reunion dinner where they drank, danced and reminisced. When I happened across the story, the Guinea Pigs, who were by then in their eighties, had decided that as their numbers were dwindling rapidly year on year, it was getting too sad to meet. The fact that their next reunion would be their last was a compelling reason to film it: if the occasion weren't recorded for posterity, the opportunity would be lost forever. That idea was commissioned by the BBC within a week and was the second fastest commission I ever had. (My fastest commission had little to do with the idea—which was about surgeons working aboard a hospital ship moored off the coast of Sierra Leone—and everything to do with it solving a problem for the commissioning channel, BBC3. They had an "Africa Season" planned and one of their films had fallen through at the last minute. My idea was set in the right geographical area and pitched at precisely the right time to fill the gap and so was commissioned overnight.)

Alastair Fothergill, producer of the BBC's blue-chip natural history series *Frozen Planet*, which focuses on the wildlife of the polar regions, said he "wanted to do it now because those regions are changing very fast. No one else will have the resources to do anything similar for a long time and when they do, the landscape will have changed a lot." In other words, "this is the last chance." No one likes to miss the last chance to do something, so it's a powerful argument to use in a pitch.

Conversely, "I've read grant applications that start off, 'I am thinking of making a film about the secret lives of moths. What do you think?'" says US grant maker Carole Lee Dean. "The filmmaker's lack of confidence and commitment to the project makes me (along with every other funder I know) nervous enough to pass."

Having absolute belief in *why* your story needs to be told instills confidence in potential buyers.

Is Film or TV the Best Medium for Your Story?

It is time-consuming and expensive to make a documentary film or TV series. If you want to raise awareness about an issue you should ask yourself whether it's really worth making a film. Might it be quicker, cheaper and have greater impact as a photo essay, magazine feature or book? Not all stories lend themselves to film. By its very nature film demands that there is something to see; a successful film is visually interesting, with lots of action to follow. If your story will be told through a series of talking heads consider making a radio documentary instead, or finding a way of making it more visual.

Sometimes you know that your subject will look great visually, but it's hard to get it across on paper. The best way of getting around that problem is to film something. For example, when filmmaker Hugh Hartford had the idea of making a film about octogenarian ping-pong players, he went to film the European table tennis championships, and came back with some scenes that proved beyond all doubt that the characters were engaging, lively and funny. That footage was a cost-effective way to give potential funders a feel for a competitive event and its characters in advance of the World Championships, which was the real focus of the film. Wildlife filmmaker Peter Lamberti, CEO of Aquavision TV Productions in South Africa, usually pitches his ideas only after he's filmed a climactic action sequence, around which he can build a story. Once he has his "money shot" he can prove to commissioners that he has a story worth telling.

Interactive producer and first-time director Lotje Sodderland originally intended to pitch her film to TV channels. *Boomtown Babylon* is a documentary project that interweaves stories from ten cities around the world, so Lotje decided it would "enhance the story" for it to be an online documentary, which would allow her to include interactive elements so viewers could choose which of the video streams they engaged with. She teamed up with Paris-based production company Honkytonk and Vincent Moon, the co-creator of a successful web series, to give the project credibility. The switch from TV to online meant that new funds opened up to her (funds are increasingly keen to promote interactive projects), and the participation of her more established partners in the project helped Lotje secure funding from France's Centre national du cinéma (CNC) and Media Fund Interactive. So not only did Lotje find the right medium for her project, the right medium helped her find funding.

Is There a Market for Your Idea?

Rare is the film or program that appeals to everyone, and advertisers and TV broadcasters are acutely aware of the segment of the audience that are watching and whom they are trying to reach at any given time.

"Producer optimism is your biggest, biggest problem," says Chris Hunt, CEO Iambic Media. "Every producer knows they've got a thing that everybody in the world needs to see—not merely wants to see, but must see—in order for their lives to have meaning ... and it's a bit of a shock when that turns out not to be the case." Elizabeth Radshaw also cautions filmmakers against the assumption that people will want to finance, license or even watch your film, however passionate you are about your subject matter. If you need to raise serious money, she says you need to "know that there is a marketplace. And that's a hard question for a filmmaker because sometimes the answer is 'no.' Even if it's a resounding massive 'yes,' you have to go and grab that market, engage with it and make it happen, it's not just going to come and lie at your feet."

Once you've identified a specific audience you can target the funding bodies that cater to that audience. But how do you know if there's an audience for your film? It's likely that a film or program similar to yours has already been made. If so, it proves that someone has already funded something similar, which is a good sign. "Having been around pitching for so many years, one thing I would say to producers is that broadcasters are always saying they want something brand-new that no one has ever seen, but what they really want is the same thing that is already successful, just slightly different," notes Véronique Bernard, president of Iliad Entertainment in New York.

If an existing program or film got good TV audience figures or high box-office receipts, it proves there is an appetite for the subject. It might also mean that you've missed the boat. *Enemies of the People*, a Sundance Special Jury Prize-winning feature-length documentary, in which Cambodian Khmer Rouge leaders talk about the decisions that led to the Killing Fields, struggled to find TV funding because at the time it was being pitched, several filmmakers were making documentaries on the same subject. If you've identified similar films to yours, work out your film's USP (unique selling point). Do you have access to a place or interviewee that no one else has? Have you uncovered new evidence that turns a long-held belief on its head? Or do you have never-seen-before archive footage that gives us a new point of view on a familiar story?

In every part of the industry, whether commercial television or independent documentary, there are trends that emerge and dominate for a few years. When there is a new breakthrough a rash of "copycat" programming usually follows. For example, at the time of writing all the US cable channels are awash with character-driven docuseries, in which larger-than-life blue-collar characters go about their daily jobs: from *Deadliest Catch* (Discovery), *Ax Men* (History) and *Miami Ink* (TLC) to *Pawn Stars* (History), *Hardcore Pawn* (truTV) and *Dog the Bounty Hunter* (A&E). It's inconceivable that you could successfully pitch a film about experimental dance to any of those channels. But come up with a character-based series set in a military or law-enforcement environment and you might have a chance.

Although noncommercial subject matter can disqualify you from mainstream TV funding, some niche subjects have a ready-made fanbase hungry for content. For example, Jon Spira's film, *Anyone Can Play Guitar*, about the Oxford music scene that spawned bands such as Radiohead, Supergrass and Foals among others, raised $32,569 via an IndieGoGo crowdfunding campaign (he met his original $15,000 target within three weeks). Identifying that you have a niche film that needs niche funding means you can concentrate on building an appropriate funding strategy rather than one that is dependent on mass-market funders.

If you truly believe in your project you can make it work, says US-based independent documentary filmmaker Jilann Spitzmiller. "I don't think we have ever tossed out an idea because we thought it would be difficult to fund. We know that making films is a several-year-long process for each film; we just have to be completely captivated and compelled to make it and that's what ensures our success, not whether or not we think it's fundable. I think it's our own drive and our own tenacity that actually gets us through to the finish. In the end, everything comes down to you. One funder is not going to be enough: you are going to have to keep going and get many different sources of funding."

Fortunately, documentary seems to be experiencing something of a renaissance with new festivals springing up, like Open City Documentary Festival in London (which launched in 2011), and ARTE (a Franco-German TV channel) opening up new documentary slots in 2012, which in turn opens up more funding opportunities. "In France in 2010 there were four times as many documentary movies in cinemas than the year before," noted Yves Jeanneau, CEO of Sunny Side of the Doc in La Rochelle, France. "And it's not just in France that we're seeing this—in Taiwan, Hong Kong, in Latin American countries ... not all over the world, but it is a trend."

How Are You Going to Tell the Story?

Once you've worked out the story you want to tell, decided on the most appropriate medium to use and identified a market, you can think about the best way to tell your story. "There are actually very few new ideas and new stories out there but there are different ways of telling that story and that's where the energy should be," says Véronique Bernard. Think about "how to tell this story differently, whether it be using tools or technology or just a different approach or angle." This is where you can get creative and choose one approach or combine several, including:

- **Observational** e.g. *One Born Every Minute, 24 Hours in A&E, Deadliest Catch*
- **Archive footage** e.g. *The Reel History of Britain, Tarnation, Senna*
- **Format** e.g. *The Apprentice, Project Runway, Undercover Boss*
- **Reconstruction** e.g. *Man on Wire, Touching the Void, Brazil–France: The Mystery of Flight 447*
- **Animation** e.g. *Waltz with Bashir, Persepolis, The Trouble with Love and Sex*
- **3D** e.g. *Pina, Caves of Forgotten Dreams, Flying Monsters*
- **Interviews** e.g. *Project Nim, Bobby Fischer Against the World, Enron: The Smartest Guys in the World*
- **Audio recordings** e.g. *9/11: Phone Calls from the Towers*
- **Covert filming** e.g. *Undercover Nurse, My Big Fat Fake Wedding, Undercover Mosque*

Sometimes someone comes along and ignores all genre conventions, such as Alma Har'el. She's a music video director who decided to make a feature film after stumbling across the residents of Bombay Beach, an impoverished community living on the edge of Salton Sea in southern California. Alma filmed an observational documentary in which she included the main characters performing choreographed dance sequences, but its unconventional approach meant it was a hard sell. "I tried to get money for a year," says Alma. "Funders laughed at me, so I ended up moving out there for five months with a small consumer HD camera and just started shooting." The resulting film, *Bombay Beach*, won the best documentary feature award at the Tribeca Film Festival.

What's the Genre and Format?

However much you don't want your film to be "put in a pigeonhole," if you want to get your work on TV it's important to pinpoint the genre of your program or film, as that will help you find the right buyer.

Some channels, particularly cable and satellite, are genre-specific as (often but not always) signified by their name. For example *Science*, *Animal Planet*, *Travel Channel*, *Food Network* and *DIY Network*. But beware: names can be misleading as channels evolve and their remit changes. For example, you might not expect the History Channel to be home to the heavily character-driven *Pawn Stars* and *Ice Road Truckers*, as they have little to do with history. Likewise, Animal Planet is no longer looking for programs about animals and the Food Network is no longer looking for shows about food; instead, both are chasing ratings-winning character-led observational docuseries that have a more tangential relationship with animals (e.g. *Heidi Fleiss: Prostitutes to Parrots* and *Rat Busters NYC*) or food (e.g. *Ice Brigade* and *Pioneer Woman*).

The bigger networks transmit a broader range of shows, with specific slots in the schedule dedicated to science, history, lifestyle or documentary. The networks generally have a number of commissioners or development executives who each work in a particular genre—history, science, art etc.—and so you must target your pitch to the correct person. If your idea straddles two genres, like my *Guinea Pig Club* (which could have been equally classified as a history or a science documentary on account of the medical content), you can pitch to both kinds of buyers, doubling your options. However, a program idea that doesn't neatly fit into a genre can too easily fall between commissioning departments, making it more difficult to get a commitment.

Once you've pinpointed the right person at the right channel to pitch to, you must ensure that the proposed length of your film, episodes and/or series fits their schedule. Channels have specific slot lengths to fill, so there's no point suggesting a fifteen-minute makeover series to a television broadcaster that has thirty-minute slots; if they don't have a suitable space in their schedule they will automatically reject your idea. It is possible, if you've come up with something so unique and compelling that they must have it, that they will ask you to rework your idea into a thirty-minute format. However, there are very few "must-have" programs, and a channel executive is more likely to take your suggestion of a fifteen-minute program as an indication of your inexperience and lack of market knowledge. Equally, it is unwise to pitch an eighty-two-minute documentary and insist it can be made only at that length, when the longest slot on a channel is one hour. It is usual, therefore, for a filmmaker to make a short version of their film for TV and, if appropriate, a feature-length version for festival and/or theatrical distribution, but that compromise doesn't please all buyers. "We have an hour-long slot, which in Canada means forty-five minutes' running time after commercials," says Mark Starowicz, executive director of documentary at CBC. "People often come to us saying, 'This is a feature length film, it's going to be ninety minutes'—well we are not going to move the national news just because you have come up with an idea that deserves to be ninety minutes. Then they say, 'OK, I understand why you can't run a ninety-minute film, but I need television funding in order to get this film made so I'll give you a forty-five-minute cut-down version.' On the whole that's a really bad idea, because the version that the producer cares about is the ninety-minute one and the television version is basically the hacked-down version just to get money."

It is easier to sell a TV series than a one-off film; channels have a lot of slots to fill so it's more economical to commission a series as a single documentary, both in terms of cost (formats tend to be cheaper than documentaries) and time (dealing with the producer of a series of twelve programs is easier than dealing with twelve different filmmakers). Research a particular channel to see how many episodes and what length of slot is usual for them and either adapt your proposal to fit or find another, more appropriate, channel or outlet.

Why Are *You* Making This Film?

Your idea and its place in the market is only part of the story: the other part of the equation is you, the filmmaker. Most funders want to know why they should fund *you* to make this film rather than someone else (because chances are they've heard your idea before, often many times). Danae Ringelmann, co-founder and COO of crowdfunding platform IndieGoGo, says, "The biggest thing filmmakers need to realize is that they need to think of themselves as a brand and that's the thing that people are supporting, not just their story." Production companies work very hard at building their brand, so that they become the "go-to" company for a certain type of programming; for example, Magical Elves has a track record of making competition reality shows such as *Top Chef* and *Project Runway*. Testimony Films concentrate on making historical documentaries that feature archive and personal testimony such as *Last Voices of the Great War*. Darlow Smithson Productions have a reputation for making high-quality feature documentaries such as *Touching the Void* and specialize in disaster documentaries: they were one of two companies Channel 4 commissioner Simon Dickson called when a passenger plane crash landed in New York City's Hudson River. Their reputation (and the fact that they were the first to return the call) resulted in *Miracle of the Hudson Plane Crash* (Channel 4/Discovery). Why are you the best person to make your film?

As an independent filmmaker, you present a much stronger case if you have a personal connection to your subject. TV commissioners and other funders are often wary of producers who pitch a "laundry list" of ideas in the hope that one will stick; they want to feel they are getting a product driven by passion not profit. So, for example, Lindsey Dryden's partial deafness inspired her to make her documentary *Lost & Sound*. Her biggest fear is that she might suddenly lose all her hearing and no longer be able to enjoy music, so she set out to film three deaf people—a dancer, a musician and a music journalist—who are all deaf but are still able experience music in different ways. Her idea was to follow three personal stories and interweave scientific information using animation and sound design to help illustrate how her main characters could still sense and enjoy music. There is clearly a very real connection between filmmaker and her subject, and a compelling reason for her to be the person to tell that story.

Gemma Atwal got the idea for her documentary, *Marathon Boy*, from the BBC News website. "They ran a story on a small kid from the slums of India who was running huge distances on a daily basis. It was both astounding and shocking," she recalled in an interview with one of her grantors. But Gemma, who is part Indian, also had inside knowledge that meant she had real empathy for the four-year-old runner. "I've run upwards of a dozen marathons and the type of training that Budhia Singh was engaged in seemed extreme, if true."

To work out your unique connection to your proposed subject Jilann Spitzmiller advises sitting down with a pen and paper before you commit your idea to a formal proposal. "Brainstorm your project: what it's about and how it personally moves or affects you, really heart-centered free writing," she says. "You are not censoring yourself, not trying to fit into a certain word count, or trying to answer a certain question, you are just writing from your heart about your project, what it is, the merits of it, and how you are connected to it." Doing this exercise will help identify the key theme(s) of your film and point you toward potential special interest funding sources.

Do You Have the Right Skills?

As an independent filmmaker, you must be able to show that you have the skills and experience to produce the film you are asking someone to fund. Obviously if you are making a personal project funded by your credit card or "the bank of Mum and Dad" it doesn't matter that you've never picked up a camera (and your mum will be very proud, whatever the outcome), but if you want other people to buy into your project you won't get far without the right credentials.

If you are working for an independent production company, it's likely you'll have the skills in-house to make any program you propose to TV channel executives. If your company has already successfully made a show similar to the one that you are proposing, it gives buyers the confidence that you can deliver, and that— sometimes more than the idea—is what is important to them.

The flipside is that it can be difficult for an established production company to break into a different genre. I once worked for a production company that made lifestyle formats such as house makeover and travel shows; my executive producer asked me to develop a quiz show in response to a channel brief. I spent the weekend frantically pulling together a format and sent it off to the channel. The response? You've never made a quiz show—why would we ever commission this from you? As it happened they liked the concept enough to invite us to a competitive pitch, but we were ultimately unsuccessful. The feedback was that the pitch was great, but they preferred to commission a company with a track record. Lesson learned.

What proof do you have that you are competent? Perhaps you've spent several years working on undercover documentaries for TV networks and now you are striking out on your own to make an investigative documentary? Or films you've worked on have won industry-recognized awards? Or a series you produced has rated highly with audiences and critics? Collect and keep any good reviews to attach to funding applications.

What if you don't have the requisite skills? Get someone on your team who does. That might mean partnering up with a production company who will provide all the editorial, legal and compliance resources that will reassure a TV channel that their money will be spent wisely. Or you could find a well-respected producer or executive producer to come on board and lend their name and expertise to your project—and the more award-winning credits they have to their name, the better. When Julia Redwood and Ed Punchard formed Prospero Productions in Fremantle, Australia, neither had any TV experience. She was a Shakespeare scholar, and he a deep-sea diver turned marine archaeologist. Their first film—*No Survivors: The Mysterious Loss of HMAS Sydney*—came out of Ed's archaeology knowledge and was structured using Julia's storytelling skills. As they lacked filmmaking skills they teamed up with a well-known director to secure the interest of commissioners. Sometimes, if a TV channel executive likes your idea but is nervous about commissioning you or your company to make it, they will introduce you to their preferred production partners or showrunners (executive or series producers).

Bear in mind that a production, and therefore any production partnership, is likely to last for months if not years, so choose your partners carefully. Lindsey Dryden advises you to "Partner with people whose skills and experience complement yours. So, say you are a really brilliant storyteller but you are not hugely technical, partner with someone who is technical. If you are a relatively new storyteller, partner with an editor who has proven storytelling skills."

Do You Have Business Acumen and a Fat Contacts Book?

Finally, it's unlikely that you will find all your funding from one source. You'll have to call on all your networking and co-ordination skills to finance your project, which means you'll have to remove your "artist" mantle and don a more businesslike persona for a while. However, it is possible (and advisable) to channel just as much creativity into your fundraising as you will into your film. In fact, one participant at a documentary festival is reported to have observed that "the most creative thing about making docs today is building the business plan."

All businesses (including film and TV projects) need a plan. Even a skeleton budget outline in the early stages will help you focus on what *needs* to be done rather than what you want to do. It will also prevent nasty surprises that can throw you off course. "Write yourself a list," says Lindsey Dryden. "It's much easier to go through the stages when you are expecting them, and it's satisfying to be able to tick them off."

Rachel Wexler, producer of Emmy-winning *The English Surgeon*, agrees that as a filmmaker, you are "running a business. We are a creative industry but I think there are a lot of problems with being businesslike. Alan Sugar was interviewed on Radio 4, and he said he found it extraordinary when he was working on *The Apprentice* [he takes the place of Donald Trump in the UK version]. They'd ask him to turn up at 8 a.m. and then make him wait around for two hours while they lit the set. He'd say, 'Don't call me at 8 a.m., call me fifteen minutes before you need me and I'll walk on set and do my job and then I'll leave.' He said he couldn't believe the attitude in our industry and how people didn't equate his time with money. I'm certainly not Alan Sugar, but I think we can learn to be more businesslike when we account for our time." New York-based documentary story consultant Fernanda Rossi has been quoted as saying, "there was a Harvard business book that said a filmmaking project is nothing else but a temporary corporation. A film project and a regular corporation share more characteristics than we want to admit. Filmmakers should take all the same workshops as a CEO takes!"

Filmmaking—and fundraising—is a long-term endeavor so it's likely your project will evolve. As you develop your idea, your perspective and ambitions will change: you might decide that your short documentary has feature potential, or that the addition of a new character will give a domestic story international appeal. You might discover that a similar TV series has recently been commissioned from a rival production company, or come to recognize that your passion project is unsuited to a commercial marketplace and therefore you must think about alternative methods of funding. It's also possible, in being forced to think about your project in micro detail, that you fall out of love with your film: that's OK. It's better to realize at an early stage that you don't want to pursue a particular project than to spend time and money on production only to find yourself in debt and hating every moment of filming.

Equally, if your project continues to excite you after you've put it under the microscope, there's an excellent chance that you'll have the necessary enthusiasm to overcome the inevitable obstacles and setbacks you'll face during your search for funding. Even if you are still as enthusiastic about your film as you ever were, you might discover you don't have the right experience or contacts to make it happen. Identifying your weaknesses upfront means you can address them and I'll give you suggestions of how to do that as we go along.

The Pitch

As you prepare your pitch I recommend you create a master proposal document to capture information and ideas as you work your way through the rest of this chapter. Your master proposal will grow and evolve with your project, and by the time you make your first funding application you should have all the necessary information at your fingertips. This document will eventually inform your press and publicity effort too.

Write a Proposal

You will need to submit a written proposal of some sort whenever you apply for funding. The process of writing a proposal is essential to the development of your idea. It's easy to believe your film or program has a workable narrative or format when it is still in your head; try to pin it down on paper and suddenly holes appear. Better now than when you are in the middle of a face-to-face pitch.

Joel Orosz, author of *The Insider's Guide to Grantmaking*, describes four types of proposal:

1. **The bad idea-bad proposal**—this one should never get as far as a funder's desk. This proposal presents a poorly developed idea along the lines of "I am thinking of making a film about domestic abuse ... " that is presented in a poorly written, rambling document that focuses on the issues around domestic abuse (or worse, is just a chunk of text about the issue cut-and-pasted from Wikipedia) rather than an outline of the film's proposed narrative.
2. **The devious bad idea-good proposal**—this is a proposal written by someone who knows how to write a good proposal; however, it promises something that can't be delivered—because of weak characters, lack of access or extortionate cost, for example.
3. **Good idea-bad proposal**—if you are a gifted filmmaker, adept at weaving a complex narrative on screen, you probably don't have a problem spotting good stories. Unfortunately, not every filmmaker is as an accomplished a writer as

they are a filmmaker. There is a particular knack to proposal writing and it takes skill and practice to be able to convey the necessary information in the most economical way.

4. **Good idea-good proposal**—this is what you should be aiming for: a succinct document that outlines the narrative, format and approach of a compelling and original idea. In itself it's not enough to guarantee that a funder will be moved to give you money—you also have to target the right person at the right organization at the right moment in their funding cycle—but it gives you the best possible chance.

A proposal doesn't set your idea in stone, rather it acts as a statement of your intent; your proposed film or TV series will evolve as development moves into production, and funders understand that. After you've had a meeting with a funder your initial written proposal might also change as you tweak it to better fit their specific remit.

All proposals look different; there is no 'standard' format. Some masquerade as letters; others are formally structured documents, some are printed on one side of plain paper either in portrait or landscape orientation, others are printed in color on both sides of a piece of card; online submission forms are constrained by the number of words that will fit in the boxes provided. Funding bodies all have their own requirements—TV commissioners subscribe to the "less is more" philosophy, whereas grant foundations expect much lengthier applications—but whatever the physical form of the application, the content is essentially the same.

TV proposals tend to be the simplest, so we'll start there. The one-page TV proposal, or one-sheet, has several functions: it concisely summarizes your idea, defines the scope of the narrative, demonstrates that you have thought about all the necessary elements and shows you understand the remit of the person to whom you are pitching. It's tempting to include as much information as possible to prove how much research you have done, but it is unnecessary. If a potential buyer is interested in your concept they will ask for more details, perhaps in the form of a budget or treatment. However, if you haven't hooked them in by the end of your first paragraph, it's unlikely that they will read to the end of the page. The trick is to give them just enough information to get them interested but to leave them wanting more. This one-page proposal will also provide the starting point for a business plan and can be tweaked later on to form your website copy and publicity materials.

Anatomy of a Proposal

Use the template below as a guide to make sure you include all the information that a potential buyer or funder needs; your proposal doesn't need to be formulaic, it just needs to express the necessary information as clearly as possible. Avoid hype and clichés such as "emotional rollercoaster" and "larger-than-life characters"; instead get the emotion and drama across with your choice of words, using the old adage of "show, don't tell." If you get stuck, look at the websites of documentaries or programs that are similar in style and content to yours to see how they convey their narratives, characters and formats.

It's often helpful to make use of bold text and bullet points to break up dense copy and draw the reader's eye down the page.

Title
Number of episodes and duration e.g. 6 x 60'

One-sentence synopsis (also known as a tagline, logline or strapline)
Think of how your film might be described in the TV listings or advertising hoarding.

One-paragraph overview
The Who, What, Where, When, Why summary of your idea.

Narrative outline
● Explain how the film or overall series will unfold
● Introduce key characters/interviewees/experts/onscreen talent
● Outline individual episodes

Approach
How the story will be told: archive, interviews, fly-on-the-wall, 3D, CGI, underwater filming, animation etc.

Ballpark budget (not always included in initial proposal)

Contact details
Include the name, email address and telephone number of the main contact—director, producer or executive producer; a production company logo.

Pitch Tape

Increasingly important, and in some cases essential, is the pitch tape. If you haven't yet shot anything you should think about doing so sooner rather than later; it's often much easier to convey your idea in a visual medium than on paper. "In 2011, I would say that 97 percent of projects submitted to Hot Docs Forum had Vimeo clips attached: more than any other year," notes Elizabeth Radshaw. She remembers being a part of the festival's Forum selection committee a few years ago, and of 200 submissions only 20 percent of proposals had a DVD attached. "It's so easy to send links to footage that we've started relying on these visual cues, so the importance of having even a little bit of footage, even if it's not a trailer, but maybe a short summary of two or three scenes, or an interview introduction or something, is critical."

A good pitch tape—sample, trailer, demo, work-in-progress, sizzler, call it what you will—introduces your key characters, proves you have access, showcases your filmmaking skills and sets up a conflict or question that you will resolve in the finished film. According to Fernanda Rossi, author of *Trailer Mechanics: A Guide to Making Your Fundraising Documentary Trailer*, the ideal pitch tape to present to film funds and foundations is "a seven- to ten-minute audiovisual pitch of the film ... it is a short without an ending ... we have to create a final scene that shows there is potential for the story to grow, namely a cliffhanger or hook ... the cliffhanger gives the promo the sense that there is something else that can be explored in the longer version of the film." For TV, the principle is the same but TV commissioners tend to prefer something shorter, two or three minutes long at most.

Early in the development and pitching process the pitch tape doesn't have to be broadcast-quality and can be filmed cheaply on a domestic video camera or iPhone (although if you are filming key scenes that you want to include in the finished film you will have to shoot to broadcast standard). Once you've got something to show potential funders you might get some development money that allows you to make a more sophisticated trailer that will, in turn, help you raise production funds. Once your project is more advanced you'll need to update your pitch tape and include carefully selected sequences from the finished film to demonstrate your storytelling and the quality of your filmmaking skills, before applying to film funds and foundations for finishing funds.

If you really can't film anything before you pitch, perhaps because your subject is located on another continent, you could make use of photographs, archive or a storyboard to help potential funders visualize your idea, as producer Hilary Durman did. She stumbled across the story for feature documentary *Donor Unknown: Adventure in the Sperm Trade*, when she was producing *All About Me*, a BBC Radio drama about the son of a sperm donor. "Our first trailer mostly used stills and radio interviews but More 4 loved the idea. We really needed to do some filming to bring other financiers to the project so More 4 released development funding and we spent two weeks in the US in 2009 filming with Jeffrey [the sperm donor] and [his children] Ryann in LA, Rachelle in Memphis, and then traveling simply to meet Fletcher, Cathy and Sue in Colorado. ARTE and NRK came on board in early 2009 and we then pitched *Donor Unknown* with ARTE at IDFA 2009 and found our Dutch co-producer VPRO."

Additional Information for Grantmaking and Other Funding Bodies

Longer grant application forms require more detailed information about your idea, including information about the production team, schedule, budget, finance and distribution plan.

Production Team

Aiming high when you put together your team gives you the best chance of attracting funding. Don't just rely on that guy from film school to be your editor (even though he might be cheap), because he won't impress potential funders if he doesn't have some serious credits. Yes, it's intimidating to approach industry names, but what's the worst that can happen? Even if they say no, you have potentially started a relationship with someone who might be willing to work with you in future. Also, some funds are open only to people of a certain gender, nationality or ethnic background and in the UK there's a push toward commissioning TV programs from the nations (Wales, Scotland and Northern Ireland) or English regions, which means that some clever strategic alliances could open up additional sources of funding.

● **Director**—A well-known, respected director adds weight to your proposal (especially on high-end factual TV programs). "That is something that is crucial in the international market," says co-production executive Lilla Hurst, founder of LillaVision. "If, for instance, a production company comes to me that I haven't worked with before, and they haven't produced anything that the international market has bought, it's useful for me to know who the director is, and whether they will have some impact."

- **Executive Producer/Producer**—The most important person's name on a TV proposal is often the executive producer, because their reputation and experience of delivering productions on time, and to budget, reassures TV channel executives. If you are an independent filmmaker, your name and reputation has to do the same job. But what if this is your first film and you don't have a track record, or the right contacts? You attach the right names to your project. For example, if you are directing your own film, you can find an experienced producer to focus on the budget and fundraising side of the production while you concentrate on filming. To find a partner, independent producer Leigh Gibson suggests you ask around, or network at one of the big markets like MIPTV* or MIPDoc in Cannes. "You need to find somebody you can get on with, who has the same kind of outlook in terms of filmmaking and who has the same ambition for the project. You want them on board from a development stage so that they are thinking along the same lines as you are." A producer or executive producer who specializes in the kind of film that you want to make will have extensive contacts in the funding world and will also be able to steer you editorially. "Good advice from older, wiser people is really helpful," agrees Kat Mansoor, who produced the double Grierson Award-winning *Here's Johnny*, "they gave us the structure and advice at key moments when we were floundering a little bit. So finding those people with that kind of experience is important." An executive producer's role is negotiable, depending on the level of input you need. "Having an exec on board is a lot to do with reassurance," says Rachel Wexler, producer of *My Perestroika* and *Out of the Ashes*. "Sometimes you have one phone call with them, and other times they are constantly in the cutting room. The broadcasters will often put their own execs on a project in order to oversee a director or producer just so that they can back off and know it's still going to happen."

- **Production Manager**—While a production manager rarely (never) gets star billing, an experienced production manager can oversee the budget, and ensure your film is deliverable and compliant with all the correct contracts, release forms, insurance policies and delivery formats in place. If you are a one-man-band filmmaker it's likely that you will look after the budgeting yourself,

*Marché International des Programmes.

but it might be worth investing in a day or two of a production manager's time to help you set up the budget. They will be able to advise on standard crew rates, scheduling and will have relationships with post-production houses that might be persuaded to give you a discounted rate.

- **Editor**—An award-winning editor reassures funders that your film is being crafted by a master storyteller, so it gives you an advantage if you can attach someone with heavyweight credentials. This is less critical at the development stage than when you are applying for completion funding.

- **International Co-producer**—If your program or film has a big budget and is aimed at an international audience there are advantages to partnering with a producer or production company in another territory; they have ready-made relationships with TV channel executives in their home country and an international partnership can give you access to various tax treaties and incentives.

- **International Co-production Executive/Agent**—There are a number of companies that can act as intermediaries to help you find international finance and co-production partners. These companies can help you with development, pitching, budgeting and act as executive producer on the project. The advantage of working with one of these specialist companies is that they have ongoing relationships with broadcasters around the world, which saves you the time and legwork it would take to build and maintain those relationships.

- **Media Lawyer**—An experienced media lawyer or attorney is an expensive addition to the budget, but is a worthwhile—and essential—investment if you find yourself patching together different kinds of legally complex funding, such as international co-productions and private equity investments. An attorney can prepare legal documents ensuring that the proper disclosures are made, risks explained and all other legal requirements met. It's important to ensure all your various finance and distribution contracts are in order, as well as those agreements between producer, director and any other crew, so it's clear who owns the finished film and exactly who has which distribution rights. An attorney can also advise whether you should set up a limited company (known as a Ltd company in the UK or LLC in the USA).

- **Fiscal Sponsor**—If you work in the USA you might want to add a fiscal sponsor to your team. A fiscal sponsor allows you to receive money from private foundations. A fiscal sponsor charges an administration fee of around 5 percent, which you can factor into your budget (there is more on fiscal sponsorship in Chapter 6 and Part III).

Schedule

A production schedule is the foundation on which your whole budget rests. A well-constructed schedule saves you money. A schedule also drives the production forward when you hit inevitable roadblocks. As a schedule always has an end, the end is always in sight (even if you have to move the end a little further away as your film evolves). Having a finite schedule also forces you to think about the best way to tell your story. For example, do you really need to follow your characters for five years or could one year be just as effective?

Your first schedule will be based on a best-case scenario, but it needs to be flexible enough to accommodate unforeseen circumstances: family bereavements can affect contributors and crew, volcanic ash clouds can ground flights and an unexpected turn in your narrative can extend your filming schedule by weeks, months or even years. Whatever happens, with a good schedule in place you'll always have a plan, or at least a starting point on which to build new a plan. As well as helping to define the budget, a schedule also acts as a to-do list that will alert you to book locations, hire cars, hotels and flights in plenty of time. It can also be extended to help you plan and organize your distribution and outreach efforts.

If you are working on a TV program or series, a production manager will draw up the schedule with the producer/director, and it will be constructed to deliver the finished film in the most cost- and time-effective way, with editing following straight on from (or sometimes parallel to) filming. If you are working independently, possibly working other jobs on the side to fund your film, your schedule might be broken up into segments that allow you to pause production while you raise further funding. The basic building blocks of a schedule are:

- **Development**—securing access, building relationships with contributors, research, writing and pitching
- **Production**—filming
- **Post-production**—offline and online editing, voiceover, sound mix, graphics
- **Distribution**—festival submissions, marketing and outreach partners

Every project is different and therefore every schedule is unique, but when stripped bare all schedules include an anticipated number of travel/filming days and a set number of weeks in the edit—once you know those things you can start to work out the cost of crew, kit and post-production facilities hire, which are often the biggest items in the budget. Be alert to anything in your proposal that might have an impact on your proposed schedule. For example, if you are intending to film in Antarctica, it is accessible only at certain times of year; if you miss your window due to lack of funding you will have to wait another eight months until the ice melts (by which time you might have lost your access).

Budget

Budgets vary wildly, from the micro-budget self-financed documentary, such as *Tarnation*, which was made for $218 (although music and archive clearance costs added another $400,000), to the studio-backed mega-expensive theatrical films, such as *Oceans* (2010), which had a reported budget of $80 million.

An accurate budget allows you to see where and when your main costs are going to be, and then put together a finance plan to match your budgetary needs. Most potential funders will want to know the ballpark budget for your film or series, but some will require a full line-by-line breakdown. Funders often see proposals where the "budget doesn't reflect the ideas that are articulated in the treatment," says filmmaker Jilann Spitzmiller, who has sat on grant juries, "so for example, the treatment might talk about a bunch of aerial footage but in the budget there won't be any allowance for aerial footage. When you submit a budget that is not accurate, it says to me that you don't really know what you are doing, and I question your ability to pull off your idea. It's OK to not know what you are doing, but then you have to get help and you have to get advisors to make sure that everything is adding up."

Using your proposal and schedule as a starting point, you can start to put together a budget which, like the schedule, can generally be split into four:

1. **Development and Pre-production**
   - Research
   - Pitch tape—equipment, travel, editing
   - Pitching—festivals, including delegate fees, travel and accommodation

2. **Production**
   - Crew
     - Director
     - Producer
     - Camera
     - Sound

- ○ Fixer
- ○ Executive Producer
- ○ Production Manager
- Travel and accommodation
- Camera and sound hire
- Archive footage
- Music or composer

3. **Post-production**
    - Edit suite hire
    - Editor
    - Voiceover artist
    - Online, grade and sound mix

4. **Distribution and Marketing**
    - Distribution is beyond the scope of this book, but it's worth noting that distribution costs for a theatrical release are substantial. For example, *The Age of Stupid* cost £450,000 to make, and a further £400,000 to distribute.

Every film is different so there are no easy answers as to what a film or series should cost. You may be hiring a full crew or shooting it yourself; you could be shooting it all within a twenty-five-mile radius of your home base or traveling the world to do interviews—every creative decision you make comes with a cost. Let's take the budget for a pitch tape as an example:

- When Hugh Hartford filmed his taster tape for *Ping Pong* he chose to fly by budget airline to Croatia, and did all the camera and sound work himself. The total cost was a few hundred pounds.
- Leftfield Pictures made a seven-minute pitch reel for *Pawn Stars*, an observational reality series featuring a family-run pawn shop in Las Vegas. Filming (two days) and editing (two weeks) the tape cost them $15,000–$20,000 (which they said is typical for them).
- When Tom Gutteridge wanted to pitch his TV series *Robot Wars* to the BBC he decided not to film a pitch tape; instead he flew six robots from the USA to London and staged a Robot Wars event, complete with a live audience. That pitch cost £95,000 ($150,000).

Check the budgets of other films, of similar scale and scope to yours, to find out if your overall budget seems to be in the right ballpark. The-numbers.com or boxofficemojo.com are good places to start. If your budget is way under or way over those of similar films, it's likely you've got your calculations wrong somewhere.

Look out for hidden costs, such as the cost of making several different versions of a film for several different funders who all have different delivery requirements. Jo Lapping, strand executive for BBC *Storyville*, was quoted as saying, "A lot of productions get caught out. They've got four or five different broadcasters involved in something, and they get to fine-cut stage and they're suddenly getting very mixed messages coming back about what each investor wants. If you've made contingency in your budget, at that stage you can say, 'Okay, we're just going to have to do a version for France, a version for the UK, a version for the US, and we'll have our festival cut' ... most of the filmmakers we work with do end up making at least two versions of their films, if not three." Theatrical documentaries bump up the budget because of the cost of the film print and physical distribution of the film (at least until digital distribution is more widespread). And 3D filming also costs a lot more than regular HD (high-definition) filming. In 2011, Peter Hamilton asked Hoff Productions to calculate how much it would cost to shoot a (hypothetical) crime program. They drew up a budget of $325,000 for HD and estimated that making the same program in 3D would require a total budget of around $621,000 (an increase of $296,000). It's worth noting that when they did the same calculation a year earlier the costs were $44,000 higher, which indicates that the cost of 3D production is falling.

Also, remember to factor in the "cost" of each type of funding you are considering. That might mean actual dollar cost in the case of commission, interest or professional fees, or sweat equity cost (unpaid time and effort you have to put into pursuing a particular type of funding). Veteran entertainment lawyer Peter Levitan is an adjunct professor at Loyola Law School, Los Angeles, where he teaches a course on entertainment financing (covering TV, music, theatre and new media as well as film) to both filmmakers and law students. "As we go through the different financing methods in my classes, we talk about which ones are costly to administer, both in terms of time and resources and in terms of actual money," he says, pointing out that many finance agreements require input from a lawyer. "Co-production and co-financing might be as simple as phoning up the organizations that are likely to be interested in co-producing your project, but it's important to have an experienced attorney negotiate the documents to make sure that they are perfectly precise, and anticipate all the issues that can and, often do, arise. Private equity by investors, if anything, is likely to be even more cost-intensive in terms of attorney fees."

Your first budget should assume you will get full funding for everything you need, including crew and equipment at standard industry rates. In the UK, the broadcast union BECTU has a list of agreed crew rates for members, and *Televisual* magazine publishes an annual salary survey; the *Showbiz Labor Guide* gives rates for the USA and Canada. Ask around to find similar resources in your territory. If in doubt, ask a production manager to help you.

Next you should prepare a second pared-down version (sometimes known as a cash or "Go" budget), where all of the third-party, essential costs are itemized. "The thing to know, internally, is what's the bottom line? What can you actually make it for?" says Rachel Wexler. This is your worst case-scenario budget, one on which you are likely take on more of the work yourself, beg and borrow kit and defer certain fees. With these two budgets in place you can aim to raise the full budget, safe in the knowledge that as long as you manage to raise the lesser amount you can still produce your film. Any money raised above that figure will allow you to pay everyone their proper fees during, rather than after, the production.

Once you get into the fine detail of your budget you can start seeing where there might be discrete amounts of money that you could solicit from particular funding sources. For example, some funds are set up specifically to finance development or the creation of a pitch tape. Others are designed to help with post-production (completion funds) or outreach (a term used in the independent documentary world for the marketing and distribution of issue-based films). Some foundations can award only small amounts of money, but are better able to justify funding your project if you can specify exactly what their $5,000 will pay for, so being able to slice and dice your budget in different ways can open up new potential sources of finance.

Finally, work out how you are going to cover your living and filming costs before you manage to secure some initial funding. There can be a gap of several months between applying for funding, being accepted and the money being released to you. "You've got to stay in business during that period," says Andrew Jackson, head of the BBC's Natural History Unit, who advises producers to "think about the amount of time that it's going to take and secondly, not to underestimate the amount of budget." For filmmakers with good contacts and a track record, it can take an average of nine months to get funding together. Beginner filmmakers can double that figure, and most are raising funds as they go along, as and when they can.

A simple budget template is provided in the Appendix.

Production Budgets

As you can see from this table, production budgets vary enormously; even two seemingly similar films can have wildly different budgets. For example, two animated feature documentaries were released in the same year, one with a budget four times the amount of the other:

Film	Format	Production budget
Oceans French ecological docudrama	Feature (2009)	$80m
Jackass 3D Live action stunts	Feature (2010)	$20m
Persepolis Animated documentary based on autobiography	Feature (2008)	$7.3m
Fahrenheit 9/11 Michael Moore	Feature (2004)	$6m (+ prints and advertising $12m)
Dolphins and Whales 3D: Tribes of the Ocean Underwater documentary	Feature (2008)	$6m
In the Shadow of the Moon Interview and archive-driven documentary	Feature (2007)	$3.2m
Inside Job Documentary about the financial crisis in the late 2000s	Feature (2010)	$2m
Waltz with Bashir Animated documentary	Feature (2008)	$2m
End of the Line Ecological documentary	Feature (2009)	$1.6m

Jig Irish dancing documentary	Feature (2011)	$875,000
Hoop Dreams Observational documentary	Feature (1994)	$700,000
Murderball Observational documentary	Feature (2005)	$350,000
Super Size Me Investigative/stunt documentary	Feature (2004)	$65,000
Tarnation Archive documentary	Feature (2003)	$218 (+ music and archive clearance $440,000)

TV Series

Planet Earth Blue-chip natural history series	11 x 60' TV series (2006)	$25.5m $2.3m per hour
Death of the Mega-beasts CGI-rich	1 x 90' TV special (2009)	$2.3m
Dino Stampede CGI-rich	1 x 60' TV (2011)	$1.2m
One Born Every Minute Fixed-rig observational series set in a maternity ward (40 cameras)	8 x 60' TV (2010)	$400K per hour
Globe Trekker Travel series	13 x 60' TV series (1994–)	$3m per season $220K per hour
Pawn Stars Character driven observational reality series	13 x 30' TV series (2009–)	$250-300K per half hour (estimated)

Finance Plan

A finance plan lists all the funding you already have in place from broadcasters or other financiers, any contribution you've made as a production company or producer, and the shortfall that you are asking a potential funder to cover.

Some funders, such as broadcasters, provide production money in return for the right to première the program on their channel. Others, such as investors, give you money in the expectation that it will be paid back and that they will share in the eventual profits (if any). Still others, such as banks, offer loans that must be paid back with added (and often high) interest. Other money, such as government tax incentives and regional film grants, is given in return for fulfilling a specific set of criteria, usually based on the geographical location of the production. This money is paid to you once it has been proved that the criteria have been satisfactorily met, i.e. at the end of production. Unless you are able to get a single TV channel to fully fund your project, your finance plan is likely to include some, or even all, of these types of finance.

As well as thinking about the sources of funding you have to take into account application deadlines or other constraints that will affect your finance plan. Rachel Wexler begins by thinking about what she's trying to ultimately achieve. "Do I think this film should be released theatrically, does it have that potential? What festival am I aiming to première at? That's where I start, and then I work backwards," she says. "So if I say I'm aiming for Sundance or London Film Festival in 2015, then I know I've got to get a film in good shape by summer 2014. Then I'm looking at my schedule and my funding deadlines, potential international equity—I'm putting the pieces together like a jigsaw. I'll have three or four scenarios in my head and I'll try them all. Some will work and some won't, so I try to find the best match." Some of the figures, particularly early on, will be speculative. "I'll ask: what would be realistic if I put in an application with this foundation—what do they give?" says Rachel. "So that would be one chunk of money. And then: how much money could I possibly raise from so-and-so? And then you put it all together."

Each potential funder will want to know who else has a financial stake in the project, to what extent, and if—and how soon—they expect to be repaid. This is important, because certain types of financiers insist on having priority over the repayment of loans. So a financier in first place for recoupment will get their money repaid before anyone else. Those further down the ladder are paid in the order agreed in the contract. A producer who has deferred their fee will likely be in last position, and therefore risks never being paid if the film doesn't sell well.

Executive producer Tom Roberts likens the challenge of getting all the funders in place to running a boat trip. A few people buy their tickets in advance and get there early so they can choose the seat that gives them the best view. By the scheduled departure time there are still some empty seats and the skipper doesn't have enough money to pay for the fuel. The boat can't leave until those final tickets are sold, so the skipper goes out on to the dock and finds some people who are willing to join the trip. However, they will agree to buy a ticket only if they can sit in the seats with the best view. A long negotiation ensues during which the skipper has to persuade the people who bought their tickets first to move to inferior seats; understandably they don't want to move, but if they don't the whole trip is in jeopardy. Eventually the skipper is forced to offer them a free lunch at his own expense to compensate them for the inconvenience of moving seats, the new arrivals get settled and the boat finally leaves the harbor. The negotiation of a recoupment schedule is a similar exercise in logistics and diplomacy that is never fully resolved until every funder is satisfied and safely on board (with a contract signed).

Finance Plan Example*

Dino Stampede
Prospero Productions, Australia

Budget US$1.2million

TV Channels

ABC Australia	US$150,000
BBC Scotland	US$100,000
Smithsonian Channel	US$155,000 (est.)

Screen Agencies

Screen West	US$150,000
Screen Australia	US$380,000

*This example has been constructed from the actual and estimated funding received by the program, as reported by Peter Hamilton of documentarytelevision.com, but the original finance plan may have differed from this.

Tax Incentives	
Producer Tax Offset	US$170,000
Distributor	
National Geographic Television International advance	US$45,000 (est.)
DVD	US$5,000
Deficit Finance	
Prospero Productions	US$45,000
Total	**US$1.2million**

Putting Together a Funding Application Schedule

Think strategically about which funds you can apply to and in which order they are best approached. It is usual these days for production companies to fund development, and often a pitch tape, before trying to get production funding. However you can get financial support at all stages of the production process:

- **Development funding**—for research, casting and producing a pitch tape that will allow you to pitch your idea more effectively. For example, Sundance Documentary Fund offers grants up to $20,000 for development (although a pitch tape is not required they do encourage applications that have some footage).
- **Travel bursaries**—to help with travel costs associated with production. For example, British director Hugh Hartford won some money to pay for flights to Australia from the PUMA Mobility Award so he could capture the 100th birthday celebrations of one of his key contributors.
- **Production funding**—for making the film, program or series. Some funding programs insist that you have a certain percentage of your funding in place before they will consider giving you money. Getting the first funding is always the biggest challenge; once you have a major funder on board others will (usually) follow.
- **Completion or finishing funds**—for post-production: offline and online editing, sound mix, voiceover, grading etc. "Then there are lots of funding companies or organizations that you can apply to to get your completion funding," says

producer Leigh Gibson. For example, "The Sundance documentary fund provides completion funding, but they require between twenty and seventy-five minutes of continuously edited footage so you should be quite far down the line with edit by that stage. But if you've been continuously filming from your development stage then you should have some footage that you can put together." Some funds will only fund a specific cost, such as a composer, or only fund a set percentage of your post-production budget.

● **Distribution and outreach costs**—marketing, DVDs, film prints etc.

Make a list of all appropriate funding bodies and then find out about their funding cycles, and mark any key submission deadlines on your production schedule. This will help you map out where and when your application and grant writing efforts should be concentrated. It's easy to miss opportunities or end up submitting poorly written proposals because you spotted a funding deadline only twenty-four hours before the cut-off date. "Absolutely, there should be a strategy, otherwise you could spend years on one project," says producer Leigh Gibson. "If you are aware of those key deadlines, there will always be three or four options."

You should also factor into your schedule how long it takes each funding source to review applications—it's no good applying for urgent production funding to an organization that makes grants only once a year if you've just missed this year's deadline. It can take as little as two months (rarely), or as long as eighteen months to get a decision and, if you're successful, it's likely to be at least several more weeks until you actually get any money. Typically larger organizations move more slowly than smaller ones. For example, the BBC promises to respond to applications via its e-commissioning website within twenty weeks, but small cable channels are often much more responsive. I've had "thanks, but no thanks" messages by return of email; disappointing but also hugely helpful as you know exactly where you stand and can move on to the next potential funder.

Although not directly related to writing your proposal and finance plan, there are several other things you can do in the development stage to set yourself up for success further along the production process, including planning your outreach (if appropriate), developing your professional network and building an audience for your film.

Distribution and Outreach Plan

If your film or series is intended for TV then initial distribution (i.e. transmission), is taken care of by the channel(s) that fully funded or co-financed your project. You may then grant a distributor a license to distribute, that is, sell the transmission rights of your program to channels in territories outside those that have already been granted to the co-funding broadcasters. Other distribution outlets include pay-TV, DVD, festival, theatrical, non-theatrical (airlines and prisons), VOD (video on demand).

Issue-driven independent films can find distribution and outreach (NGO-speak for publicity and marketing) partners via the larger documentary forums, such as IDFA and Hot Docs and initiatives like the Channel 4 BRITDOC Foundation's Good Pitch. Foundations and charities can help filmmakers market their film to their supporters and to schools and other educational establishments via their email databases.

Although distribution and outreach might seem like a long way off, "If you get your outreach set from the beginning, that then feeds into production money," says filmmaker Hugh Hartford. "If you can show that you have a budget for marketing, it means people will definitely see this film. So in that sense you are working backwards, guaranteeing that it will get out there and then going back to the foundations and saying, 'We've got all this interest, we just need the production funding.'"

Building Contacts

Building useful contacts takes time, so the earlier you start the better: certainly as soon as you first think of your idea, preferably a long time before. Film festivals, markets and conferences are one—if potentially expensive way—of building up your contacts book. "The key thing is to see who is attending," says Elizabeth Radshaw, director of the Hot Docs Forum and Market. "We print up books, we put all this stuff on the website—filmmakers should do some serious trawling and research and set aside a minimum of six to eight hours, and know who the heck is coming, who they are, what they do, why they do it. These are resources that people don't access nearly enough; at every single event around the world that I've attended, people just show up and look for the party. Passive networking can be successful, but active networking, with a lot of preparation and good groundwork, sets you up for better serendipitous happenstance. The documentary community is small and tight-knit, even though it's very global and we are very supportive of each other, but it's personality-driven, so you can't just rely on your filmmaking skills to get you noticed."

Ask everyone you meet at festivals and conferences for their business card and keep a database of names and contact details. It's useful to make note of when and where you met them, and any memorable details about your meeting, as that will give you a memory-jogging opening line when you need to contact them. Another potential source of useful contacts is through workshops and seminars. It's obviously beneficial to sign up for development, pitching and trailer workshops so that you fully understand the process of getting a project off the ground, but an added bonus is that you meet other people in a setting that is conducive to chatting over coffee and lunch. You might find a producing partner or someone who knows the inside track of applying for a particular source of funding, or the tutor may be able to open doors for you. That strategy worked for Geoffrey Smith, director of *The English Surgeon*. He was an experienced British TV director, but was new to the international documentary funding circuit. He signed up for several pitching and trailer workshops through the European Documentary Network and as result met some European commissioners. "It also just gave me new friends and contacts and that is so important when you are starting out like I was, in a brave new world," he said.

Debra Zimmerman, Executive Director of Women Make Movies, recommends looking at the end credits of documentaries that are similar to your own and approaching the producer and/or director to see if they might suggest some relevant contacts and perhaps even make introductions. If your film has a certain theme—sport, perhaps—or is issue-based, keep your eye on the press for celebrities or special interest groups who might be curious to see your film. You can approach them to ask for a donation or help in publicizing your fundraising mission and start building your audience in advance of the film's release.

Send all new contacts an email to say how much you enjoyed meeting them and that you hope to cross paths with them again. A slightly less personal way of keeping in touch is to set up a profile on LinkedIn and send a connection request to everyone you meet. Most people have a LinkedIn profile and it can be easier to keep track of people if they move jobs often (assuming they keep their profile updated). Alongside keeping up to date with changes in the industry via the trade press it should be relatively easy to keep your contacts current and ready for when you want to make your first pitch.

Don't forget to get your own business cards made (and carry them with you at all times); it can be done cheaply and quickly through online printing services and most allow you to upload your own designs for a small fee. It's a good idea to buy your own domain name (which will cost approximately $6–$20 for a couple of years and generally comes with free email account), so that you don't have to use an amateurish-looking yahoo or hotmail email address. If you already know the title of your film you could buy that domain name, and then you are all set for when you want to build a website to publicize your film. Otherwise, a more flexible and perhaps a more permanent option is to buy a version of your name, such as Joe@joebloggsfilms.com. Put your email address, website or LinkedIn profile and telephone number on your business cards. Further down the line you can get a set of business cards made with your film's title, logline and website address.

Building Buzz

When Geoffrey Smith was thinking about outreach and distribution for *The English Surgeon* he discovered, "The most useful thing you can do with the internet is to try and build an audience for your own film." First, he brainstormed all the different groups that might be interested in his documentary which followed Henry Marsh, a British neurosurgeon, who traveled to Ukraine to perform delicate brain surgery on a man who had been told his brain tumor was inoperable. "We reached out to medical groups, people involved in caring in the community (Obama's big pledge was "what can you do for your neighbor" and we picked up on that theme), doctors, nurses, patients, universities, and even Nick Cave fans [Cave wrote the film's soundtrack]. It was a big list, particularly when you are going global. On top of that just ordinary people want to see it, of course, as we are all patients at the end of the day."

Building buzz can help not just your film but your longer-term career too. Paul Tucker, of Monkeypuzzle Productions in Scotland, made a critically acclaimed film about singer-songwriter Edwyn Collins, but he wasn't ready to capitalize on the momentum. "The sort of people who are Edwyn Collins fans are the kind of people who are influential in the creative industries and may be inclined to say, 'If he made that, he might like to make this ...' I was very slow to make the most out of the positive feedback we got when we finished the film because my website was only made fairly recently, so that was a great loss of potential work."

Decide whether you should set yourself up with a personal website where you can post your credits and showreel, adding to it as your career progresses, or whether you need to set up a standalone website dedicated to a single film. The former is probably better suited to a jobbing producer/director who is employed at a series of production companies or someone working on a series of more commercial TV projects that are owned or licensed by production companies or channels, and the latter better for an independent film project that needs to build its own buzz.

It's worth setting up a Twitter account as soon as possible, too. Once you have a reasonable Twitter following you have a ready-made community who can spread the word about your work (and need for funds). Again, you need to decide whether to tweet as yourself, or as your film. I'd advise the former, so you can build real relationships with people before you start pushing your marketing message. Personally, I'm unlikely to follow anyone back who is tweeting as a film or a brand as I know they aren't following me because they think I'm witty and interesting: they want something from me, and that's a turn-off.

To start building a Twitter following begin tweeting interesting observations on your area of interest or expertise, share useful links and answer questions. Whereas LinkedIn is resolutely professional in tone, on Twitter you can add more personality. There is a search function where you can find people with similar interests; when you find people you want to build a relationship with you simply press the Follow button and it's likely that they will follow you back. To optimize your account, fill in your Twitter profile with a short biography and post a picture. People like dealing with people and will suspect you of being a spammer if you don't identify yourself. It's not necessary to spend all day tweeting, but you do need to be consistent, so put aside a few minutes every evening or a couple of evenings a week. Twitter is usually at its liveliest when there is a big TV show airing, so that's a good time to get caught up in a real-time conversation as people swap opinions about the latest *Dr Who* episode or *X Factor* contestants.

A word of warning: if you are planning to pitch an idea in the more lucrative and cut-throat world of TV formats you should keep your idea and its production under wraps for as long as possible. The threat, real or imagined, of idea theft requires the format creator be much more cautious; posting it on the internet is unwise, and won't help your case should you later feel someone has stolen your format. There are a number of script and format registration services with which you can log your format (such as the Writers Guild of America or BECTU in the

UK), and you should do due diligence to find out who are the most reputable production companies and channels to approach with your idea. In the US it is usual for format creators to appoint an agent or entertainment attorney to represent them; indeed many US networks will not see someone who does not have such representation.

By now you should know your project inside out, and have identified where you need to develop it further. A couple of sample proposals are provided here for reference.

Sample Proposals

How to Re-establish a Vodka Empire *
by Dan Edelstyn, Optimistic Productions

The Story

This feature-length film is about three of the great events of the twentieth century: the Bolshevik Revolution, the Holocaust and the collapse of Communism. It is told through the story of the filmmaker Dan Edelstyn, whose Jewish grandmother fled the Bolshevik Revolution as a twenty-year-old, to end up in turbulent Belfast in the early 1920s. Dan, discovering her diaries a few years ago, decides to investigate her life. He discovers that most of the remaining members of his family died at the hands of the Nazis in Kiev, but the family vodka factory still exists—tottering on the edge of bankruptcy. To save it—and the village on which it depends—he decides to import its high-quality vodka to the UK. The film will interweave Dan's attempts to get the business going, with his historical investigation into the history of his family— including his father, who became an eminent cancer specialist in Northern Ireland. This is a film about identity, belonging, cultural integration and the Jewish experience of the twentieth century, told with wit, insight and a gripping unfolding narrative.

*This is the original proposal that filmmaker Dan Edelstyn used to pitch his feature documentary. The full story of how he raised money can be found in Part III.

The Style

This is an authored journey, which takes in a massive sweep of European history. On the one hand, it's a quest by the filmmaker to discover his European Jewish identity and balance that with being British—on the other it's a serious tragic-comic adventure story in which Dan's grandmother is brought to life—last of all—it's a business story involving high stakes, where success carries a huge reward. As this is an undertaking in process, the film will comprise recent footage from the Ukraine, shot in February, where Dan discovers the factory, and then it continues as he returns to negotiate the import of the first 1,000 bottles, the development of the brand and the forging of partnerships with distributors, PR gurus, and financial backers. It's a film which combines dramatic re-enactments of the Bolshevik Revolution, based on Maroussia's manuscript, with the modern-day Ukraine. The film interweaves the story of the rest of the family, who disappeared under Stalin and were never heard of again after Hitler's invasion of the Ukraine in 1942. Ultimately it charts the full circle of migration.

Why Now?

Business is a hot topic, it's been made sexy by such TV stories as *Willie's Wonky Chocolate Factory* and the hit format *The Apprentice*. This story trumps the lot, however, with its back story of the Russian Revolution, the whole thing coming to life out of a manuscript discovered in a slumbering old suitcase in the attic of my mum's house. This film taps into the verve for business stories—but also the massive interest in roots and family history. It also paints a unique picture of the Ukraine just as it begins to look towards integrating with Europe.

The Rock*

6 x 60'
Channel 4
Fixed rig documentary series

Delivery: November 2013
Executive Producer: Nicola Lees
TV Mole Productions
tvmole@tvmoleproductions.com

It's Britain—but not as you know it
This ambitious observational series expands the fixed-camera format to provide unprecedented access to an entire country: Gibraltar. Fiercely British, and united in its antipathy towards neighboring Spain, this is a community like no other. Its 30,000 residents—crammed into less than seven square kilometers—live in one of the most densely populated places on Earth and Gibraltar's location on the border between Europe and Africa make it a hotbed of political intrigue, international crime and small-town gossip. We follow the everyday dramas of Gibraltar's residents over the course of one hot summer.

Over three months we get to know a number of key local characters as they cope with the annual influx of holidaymakers and prepare for a rare, and much anticipated, visit from the Royal family. We meet people like:

- Jo Cartwright, mum of one, and daytime presenter with BFBS radio—she knows everybody and is at the centre of everything that happens on the Rock;
- Tim Montgomery and Conchy Lopez, owners of Dolphin Safari tours— who have to avoid the regular skirmishes between the British Ministry of Defence and Spanish Guardia Civil vessels in the Bay of Gibraltar but hope to persuade the Earl and Countess of Wessex to hop aboard for some sightseeing;

*This is a proposal for a hypothetical series designed to show the information that TV commissioners expect to see in a "one-sheet."

● Traffic cop PC Paul Davies, who was recently awarded the title of Constable of the Year and has the huge responsibility of chaperoning the Royal couple.

As well as following the lives of our main characters, a hundred fixed-rig cameras capture unfolding dramas at key sites around the Rock, day and night. Fast-response camera operators shadow police and customs officers as they move around by land and sea to combat crime and rebuff hostile behavior from the Spanish authorities. CCTV cameras capture funny—and potentially dangerous—encounters between unwary tourists and the wild Barbary macaques that populate the Rock.

As the summer wears on, tourists arrive and leave and political tensions with Spain wax and wane, we explore the motives behind Gibraltar's very British battle to maintain its independence from Spain and offer an entertaining—and sometimes dramatic—insight into this tight-knit community.

Further Reading and Resources

Proposal Writing
Greenlit: Developing Factual/Reality TV Ideas from Concept to Pitch by Nicola Lees (Methuen Drama, 2010)

Pitch Tape
Trailer Mechanics by Fernanda Rossi (Magafilms, 2nd edn., 2012)

Fiscal Sponsors

Arts Engine	www.artsengine.net/fs
Center for Independent Documentary	www.documentaries.org
Documentary Educational Resources	www.der.org
Fractured Atlas	www.fracturedatlas.org
From the Heart Productions	http://fromtheheartproductions.com
International Documentary Association	www.documentary.org
New York Foundation for the Arts	www.nyfa.org
Third World Newsreel	www.twn.org
Women Make Movies	www.wmm.com

Scheduling

Movie Magic Scheduling (previously known as EP Scheduling)
http:www.entertainmentpartners.com/Content/Products/Scheduling.aspx

Budgeting

Film and Video Budgets, and *The Independent Film and Videomaker's Guide* by Michael Wiese (Michael Wiese Productions, 2010)

Documentors—http://www.documentaryhowto.com/—have a range of inexpensive budget templates and samples to download, including:

- Simple budget template—one page
- Detailed line item budget—six pages
- Budget samples from five documentaries with budgets ranging from $10K to $545K
- Budgeting tutorial

Reelgrok—www.reelgrok.com
Inexpensive (and free to members) sample budgets, including:

- Reality TV pilot
- $150K documentary
- $550K primetime TV history documentary with re-enactments
- $1.5m documentary series

Celtx—http://celtx.com
Free budgeting and scheduling downloads

Movie Magic Budgeting software—http://www.entertainmentpartners.com/Content/Products/Budgeting.aspx

Film Budgeting Yahoo! Group (forum for all things budgeting)—http://movies.groups.yahoo.com/group/FilmBudgeting/

The Numbers—a list of budgets for theatrical documentaries—http://www.the-numbers.com/movies/series/Documentary.php

Showbiz Labor Guide—details of pay rates for the USA and Canada, including plain English explanations of labor law.
http://www.showbizsoftware.com/Showbiz_Labor_Guide_Rates_eBook_2010_2011_p/1008.htm

Televisual magazine run an annual salary survey of the UK TV industry every April.
http://www.televisual.com/blog-detail/Who-earns-what-in-TV_bid-261.html

General

The Biz: The Basic Business, Legal and Financial Aspects of the Film Industry by Schuyler M. Moore (Silman-James Press, 2007)

Production Manager's Handbook: Production Management for TV and Film by Linda Stradling (Methuen Drama, 2010)

TV and Documentary Trade Press

Broadcast	broadcastnow.co.uk (UK)
CableU	cableu.tv (USA)
Cynopsis	cynopsis.com (USA)
DOX	dox.mono.net (Europe)
Realscreen	realscreen.com (N. America)
TVMole	tvmole.com (UK/USA)

PART II:
The Funding

Having focused on getting the idea into shape, we can now look at the various sources of funding that might be appropriate for you and your idea. The funding landscape changes on an almost daily basis as TV schedules get filled, funding deadlines pass, new funds open and others close, new players come into the market and governments are elected in and out, so it is impossible to produce an accurate guide to funding sources. Instead, I'll present an overview of the different types of funding so that you can make an informed decision about which one(s) to pursue.

The funders are split into ten different types, roughly by what kind of organization they are—broadcaster, distributor, foundation—but, perhaps more importantly, also by their funding motivation. Once you have identified what a particular type of funder wants to get out of funding a film you can approach them in a way that shows them how funding your idea will satisfy their needs. Each chapter concentrates on one type of funder, outlining its pros and cons and sharing tips from people who have secured money from that kind of funding source. I've also indicated for which kind of program/film and producer/filmmaker each type of funding is most appropriate. Where possible I've also provided examples of actual proposals or application forms to illustrate what constitutes a successful submission.

If you are an experienced TV program maker and have a commercially viable program idea it's likely that you will find funding from one or more of the funders at the start of this section. If you are a beginner filmmaker or are making a project for a niche audience it's likely that your funding will come from one or more of the funders in the second half of this section. Some projects will be funded from just one source (the ideal scenario), some from a couple of sources within the same funding type, others will stitch together a patchwork of funding from several different types of funding. Every project is different so there are no hard and fast rules; the trick is to ascertain what works best for you in your particular situation. The different sources of funding we'll explore are, in order of appearance:

1. TV channels
2. Distributors
3. Brands
4. Banks and investors
5. Government
6. Nonprofit organizations and charities

7. Educational institutions and grant foundations
8. Film foundations
9. Crowdfunding
10. Friends, family and acquaintances

1
TV Channels—Ratings Addicts

TV broadcaster and co-production funding is best suited to experienced program makers with:

- An entertainment, factual entertainment, specialist factual, reality or documentary series with hour long or half-hour episodes
- An expensive TV program idea with international potential
- A returnable format with global appeal
- Established relationships with TV commissioning (development) executives
- A proven track record in the type of program being pitched

Independent filmmakers with:

- Proven experience on TV productions as an associate producer/director
- Credits on award-winning films
- Authored one-off documentaries with international appeal
- An idea that matches the remit of one of the specialist documentary strands e.g. *First Cut* on Channel 4 or *POV* on PBS
- Good relationships with channel commissioning executives
- A partnership with an established production company or executive producer who already has existing relationships with channel executives

> *We're up against* Grey's Anatomy, Survivor, The Office,
> *and* The Big Bang Theory: *we're huddling in the trenches*
> *firing at the armed might of the entire American cultural*
> *empire coming at us ... don't come into the office saying*
> *you've got a gentle tale about a dog."*
>
> —Mark Starowicz (Executive Director, Documentaries, CBC, Canada)

In the USA the networks and cable channels hold annual "upfronts" in fancy New York City locations such as Lincoln Center and Carnegie Hall. These events are an opportunity for the advertisers to view the upcoming season's programs. The networks often put on a real show, wheeling out their top executives, actors and comedians, alongside specially shot spoof videos and genuine program trailers in an attempt to whip up as much excitement as possible. The networks' aim is to get the advertisers to pay top dollar to advertise their products in the commercial breaks in and around their upcoming shows.

The price the advertisers pay for an advertising slot is calculated using the audience viewing figures during a few key months (November, February, May and July), known as the "sweeps." The more people who watch a particular program during sweeps the more the channel can charge advertisers to advertise in the commercial breaks in that program and/or slots in future. The channels schedule their programs particularly aggressively during those weeks in an attempt to get the highest possible audiences and keep the advertising rates high. If they lose their audience to a rival channel during those weeks, they lose advertising dollars, which means they don't have as much money to spend on future programs, which in turn means they might not be able to attract audiences during the next sweeps, and they get sucked into a dangerous downward spiral.

Channel executives can track exactly when viewers tune in, turn over to a different channel or switch off their televisions. They do everything they can to get people to come to their channel and stay there for as long as possible. Advertisers pay thousands, and sometimes hundreds of thousands, of dollars for a thirty-second advertising spot and, understandably, they want to buy advertising time during the most watched programs so as many people as possible will see their expensively produced commercials. When viewers respond to the ads by purchasing the brand's product the advertiser gets a satisfactory return on their investment (ROI). Thus, TV channels the world over are driven by their audience ratings and data are gathered, analyzed and agonized over on a daily basis.

Some slots, on niche cable channels and in the daytime schedule for example, attract fewer viewers, so it is cheaper for brands to advertise there. The channel therefore has less ad money coming in and less to spend on funding programs. Other advertising slots, notably in primetime (and particularly around hit shows such as *X Factor* or live events such as the *Superbowl*), command a much higher price, as advertisers are guaranteed a big audience.

Channels that work on a subscription model are less reliant on advertising revenue as their subscribers provide a regular income, but pay-TV channels must still attract a large audience so they can continue to fund quality programs and in doing so retain current subscribers and attract new ones. Public service television typically doesn't carry advertising and is funded by the public via license fees (for example, the BBC is funded by a compulsory license fee that must be paid by everyone who owns a television in the UK) or directly from the government or other organizations, but those channels still have to prove their worth in a competitive marketplace in order to justify and maintain their funding, which means that they too must attract large audiences. The upshot of all this is that TV executives, whether at networks or cable/satellite channels base all their commissioning decisions on whether they think a program will rate, that is, attract a large audience.

Anyone who has ever attended a panel at an industry conference will know that commissioners speak their own special language, which often seems to consist of no more than a handful of words, like "fresh," "noisy" and "original." What they really mean is that they want programs that will get them column inches in the press, which in turn will drive viewers to their programs. Documentaries with titles such as *My One Hundred Thousand Lovers*, *My Monkey Baby* and *My Big Fat Gypsy Wedding* are all likely to attract media interest. Once a channel has caught the attention of viewers they want to keep them coming back for more. The preferred method of doing that is to commission series rather than one-off programs, which is why formats like *The World's Strictest Parents*, *The Apprentice* and *Undercover Boss* and reality series such as *Keeping Up with the Kardashians*, *The Only Way Is Essex* and *Jersey Shore* dominate the schedules. Of course, not every channel is wall-to-wall reality; there is a place for high-end documentaries, particularly in the specialist factual genres, but channels still prefer to commission science or history series over one-off science or history documentaries and they keep returning to subjects that rate such as World War II, dinosaurs and lavish *Planet Earth*-style spectaculars.

Sometimes, a broadcaster makes a strategic decision to spend more money on a certain type of program in an attempt to maximize impact. For example, about a decade ago, the mantra in the BBC's specialist factual commissioning department was "fewer, bigger, better." More recently, Channel 4 decided to pump more money into ambitious fixed-rig documentary series, such as *One Born Every Minute*, which observed the staff and patients on a busy maternity ward. The budget for that series was a very healthy £250,000 per hour. At the time, the then deputy head of documentaries, Simon Dickson, said, "There's no point in having the right idea and being unable to realize it. The imagination of the indies shouldn't be restricted by what they think we'd pay for it."

As broadcasters commission more series, competition for the few remaining slots for one-off documentaries gets tougher. A commissioner at TVOntario (TVO), a regional Canadian channel that transmits approximately twenty-eight hours of documentary programming a week, saw an increase in submissions from 350 proposals in 2007 to 500 in 2010. Unfortunately, she is able to commission only eight or ten documentaries a year. But it's not all bad news. While some markets have reduced the number of slots for documentary, other markets are opening up to provide new opportunities. In South Korea, for example, a number of new channels (launched in 2012) are run by newspaper publishers and focus primarily on news and documentaries. The more traditional South Korean channels are also embracing documentaries. Jae-Heon Song, head of co-productions at South Korea's national broadcaster KBS, told reporters, "KBS1 runs no commercials so there are lots of slots for documentaries on the channel."

Fully Funded

The simplest, most efficient way of funding your TV series or documentary is to get it fully funded by a single broadcaster in your home territory. For the right idea—cheap and long-running, or expensive and ambitious—channels are still willing to fully fund programs. This is the way television programs have been funded for decades and is still the way most producers prefer to work. The obvious advantage is that you only have to deal with one buyer, which streamlines both budget and editorial negotiations.

The disadvantage to having a program fully funded by one broadcaster is that many channels, particularly in the USA, insist on taking all the rights in a program, so they can transmit and exploit it as they like; many channels are now part of international networks, so it's extremely cost-effective for them to be able to fund a program and then transmit it around the world without having to pay extra licensing fees in each territory. In this situation the producer is effectively employed on a work-for-hire basis. They are given the budget to make the program, from which they keep a 10–15 percent production fee. This "profit" can quickly disappear if unforeseen costs cause the production to go over budget.

In the UK, independent production companies have collectively negotiated terms of trade with the channels, which means the broadcasters don't hold all the rights to programs they fund. Instead, they license a program for a number of years during which they can transmit the program an agreed number of times. If they broadcast the program more times than originally specified, they have to pay the producer an additional license fee. All other rights in the program are retained by the producer, which allows them to exploit, that is, make money from selling the program and/or the format, new media and merchandising rights around the world (sometimes referred to as the "back end"). This provides independent producers with an important source of income on top of the 10 percent production fee: according to a 2010 survey, "the average [UK] indie derived 11.5 percent of its total turnover from rights exploitation." US production companies are starting to set up offices in the UK so they can produce programs under the UK agreement, and then sell the North American rights to US broadcasters, keeping all other rights to exploit around the world.

There are also other opportunities to get your program fully funded. Some large independent production companies fully fund their own productions, only taking them out to market once fully completed. Celine Payot, VP international sales and marketing at Paris-based blue-chip wildlife producer ZED, told Realscreen, "Now instead of knocking on broadcasters' doors, which we're still doing but it is difficult, we're knocking on producers' doors." It's not as crazy as it sounds because some of the so-called "super-indie" production companies have more money than broadcasters: at one point it was reported that the then RTL-owned Channel 5 in the UK had a revenue of €212m and an operating profit of zero; FremantleMedia, a production and distribution company also owned by RTL, had a revenue of €567m and an operating profit of €97m for the same period (during the first six months of 2008). Looking beyond TV, Netflix, the subscription-based online video rental company, is moving to video streaming and looking to commission original programs (they were reportedly offering to pay around $4–$6million per episode for a political drama starring Kevin Spacey).

How to Pitch to a TV Channel (or Independent Production Company)

There are several ways to pitch to a TV commissioner—from least likely to most likely to succeed:

1. Submit unsolicited idea via the channel's e-commissioning website (their preferred method of contact)
2. Send unsolicited query via email to commissioning executive you've never met
3. Take part in competitive public pitch to at TV conference or festival
4. Submit a proposal via email to a commissioner you met at industry event and who expressed a vague interest your idea
5. Be selected to take part in a series of one-on-one meetings at an organized TV/film festival pitch forum (good for pitching to international commissioners)
6. Be invited to a one-on-one meeting with a commissioning executive at a broadcaster
7. Discuss your idea during your regular monthly meeting with a commissioning executive at a broadcaster (best-case scenario)
8. A commissioning editor calls you to ask if you'd like to produce a program s/he's just dreamt up

Commissions are usually born out of a dialogue (often several conversations over weeks or months), so your best bet is to try to engineer a face-to-face meeting with a commissioning executive. If you can't get a meeting with a commissioner you can try pitching your idea to a reputable production company which already has a relationship with the relevant broadcasters.

If approaching a commissioner or production company for the first time, write a brief email that outlines the subject of your project and its format, e.g. "a one-off hour-long documentary about a unique pop-up police canteen in London," which gives them enough information to know whether they might be interested, but not so much detail that they can walk off with your idea or give it to someone else. Say why you think it is a good fit for their channel/production company and ask for a meeting to discuss it further. Keep it brief and professional. If they are interested they will ask for a written proposal and invite you to a meeting. If at all possible avoid sending your full proposal/treatment until after you've met with them; that gives you the opportunity to incorporate any changes that were discussed in the meeting.

If you are invited to a face-to-face pitch do some preparation to make sure you make the most of the meeting:

1. Who will be in the meeting? Do you have any previous connection to them that might act as an icebreaker? What kinds of programs have they commissioned/produced in the past?
2. Where does your program fit in their schedule and why?
3. Have they commissioned something similar in the last few years? If so, why is yours different? If not, why should they?
4. Can you describe your idea clearly and with enthusiasm? "Most people start off pitching the research or pitching the background, pitching the context, everything except the story," says Rudy Buttignol, President of Knowledge Network, Canada. They want to know about the narrative, your key characters and your approach; they don't want to listen to a lecture about an issue or hear about your exhaustive research efforts.
5. Think about using visual aids—pitch tape, photographs, newspaper clippings or anything else—to bring your story to life. If you are showing a DVD make sure it plays properly, and doesn't have too much "black" at the beginning before the clip starts. If you are using your laptop, ensure it's fully charged and is switched on and ready to go before you go into your meeting. Waiting even thirty seconds for your computer to fire up feels like a lifetime in a stressful pitch situation.

Mark Starowicz

Executive Director, Documentary Programming, Canadian Broadcasting Corporation, Toronto

"I work at a television network that believes documentaries should be on television in primetime. We have a broad audience and we are operating in primetime up against all the US channels. We have all of the television channels that NYC has, plus Canadian television channels are allowed to carry 60 percent American content, so we are competing against more American programming here in Toronto than a program in New York.

"Before you set up a meeting, know what the buyer is looking for. Make sure you've seen and understand the strand. There's nothing more offensive to a commissioning editor than somebody coming and saying—it happens to me about 60 percent of the time—"What does your strand carry? Is this public television in Canada?' I wouldn't dream of going and seeing someone in Hungary without having seen their strand. That's the big mistake made by most people.

"If you know a strand exists and you've watched a couple of films, take the next step and find out what we are specifically looking for. We are not looking for history: we show hosted programs that have a single narrator, so don't come to us with your personal story of how you are looking for your ancestors, because it's the wrong strand for that. We are paying producers to bring us a television program that will compel people."

Try to take notes during the meeting if you can (or immediately afterwards) so you have a record of what was discussed, and a paper trail should there be any future dispute. The meeting will lead to one of three outcomes:

1. No thank you, it's not right for me
2. I'm interested, but I have some questions/doubts—let's talk again in few weeks/months when you've done some more development (this is often used interchangeably with "No," when the commissioner doesn't want to upset the person pitching the idea)
3. Yes—I love it and I want to commission it immediately (least likely)

If you are lucky enough to get a positive response, it is increasingly likely that you will be offered only a proportion of the money you actually need for production. The traditional way to make up this budget shortfall is via a co-production—an arrangement where another broadcaster puts in the rest of the money. It's been suggested that UK channels are now using co-productions to fund one-third of their commissions, with channels in the USA, Canada, France, Germany and Spain the most likely to provide co-production funding.

Co-production between International TV Channels

Co-production is a slightly confusing and potentially misleading term, as it can mean two production companies working together to make a TV show or, more often, it refers to a co-financing agreement where two or more channels share the cost of funding one program, which is what we're talking about here.

In a two-channel co-production it's usual for one channel to put in 60 percent of the budget, and the other channel to contribute 40 percent; in some instances, where the producer wants to retain some rights, the split might be 40/40 between two broadcasters and the producer puts in the final 20 percent. The channel that puts in the most money takes the lead editorially, but the other channel also expects to exert some editorial control over the program content. In return for making up the budget deficit, the co-producing channel gets the right to exclusively transmit the program in their home territory (and any other territories that they've negotiated as part of the deal).

Many of the US channels that traditionally co-produced the "fewer, bigger, better" science and history documentaries have moved on to fully funding cheaper, long-running character-driven shows, such as *American Restoration* (History), *JUNKies* (Science), and *Swamp Brothers* (Discovery). If they commit to a big co-production special, it's likely that their contribution will be relatively small, forcing the producer to do deals with several channels to raise the budget. For example, feature-length CGI documentary *March of the Dinosaurs* had funding from National Geographic (USA), History Television (Canada), France 5 (France) and Super RTL (Germany). Everyone who's ever been involved in a co-production advises that the fewer partners there are, the better. "In an ideal world you don't want more than two co-producers on one project," says Lilla Hurst, founder of LillaVision, but "sometimes you are forced into a situation where you have to have more than two co-producers, because you require that money and that's the only way you are going to get it." Some channels, such as France Télévisions, won't even consider a co-production proposal unless two other channels are already committed to the project.

Co-productions work best when all the participating broadcasters have broadly similar editorial remits. I was once tasked with developing programs that could be co-produced by TLC and the BBC. At the time, the BBC channel with the closest audience demographic to TLC was BBC3. TLC's schedule was full of observational series about large, wholesome mid-western American families: *Jon & Kate Plus Eight*, *Sixteen Children and Moving In*; and *Little People, Big World*. Meanwhile, BBC3 was commissioning shock docs focused on British-born characters and programs with in-your-face titles, such as: *My Penis and Everyone Else's, Help I*

Smell of Fish! and *F*** Off I'm Ginger.* There was no common point of reference between the two channels editorially and so neither channel was willing to co-operate financially.

One of the biggest risks of co-production is that two channels agree to a deal but the producer makes something that one of the channels isn't expecting. "It's quite easy for there be a cultural breakdown in communication," warns Lilla Hurst. "The first co-production I ever worked on was between a British producer making a series on cruises for a UK channel and the Travel Channel in the US. In the initial pitch to the US channel, my predecessor hadn't appreciated that cruises in America are very different from cruises in Europe. In the States, it's a young person's pursuit, whereas here in the UK, they're for older people. So I walked in at the point where the US channel had seen the first rough cut and gone completely mad—'there's a bunch of seniors playing quoits on the deck of a ship on a wet and windy day ... what the ***?!'" It's tempting to cast the channels in the role of the bad guy, but keeping everyone informed all the way through production is important, says Lilla. "Very often I think people have been quite rude towards their international partners and just have taken the money and run. Even though the international partner might be investing just as much as the UK partner they treat them as a secondary channel and don't keep them up to speed or involve them enough."

CASE STUDY
Wojtek: The Bear That Went to War

Kat Mansoor
Co-Founder/Producer/Director, Animal Monday (a multi-award-winning independent documentary production company).

"We are making an international co-production at the moment and that's much more challenging than an independently funded film. I think if you get the opportunity to get funding from an organization, it's such a gift, especially for your first film, because getting funds from the Channel 4 BRITDOC Foundation and the Wellcome Trust was a walk in the park comparatively to getting small amounts of money from several broadcasters. Dealing with an international co-production is much more serious and there are a lot more personalities to work with,

"The documentary, *Wojtek: The Bear That Went to War*, is a film about a bear that became a soldier and fought alongside the Polish allies in World War II; he shared their beer and cigarettes and eventually their fate. The film is a kooky look at the Polish contribution to the war effort and what they went through—they were really badly treated and lost their independence until 1989—which is told through this amazing character—Wojtek the bear. We found the story through Pinny Grylls, who made a fantastic short film called *Peter and Ben* about a man who lives with a sheep. She was meant to be the director on this film, but she got pregnant so we ended up taking it on and she's acting executive producer/co-writer.

"When we pitched the idea commissioners loved it, but they all wanted to know how we were going to bring it to life, so we were drip-fed small amounts of money, to prove we could do it, before the production money came through.

"Our previous film, *Here's Johnny*, was our film, our point of view at all points. But for *Wojtek*, we had Polish production partners, and they've got their own ideas, the Polish funders also have their ideas, and the BBC have got their ideas too: so at times it seemed that everyone had different ideas."

Wojtek: The Bear That Went to War was a co-production between Animal Monday and Braidmade Films for BBC Scotland, TVP the Polish Film Institute and MDR.

Co-production between Two Domestic Channels

Less commonly, a co-production deal is brokered between two channels in the same country. The channel that puts in the larger percentage of the budget gets to première the show; the channel that puts in the smaller amount gets the "second window," that is, they are allowed to transmit the program on their channel after an agreed delay. When Darlow Smithson pitched *Concorde's Last Flight*, a one-off documentary to mark the tenth anniversary of the Paris crash, they struck both domestic and international co-production deals. Channel 4 were the first broadcaster to commission the film, and Discovery Networks UK took the second transmission window in the UK, while Smithsonian Channel in the USA became the international co-producer.

Competing broadcasters are discovering the benefits of collaboration and channels such as Channel 4 and National Geographic International sometimes negotiate directly with each other about programs that have domestic co-production potential. Scandinavian channels also regularly talk to each other and if they invest in the same programs they all like to transmit the program around the same time.

Co-production between International Production Companies

Another type of co-production occurs when two international production companies join forces to produce one show: they can combine their different areas of expertise and capitalize on their individual commissioner relationships to secure a commission in their respective countries. Such an arrangement typically involves splitting the production responsibilities (and any potential revenue). For example, when Indian producer/distributor Shemaroo wanted to make a 3D version of *Fruit Salad*, an Indian children's program, they partnered with South African animation specialist Astral Studios.

Those collaborations can turn into longer-term partnerships. Arthur Smith of A. Smith & Co. in the US told *Realscreen*, "We did a show for ABC called *I Survived a Japanese Game Show* that was the first American series to be shot entirely in Japan. So we worked with a company called Taiyo Kikaku, which is one of the largest commercial production companies there. We got along so well with them that last year we built a development structure—an exchange of programming ideas. We set up this unit and there's a game show that we've developed together, and we'll start rolling it out by the end of the summer."

Aside from creative collaboration, one of the main reasons that international production companies team up is to take advantage of a co-production treaty arrangement between the governments of two countries (which is discussed in more detail in Chapter 5).

How to Pitch for International Co-production

Before looking to international broadcasters for money, it's important to prove there is a market for your idea by securing some funding from a domestic broadcaster. This gives your idea a stamp of approval, and immediately raises its value in the international marketplace.

To attract co-production money your film or TV series needs to have themes that are relevant to international audiences. Love, survival, transformation, triumph over adversity and other recognizable themes work well the world over. "*Guilty Pleasures* was a no-brainer for me," says Bungalow Town Productions' Rachel Wexler of her decision to produce and raise money for the film, "because it's about Mills and Boon books, love and romance, and these things cross all boundaries. It's shot in India, Japan, America and the UK so I could see that it had good international potential right from the start; I thought it was quite a commercial project." Other genres such as travel and food also work well globally, as does specialist factual content. As co-production consultant Lilla Hurst points out, "Science and history have done very well in international co-production for years, because they tend to deal with universal subjects and name recognition. For example, with a story about World War II, you're generally always going to be able to find a handful of countries that will be interested, that's why there are so many documentaries on the Nazis—they rate well. Equally, science deals with universal themes. In science, it's quite easy to generate imagery that is going to work across different cultures, so it lends itself very well, as does natural history."

Some subjects, however, have to be treated with care in an international market, warns Danny Tipping, Director of Production at Parthenon Entertainment: "History programmes are very difficult because, if you do a Vietnam War special for Europe and America it will have a certain point of view, but if you want to sell it to Vietnam or south-east Asia they will see it slightly differently."

There are other editorial considerations too, such as whether or not to have a host or presenter onscreen, for example. "Generally you want a program to be presenter-free, because presenters can become a big stumbling block, internationally," cautions Lilla Hurst. "You can have some talking heads, but if you've got a project that's too talking-head heavy, that's more difficult. Narrator-led tends to be ideal."

There are a number of ways to pitch to international broadcasters:

1. **Via a broadcaster's co-production department**—Some channels have in-house departments that can help foreign producers find a home for their programs. For example, ZDF Enterprises in Germany, which is part of the public service broadcaster ZDF, was set up as a one-stop shop to help producers pitch their ideas to ZDF commissioners and also acts as their distributor. Nikolas Hülbusch, project manager of documentary co-productions at ZDF Enterprises,

told *Realscreen*, "If the producer needs both a partner in Germany and an international distributor ... the producer only needs to sign one contract and we take care of it."

2. **At a TV market or documentary festival**—You could go it alone and travel to the various TV and documentary markets such as MIPDoc, Realscreen, Hot Docs and IDFA and to meet with channel executives (it's highly recommended that you set up meetings at least a month in advance). Some markets, such as Sheffield Doc/Fest's MeetMarket have an official selection process for producers who want to pitch. If selected, you are scheduled to meet with a number of broadcasters who have seen your written pitch/video and have expressed an interest in hearing more. The advantage of these markets is that it's an efficient way of meeting lots of people, but it's hard for an emerging filmmaker to get traction. Building a relationship to the point where a broadcaster feels confident enough to invest hundreds of thousands of dollars in your idea can take many meetings over several years.

3. **Partner with an established production company in another country**—By partnering with an established and well-respected production company in the country in which you want to pitch your idea, you are giving a foreign channel reassurance that you will be able to deliver the program, to budget, and with all the necessary legal documents in place. The drawback is that you will have to split any revenues with the other production company. While some production companies do accept ideas from outside producers, many don't, so check their website before approaching them.

4. **Engage the services of a co-production agent**—Specialist co-production companies, such as Iliad Entertainment in NYC and LillaVision in London, already have an established network of international contacts, and can represent you and your project at the markets. A co-production agent might also act as an executive producer, to further reassure broadcasters. Co-production agents are receptive to people approaching them with ideas, but they often have relationships with broadcasters in certain geographic areas and will therefore be better at raising finance in those territories. You pitch to a co-production company in the same way as you would to a channel or production company—with a paper pitch, followed by a verbal pitch if they are sufficiently interested—but you have to satisfy them that there is a genuine international market for your idea. Some co-pro agents like to be involved from an early development stage, so they can help you shape your idea so it is

appealing to a wider market; others will take your project on only if you have already got a certain percentage of funding in place already. "Number one question for me, is what money is already attached?" agrees Lilla Hurst. For her, "a perfect pitch would be:

- A (no more than) three-page document, with a good strong outline of not just what the story is going to be but what I'm going to see, and the style of the film;
- A synopsis of the budget, and information on what's been raised to date—approximations are fine;
- Details of the production team, including director;
- A trailer is always good—something that best articulates what you are trying to do with the project, and it gives you a feel of the project.

"The thing you want from any co-production project is that when you pitch it to a broadcaster the broadcaster thinks: 'I've got to have this, I'm going to take a risk and I'm going to throw my money in the ring now.' The proposal and trailer have to convey that there aren't lots of films like this already out there in the distribution catalogues, it's something new and hasn't been done before, or it has been done before but this is a new angle and there's something exclusive about it."

When looking for a partner production company or co-production agent, word of mouth and recommendation is the best place to start. Industry intelligence can be gleaned from conferences, festivals, workshops and seminars. Talk to everyone you meet in the course of your work; you never know when someone might have a key piece of information or could make a valuable introduction.

Whoever you approach, check what their submission procedure is and adhere to it. As much as people want to work on great programs that sell well, they also want to work with people they like and can rely on to be pleasant and professional. "It's very important that I like the production company, because you invest quite a lot of time and energy in people, so you want it to be a natural meeting of minds," says Lilla; "if I'm starting a new relationship I want it to be one that continues."

While co-production can plug the hole in your budget in the short term, having a program that has international appeal can also provide income over the longer term too. According to Thomas Dey, head of corporate finance at Grant Thornton, international distribution makes up just 10 percent of a typical TV production company's turnover (total sales) but it provides approximately 50 percent of its profit. In the next chapter we'll get to know the distributors.

Advantages of Co-production Funding

1. Producers, working in a market where domestic broadcasters are reducing the amount of money they are willing to put into a budget, can find funding from overseas markets either through co-production or presales.
2. Channels are able to invest in programs that they wouldn't otherwise be able to afford.
3. Contributing part of the budget means broadcasters can invest in a broader slate of programs, thereby reducing the risk of failure of a single expensive program.
4. Producers can start to build a global reputation, opening up possibilities for expansion into new territories.
5. TV channels don't expect the production to be underway prior to funding; you can pitch with a proposal/treatment and a two- or three-minute pitch tape.
6. Fully funded and co-produced programs receive the funding at the start of, and at various milestones during, the production process, which reduces cash flow issues.

Disadvantages

1. Producers have to deal with the editorial demands of two or more competing channels; the involvement of more channels increases the budget (through legal fees and the production costs of making different versions of the program).
2. When there are a number of contracts to be negotiated and signed off by several channels it can delay production.
3. The more channels involved in a co-production the more territories you have tied up, and therefore fewer territories into which to sell the completed program (which reduces any potential future revenue).
4. Channels in different countries deal in different currencies, so an unfavorable exchange rate fluctuation could trigger a sudden and unexpected shortfall in your budget.

Next Steps

1. Work out your whether your program's content is better suited to being fully funded by a domestic channel or whether it has enough international appeal to make a co-production a viable option.

2. Research domestic and international channels that might be a good fit editorially.
3. Write a full treatment for your idea. A treatment is a narrative description of your film or series, that outlines the program from start to finish; it introduces the reader to the characters and plot and explains how the film will be shot, structured and edited, including any notes on tone and style of the finished program. A treatment is typically between four and ten pages long.
4. Start a contacts book or database to record useful industry. Split it into:
   a. Commissioning/development executives
   b. Independent production companies
   c. Co-production companies

Sample Treatment*

The Guinea Pig Club

Synopsis

This one-hour documentary tells the story of the Guinea Pig Club, a WWII drinking club so exclusive that membership was restricted to fighter pilots and their bomber crews who had cheated death and sustained horrific facial burns. Sixty years on, they still gather every year for a weekend of eating, drinking and remembrance, but this year the remaining eighty Guinea Pigs will meet for the very last time. They (along with 570 others) underwent weeks, months and years of experimental plastic surgery under the care of a maverick surgeon, Archibald McIndoe. He rebuilt their faces and restored their confidence, and the men went on to lead full and active lives, many of them marrying women they met at the hospital. This film tells the story of three Guinea Pigs, from the dramatic moment when they were shot down in flames, through their long and painful treatment—during which they had to come to terms with their terrible injuries—and their re-entry to civilian life (and love). Using first-person testimony, archive footage and expert interviews we explore how McIndoe's unconventional approach to his patients' care revolutionized plastic surgery and created a group of men who would, given the choice, go through it all again.

*This is an example of a treatment that might have been written for *The Guinea Pig Club*, a 1 x 60' documentry transmitted on BBC4; it's not the original treatment.

Treatment

The film starts with black-and-white archive footage of young men in military uniforms gathered around a piano, singing a song. Many of them have an obvious facial disfigurement. The scene dissolves to a jovial banquet scene in the present day, where a group of elderly men in black tie are eating a three-course dinner. Most of them have facial scars; one has no fingers; another deftly manipulates the silverware using a hook instead of hand. The mood turns somber as a telegram is read out.

Historian **Emily Mayhew** explains that these men are part of a unique club called the the Guinea Pig Club and were the patients of a pioneering surgeon, **Archibald McIndoe**. A black-and-white photo shows a group of smiling young men standing around a hospital bed. One of them is smoking a cigarette; others have strange elephant-like 'trunks' of skin strung between their upper arms and their noses. Guinea Pig **Jack Toper** explains that the plastic surgeons learned their craft by trying out new surgical techniques on the men.

We cut between WWII archive of Spitfires, the modern-day banquet and interviews with some of the men at home. At its height, the Guinea Pig Club had 650 members and their stories are heroic and inspiring, devoid of self-pity. The men, aged eighteen or twenty, joined the Royal Air Force to fight for their country, but also enjoyed the glamour of being pilots, choosing to ignore the danger. The odds weren't good: only one-fifth of aircrews would avoid being shot down, killed, captured or badly injured.

Jack Toper was a wireless operator. On his sixth raid, to München-Gladbach, the propeller was damaged by anti-aircraft fire and the pilot struck in the leg by shrapnel. The plane made it back to England on the remaining engine, with Jack holding the pilot's foot on the rudder bar, before they crash-landed. The plane bounced but landed safely. As they made their escape, the navigator panicked. As Jack struggled to help the navigator escape the plane the oxygen bottles exploded, engulfing Jack in flames, like "a human candle." He woke up in hospital with third-degree burns to his face and fingers.

The kind of injuries Jack sustained were usually fatal, so plastic surgeons had never encountered, let alone treated, them before. Enter Archibald McIndoe, a Kiwi surgeon, who came to be known by the men as "The Maestro," "The Boss," and even "God". **Mr Iain Hutchison**, a maxillofacial surgeon at

St Barts Hospital, London, explains that McIndoe was part surgeon, part counselor and part support worker. An aspiring abdominal surgeon, he moved to London on the advice of his uncle Harold Gillies, a plastic surgeon (known today as the father of plastic surgery), and ended up training alongside him, before presiding over Ward III at the Queen Victoria Hospital, East Grinstead in the south of England. McIndoe describes seeing Jack Toper for the first time, and "God somehow came down my right arm."

We see the Guinea Pigs assembled outside a pub named after them, all dressed in dark blazers and ties bearing the Guinea Pig Club insignia. The club was formed in 1942 by McIndoe's patients. **Dennis Neale** (known as "Eyes Higher," due to one eye sitting higher than the other after he was struck on the head by a moving propeller), explains that McIndoe taught the men that they had strength in numbers and encouraged them to keep in contact. **Vanora Marland**, McIndoe's daughter, describes the Guinea Pigs as troublesome, outrageous and infuriating, and remembers that they were all part of McIndoe's family.

Paul Hart is the only surviving founding member of the Guinea Pig Club, which was originally twenty-eight strong. He sustained his injuries in a training exercise in 1940 when his plane flew into the side of a mountain obscured by cloud. He staggered down the mountain "in a ball of flames." He spent weeks in agony and despair before he became one of McIndoe's first patients. McIndoe saved Paul's sight by performing a rarely used procedure to replace his eyelids with undamaged skin from under his arm. McIndoe went on to save the sight of hundreds of men using this technique.

Jack Toper needed a total facial reconstruction as he'd lost his nose, ears, eyelids and chin. To tackle this McIndoe tried a radical new approach, the tube pedicle. This involved taking a strip of skin from Jack's stomach and attaching the free end of the flap to his forearm, where over the course of two weeks it would heal, using blood from the vessels in the portion of the skin that was still attached to his abdomen. Once healed, McIndoe cut the skin from the stomach and attached the free end further up Jack's arm, and waited for it to heal. The flap of skin was gradually "walked" up his body until it could be attached to where his nose should have been, and eventually fashioned into a new nose. (Today, Jack has to shave his nose as it still sprouts hair as if it's located on his abdomen.) McIndoe was soon performing thirty such operations a day and Ward III looked like the set of a science-fiction film, with men sporting these strange "trunks" or swaddled in bandages like mummies.

At the age of seventeen, **Alan Morgan** was a toolmaker, making parts for Lancaster bombers, but he had hankering to do more. He joined the RAF as bomber crew. On his twenty-first birthday a bombing raid went wrong when the doors of his plane were blown open. He was sent to close the door, but with his oxygen dangerously low, he blacked out and collapsed against the side of the plane, his hands resting against the side of the plane. By the time they landed he had severe frostbite to his fingers. He was rushed to hospital and his fingers warmed up but gangrene set in. McIndoe found Alan during one of his regular visits to RAF hospitals on the search for new patients. Alan recalls being surprised by the party atmosphere on Ward III, with a piano, card games and beer on tap. This was all part of McIndoe's plan: to boost morale and get the men used to socializing in readiness for their discharge into the outside world.

Joyce Crane was one of the nurses and looked after hundreds of Guinea Pigs. She was one of many highly qualified nurses recruited by McIndoe for their good looks. Many Guinea Pigs fell in love with their nurses, and Joyce went on to marry Derek, one of her patients. They have been married for sixty years.

The nurses needed great fortitude as they dealt with the terrible injuries of their charges. The worst part of the day's routine was the changing of the bandages, which stuck to the burns and had to be soaked off. The traditional treatment for burns—tannic acid baths—was supposed to reduce infection and fluid loss, but it made the skin tough and resistant to reconstruction. McIndoe noticed that men who had ditched their aircraft in the sea healed much better so he started to prescribe salt-water baths instead and other hospitals soon followed suit.

He tried a different tack with Alan Morgan's damaged fingers, treating them with ice, but it was no good; Alan's fingers were amputated—a devastating loss for an engineer reliant on his hands for his livelihood. McIndoe fashioned stumps out by separating Alan's knuckle joints to give him some movement in his hands.

As the men underwent their various surgeries McIndoe allowed the other patients into the operating theatre gallery to watch. This ensured they were well informed and were able to discuss their proposed surgery with McIndoe, often making their own suggestions. This level of control reduced fear and pain, explains Iain Hutchinson.

McIndoe also forced the men to go out into the town centre, so they could get used to people staring at them (although East Grinstead would soon be known as "the town that doesn't stare," when McIndoe asked the locals to treat the men normally).

Jack Toper and Paul Hart visit Marchwood Park, where the Guinea Pigs went to recuperate between operations with rugby, soccer and gym sessions. There's an emotional moment as they realize how few Guinea Pigs are still alive. While there was fun, there were also accidents. Paul remembers getting back to the ward late at night after a few beers; he tried to catch a plate he dropped while washing up, forgetting the pedicle that joined his arm to his abdomen ...

There were many dances, which introduced the men to women who were seeing the disfigured men for the first time. **Mary Perry** recalls her initial shock at their appearance; she went on to marry one of the Guinea Pigs. But some of the men suffered relationship and marriage breakdowns as they struggled to adjust to their new circumstances. Alan Morgan was engaged to his childhood sweetheart **Ella** when he lost his fingers. He told her to walk away as he couldn't wear a wedding ring with no fingers and wouldn't be able to earn a living. She told him not to be ridiculous. They've been married for fifty-nine years.

As well as facilitating the Guinea Pigs' social lives, McIndoe helped them get jobs. Alan Morgan exercised his hands daily, slowly regaining his dexterity. After being turned away by employers who didn't believe he could work, he secured a job by keeping his hands in his pockets. His manager only realized Alan had no fingers after three weeks, but by that time he'd proved himself.

The men continued to help each other through times of hardship in the years after war, offering financial support or a place to stay for those that fell on hard times. McIndoe's blend of pioneering surgery, psychological care and social support ensured the men who came under his care not only survived the war but thrived for many decades afterwards. McIndoe died in 1960 at the age of fifty-nine.

Main Characters

The Guinea Pigs are mostly in their eighties but are bright, articulate and interesting, and enjoy spinning a yarn. The are due to meet up for what is likely to be their last reunion when approximately eighty Guinea Pigs will attend and share their news and reminisce about their experiences. We will film the reunion and then concentrate on telling the stories of three of the Guinea Pigs, with a couple of the wives, McIndoe's daughter and a nurse also making an appearance.

The Guinea Pig Club was originally set up as a drinking club. They dealt with their terrible injuries by developing a dark sense of humor, endlessly teasing, provoking and playing tricks on each other.

The positions on the Board were appointed according to injuries. For example, a man with no legs was given the job as Treasurer so he couldn't run off with the money. This sense of humor stays with them today.

Jack Toper—An idealistic and patriotic young man, he joined the RAF in response to Coventry and London being bombed in the Battle of Britain. He was a skilled Morse code operator but once got caught tapping out expletives. He arrived at the hospital in 1944, and spent a long time with his head and face swathed in bandages. He managed to fashion a hole through which he could smoke, flicking ash into a bucket. One time he missed and set his bed on fire.

Paul Hart—One of the founding members of the Guinea Pig Club, he suffered terrible burns to his face and thought he was blind. However, when his bandages were removed, he remembers seeing a nurse like a vision in her starched white apron. He has a reputation among the Guinea Pigs as being a bit of a ladies' man. One of his memories of his time at the hospital was of an air raid when bombs dropped on East Grinstead. The Guinea Pigs hid under their beds and the nurses sprawled on top of them to protect them from falling masonry. He's married to Vera.

Alan Morgan—A toolmaker who enjoyed building model airplanes. When he joined the RAF he left his sweetheart Ella behind in Stockport. She arranged a twenty-first birthday party but he didn't turn up as he was in hospital after suffering severe frostbite to his fingers. She only found out what had happened when his parents received a telegram. He tried to break off their relationship, but she refused to let his injuries stand in their way. They got married four months later. Today they enjoy traveling the UK in their campervan.

Experts

The experts provide objective historical and medical context to the subjective accounts of the Guinea Pigs.

Emily Mayhew—A historian, she is the granddaughter one of the nurses who worked at the hospital, and the author of *The Reconstruction of Warriors*. She explains how McIndoe's approach to his patients differed from surgeons who came before him, and the impact that his holistic care had on the men.

Iain Hutchinson—A consultant plastic surgeon at St Barts Hospital who talks about the surgical techniques used by McIndoe and compares and contrasts them with techniques used in modern-day reconstructive surgery.

Vanora Marland—Archibald McIndoe's daughter. She describes her father's charismatic presence and the impact that his work had on the family when she was a small child

Structure

The documentary is structured around a rough chronology, from McIndoe's early training through to his first operations on the Guinea Pigs, and how his techniques were adapted and evolved as the years passed.

The film explores three aspects of McIndoe's work in turn: the pioneering surgical techniques, his careful attention to the psychological welfare of his patients, and the ongoing aftercare he provided (and the Guinea Pigs themselves later took on) that helped the men into long-term jobs and relationships.

This narrative unfolds through the personal testimony of three main characters: Jack Toper, Paul Hart and Alan Morgan. Each one describes how they sustained their injuries, illustrated by archive, photographs or stylized reconstructions. Formal interviews take place at their respective homes, but we also see them at an aircraft museum, medical museum, driving along country roads, and at the Guinea Pig reunion dinner.

Style

The documentary is narrator-led, and the tone is respectful. Black-and-white archive film and rostrum photographs that take us back into the past are juxtaposed with color footage of the Guinea Pigs in the present day. Actuality of the Guinea Pigs singing in the present day alongside bursts of 1940s music adds authenticity and atmosphere.

Context

The membership of the Guinea Pig Club has fallen in recent years from 650 to approximately 120, due to the advanced age of the men, who are now in their eighties. They have held an annual reunion every year for the Guinea Pigs and their wives at a hotel close to the hospital. Over the course of a weekend they have two dinners (one with their wives and one exclusively for the Guinea Pigs), visit the Guinea Pig pub and other local landmarks and attend a memorial service. This year, due to their dwindling numbers, the Guinea Pigs are planning their last reunion. This film will form part of an important historical record, which also includes hundreds of medical before-and-after surgical photographs, autobiographies, and a Canadian public information film in which the Guinea Pigs played themselves as patients on the ward.

While the documentary is a historical account of WWII, it also has a relevance today. Many soldiers returning from the war in Iraq today struggle to overcome the social isolation brought by their injuries. While medical and surgical techniques have advanced, McIndoe's three-pronged surgical-psychological-social approach to the care of his patients has much to teach us about how to care for the men and women who fight for their countries today.

Jargon Buster

Term	Meaning
Acquisition	When a TV channel buys a finished TV program "off the shelf." Channels usually employ dedicated acquisitions executives who attend the big global markets to look for completed programs to buy.
CGI	Computer-generated imagery.
Co-funding/ co-financing	When two or more funding bodies share the cost of producing a TV series or documentary. Often used interchangeably with the more commonly used co-production.
Commissioner	A TV executive who funds TV programs through a full commission, co-production or presale. Also known as a Development Executive in North America. At the annual TV industry markets they are likely to be referred to as buyers.
Co-production	Usually refers to an arrangement in which two or more TV channels share the cost of funding one TV program. Also refers to an arrangement in which two production companies are involved in producing one program.
Format	A TV series in which every episode's narrative has the same structure, but each week the contributors, characters or contestants change. A proven (produced and successfully transmitted) format can be sold to TV channels around the world.
Hold-back Window	A period of time stipulated in a contract during which a program cannot be broadcast or exploited in a certain territory or on a certain format, e.g. DVD.
Pre-buy/presale	When a broadcaster makes an early commitment to buy a proposed program on completion. Payment is made on delivery and the broadcaster has no editorial input.

Returnable	A TV series that has the potential to return for several series/seasons.
Specialist Factual	A term used for programs that focus on history, arts, science, religion or natural history.
Strand	A series of individual documentaries can be grouped together by theme in a channel "strand," e.g. *Horizon* (BBC2) or *POV* (PBS).

Further Reading and Resources

Channel 4 Alpha Fund—Designed to support the development of ideas, talent and innovation from emerging UK production companies. There's no application process (or website)—just call a Media Project Manager to discuss the idea. Tel: 0141 568 7106.

EDN Television Handbook—The European Documentary Network is a membership organization that publishes a useful directory that lists the names and contact details of documentary commissioners around the world.

Sweet Spots Study—US factual TV network budgets as compiled by Peter Hamilton. Includes figures for twenty-five channels including Discovery, Nat Geo, Sundance, Documentary Channel and A&E with "signature, high, sweet spot, low" budget figures for each channel, along with target demographics and number of hours commissioned annually. Available from: http://documentarytelevision.com/store/.

Festivals, Markets and Forums

Channel executives and buyers travel to all the big markets to meet with producers and find new projects. They are a good place to meet with commissioning editors, potential co-production partners and you can apply to pitch projects in the various markets and competitions. There are also a number of training initiatives that help filmmakers develop and pitch their projects to buyers over a series of structured workshops and pitching forums.

January

DocedgeKolkata
http://docresi.org/docedgeKolkata_about.html

India

Docs Barcelona
http://www.docsbarcelona.com/

Spain

Dragon Forum
http://www.dragonforum.pl/

Poland

NATPE (National Association of Television Program
Executives)
http://www.natpe.org/natpe/

USA

RealScreen Summit
http://summit.realscreen.com/

USA

February

AIDC (Australian International Documentary Conference)
http://aidc.com.au/

Australia

Documentary Campus Masterschool
http://www.documentary-campus.com/v2/

Germany

Documentary Edge Festival
http://www.docnz.org.nz/

New Zealand

EURODOC
http://www.eurodoc-net.com/en/

Residential workshops
in Europe

Zagreb Dox
http://www.zagrebdox.net/en/

Croatia

March

EAVE (European Audiovisual Entrepreneurs) European
Producers Workshop
http://eave.org/

Luxembourg

Ex Oriente Film Workshop http://www.dokweb.net/en/ex-oriente-film/	Czech Republic
MIPDoc http://www.mipworld.com/mipdoc/	France
MIPFormats http://www.mipworld.com/en/mipformats/	France
Sofia Meetings http://www.siff.bg/sofiameetings/	Bulgaria
April	
HotDocs http://www.hotdocs.ca/	Canada
MIPTV http://www.mipworld.com/en/miptv/	France
Visions du Réel Pitching Forum http://www.visionsdureel.ch/en/market.html	Switzerland
May	
COPRO—Israeli Documentary Screen Market http://www.copro.co.il/	Israel
ESoDoc (European Social Documentary) http://www.esodoc.eu/	Italy
Good Pitch New York http://britdoc.org/real_good/pitch/	USA
June	
Banff World Media Festival http://www.banffmediafestival.com/	Canada

Sheffield Doc/Fest http://sheffdocfest.com/uk/	UK
Sunnyside of the Doc http://www.sunnysideofthedoc.com/uk/	France
July	
Durban FilmMart http://www.durbanfilmmart.com/	South Africa
August	
Lorcano Film Festival http://www.pardo.ch/jahia/Jahia/home/lang/en	Switzerland
September	
Baltic Sea Forum http://www.mediadesklatvia.eu/archive-baltic-sea-forum/	Latvia
Doc Meeting Argentina http://www.docmeeting.com.ar/english.php	Argentina
Good Pitch San Francisco http://britdoc.org/real_good/gpsf2011	USA
Westdoc http://www.thewestdoc.com/	USA
October	
Archidoc http://www.lafemis.fr/	France
CNEX Chinese Documentary Forum http://www.cnex.org.cn/	China
Dok Leipzig http://www.dok-leipzig.de/	Germany

East European Forum http://www.dokweb.net/en/east-european-forum/	Czech Republic
Good Pitch http://britdoc.org/real_good/europe2011	UK
Lisbon Docs http://www.doclisboa.org/lisbondocs/en_home.php	Portugal
MIPCOM http://www.mipworld.com/mipcom/	France
Wildscreen Festival http://www.wildscreenfestival.org/	UK
November	
CPH:DOX http://www.cphdox.dk/d/a1.lasso	Denmark
IDFA http://www.idfa.nl/industry.aspx	The Netherlands
Miradas Doc http://miradasdoc.com/	Canary Islands
World Congress of Science & Factual Producers http://www.wcsfp.com/	Various
December	
Asia Television Forum http://www.asiatvforum.com/	Singapore

2 Distributors—Traveling Salesmen

Distributor funding is best suited to TV producers with:

- An entertainment, factual entertainment, specialist factual, reality series or documentary with international appeal
- A lack of experience and contacts in the international market
- A lack of time to build relationships with international commissioners

Independent filmmakers with:

- A documentary that has international appeal
- A need to prove to foundations and other funding bodies that there is a distribution plan in place
- The need of a "heavy-hitter" backer that can negotiate contracts with broadcasters' legal departments
- A lack of international market intelligence
- The wish to start making their next film instead of distributing their last one

> *Rights are what allow you to make what you make. Rights are what people will want to buy and what you want to sell. Rights can make you rich or stop you from making any money at all."*
>
> —Rights.tv

Distributors are the traveling salesmen of the TV and documentary world. They roam the globe, schmoozing TV executives at the annual markets in Cannes, Washington DC, Amsterdam and Toronto, to sell programs on behalf of producers and filmmakers. Distributors and sales agents (terms that have specific meanings but are sometimes used interchangeably) sell TV programs and feature documentaries in the foreign/international/worldwide/domestic markets.

According to Adam P. Davies and N. Wistreich in *The Film Finance Handbook*, in the USA the following definitions are typically used:

- **Domestic distributor**—appointed by the producer to sell the rights to their film or series within the USA and Canada
- **International sales agent**—works on behalf of the producer to sell to buyers, sometimes local distributors, in territories outside of North America
- **Worldwide distributor/sales agent**—is engaged to sell the film both within and outside of North America

Inevitably it all serves to confuse. For the purposes of this book, a producer grants a distributor a license to distribute (sell or exploit) their program for a specified period of time. Once the terms have been agreed, the distributor doesn't have to seek permission from the producer to sell the program to broadcasters or other exhibitors. A sales agent, on the other hand, doesn't get assigned the rights in a program, they merely act on behalf of the producer to license a program's rights to foreign/domestic distributors, broadcasters or other exhibitors, and so does need to consult with the producer on each deal. Sales agents are more typically used by feature film producers and so we'll stick with using the term distributor. A TV distributor might be attached to a broadcaster, such as BBC Worldwide or part of a production company, such as Cineflix International; some have enormous catalogues covering every genre, and others are boutique operations that specialize in a niche market. Suffice to say, every distributor and every deal is different.

What Does a Distributor Do?

A producer can grant a distributor the worldwide distribution rights to their film or program in all formats, or they can "unbundle" the rights and split them between specialist distributors in specific territories and/or formats. For example, the rights might be split by:

- **Territory**—either a single country or larger territory, e.g. Europe or North America (US and Canadian rights are typically combined), Africa, South America, Middle East, Asia
- **Language** e.g. English- or Spanish-speaking territories
- **Media**
  - ○ Theatrical e.g. cinemas and drive-ins
  - ○ Non-theatrical e.g. college campuses, airlines and military bases
  - ○ Television e.g.
    - ■ Terrestrial—Analogue
    - ■ Terrestrial—Digital
    - ■ Pay-TV
    - ■ Interactive TV
    - ■ Video on demand
  - ○ DVD
  - ○ New media

For example, theatrical feature documentary *Inside Job* had a number of distributors who looked after the various rights in different territories.

Inside Job distribution partners

North America		
Canada	Mongrel Media	Theatrical
USA	Sony Pictures Classics	Theatrical
	Sony Pictures Home Entertainment	DVD Blu-ray
Europe		
Finland	Sony Pictures Home Entertainment Nordic	DVD
France	Sony Pictures Releasing	Theatrical
Portugal	Columbia TriStar Warner Filmes de Portugal	Theatrical
Asia		
Japan	Sony Pictures Entertainment	All media

Whichever way the rights are split, each distributor requires an exclusive license within a territory or format so they aren't competing directly with another distributor in the same market. In return the distributor might offer the producer an advance against anticipated sales. The distributor will then try to obtain the highest possible price from third parties—usually network or cable TV channels in the first instance—in return for the exclusive right to transmit or screen the program in their territory. Once the distributor has recouped their advance from sales of the program or film, they pay any profits to the producer minus their fee, which is typically 30 percent. Once the distribution license has expired—after ten years or so—the rights revert back to the producer and the distributor can no longer exploit the program (also known as property). It's in the producer's interest to grant a distribution license that is long enough to give the distributor enough time to fully exploit the program, but not so long that it is tied up with a distributor that isn't proactively selling the program (a clause can be written into the contract that allows the producer to take back the rights if the distributor is underperforming).

Traditionally, distributors dealt only in the sale of finished programs, but today they are involved helping producers raise production money too.

How Can a Distributor Help with a Budget Deficit?

Over the last few years broadcasters have increasingly expected distributors to step in and cover the budget deficit left by a channel and so the role of the distributor has evolved. Fortunately, in the UK, at least 94 percent of distributors are willing to deficit finance programs. "Since full commissions have dwindled and broadcast license fees have got smaller, the distributor has come in almost as a producer, deal broker and financier," says Danny Tipping, director of production at producer/distributor Parthenon Entertainment. "Nowadays we are very rarely dealing with selling a finished product where we've had nothing to do with the financing of the project."

Distributors can get involved from the development stage to secure presales, find co-production money, cash flow production and even invest equity in a program, as well as providing the traditional advance against future sales. Some of the ways a distributor can help finance your program or film include:

Development Funding

In 2010, eight UK distributors spent £1million or more on development. As a producer, "you've still got to pay a 30 percent fee whether you get a distributor in at the development stage or at the end, so why not make them work for you?" asks Danny Tipping. "Use their knowledge and their network from the beginning and make the most commercially viable product you possibly can." If a distributor contributes to the development of a project they may also insist on sharing the rights (and therefore any profits) with the producer.

Some producers enter into an agreement to give a distributor the "first look" at their ideas (sometimes referred to as an "output deal"; broadcasters sometimes do similar deals with producers). The producer may get a lump sum of money from the distributor upfront to develop content ideas and the distributor gets to see those ideas before anybody else. If they choose not to take on a program, the producer can usually take it elsewhere. "Some production companies will do a first look deal with a distributor in return for a large advance, but personally I won't do that," says Lucy Styllanou, MD of Furnace, "because it ties you to that distributor and you won't see an income on any of your projects until they've recouped their advance, added to which, not all distributors are necessarily right for every project."

Some distributors have even set up special development funds. For example, the Ignite Factual Development Initiative was set up by Canadian distributors Partners in Motion and Breakthrough Films & Television and as long as a project already has interest from one TV broadcaster, they will contribute $5–$30K (USD) in development funding.

Presales

Presales, also known as pre-buys, are an important part of the funding jigsaw, but crucially for the producer, a presale is merely an early commitment to buy the finished program and the buyer does not normally pay anything until the film has been delivered to the channel. However, a producer might be able to use presales to leverage an advance from a distributor (or a loan from a bank) to cover production costs until completion and delivery triggers the release of the presales money from broadcasters.

The advantage of presales is that the broadcasters require, and are given, little if any editorial input, so it's less onerous than dealing with several co-producers who all expect their opinions to be taken into account. However, *Broadcast* reported that broadcasters have been abusing the system, "pre-buying rather than commissioning to avoid [paying] the minimum tariffs, but at a stage when they can still have editorial control."

A disadvantage of a presale is that it is worth less money than a co-production deal and therefore requires more partners. If you have to presell your program to every available country in order to raise the production budget, there will be nowhere left to sell the finished program and therefore no opportunity make any profit on the "back end."

If you have a feature-length documentary that is aiming for a cinema release, another disadvantage of making a presale to a TV channel is that a theatrical distributor will insist on the right to première the film in that territory; if it's already been sold to a TV channel without an agreement (a "hold-back window") in place that ensures the broadcaster will not air it before it's been screened in cinemas, the theatrical rights are worthless. Conversely, for a television channel, there is no advantage in them waiting until a film has screened in the cinema, as that will potentially cannibalize their viewing figures.

Distribution Advance

The traditional way for distributors to help plug a budget deficit is to provide a distribution advance (typically 5 to 30 percent of the budget), which can be given at any time unless the program is already finished. An advance signifies a level of commitment from the distributor—they have to be willing to put in the work to make sales otherwise they won't recoup their investment. If a distributor gives a producer an advance, the distributor recoups that money first from any sales (i.e. before giving the producer any money). For a large advance they might also insist on taking a share in the back end, which means they share a proportion of future profits with the producer (on top of their standard distribution fee).

A specialist DVD distributor might also be willing to offer an advance against DVD sales for high-end factual projects such as blue-chip natural history series or documentaries with broad market appeal.

Securing Co-production Funding

Some distributors will pitch your idea to international broadcasters even if you haven't got a domestic channel onboard. Paul Heaney, MD of Cineflix International, London, described being pitched an expensive, high-end docudrama called *Nazi Hunters*, which hadn't managed to secure funding from UK or US broadcasters. World War II documentaries, if done well, will always attract an audience, so he was confident that he would be able to sell it and that the film would have a long shelf life, but without an upfront investment it wouldn't get made. Cineflix managed to negotiate a co-production deal between History (Canada/International), Historia (French Canada), and National Geographic (Latin America) and presell the show to broadcasters in Australia, Ireland, Finland and New Zealand. "If a distributor is passionate about the show and the rights are available, distributors like ourselves will tend to push a show over the line by hook or by crook," he says, "because they'll see that there is money to be made at the end of it, which is good for the producer as well." In a situation where a distributor has raised the entire budget, they are likely to require more than their standard 25–30 percent distribution fee and expect to get some of the back end too, says Danny Tipping.

Completion Funding

Productions, particularly independent documentaries, often run out of money at the post-production stage due to unforeseen production costs or because the film has been shot on a shoestring budget, but the filmmaker needs to hire an experienced editor and an edit suite to finish the film. Some distributors are willing to provide completion funding in return for being given the distribution rights. For example, Cactus Three, a New York-based producer/distributor, launched a completion fund specifically for "films that focus on social issues in need of a voice, as well as films that capture the essence of the human spirit," said executive producer Caroline Stevens.

Some more indirect ways a distributor can help you raise money include:

Increase International Appeal

For a distributor to be able to sell a program globally it must have international potential and distributors can help guide the producer and shape the content so it is as commercially viable as possible. Some producers see this as an—albeit enforced—opportunity. "In a way, a process that starts out with a shortfall actually becomes a bit of an advantage, because it gets you thinking beyond the Channel 5 commission and about how the project might do internationally," noted Richard Bradley, Managing Director, Lion Television. A distributor that "thinks globally and thinks how he can recoup the money that the producers want" makes the producer more money in the long term.

Parthenon Entertainment had a documentary series on the Berlin Wall that a German broadcaster was interested in. "The Germans wanted ten one-hours on literally every aspect of the Berlin Wall—loads of politics, what happened the day before, the day after and since, the Cold War—but we had to find a different angle," says CEO Carl Hall. The in-depth series wasn't viable internationally, so they turned the series idea into a more commercial one-off documentary idea. "It's easier to close the final 20 percent of the budget on a one-hour that appeals internationally, than close the budget on a series that appeals to nobody," says Danny Tipping. Parthenon will also sometimes make a program more saleable by funding extra filming to turn a UK or US hosted program into a presenter-less version for the rest of the world.

International Market Intelligence

Leila Monks, International Director at TVF International, says distributors provide producers with "eyes and ears into the international market," something that will free you up to do what you do best: produce TV programs. Chris Bonney, Managing Director, Outright Distribution, advises finding a distributor you can bounce ideas off before putting too much work into an idea. "You should be having monthly development meetings with a distributor who is giving you useful strategic input into the slate that you've got going and they will give you a view whether it has potential to generate income, over and beyond the amount you actually need to get it done."

Credibility

Having a distribution deal in place gives a project added credibility because a distributor is, by agreeing to distribute, saying that they believe that there is a market for the project. This in turn reassures potential buyers about the quality of the film or series, which might persuade them to come onboard as co-production partners or in a presale agreement. If you are planning to apply to film funds or foundations, such as, "MEDIA, grant foundations and Canadian funding, they require distribution and a funding and marketing plan for that project," says Danny Tipping, "so it's essential for some of these funding bodies that a program has a distributor onboard, because they want to know that you have got a plan to sell that show internationally. We will provide a letter, a marketing plan and sales projections."

Rights Protection

Having a distributor onboard can also help you retain rights in your project— particularly useful when dealing with broadcasters who want to own all the rights. To avoid broadcasters taking worldwide rights in a program, some producers report getting a distributor onboard to give them an advance against the rest of the world before pitching to a channel. That way the broadcaster can only buy the program for transmission in their own territory and, once the distribution agreement has expired, the producer regains the rest of world rights that they can then exploit themselves.

Unfortunately, as more and more producers are forced to stitch together their budgets from a variety of sources, it's making it harder for distributors to help. Quite often producers can raise 80 percent of their budget themselves through a series of TV co-productions and presales, but the last 20 percent can be impossible to raise, because there are no rights left for a distributor to sell. Producers might resort to using their production fee (which is typically 10 percent of the budget), to get their film made, but that means they will have no income from future sales because all the rights have already been sold. Without an income it's hard to cash flow your next production. "Make sure you are closing the gap without selling the farm," advises Danny Tipping. "If you have sold 80 percent of your project by going to ARTE, or S4C and RTE and a cable-satellite channel in the US with a little bit of film funding from the Irish, and all that is left is central and eastern Europe," he says, and you are asking the distributor to "get the final 20 percent of your budget from there, and then after a fifteen-month hold back they can go to the other territories and sell that product—that's not hugely appealing."

Another pitfall is that producers can unwittingly sign away all their rights in early deals, meaning a distributor can't sell their program in other territories. "Sometimes we've got very excited about a project," says Danny Tipping, "and then we look at it and see that they've given the domestic broadcaster the European rights, even though they are not broadcasting it in Europe; they've given away the DVD rights; and they think they've sold it to Canada, but they've actually sold it to North America. You can't unpick those deals once they're done, so we've had to say no thanks, but come back to us in two years ... Often the buyer is lovely, but the legal department that sits behind them at the broadcaster is often less than lovely. Especially the US ones, because quite a few channels in the US are owned by much bigger corporate entities so you get network lawyers who've just been doing a $2m-an-episode deal with an LA agent, and you have to say, 'Hold on, it's only a documentary from England. Calm down!'"

How to Pitch to a Distributor

It's been estimated that only 10–25 percent of UK TV programs have the potential for international sales. If you are thinking of approaching a distributor to help you finance your film or series, first refer back to your proposal and check that it is suitable for a distributor:

- Does it have content or themes that will be of interest to an international audience?
- Is it narrator-led rather than presenter-led/hosted?
- Is it deliverable at a broadcast length, i.e. to fit a thirty- or sixty-minute slot?
- Does it have a standard number of episodes? For example, one, three, six, twelve, thirteen or twenty-four?
- Does it offer something unique? For example, access, archive or a new take on a familiar subject?
- Is all archive and music cleared or clearable for international use?

The same pitching rules apply as if you were approaching a production company or TV broadcaster. Research, via other producers, channel contacts, websites, festivals and markets to find distributors who deal in similar programs or films to yours. Some specialize in high-end, blue-chip science, history or wildlife; others in reality series, or cooking or travel shows. "Some distributors will take on anything and everything," says Danny Tipping, "but there's probably two or three distributors you would choose to go to with a big natural history or science project. Broadcasters will be attracted to talk to that distributor because of their particular type of programming. The distributor will understand the program you are trying to make and will have the contacts who will be interested in buying it."

Try to find out what kind of reputation the distributor has in terms of transparent accounting and prompt payment. Also have a look at the films they have in their catalogue and contact some of the producers who have previously worked with them and find out how pleasant they were to deal with and how hard they worked on the filmmaker's behalf. Some other things to consider when researching distributors:

● What do you want them to do? Find co-production funding, help you with development, or just sell the rights outside of your own territory?
● Do they have expertise in they type of program you are offering?
● Do they have good relationships with the key international channels that are likely to be interested in your film? That is, have they sold programs to them before?
● How aggressively are they likely to market your program?

Next make a telephone or email enquiry to the distributor's programming division to ask if you could discuss your idea with them. If they are interested you'll most likely be invited to a face-to-face meeting where you can pitch your show. Different distributors will prefer a particular type of pitch, but it's much like pitching to a TV channel, where a paper proposal will be supported by a verbal pitch, and where appropriate, a pitch tape of some sort. "If we don't have an existing relationship, I'd like to see a treatment. Otherwise, a paragraph is usually enough and then a meeting is the best way to do it," says Danny Tipping. Caroline Stern, Director of International Sales and Acquisitions at Kaleidoscope Home Entertainment, also prefers a brief introductory email with genre of film, name of the director and an overview of the current funding situation; if she's interested she will request a treatment, series breakdown, budget and director biography. Independent documentary distributor Dogwoof want to see a trailer (not a full-length screener as they receive thousands of submissions and don't have time to watch them all) and also an indication that the filmmaker has thought about how they are going to help market their film: do they have a website, thousands of email subscribers and Twitter followers, a Facebook fan page?

When meeting with a distributor for the first time you are selling your ability to make the project as much as you are selling your idea. "You need confidence because I'm going to ask you all the questions that a broadcaster is going to ask me, so I will feel a lot happier if you can answer those questions," says Danny

Tipping. "Have you got access? Have you already established a relationship with these characters? What's the budget? Are you absolutely sure you can do it for £300,000? Can you definitely do it by December? I want confident answers, so that when I am repeating that to broadcasters I am able to back it up. I'd like to come out of that meeting absolutely loving that project. If I don't feel strongly about it, there's a good chance no one else will either, so I'd like to come out of that meeting feeling really enthused, and confident that you can deliver, and excited about the potential."

Make sure that you have all your materials and information ready before your meeting, knowing exactly "where's it already been pitched to, what rights are available, what the budget is," says Danny Tipping. "It's frustrating taking meetings and the producer says, 'Oh I don't really know, my partner's pitched it but I don't know who to ...'"

Sometimes a distributor isn't interested in your idea because it doesn't quite fit what they are currently looking for, but they might be able to point you in the right direction, says Carl Hall. "If producers come along with great ideas that just don't fit, we pass them on to other distributors who are specialists in that genre ... we collaborate with each other."

Once a distributor has decided that they like both you and your project, your contact at the distributor will pitch your project to their sales team, who will do a sales projection that predicts which buyers in which territories might be interested in licensing the show and how much they are likely to pay either in a co-production deal (more money, more editorial input, release money during production as triggered by agreed milestones) or presales (less money, less editorial input, release money on delivery of finished program). Once the distributor has a sales projection they will offer you a deal based on how much money they think they can raise, which is usually a cash advance that will help you fund production, and which they will recoup once the money from the presales is paid by the channels.

If you are working with an entertainment attorney or producers' agent (as is common in the USA) they are likely to be able to make recommendations and negotiate with distributors on your behalf. In the UK, Rights.TV, a legal and business affairs company, acted on behalf of Glasshead for their documentary *My Monkey Baby*, a film about people in the USA who treat pet monkeys as if they are part of their family, and pitched the idea to a number of distributors. They managed to generate so much interest that they were able to strike a deal for five times the original offer.

Finding the right distributor is like entering into a marriage partnership: it has to be based on trust and mutually beneficial to both parties. Some producers work on an exclusive basis with one distributor; some distributors work with producers on project-by-project basis. It depends what best suits you, as the producer.

On the plus side, partnering with a distributor means that they can do a lot of the legal heavy lifting. "These contracts now are so complex with multimedia rights, your average local solicitor is not going to pick up the nuances of the Italians asking for VOD rights exclusively, on page ten on the standard agreement; producers just want to sign it so they can get into production, but lawsuits can be horrific if you inadvertently break the terms of your contract," warns Carl Hall.

Equally, make sure that you understand any deal that you agree with the distributor. Does the commission they charge you on sales include all their overheads, or will you be charged distribution costs (DVD screeners, shipping costs, clearances, marketing etc.) too? When will you get the money? Are they seeking partial ownership in the project? How long do you agree that they can keep the rights to sell your project? If in any doubt at all, consult a rights consultant or entertainment lawyer.

Once you've entered into a partnership with a distributor, it's essential to keep talking to them throughout the production process. "I know too many distributors who come to me and say independents just take our money, run away and then we don't hear about it until it turns up and it's something completely different, so I think that communication is really important," says Andrew Jackson, head of the BBC's Natural History Unit.

Advantages of Working with a Distributor

1. A distributor can help you shape your film so it has a greater chance of finding international funding.
2. A distributor might contribute money toward development (possibly in exchange for some ownership of the idea).
3. Some distributors have a production arm that can "warehouse" you if you are not an established filmmaker. "The idea is the important thing to us, not necessarily the track record of the producer," says Danny Tipping, but a track record of a producer "does matter to the networks, so what we provide is a track record and a guarantee that this program will get delivered—we provide all the infrastructure and resources to make this real, which allows them to take

a punt on it—rightly or wrongly they probably wouldn't take a risk on a less well-known producer."

4. They can offer a cash advance against future sales that you can use to make your program.
5. They are out in the market and know exactly what different channels are looking for at the moment.
6. They have ready-built contacts with TV executives around the world.
7. They can help you negotiate with TV channels, and chase up slow payments.
8. They bring access to legal and business affairs advice. "For a first-time producer doing a co-production for the first time, just wading through those contracts, they are about forty-three pages long with twenty-eight pages of deliverables: producers don't have the resources and the time to wade through that," says Danny Tipping.
9. They can manage and keep on top of complex agreements with dozens of different buyers, and provide E&O (errors and omissions) insurance under a blanket policy.

Disadvantages

1. Distribution costs and distributors have large overheads, so it's usual to pay a distributor 25–30 percent commission on sales and they might not include marketing and other overheads in that fee.
2. Choose the wrong distributor and you might feel as though the distributor is being complacent and not putting in as much sales effort as you'd like. This is more likely with a large distributor that has an enormous back catalogue, in which a single film is likely to get overlooked. If you are a small indie, or working in a niche genre, it's better to seek out a smaller boutique distributor who will give you and your film more personal attention.
3. One-off documentaries that are focused on a domestic story are the hardest to fund via a distributor, as they are less attractive to international buyers.
4. If you make a lot of presales in order to raise money against which you can get a distributor's advance, there will be no territories in which to sell the finished film; so you might be able to fund your production, but be able to make no more money on completion. This is fine if your only objective is to get your film made, but is no good if you are trying to build a business or are also trying to interest equity investors (who require the project to make a profit in which they can share) in your project.

5. "You are handing over your baby to someone who will sell the show to the highest bidder," says Danny Tipping; if they are "over-promising, then your reputation is on the line because you are beholden to delivering. You need to have a relationship of trust."

Next Steps

1. Research distributors who handle films or programs like yours.
2. Once you have a shortlist, ask to see their catalogue or press kit to get a feel what kind of films will be sitting alongside yours.
3. Contact the producers of films distributed by each company and ask if they recommend their distributor. Find out if the distributor marketed their film enthusiastically, kept good accounting records and paid any monies due promptly.
4. Call up the programming division of your preferred distributors to discuss your project and set up a meeting.

Jargon Buster

Term	Meaning
Advance	An amount of money given to a producer in anticipation of future sales of a program or film. The producer receives no money from sales until the distributor has sold enough to cover the advance, at which point the producer will start to receive money from sales less the distributor's fee (commission).
Back End	Income from sales of a completed TV program, DVDs, theatrical distribution, books and merchandise related to a program etc.
Minimum Guarantee	The minimum amount of money a distributor will pay to a producer in order to license their program or film for an agreed number of years, formats and territories. This money typically is given to the producer in the form of an advance. If the distributor doesn't sell enough programs to recoup the advance they gave to the producer they lose that money; the producer doesn't have to pay any money back.

Primary Rights   Relates to the exploitation of a program or film in its primary medium, e.g. television for a TV show or cinema for a theatrical documentary.

Recoup   Recover.

Rights   Refers to the legally contracted "right" to copy, transmit or otherwise exploit a film or TV program, e.g. a broadcaster licenses the right to transmit a TV program, or a distributor licenses the right to sell a documentary in English-speaking territories.

Secondary Rights The sale (licensing) of a TV program or film in other territories and formats such as DVD. Sometimes known as ancillary rights (along with tertiary rights).

Territory   Individual countries; geographical regions, e.g. Europe, North America, Asia, South America, Africa and Middle East; or regions united by a language, e.g. English-speaking or Spanish-speaking territories.

Tertiary Rights Relates to the licensing of books, soundtracks, toys and other non-media merchandise relating to a program. Also known as ancillary rights (along with secondary rights).

Further Reading and Resources

Cinando—subscription database for the global cinema industry.
www.cinando.com

Film Distributors' Association—trade body for UK theatrical film distributors with a list of current members.
http://www.launchingfilms.com/fda-members

Filmmaker's Clearinghouse—an evaluation of US distributors in respect of the quality of their marketing, timeliness of payments and honesty and integrity.
http://www.marklitwak.com/resources/results.php

Film Specific—subscription site about all things distribution. Includes worldwide distributor and sales agent databases, sample contracts, sales projections and other useful resources mainly aimed at narrative (fiction) filmmakers.
www.filmspecific.om

Independent Film and Television Alliance (IFTA)—global trade association of the film and TV industry. Provides information disputes and arbitration awards against distributors. IFTA Arbitation Awards

Out-Law—guide to the law relating to film and TV distribution and co-production in the UK.
http://www.out-law.com/page-6400

3 Brands—Dirty, Sexy Mad Men

Brand funding is best suited to TV producers with:

- An entertainment, factual entertainment or reality series that appeals to a specific demographic.
- A program that focuses on a subject where there is clear product placement potential, such as DIY, food, travel, homes or fashion.
- A high level of comfort when working with lots of partners with different agendas.
- A broadcaster that is supportive of brand-funded programs (or indeed, insists on them).

> *I've put myself in some pretty horrible situations over the years, but nothing could prepare me for anything as difficult or as dangerous as going into the room with these guys*
>
> —Morgan Spurlock (*POM Wonderful Presents: The Greatest Movie Ever Sold*)

If you sit down to watch a reality TV show in the USA you'll see more ads than program: in a typical one-hour program, thirty-one-and-a-half minutes is given over to thirty-second adverts ("spots"), product placement, promos for other shows and other sponsored or branded content. For über reality producer Mark Burnett, brands are central to his shows and he even went so far as to say the products featured in the second season of *Survivor* were the "seventeenth character." "*Survivor* is as much a marketing vehicle as a television show," he told *Esquire* magazine. "My shows create an interest, and people will look at them, but the endgame here is selling products in stores—a car, deodorant, running shoes. It's the future of television." Indeed, it's been noted that many of Burnett's shows (and *American Idol*) would never have been born without brand funding.

Ten years later, Morgan Spurlock pushed Burnett's assertion that marketing was the future of television to its limit by making a feature-length theatrical documentary about product placement which was itself paid for by brands. *POM Wonderful Presents: The Greatest Movie Ever Sold* follows Morgan as he learns about marketing and sponsorship and simultaneously tries to fund the documentary through brand sponsorship. The film was funded by twenty-two brands, including the pomegranate juice drink in the title (who sponsored the film for $1m), Ban deodorant ($50,000), Merrell shoes and Mini cars. But he had to work hard for his money: he approached, and was rejected by, around 500 brands that declined to get involved in a film made by a man famous for skewering another brand, McDonald's, in *Supersize Me*. Like many filmmakers, Morgan and his team ended up "burning money out of our own pockets" until the first sponsor, Ban deodorant, signed up (although, frankly, his pockets are probably deeper than most filmmakers').

As each brand agrees to give him money Morgan has to work out how to insert that brand into the narrative of his film through verbal mentions and product placement. We see Morgan wearing Merrell shoes, drinking POM Wonderful in meetings, flying Jet Blue, staying in Hyatt Hotels and filling his Mini with gas at Sheetz convenience stores. He also punctuates the film with a series of advertising "spots" that he creates for his sponsors. Morgan insisted that no sponsor would have editorial control or final approval over the film, but his sponsors had their own ways of asserting control. For example, POM Wonderful paid $500,000 upfront plus $100,000 to make a commercial featured in the film, but to get the remaining $400,000 of the $1million sponsorship deal the film has to generate 600 million media impressions (which it achieved at its Sundance première in 2011); gross more than $10 million at the box office worldwide (as of August 24, 2011 it had grossed $638,000 at the US box office); and sell 500,000 DVDs and downloads.

Broadcasters have been reliant on advertising dollars for decades, but it's now becoming more common for advertisers to fully or partially fund whole programs, rather than just buying commercial time in which to show their ads. Some channels, such as Channel 5 and Channel 4 in the UK, have parts of the schedule set aside purely for programs funded by brands. Some producers emerge from a successful pitch meeting knowing that the channel wants to commission the program but will do so only if the producer can find a brand to fund production. "We were told our pitch was good, but to get some funding first and come back to them afterwards. We left the meeting feeling it was a blatant attempt to see how little they could get away with paying us," complained one producer. "It really does feel like you have to try and buy your way into the slots with cash, rather than ideas, when you are pitching," said another.

On February 28, 2011 product placement was made legal on British television and on the same day Nescafé put its Dolce Gusto coffee machine on the set of *This Morning*, a long-running daytime magazine show on ITV1; they paid £100,000 for a placement lasting three months. For the first time in the UK, ads are no longer just in the breaks: programs *are* the ads. Producers and brand managers, who both want ownership over the content, suddenly find themselves thrown together in a new and uneasy relationship.

A Brief History of Brands on Screen: Back to the Future

Product placement on TV is nothing new. In 1929, more than half of radio programs in America were created by ad agencies and paid for by advertisers, such as: *Maxwell House Hour, Palmolive Hour, General Motors Family Party,* and *The Wrigley Review.* By 1957, US advertisers were creating around 33 percent of TV programs, including the unimaginatively titled *Firestone Orchestra, Kraft Television Theatre, United States Steel Hour, Colgate Comedy Hour* (an extra point here for alliteration) and the *Pepsi-Cola Playhouse.*

It wasn't just entertainment shows that were fair game for the Madison Avenue advertising guys: even the news was branded. In 1950, viewers of *Camel News Caravan* were invited to "sit back light up a Camel, and be a witness to the happenings that made history in the last twenty-four hours." During the newscast there were two ad breaks featuring Camel cigarettes, and news anchor John Cameron Swayze had a lit cigarette in front of him for the duration of the show. A close-up of the cigarette was shown as Swayze signed off, "saying good night for Camel cigarettes." To avoid any possible dilution of the marketing message, news cameramen had to avoid including "No Smoking" signs in shot.

Brands controlled almost every area of programming. When it was revealed that Revlon were telling the producers of a quiz show which contestants should be allowed to stay in the competition "and which should be helped off air," it caused a national scandal. Sore at a lack of control over their own schedules, channel executives rebelled. When Sigourney Weaver's father, Pat, became president of NBC in 1953 he promptly made the cost of funding a whole show too expensive for brands by insisting that programs were longer than the customary fifteen-minutes. Instead he invited a number of advertisers to buy advertising spots within a single show. By 1968, advertisers were creating fewer than 3 percent of network television programs.

Although the UK has only recently allowed product placement in British TV programs, the return of greater brand involvement to US television around the turn of the new millennium is blamed on successful British exports: quiz show *Who Wants to Be a Millionaire* (ABC) was one of the first shows to take advantage, with telecom company AT&T sponsoring the "friends and family" telephone lifeline.

The Future of Brands on Screen

TV broadcasters have become increasingly reluctant to fully fund programs at a time when brands are looking for new ways to engage with consumers. "With [On Demand platforms such as] Sky+ and with [the BBC] iPlayer, and the internet explosion, no one's gong to be interrupted by ads," says Mark Wood, founder of Krempelwood, an agency that represents producers looking for ad funding or product placement, "so advertisers have got to find another way of funding television and sponsoring or funding content is a very important part of that." But as producers wake up to the funding opportunities in brand partnerships, brands are fighting shy of merely being "funding sex objects" (as a commissioning editor once described himself) and are looking for content that truly engages consumers with their brand. In the UK, at least, the two sides haven't yet come up with a comfortable and mutually beneficial way of collaborating. However, there are signs "that's starting to happen now, rather than TV companies just saying to advertisers, 'Do you want to fund our TV show?'" says Mark Eaves, co-founder of Gravity Road, a content creation company that develops ideas to address the needs of brands.

TV is by no means the only answer for brands which want to reach out to consumers. "Most people in television think brands are the future of funding," says Mark Wood; "one of the key problems is no one's told the brands yet." There is a place for television but only as a support medium. "The actual involvement happens not on TV but online," says Frank Rose, author of *The Art of Immersion*. Producers need to rein in their egos if they imagine brands are going to fall over themselves to fund a program just because a producer needs to find funding; any partnership has to be of mutual benefit. Particularly in markets where brands and TV producers are working together for the first time, producers have to learn to listen to (yet) another partner who wants creative input, and marketeers have to learn to relax a little. As Frank Rose notes, "the MBAs who populate ad agencies and corporate marketing departments spend years learning the art of control—what their cleverly calibrated messages should and shouldn't say, where they should appear, how often they should appear there, and what should appear nearby. Empowering people [including TV producers] has never been on their agenda."

Scott Donaton, president-CEO of Ensemble Branded Entertainment in the USA, predicted another model that is beginning to filter through, in which, "sponsors take equity positions in shows, to become owners. That could increase the risk for the sponsor, but it also increases the potential upside if the show is a success. And it gives advertisers a chance to have more say in how their products are written into scripts. That happened with *The Restaurant* on NBC, in which media agency Magna Global took an ownership position in exchange for getting its clients global exposure on the series. The head of Magna Global's entertainment unit even appeared in the credits as an executive producer of the show."

Producers are beginning to think like brands too, seeing a TV program as one part of a much larger offering. For example, in the UK, Lime Pictures registered a trademark for clothing, nightwear and headgear as part of plans to develop a branded clothing range to accompany its ITV2 "structured reality" series *The Only Way Is Essex*.

What's in It for Brands?

Broadly speaking, advertiser funded programming involves brands either directly funding programs, or paying for product placement within shows. In return they might get their brand's logo featured on "bumpers" (the couple of seconds of video that separates program content from the adverts), on the title sequence, and/or the use of their products in the program. But what exactly are they hoping to achieve by funding a television program?

Despite the dubious practices of some sponsors in the past—Revlon manipulating the outcome of a game show, for instance—being seen on TV gives a brand credibility and means it is regarded by consumers as more trustworthy (which is the reason brands put "As seen on TV" on packaging and in newspaper ads). Consumers still tend to regard the internet with a certain mistrust so brands that live online, such as insurance companies and comparison websites, typically spend more on television advertising than brands that also exist on the high street.

Brands are drawn to TV for a range of reasons. A brand might want to:

1. **Build their market share** in a particular part of the country and so will be interested in programs that transmit in a certain geographical region;
2. **Promote a seasonal product**, and therefore want to be involved in a program that is guaranteed to transmit at a certain time of year;
3. **Target a particular demographic** who are known to watch certain programs or at specific times of the day;
4. **Connect with viewers who have a niche interest**, for example, cooking or DIY, and will therefore be drawn to programs on niche channels such as Food Network and DIY Channel.

You'll notice that none of the things that preoccupy TV producers—story arcs, great access, compelling characters, transformative journeys etc.—features in this list. Brands are focused purely on their own needs, and every brand hopes to get something different from their involvement in a TV program. That "something" is the $64,000 question, says Chantal Rickards, head of programming and branded content at media agency MEC in London. "From my perspective it has to be a program that works for and will reach the audience I am trying to get to, because otherwise it's simply pointless. If I am trying to sell deodorant to women over the age of forty-five and the only people who watch the show are men over the age of sixty-five, I have completely and utterly failed. It's a total waste of money, and there will be no return on investment, because, quite simply, the message has got to the wrong ears and the wrong eyes."

Brands also consider other ways they might benefit from being involved in a show. A TV program itself is a mere springboard to more exciting promotional activities that can be manipulated more freely than in the highly regulated TV world. A brand that provides funding for a TV show might use clips from the show on their own website or in multiplatform apps; have the celebrity presenter do in-store demonstrations or public appearances; use the show's name on product packaging and promotional material and even share in the revenues from international sales of a program format.

Brands willing to pay £500,000 to fund a ten-part series of *Dream House in the Country*, in which viewers had the chance to win ownership of a newly renovated four-bedroom country house, were offered a range of promotional opportunities including:

- On-air sponsorship banners around each episode and on the broadcaster's website (which click through to the brand's own website or online store)
- Product placement for home electronics, DIY tools and furnishing products
- Use of the show's DIY guides on social networking sites
- Use of the show's branding and "As seen on TV"

It was suggested that several brands might want to share the cost of the series, with DIY retailers, bathroom and kitchen brands, real-estate agents and product placement agencies proposed as the best fit.

Aaron's Tour de France: French Cooking Made Simple was looking for brand funding partners in food and French brands. *Win a Dream Holiday* sought three funding partners to each match the 25 percent of funding the broadcaster was putting into the budget, by targeting airlines, hotels or package holiday companies.

It's important that any brand involvement with a program is authentic, otherwise a show misses its mark both in terms of entertainment and advertising. Mark Burnett made a rare misstep when his reality boxing show, *The Contender*, was partnered with US DIY store Home Depot as part of a multi-year, multi-program integration deal between Home Depot and Mark Burnett Productions. As Jean-Marc Lehu notes, "*The Contender* is often named by professionals of branded entertainment as a case of out-and-out failure, since no coherence between the brand and the program was ever found."

Morgan Spurlock underwent a "Morgan Spurlock brand" analysis as part of his quest to understand brands and branded content. He consulted Olson Zaltman Associates, a company that helps brands like Hallmark, Audi, Pfizer and Sears identify and define their brand personality. He was told by Lindsay Zaltman that he has "two distinct, but complementary, sides" to his brand personality—"the Morgan Spurlock brand is a mindful/playful brand. There are playful brands and mindful brands ... but a playful/mindful brand is a pretty powerful thing," she said.

Perhaps then it comes as no surprise that the brands who felt comfortable taking part in Morgan's documentary included Mini and JetBlue, which also have playful/mindful brand identities. (Although Morgan's assertion that "I have funded this entire film with money from some pretty strait-laced companies," suggests he's not averse to perpetuating his own "brand story": Morgan Spurlock gets one over on corporations.)

For Lynda Resnick, CEO of main sponsor POM Wonderful, playfulness was definitely part of their motivation for taking part: "For us, it's like we're in on the gag. And it was fun working with Morgan. He's clever." This also hints at a common, but less obvious motivation for brands to spend money on TV programming, which has less to do with consumers and more to do with enhancing a brand's self-image and motivating its employees. Jean-Marc Lehu reports that some "studies even claim that this can lead to an improvement in morale and productivity" among staff.

When co-production is agreed between several broadcasters there's usually a common motivation (to win viewers) and broadly similar editorial agenda. One of the things that makes branded content so complicated to execute (beyond the legislation in force in a particular territory) is the number of people, with often wildly diverging agendas, who have to collaborate and agree throughout the process. "The way that branded content should work is that it has to be a collaborative relationship. It can't be solely a badging exercise on behalf of the brand; the editorial cannot be compromised," says Jason Hughes, head of branded content at BSkyB. "It is very difficult to get these things off the ground because there are a lot of stakeholders and there are a lot of hurdles to cross." John McVay, CEO of the UK producers' trade association Pact said, "You are dealing with a trinity of brands—broadcasting, product and program brands. Everyone guards [their brand] jealously and is absolutely focused on the integrity of those brands. If we don't get it right, the viewers won't watch and so we'll all be wasting our time." To those three brands who have a self-interest, I'd add a fourth, the producer's brand. In the case of successful producers such as reality show king Mark Burnett (*Survivor, The Apprentice, Shark Tank*), or blue-collar champion Thom Beers's Original Productions (*Deadliest Catch, Ax Men, Ice Road Truckers*), they've gone to a lot of trouble to build their brand and become the "go-to" company for their respective kind of programs.

As with everything to do with TV and documentary funding the terminology is tricky. At the time of writing there's advertiser funding, branded content, sponsorship, product placement, brand integration, prop placement, trade outs and more to contend with. Certain terms are used specifically by different TV producers and broadcasters, and interchangeably by others. As Twitter user@_mip_noted during an MIPTV festival panel in 2011, "The def[inition] of branded content changes by who you talk to + is changing from MIP* to MIP ... it's a moving target right now."

Here's an attempt to unravel the different forms of brand funding you might encounter—you can work out what best to call it in any given situation.

Sponsorship

"Genius brand pairing this week—*Kerry Katona: The Next Chapter* is sponsored by Mattressman.co.uk—I don't even need to write a punchline," noted comedian Jimmy Carr on Twitter, in reference to the ex-Atomic Kitten singer turned reality TV road wreck whose colorful love life provides regular tabloid headlines. Someone in the channel's media sales team clearly enjoyed a sense of mischief.

Sponsorship is of less interest to program makers looking for money to top up their program budget, as it's something that is generally negotiated between the channel and a brand, and the money goes to the channel rather than the production company. "Broadcast sponsorship is effectively an existing piece of content, a program that is already commissioned and probably wholly paid for by the channel, that is then sponsored by a brand," says Jason Hughes. It is "sold by the channel to whoever pays the highest price," says Claire Heys, director of commercial partnerships at Tiger Aspect Productions. "The producer has no say in who the sponsor is. This is an airtime deal based on the traditional media value of that airtime."

In entering into a sponsorship deal (which can cost anything from £10,000 to £10million in the UK), the brand buys the right to have their name featured in a "bumper" that appears before the program titles, and before and after ad breaks. There might also be a verbal reference to the brand "Brought to you by ..." and a minimum guarantee of one to three commercial spots within the ad breaks. They might choose to sponsor a program or a whole series, and a long-running series might have a number of sponsors over its lifetime. In order to find sponsors, a broadcaster will take clips of a program or series they hope to have sponsored and pitch it to media agencies, who buy advertising space on behalf of brands. In the USA all the channels and agencies converge on New York City every spring to hear the pitches en masse, at an event called "the upfronts".

*MIP refers to a series of international TV and documentary markets held annually in Cannes, France.

In some markets, where product placement isn't allowed or is still in its infancy, sponsorship is the preferred mode of brand funding for channels. "Sponsorship from a revenue point of view will have more of a recognizable value to brands and agencies than product placement, certainly to begin with," says Jason Hughes of the UK market. "Media agencies and brands know how to value sponsorship; but until there are case studies out in the market, product placement doesn't really have a specific ballpark area to give it value [in the UK]; over the next two years that will develop."

Although the sponsorship process doesn't really involve the producer, there are still some tangential benefits to a show, especially if a cool brand gives your program a stamp of approval (although I've never met a producer who wouldn't prefer a BAFTA or an Emmy nomination). A particularly useful by-product of sponsorship is that the brand might promote their involvement of the show in magazines, supermarkets and in social networking spaces, which will help drive viewers toward the program, increase viewing figures, which in turn increase the likelihood of a recommission. Any promotion that a brand can do around your show is good news, particularly as the "fewer, bigger, better" mantra has also been applied to channel marketing budgets in recent years, leaving most programs with no marketing at all. If a brand is onboard, they can do a lot of the promotional heavy lifting. For example, *Chinese Food in Minutes* (which was actually ad funded rather than sponsored) benefited from their majority funder, Sharwoods, promoting the show in magazine advertorials and newspaper adverts: the first episode got one million viewers in a slot on Channel 5 that averages 400,000. Another plus of a pure sponsorship deal is that the sponsoring brand gets no share in the program rights or any back-end revenue.

Advertiser Funded Programming (AFP)

> First of all, entertain. Second, advertise the entertainment.
>
> —Mark Eaves (Founder, Gravity Road)

Programs that have part or all of their production budgets paid for by a brand are called AFP (advertiser funded programs), but also might be known as branded content or, confusingly, sponsored programming. What sets AFP apart from sponsorship from the point of view of the viewer is that "sponsorship 'interrupts' the program and is separate from the program's content; ad-funded content is more about engagement and integration with the content," says Claire Heys, director of brand partnerships and licensing at Endemol UK. And importantly for the producer, the money that a brand pays for AFP goes to the producer rather than the channel (although it's possible the money will be routed via the commissioning executive at the channel), and can therefore be used to fund production.

A potential brand funder has zero interest in how much money a producer needs to make a TV series and will instead calculate how much they are willing to give to the production by working out its "media value," that is, how much impact the money spent on the show is likely to have in comparison with other forms of marketing such as billboards, advertising spots, magazine advertorials etc. There are a number of elements of AFP that have media value:

- Great editorial content helps them sell their brand message
- TV progam content and onscreen talent can be exploited across multiple platforms, such as smart phones, social networking sites and instore promotions
- The brand might take a share in the show's rights and back-end revenue
- Association with TV can make the brand feel pioneering and noisy ('noisy' being a word that TV executives love); and link the brand to TV celebrities familiar to consumers

Advertiser funded programs have to fit with a brand's values and expertise for it to be an authentic match. For example:

- *The Vue Film Show* on Channel 4 is, as the name suggests, a film review show set on location in a Vue cinema in west London. Containing reviews of hot new releases, interviews with celebrity cast and crew and glamorous red carpet reports, the brand and content are completely integrated and designed to drive people to the cinema.
- Lakeland, a much-loved family-owned kitchenware business based in the UK's Lake District, funded *The Lakes on a Plate* on Channel 4. The 20 x 30' series saw host Peter Sidwell traveling around the picturesque Lake District discovering fantastic local ingredients that he turned into mouthwatering dishes. Lakeland's Managing Director, Tony Preedy articulated the company's

motivation for funding the program when he said, "We hope viewers will be inspired to get into their kitchens and try [the recipes] out." Obviously he hopes they will do so using Lakeland kitchenware.

Sometimes a dream partnership can turn sour, leaving the brand associated with a program or celebrity that attracts negative press. Some brands, however, aren't averse to capitalizing on notoriety. Abercrombie & Fitch were reported to have offered Michael "The Situation" Sorrentino, one of the cast of the hit reality series *Jersey Shore*, money to *stop* wearing the brand's clothing range because "we believe this association is contrary to the aspirational nature of our brand, and may be distressing to many of our fans." It was soon rumbled as a ruse to rustle up some free publicity for the brand off the back of the TV show.

A potential trip hazard for anyone considering AFP is that the people responsible for overseeing the project for the brand have neither experience nor understanding of production schedules, and so things might get held up when you need someone to agree or sign off on something. Claire Heys recommends building all the stakeholder meetings, viewings and sign-off dates into the production schedule well in advance so everyone knows the timetable. Find out when your key agency and brand contacts are on holiday and build that into the schedule too and then stick to it as much as possible.

If you are considering testing the waters of ad funded programming, Claire Heys advises (with the now familiar mantra) "advertiser funded programming won't replace all channel funding across your whole slate. Aim to do one big deal a year: fewer, bigger, better."

CASE STUDY
The TV Book Club—Channel 4
Fully funded by optician Specsavers
Produced by Cactus Television

Chantal Rickards, Head of Programming/Branded Content at media agency MEC, London

"*The Richard and Judy Show* [a magazine/chat show] on Channel 4 used to have a small section on books, so we recognized there was an appetite for this type of programming. We took this thought and created a half-hour TV program after a brainstorm with Specsavers and the original producer of the show and created a brand-new format with books fully at its core. Specsavers want to be recognized as experts in their field; because of the association of spectacles with reading and erudition this helped them achieve that aim. They wanted to get their message across to up-market people over the age of forty-five, keen readers who are beginning to lose their eyesight; the audience that Channel 4 and More4 could offer were the perfect target.

"It's a three-year deal with two series a year on Channel 4 in the afternoons, and on More4 in the evenings, making sure we get to as wide a book-reading demographic as possible.

"Specsavers don't get involved in the content of the program per se but they do have influence and they are interested in the look, feel and tone of the program and the types of people who present it. They wanted a cross-section of people—they wanted regional as well as urban, different age groups and ethnicities—so they wanted a very rounded set of presenters and they were able to voice that at the beginning.

"They didn't have a right of veto over what has been created because Channel 4 are the only people who are allowed editorial control over a program that they broadcast, which is why the creation has to be a collaborative process from the start. It's got to be a symbiotic arrangement, not parasitic, because if it isn't people don't feel that they have engaged in a meaningful way in the process; you have to make sure that the brand and the agents feel that they are all being involved. If you've got a production company that is trying to sideline either the brand or the agency it simply won't work because everyone has to be singing off the same hymn sheet. There are some producers who don't understand that, they think that the brand is just going to come up with a cheque and they can run away with it. Those are producers that I will not work with again, because the brand and I need to be part of a collaborative process all the way through.

"When I'm in production I always make sure that there is at least one weekly meeting with everyone involved—the client, the production company, the channel. If one week we are talking about PR then I would expect the channel PR to be there, if another week we are talking about the website then I would expect a representative of the channel's website to be there.

> There is often a web agency and PR agency involved so they would be at the
> table as well; by having all of those agents working on the project at the same
> time, then it turns into a highly effective TV program and thus a successful
> marketing exercise."

Product Placement

Of all the different ways a producer might raise money to make their TV program, product placement is probably the one that is most controversial (and the one most likely to be picked up and commented on by viewers).

Product placement is a contractual arrangement in which a brand pays a fee in return for a brand's product(s) featuring in a program for an agreed length of time and/or number of appearances through the use of branded segments, product branding on the set or actual use of a product. In the UK, product placement is signaled to viewers by a "P" on the screen (although four months after its introduction more than 90 percent of British adults had no idea what it meant— ironically some thought it had something to do with PayPal, which means a symbol designed to warn viewers of a product placement is itself being mistaken for product placement). In the USA, the Federal Communications Commission (FCC) requires broadcasters to disclose any paid placements, which they normally do by including a line in the closing credits along the lines of "Promotional consideration paid for by ..."

Product integration, a souped-up version of product placement, involves greater editorial collaboration between the producers and the brand, in which, rather than placing products into existing programs, program narratives are built around a product. This is a model pioneered by Mark Burnett on *Survivor* in 2000: "I worked with CBS Advertising Sales to design sponsorships instead of merely commercial time, offering advertisers on-air product placement if they put their money behind *Survivor*. The sponsorship product placement concept was relatively new for a network television series, though I had been doing it for years as a necessity for *Eco-Challenge*. I learned it through studying the financial sponsorship model for the Olympics. I was positive the sponsorship model would work with *Survivor*, too—and it did. Advertisers embraced the new show. Every sponsorship was sold before we began filming. *Survivor* was already a financial success!" The model also worked for Leslie Moonves, president and CEO at CBS, because the product references were authentic in the context of a group of people marooned on a desert island, where the show was set. "It far surpassed what you would get from a thirty-second spot, or even five thirty-second spots, to have somebody say, 'Oh, my God, a Dorito chip,' as if it were manna from heaven or, 'Oh, my God, I get to drink a Budweiser. I haven't had alcohol in four weeks. This beer tastes so good.'"

Mark Burnett continued to use product placement in his later shows, such as *The Apprentice*. In the Irish version, contestants were tasked with inventing a new Dairy Milk bar for Cadbury's. The episode was accompanied by a nationwide competition in which the public were invited to design new Dairy Milk packaging. The integration was deemed a success by both the channel and the brand. Larry Bass, CEO of Screentime ShinAwil, an independent production company that makes the Irish version of *The Apprentice*, said "brands are reaching out to us directly to feature their products in forthcoming programs. Unfortunately, it is not that simple; much as we need funds to produce shows, the show comes first, never the brand. Viewers must still be entertained by TV and not have the sitting room hijacked by an awkward placement." Brands are part of everyday life, so "A good product placement would be something that is really in keeping with the scene. When it jumps out at you and the audience is wondering 'How much did they paid for that?', it's a bad placement," says Alex Gulland, founder of Contented Brands, a London agency that specializes in digital content. Nick Price, head of content at advertising agency MPG Media Contacts, told a radio program, "The way that product placement has been shown to work in other markets is that if it's too prominent and people wake up to it, it actually has a bad effect on the brand, so it becomes about the context in which your brand is seen, as opposed to the hard sell. The hard sell can still be done in the spot ad, whereas what this allows us to do for the first time is to leverage brands within programs and then do stuff off air to give a sense of context and value and positioning."

It's difficult to generalize about how product placement works because there are many regulatory differences around the world. In the UK regulations forbid product placement in certain types of shows: children's programs, news, current affairs, religious and consumer programs. It is also not permitted to product place tobacco, medicines, guns, gambling, alcohol, baby milk and food containing high levels of salt, fat and sugar. There is also a ban on "undue prominence" of products in programs (a restriction that does not apply in the US).

If a brand has funded a program it's natural for them to want to place their products within that program too, because "if you own the program you don't pay any extra for putting your own product inside your own show as long as it is editorially justified," says Chantal Rickards. If, for example, "you are doing a cookery show, you are obviously going to have food brands inside that show, so any food brand would be able to put their brand inside that program, as long as it has an editorial justification and is not over-promotional." However, this is a tricky area as the producers of Channel 5's *Family Food Fight with Flora* found out when they fell foul of Ofcom (the UK regulatory body for the communications industries). In this instance, the program's funder, Flora, was the manufacturer of low-fat sunflower spreads and on several occasions the program's narrator referred to "low-fat" products and "sunflower spread," which Ofcom deemed to be overly promotional, and therefore in breach of the rules. In these early days of product placement UK broadcasters are wary of product placement in factual programming, unwilling to be the first broadcaster to overstep the line and incur the wrath of Ofcom, as borne out by the rather timid placement of a coffee machine on the set of a daytime magazine show. As AFP and product placement becomes more common, it's likely broadcasters will become bolder and the rules will evolve.

Factual entertainment, reality and entertainment shows are the natural home of product placement. In the USA, Nielson Media Research recorded more than 100,000 instances of product placement in TV programs (including scripted television) on the six major US TV networks during the 2004–05 season. Nielson also logged a staggering 9,136 product placements between January and June 2008 on Bravo's *Top Chef*. This feat earned them only third place in the US product placement chart, with *American Chopper* and *Project Runway* taking top spots. In 2009, *Extreme Makeover: Home Edition*, *The Celebrity Apprentice*, *America's Next Top Model*, and *Dancing with the Stars* all featured in Nielsen's top ten. More shocking, perhaps, was the news that Food Network's *Chopped* has *NO* product placement.

Interestingly, one of *Top Chef*'s main product integrations was Gail Simmons, a food critic and journalist for *Food and Wine* magazine, who serves as one of the judges, and proved to be one of the most "effective product placement" activities measured by Nielsen, which might make it an interesting area to explore. The UK version of the *X Factor* got into hot water when Mary Byrne, a middle-aged checkout operator at Tesco supermarket, became another, if inadvertent, example of "human" product placement. The singer quickly became one of the show's favorites and was regularly referred to onscreen as "Tesco Mary." Rival supermarkets called foul, objecting to the frequent name checks, especially in light of the fact that Tesco was the exclusive stockist of the *X Factor* magazine. This was tantamount to product placement, they complained (product placement was not yet legal in the UK at that point). There were also dark mutterings of vote rigging as Tesco had emailed its entire staff about Mary's participation in the show. "If all 300,000 voted for their colleague, that's an awful lot of votes," noted the *London Evening Standard.*

It's been estimated that the UK is five to ten years behind the US product placement market, but it's likely that product placement will be a little less prolific in the UK, even after everyone's nerves have stopped jangling. Rupert Brankin-Frisby, commercial director of TalkbackThames, the production company behind *American Idol*, notes, "over [in the USA] you've got the Coke cups on the table. In the UK, would that be offensive to people? I don't think so. But each week the show gets the contestants to shoot a pop video in a Ford car. Culturally, for me, that makes me feel a bit uncomfortable. I think that's the sort of thing that is definitely not going to happen here in the UK." *New York Magazine* runs a regular feature in which Paul F. Tompkins recaps what happened on the latest episode of *American Idol*. Amusingly he also includes the product placements:

PRODUCT PLACEMENT THIS SEGMENT: Ford. It's always Ford now. Oh, good news! It's another Ford music video! This time the gang are superheroes. Some of them. The rest of them are weaklings who need to be saved from falling things and fires. The only one who doesn't need saving is Scotty, because he has a Ford car! After we witness many superpowered rescues, Scotty saves his own Ford car from a falling lamppost by getting into the car, starting the ignition, driving forward two inches, and letting the lamppost fall harmlessly behind him. So if you are skeptical of buying a Ford, be sure to take into account its "forward motion" feature.

Ashlea Halpern performs the same service for *Project Runway*:

Fans of the show's choleric take-downs will be pleased to know that ... those bitch pants are riding up their cracks higher and harder than ever. Nina, Michael, and Heidi have gone from mildly derisive to downright hostile. Outfits are no longer just train wrecks—they're hideous, wacky, tacky, cheap, ugly, awful, and unflattering. Oh, and usually horrifically styled, too. Sheesh. Why so angry, guys? Is the goal to make the designers cry? To have someone *auf* themselves on-camera? Or is it just to make the last nine minutes of every show so rewardingly juicy, it compensates for the other eighty-one minutes' Second Coming—slow dialogue and close-ups of HP TouchSmart Notebooks?

You can't just knock on a brand's door and expect them to provide you with a car or laptop for next week's shoot because brand managers plan their marketing activities around twelve months in advance. If you decide that product placement is appropriate for your show, Alex Gulland advises, "You should be thinking commercially at the very early days of scripting and putting a program together; how to get brands involved in a way that doesn't compromise the creativity, but does endorse the authenticity of your project." It's also important you talk to the channel as soon as possible about any potential product placement deal, says Claire Heys: "as the channel may have sold sponsorship which conflicts with product placement opportunities."

Product placement doesn't always have to be physical, as branded goods can be digitally inserted into a shot in post-production, using technology such as that provided by MirriAd. The advantage of adding a product in post-production is that the positioning and time onscreen can be more tightly controlled. It also solves the problem of international program sales: what happens if a potential market doesn't allow product placement? Or if the placing brand doesn't want to be associated with a certain channel in a different territory because the demographic is wrong for them? Digital product placement means that product branding can be changed from English to Spanish or Chinese, and a 7-Up in one country's program can be a Coca-Cola in another country's version and Pepsi Cola somewhere else.

Calculating the Value of a Product Placement

Product placement is big business. It has "grown steadily in the US for three decades (with the only exception of 2009) across all media. In the US product placement grossed $3.6 billion in 2009 and is expected to reach $6.1 billion in 2014." But, as every deal for every program in every market is different, it can be hard for the producer to judge how much a product placement might be worth in monetary terms. There are a number of factors that are taken into account when calculating the fee paid by the brand, including:

- How well-known the brand is
- The prominence of the product within a scene
- The location of the product within a scene
- The location of the product on the screen (in which quadrant)
- The length of time on screen
- Whether or not the product is fully visible
- If there is more than one placement of the product
- Exclusivity for the brand being featured
- Whether the product is actually used
- Whether the product is used by a celebrity
- Whether there is a verbal reference to the brand
- The program budget

In the USA specialized tracking tools have been developed by a number of companies to measure the impact of a product placement on a brand's subsequent sales. That information is then used to put a monetary value on future placements. In the UK, it will take time for brands, channels and producers to work out the value of product placement activity. "The baseline for costing will be the thirty-second TV spot," says London agency BrandsonTV. "Whether the placement was valued at above or below the baseline would depend on the level of exposure." So, for example, if there is "passive brand exposure," that is the product is simply part of the set (like the *This Morning* coffee machine), the cost of that placement is likely to be 30 percent of an advertising spot in the commercial break. If, however, the product was actively integrated into the program—used and verbally referenced by the host—then the cost of that placement is likely to be 200 percent that of a thirty-second advertising spot.

Sky requires an initial fee upfront, which is the minimum value agreed for the placement. Once the show has aired, they apply quantitative and qualitative analysis to determine the actual value of the placement, which will be on a sliding scale up to an agreed maximum cap. In other words if a product placement results in greatly increased brand awareness they expect the brand to cough up more money. ITV uses a combined "brand placement" score and a "contextual integration score" devised by sponsorship agency Repucom to calculate the cost of a placement. "None of these deals are going to be straightforward," says Chantal Rickards, "because there are going to be at least three, if not four, different players around the table negotiating: the broadcaster, the brand, the agency and the independent producer." Nick Price described a simpler model in which producers do small, day-to-day product placement deals with brand agencies while broadcasters concentrate their efforts on brokering larger sponsorship and product integration deals for their biggest shows.

While product placement is a potential source of funding for producers working on the kind of shows (and in territories) that permit it, "Don't believe that [it] will open the vaults to untold riches; it won't," cautions Mark Wood. "Do understand that at best it will be one more benefit to help add value to an overall package of rights."

Prop Placement and Trade Outs

Contestants in *Britain's Next Top Model* enjoyed celebrating their first photo shoot with bottles of Freixnet Cava (alcohol is not allowed to be product placed in the UK); 85 percent of the time you see a Volkswagen on British TV it's on a BBC channel (where no advertising of any kind is allowed); Olympus 770WSW compact digital camera and its brand name were repeatedly shown on consumer program *The Gadget Show*, causing sales to increase by 200 percent and Amazon to run out of stock (when product placement was, and still isn't, allowed on consumer shows). Yet all of these placements were acceptable. Why? Because they were prop rather than product placements. "Products that are furnished as backdrops for a TV program scene do not have to be disclosed as long as they are not portrayed in an unreasonable manner that implies 'commercial intent.'"

In a prop placement arrangement, brands provide products free of charge in the hope that a producer might use them in their show; the producer is under no obligation to include that product in the program for any specified screen time, or indeed at all. The advantage to producers is that they can make budget savings by borrowing or making use of donated props rather than buying the items needed onscreen, but be sure the savings are worth it. I once worked on a show where the showrunner thought it would be fun to see the host drive up to each location in a sports car. I managed (to my subsequent regret) to persuade a classic sports car manufacturer to lend us a car, thus saving us considerable car hire fees, and spent a stressful summer making sure the car was in the right location at the right time for shoots all around the UK. In retrospect I'd have preferred to hire a basic model and leave the car out of shot, which would have saved me countless sleepless nights worrying about the logistics of transporting a valuable car around the country.

Prop placement isn't confined to territories where product placement is banned. According to director of Seesaw Media, Darryl Collis, "In America, about 80 percent of the brands you see on TV are prop placement, not product placement," where it's known as doing a "trade out." Production teams often employ a dedicated trade out producer who works with specialist prop placement agencies that look for potential opportunities for their clients.

How to Pitch a Brand Funded Program

Advertiser funded programs can originate from anywhere and pitching can take place in any direction:

- Producer → TV channel → Brand agency
- Producer → Brand agency → TV channel
- TV channel → Producer → Brand agency
- TV channel → Brand agency → Brand
- Brand → Media Agency → Production company → TV channel
- Media Agency → Brand agency → TV channel

As you can see, there are a number of players involved, who inevitably all have their own preferred *modus operandi*. Which brings us to our first problem: a program idea is often pitched to several channels before it's picked up (so at this stage you don't know the exact channel it will eventually be transmitted on, if at all); and a producer will often not know the exact transmission date (which is important for brands with seasonal products) or time (important as different demographics watch different slots) until well into the production process.

There's no reason why a brand should commit to funding a program before they know when and where it's going to be shown, which means it makes most sense to pitch to brands *after* you've managed to get some interest from a channel.

Pitch to TV Channels First

If you have a show that is suitable for brand funding, the usual route is for TV producers to pitch the idea to a channel in the normal way, get an expression of interest, and then go out to the brands to try to raise the money needed to make it. The problem with this route is that brands dislike having to work with creative content that they've not had a hand in shaping. If you manage to get interest from a channel first, a brand will need convincing that there is a real synergy between their brand values and the TV program.

Pitch to Brands First

Sometimes a producer will talk to a brand first, and then present the program as a *fait accompli* to the channel. This has the advantage of shortening the length of time between the pitch and the actual commission, as there is nothing to stop the channel commissioning it: there is a good idea, ready funded, and all they have to do is find a slot in the schedule for it. However, not so fast ... if a producer has signed some kind of deal with a brand for product placement or funding, it might conflict with existing advertising and sponsorship deals that the channel's ad sales team has in place, making the show uncommissionable. If a producer were to find a single brand funder before approaching the channel, it shouldn't be a deal-breaker, it would just mean that the channel couldn't sell advertising to brands in that same category.

In the USA it's not uncommon for producers to do funding deals directly with brands, and agree that the brand will get the sponsored bumpers and an agreed number of advertising spots in the commercial breaks, and then offer it to the channel as a show that comes with two or three out of approximately twenty-two spots in a thirty-minute program presold. The advantage of getting a brand onboard before approaching a channel is that there is proven brand interest in the program and therefore increases the chances of the channel finding other advertisers to buy advertising time. If in doubt the best advice is to not finalize any deals with a brand before talking to the channel (safer to get a letter of interest from them), and always talk to the channel sooner rather than later.

The first challenge when pitching to a brand is to find the right person within the right brand to whom you can pitch. "If you go to a large brand like Adidas," explains Alex Gulland, "they have lots of different divisions—for women, for men, for kids—and beneath all those there are other brand managers for different shapes, models, makes of clothing." Once you've managed to track down the right person, you may or may not be able to build a relationship with them. "Some brand managers are quite savvy and you can connect directly with them and they want to work with you. Other brand managers are slightly nervous about the process and don't have any experience in this area so therefore they will refer you to their media agency. Once you get into that triangle it does slow things down an awful lot. So the sooner you can start talking to them the better."

There are a number of intermediaries who can help, including those who work on behalf of a brand to find marketing opportunities. "It's better to go to the agency than to the brand," advises Christian Tureaud, co-founder of Highroad Entertainment Group, so "you can find that brand manager who represents multi-cultural, music, sports or whatever you are trying to reach within that brand." Unfortunately, this means there can be four or five different stakeholders, says Jason Hughes, head of branded content at BSkyB, "but what is of paramount importance is that there is only one person who has the ultimate power of ediorial control and that has to lie with the broadcaster under the [UK] rules and regulations."

1. **Branded Content Agencies**—Branded content agencies are a relatively new addition to the scene and might come from either a broadcasting or brand background. "We're in the middle and you're talking two completely different languages ... we're the translator through it all," explained Tera Hanks (then at Davie-Brown, a branded content agency in Los Angeles), "there are very different needs and agendas on both sides."

   One of the leading London agencies is Krempelwood. Mark Wood describes his role as being like an agent for producers. "When they get to the point when a commissioning editor says, 'That's a great idea, please go away and find some money,' and they think, 'Well how the hell do I do that?' We do it for them. So we represent about twenty different production companies and we've got four shows on TV in the last eight months that have all been funded to some degree or other by a brand."

   Independent documentary producer Leigh Gibson, has recently stepped into this world with a commercial documentary project. "We've got this matchmaking company involved—Edward Sharp at Film Tree—and he's been fantastic. We couldn't have done it without him because he's got lots of branding contacts at his fingertips, so he can call them up and pitch your project on your behalf in a language that the brands understand. Although there is an added cut that comes out of the budget pot, the deals are so much greater you can take that onboard and it doesn't make much of a difference." Obviously, branded content agencies will charge for the service they provide, typically a commission-based fee. "They have lots of different funding models, some just take commission, some want funding upfront, and the costs vary enormously," says Dan Chambers, company director, Blink Films, "and it depends on how much time you want them to spend on your projects. We spoke to some who were willing to come and work for us two or three days a week, so that was a much higher cost but the upside of that is that if they are focusing on it two or three days a week, the chances of them being able to land a brand that is interested is high." It's likely that you'll pay 10–30 percent of the amount of money an agent raises, and their involvement could continue throughout the production process and into the edit as they make sure things are running smoothly.

2. **Media Agencies**—Often a brand will prefer to deal with you via their media agency. A media agency is responsible for identifying advertising and marketing opportunities and spending the brand's marketing budget. The job of a media agency is to mediate between the brand and the broadcasters and producers. "We sit with a brand and we help them to understand what they're trying to achieve with their marketing," says Christopher Lockwood, Head of Invention at Mindshare, "that might turn into a very nice idea for a TV format, that is literally built out of their marketing needs. If there isn't a broadcaster or a production company in the market who was currently thinking about creating something like that, we do have to go to market and say, 'Look, we'd like to make this; this is what it looks like, are you interested?'" As a media agency is on the brand's payroll there will be no cost to you as producer, but that also means the best interests of their clients is at the forefront of what they do.

If you have a relationship with a media agency you might be asked to pitch ideas against a brand's brief. This is risky for you, the producer, as you might put in a lot of development work for nothing if channel interest can't be secured. "Ensure you actually have a level of funding and commitment from the brand first, don't spend a huge amount of time scoping out an idea even if they've given you £5,000 to go and develop the idea if there's never really been a commitment for the rest of the money to go forward," says Jason Hughes. "Know what broadcasters are looking for so you've got an idea in your head to start with as to whether it will work for certain channels or broadcasters."

Alex Gulland recommends bringing on an expert to support you. "If there is any way you can bring onboard a media consultant, someone who can help you put a value on the opportunity from a producer's point of view, it is very helpful. What tends to happen is that once you are bounced into the media agencies' camp they start putting a media evaluation on the opportunity. Invest in your own media consultant to do that for you." If you already have a channel interested in your project they could help with this too.

Whether you are pitching directly to a brand manager or via an intermediary you'll need to tweak your pitch to emphasize the benefits of a brand supporting your show. Ben Devlin, executive producer at Brand Sponsor, offers the following tips:

- **Can you highlight the project in a sentence?** Brands get hundreds of proposals—grab them up at the top with your idea in a nugget.
- **When is it happening?** If you're looking for more than £10,000 then most brands will need several months to allocate budget.
- **What do you want the brand to provide?** Of course brands can give money but they can also help by providing products and lending the weight of their own PR departments.
- **Who are your "audience" and how are you reaching them?** In what way are you interacting with the public? Do you have guaranteed terrestrial broadcaster coverage, do you plan content on the web, are you reliant on news/magazine coverage or word of mouth? If it's an event, are there banners over entrances, signs visible by passing traffic, t-shirts for participants, etc. The potential for logo placement can be just about anything, so use your imagination.
- **Will your project stand out? Is it PR'able?** Point out what makes your project unique, special, topical (or star-studded).
- **Leave room for the brand to have some input into the project.** While you may not wish to have brands change your plans it's a good idea to show flexibility and to be open to creative suggestions.
- **What can you offer in terms of return on investment?** Make list of tangible things that you can offer a brand in return for their investment. Product placement, logos, supporting video content etc."

The brand funding opportunities discussed in this chapter are best suited to entertainment and reality shows. In Chapter 6 we'll explore how brands are becoming involved in documentaries, often in partnership with not-for-profit and non-government organizations (NGOs).

Sample Brand Proposal

The New York City Experience

A map, a time limit and high emotional stakes make for an unforgettable experience in the world's most exciting city.

Each 60-minute episode features a couple or group of friends who are visiting New York City for a celebratory weekend break—for a special birthday, a proposal or honeymoon. We see them touch down at JFK and check in to their accommodation in an up-and-coming Brooklyn neighborhood where they are greeted by their surprise host—a famous local who gives them a handpicked itinerary of sights, tastes and experiences that will make their weekend memorable. The twist is that they have just forty-eight hours, a map and a set of clues with which to complete every activity on their itinerary. If they fail they catch their flight home; if they succeed they get an immediate upgrade to a weeklong expenses-paid luxury holiday of a lifetime.

Viewers have the chance to win the same New York break that features in each show.

Brand Partnership Opportunity

This thirteen-part series for a lifestyle channel aimed at women 25–45 is looking for funding of $1 million from a combination of sponsorship and product placement.

Ideal partners would be:

Airline

Hotel chain

Beauty brand

Clothing brand

Fashion brand

Credit card

Tourist board

Camera/Smart phone

Each partner would contribute 25 percent of the funding in exchange for a range of benefits:

- Sponsorship banners around each episode
- Verbal and visual product placement opportunities for hotels, restaurants, credit cards, smart phones, spas, luxury retail outlets, fashion brands, grooming products
- Click-through sponsorship banners on the TV channel's website
- Brand alignment with the program
- Access to opt-in data collected from competition registrations and interactive elements

To find out more contact: Nicola Lees: Nicola@tvmole.com www.tvmole.com

Advantages of Brand Funding

1. Some slots in broadcasters' schedules are given over to purely advertiser-funded programs and therefore if you have a brand onboard you have access to those slots.
2. A brand's marketing might will help drive people to the program via in-store and package promotions, posters and social media.
3. You can use product and prop placement to enhance the design of your set without having to spend money out of your budget.

Disadvantages

1. Product placement is suitable only for certain types of programs—legally and editorially.

2. A product placement deal in one country might affect sales of the program to channels in other countries that have different rules and regulations. "Brand funding is more acceptable in certain territories like the UK and USA, absolutely unacceptable in Scandinavia. Where it demands an overt brand presence could make it impossible to sell in certain territories," warns Danny Tipping of Parthenon Entertainment.

3. Brands are unlikely to fund a program that they deem negative or controversial in any way.

4. Advertiser funding or product placement might be vetoed by the channel if it clashes with other advertising deals they have in place.

5. There are more stakeholders to mange. According to Vicky Kell, Channel 4's business manager for sponsorship placement and funding content, a deal with clothing store New Look involved more than eight different parties, from the production company and the C4 commissioners to the creative agency, the media planning agency, the media buying agency and "a myriad of consultants."

6. There is no such thing as a standard deal; each one has to be negotiated indi vidually. A brand might agree to fund 100 percent of a program budget, or just 25 percent or some other proportion in partnership with the broadcaster or other co-funding partners. "In some cases, TV producers want millions of dollars from participating brands," says Scott Donaton, "in others, TV network sales forces throw in product placement as a free 'added value' element of a larger ad buy."

7. A naive or pushy brand might expect to exert editorial control over your program—managing expectations will be a core part of the production pro- cess. Every brand that funded Morgan Spurlock's *POM Wonderful Presents: The Greatest Movie Ever Sold* sent him a contract that gave them final approval over the edit. It took months of negotiation to get them to accept that they couldn't have final approval. "Every advertiser I've ever worked with starts by saying, 'We totally understand that it's your editorial product and we're not going to interfere in the process,'" says Mark Wood, "and every single one of them at some stage asks if [the character/presenter] can wear a red dress, or if the set could be a different color. And no matter how much producers are tempted to do what the brand wants because of the money, they are protected by the laws ... so no matter how much a brand wants to do it, they can't and everybody knows you can't do it."

8. The production schedule needs to take into account the length of time it takes to get sign off from all the different parties. Having a brand involved tends to

slow the process down. "Sometimes smaller brands tend to move faster," says Alex Gulland. "There is a large automobile company that is notorious for taking long periods of time to make a decision due to their internal structure—sometimes they can take up to twelve months—but if they suddenly decide that they want to do something then they can turn things around reasonably quickly."

9. It's been claimed that product placement not only irritates the viewers, but harms the industry itself. "Producers, directors, writers, actors and other creative personnel come to learn that the likelihood of their being hired is linked to their willingness to be friendly to products being placed in their work. In a business where the 'clout' to say no is fragile and elusive, 'uncooperative' or 'difficult' creative workers can be replaced by others who 'see the light,'" said Lawrence Wenner, Professor of Communication and Ethics at Loyola Marymount University, Los Angeles.

10. Having a paid product placement in a scene can give you a headache in the edit when you need to cut that scene for editorial reasons. For this reason brands may not pay any money upfront, releasing it only when they know exactly how many seconds of screen time they have.

11. Brands don't like to come onboard at the last minute, as they want to feel they are getting a bespoke program, so brand funding isn't likely to help you raise the last 20 percent of the budget.

Next Steps

1. Look at the regulations in your territory regarding brand funding and product placement.

2. Brainstorm your program idea—is there a natural potential fit with a certain type of brand?

3. Think laterally about the type of products that might be integrated. For example, in the eighth season of *Project Runway* the contestants designed a pattern using Hewlett-Packard computers. Conversely, "Just because you've got a food program it doesn't mean it's going to be right for every food brand," says Chantal Rickards, but you could think about kitchen appliances or kitchenware brands.

4. Think about what you can offer a brand: exclusive content? Talent tie-ins? VIP tickets for a special screening?

5. Research media agencies and intermediary brand agencies in your territory and set up meetings to discuss your idea.

Jargon Buster

Term	Meaning
AFP	Advertiser funded programming. A brand might fund all or part of a program.
Brand Integration	When a program or series narrative is deliberately built around a brand or product. The brand is integral to the story rather than being a peripheral placement.
Liquid Content	A term used by brands to talk about content that can exist across a range of platforms, e.g. TV, internet, mobile phones, live events, in-store promotions. Equivalent term in TV might be 360-degree content, multiplatform content or transmedia.
Media Agency	Sits between a brand and the media in which it advertises. The media agency controls a brand's marketing budget, looks for advertising and marketing opportunities in the media and negotiates advertising space.
Media Impressions	Refers to the number of people who have read an article or review, heard a radio feature, seen a TV interview or visited a website or blog etc. that mentions a product (in our case a film or TV program); uses a calculation based on the audience figures of a program or circulation figures of a newspaper.
Plinking	Product-linking (plinking): the process of adding a product or service link to a visible object in a video.
Product Placement	A contractual agreement between a brand and a TV producer, in which the brand pays to have the program feature a product for a specified length of time or number of times. The placement can be physical, i.e. the product is actually present on the set, or digital, i.e. it is added to the show in post-production.
Prop Placement	A brand supplies or lends a product to a production in the hope that they will feature it in the show. The brand doesn't

pay any money and the producer is under no obligation to feature the product.

Sponsorship   When a brand pays a broadcaster a fee to have their brand name associated with a show, e.g. have the brand name featured in the two- to three-second "bumpers" that are shown between the program and commercial breaks.

Trade Out   A barter arrangement in which a production asks a brand for free products from a brand to use on their set (typically a US production will have a dedicated trade out producer). Similar to prop placement.

Further Reading and Resources

Brands on TV—Provides free bulletins to alert brands to AFP and product placement opportunities in the UK.
http://www.brandsontv.com

Brand Sponsor—A UK resource for information on sponsorship, prop and product placement and ad-funded programming. Includes a directory of more than 2,500 marketing contacts at UK brands and services (membership required).
http://www.brandsponsor.co.uk

Contented Brands—A branded entertainment consultancy that works with brands to create film and television content.
http://www.contentedbrads.com

Entertainment Resources and Marketing Associations (ERMA)—A searchable database of product placement and marketing agencies in the USA.
http://www.erma.org/memberlist

Federal Communications Commission (FCC)—The US regulatory body for radio, television, satellite and cable communications.
http://www.fcc.gov/

IPA, the (Institute of Practitioners in Advertising)—UK trade body for marketing and communications agencies. A clickable map provides a list of member agencies.
http://www.ipa.co.uk/AgencyList.aspx

LA Office, the—Matchmaking agency between brands and entertainment producers. A free newsletter alerts producers/brands to upcoming opportunities.
http://www.laoffice.com

MEC—a global media agency operating in eighty-four countries, helping brands to plan and implement their advertising and marketing strategies.
http://www.mecglobal.com

MirriAd—Digital product placement company with a useful description and video demonstration of how digital product placement works.
http://mirriad.com/technology/

Ofcom—The product placement code for producers working in the UK.
http://stakeholders.ofcom.org.uk/consultations/bcrtv2010/statement/

Thinkbox—Marketing body for commercial TV in the UK. Extensive website with lots of research and case studies.
http://www.thinkbox.tv/

4 Banks and Private Equity Investors—Masters of the Funding Universe

Bank loans are best suited to TV producers and filmmakers with:

1. A high budget program with commercial appeal—some banks will only finance films with budgets of at least $5million
2. Committed funders onboard, e.g. broadcasters and distributors
3. A high percentage (80 percent +) of the funding secured
4. A demonstrable track record
5. A time-sensitive subject that requires you go into production before the money arrives in your account, necessitating the use of a bridging loan to cash flow production

Private equity investment funding is best suited to TV producers and filmmakers with:

1. A commercially viable project that is likely to make money from sales, such as a feature-length film with broad appeal, e.g. *Senna* or *Man on Wire*
2. An multi-award-winning director or producer attached to the project
3. A high percentage of the budget in place
4. Access to good legal advice

> Inside Job: *The film that cost over $20,000,000,000,000*
> *to make.*
>
> —*Inside Job* tagline

The *Inside Job*, a feature documentary that exposed how collusion and corruption in banking, academia and politics caused the 2008 financial crash, had a budget of $2million, of which Sony Classics Pictures, its distributor, provided just over half. It's probably safe to assume that banks would have been disinclined to fund a film that attacked the financial services industry, however banks often do help finance big-budget productions. So too do equity investors, who are rich (sometimes referred to as "high net worth" or even "ultra high net worth") individuals who invest money in order to share in the ownership of a "property" (or in our case, a film or TV show) and consequently share in any future profits. The financial crash caused many individual investors to rethink their investment strategies and pull out of the riskiest forms of investment such as film, but new specialist equity funds have sprung up to help investors spread their risk and dedicated media banking divisions provide loans to help producers cash flow productions. Neither banks nor equity investors have any interest in film as an art form or vehicle for social change; their interest is purely commercial. All they care about (as the *Inside Job* revealed) is making money, either by charging interest payments on a loan, or by sharing ownership and therefore profits.

Banks

There are a number of ways that a bank can help with production finance and they are increasingly stepping in to help broadcasters with their cash flow. For instance, *The Passion of Girls Aloud*, a 4 x 60' series about the girl band, was cash flowed by Barclays Corporate and ITV2 paid for the program on delivery. Barclays Corporate also funded indie producer Transparent Television to make *Danger: Diggers at Work* for Channel 5. The bank released the funding to the indie in four installments as the production reached agreed milestones, and Channel 5 repaid the bank at a later date. Here are a couple of the most common ways banks can help you to fund your project:

Gap Finance

If you have raised most of your budget, but are having trouble finding the final 10–20 percent that you need to actually make your film, you can approach one of the handful of banks and specialty lenders that offer film production loans that "fill the gap." "Gap financing is the financing of the gap between what a filmmaker is able to obtain from its financing package—what it's able to raise from private equity, presales and government incentives—and the balance of what it needs for the production budget," says entertainment lawyer Peter Levitan. Gap financiers "are specialty lenders who are lending against the unsold territories, and that's a substantial risk for the lender," so gap finance comes with a high rate of interest. The banks calculate the amount of money they are prepared to lend based on the projected sales estimates drawn up by a reputable distributor (of course, some distributors also offer gap finance, saving you the hassle of going via a bank). The sales estimates show best- and worst-case scenarios on a territory-by-territory basis for the territories that remain unsold. A bank will lend against these estimates only if a distributor is reputable and already attached to the project (thereby guaranteeing distribution). To further reduce the risk, the project must also have proven market appeal—in the form of presales. A bank offering a gap finance deal will recoup its loan plus interest and possibly an arrangement fee, but won't take a share of the back end (although they might take the film or other assets the producer holds as security until the loan is paid off).

There are also private gap financiers who will recoup (be repaid) their loan plus interest *and* expect a share in the equity of the film. Clearly, it's better for the producer to retain as much equity (or ownership) in the film as possible; the more people sharing the equity, and therefore the back-end revenue, the less there is for the producer if the film is successful.

Cash Flow

It's possible to raise 100 percent of your budget but still not be able to go into production because you haven't yet received any money. Simon Vyvyan, managing director of Industry Media, a company that looks after business affairs for independent production companies, says funding a production is an exercise in "constant plate spinning to make sure that you can make the money come in when you need it." Because money from a broadcaster might not come through for several months after commission, or until delivery of the completed program, many film and TV producers have to borrow money so they can actually produce the program. A bank can lend money against funding contracts issued by broadcasters and distributors; the loan, plus interest, is repaid to the bank when the broadcaster releases the money.

Sometimes this type of funding is known as a bridging loan. It comes with a high rate of interest and therefore should only be considered as a short-term loan and *in extremis*—such as on a high-budget production where receipt of money is due imminently but filming has to start immediately or the whole production would collapse because of loss of access to a star contributor or location. Bridging loans are sometimes used in high-end theatrical documentaries but the average independent documentary maker won't use bridging loans. Instead they tend to raise money in tandem with production and if they run out of funds they will typically pause production until they receive their next pot of money and can afford to continue.

If a bank is cash flowing a production they want to be sure that they will get their money back and so need to see that the producer and production company have a solid track record. They may want to see a business plan, but as ever, in an industry that relies on personal contacts, it's unlikely that the bank will rely solely on a document. "I will use all of my resources to check their credentials," says Sue Pettican, Media Relationship Director at Barclays Corporate. "I may have worked with them through another client or I can call on my contacts in the industry."

In a loan agreement, the producer is obliged to pay back the money with interest whether or not the film makes any money and the lender doesn't share in any future profits. Once the loan has been repaid, the relationship between the lender and the person receiving the loan ceases.

Banks offer a number of other services to filmmakers too, including:

- Provision of production bank accounts
- Acting as a collection agency—ensuring distributors and sales agents pay monies owed
- Providing letters of guarantee and credit—which allow the producer to obtain credit from foreign banks and other financial institutions on international shoots
- Managing the exchange rate on a foreign production to reduce the risk of currency fluctuations

Private Equity Investors

Equity investors, on the other hand, are investing their money in order to become part owners of a business (film or TV show in this instance), and are therefore entering into a long-term relationship with you. Despite the dire state of the world's finances, it is still possible to find rich people who are willing and able to take this kind of risk with their money. "I have one client, whose film was produced in London and entirely financed by private equity, by investors to whom they had access," notes Peter Levitan. An investor's main motivation for investing in a project is their expectation that they will get a cut of any future profits. The problem is that very few documentaries make a profit, which means they are an extremely high-risk investment. Film financing is inherently an exercise in predicting the unpredictable. Peter Levitan, who is also a former LA studio executive, and has more than twenty-five years' experience of representing and advising production companies, studios, banks, distributors, film funds and individual producers, writers and directors, describes predicting film performance as, "an exercise in classical chaos theory ... where you have a dynamic system of multiple independent, constantly moving parts that are interrelated, but in a non-linear manner, the result is near-total, if not total, unpredictability."

According to distributor Carl Hall, "An investor needs a return of 30 percent year-on-year and there are very few TV shows that will do that, so that's why investors tend to go to [fiction] feature films." Return on investment can be most simply calculated by dividing net profit (earnings after all relevant expenses have been deducted) by the investment and multiplying by 100 to get a percentage. So for example, if the investment is $50,000 and the net profit is $2,500: $2,500 (net profit) ÷ $50,000 (investment) = 0.05 x 100 = 5 percent return on investment (ROI).

It makes more sense for an investor to put their money into a big entertainment TV series that has global format sales potential, such as *Dancing with the Stars*, *X Factor*, *Idol* etc., but there are still no guarantees; more new TV formats fail than succeed. In the UK, the James Grant Group, a talent agency, devised a 6 x 60' TV format in which investors were intrinsic to both the funding and the narrative. Equity investors were invited to invest £100,000 in return for a 2 percent stake in a new company, Made in Britain, which in turn would take a 35 percent stake in half a dozen fledgling businesses. A TV show, also called *Made in Britain*, would follow the progress of the six entrepreneurs and leverage publicity around the show to help them launch their products, thereby creating a profit for the Made in Britain company that could be shared among the investors and reinvested in the development of new TV formats. The idea was to offer the format to broadcasters free of charge; however, at the time of writing they had not managed to secure a commission. In a statement the James Grant Group admitted, "It is somewhat chicken and egg—we need interest from a broadcaster to get investors involved and investors interested for a broadcaster to come onboard."

As viewers of *Dragons' Den/Shark Tank* know, investors bring more than just their money to a deal, such as their business expertise and valuable contacts, but by their very nature they are likely to negotiate a better deal for themselves in return for these "added extras." "By financing a film, investors are not doing producers a favor; both groups need each other," says producer/director Shamir Allibhai, in *Getting Your Documentary Funded and Distributed.* "The goal for the producer should be to find a suitable investor, to get a deal signed that is mutually beneficial to both parties, and to deliver on commitments. For financiers, the questions are: what do they want from the deal? What are the key criteria? Will this deal get their capital back plus interest, and what size returns are they looking for?" It's important to establish exactly what revenues the investor will share—just the profit from feature film box office receipts or will they take a cut of the profits from sales of DVDs, books, soundtrack or other merchandise too?

While most equity investors invest their money for hard-headed business reasons and see investment in a film as just one part of their financial portfolio, others are seduced by the perceived glamor of being associated with a feature film and, depending on the subject of a film, some have an emotional investment in a project too. For example, *Sons of Cuba*, a Grierson Award-winning feature documentary about boy boxers, was partially funded with a loan from an individual in Hong Kong who had made his fortune from technology, but wanted to get involved in the film business. Another two investors in the UK really believed in the project and wanted to support the director, Andrew Lang.

Whereas a loan agreement is a short-term arrangement (at least if you want to avoid paying expensive interest charges), investors stay involved with a project long term and—while hopeful (and expectant) that the film will produce a profit— they are taking a risk as the film might make no money at all and indeed the filmmaker might return to ask them for a further investment in order to finish the film. Having investors onboard may entail you engaging in some hands-on relationship management; one feature film producer remarked that it was the investors who invested the least amount of money who took up the most amount of her time with their frequent requests for updates.

Investment Funds

One way that individual investors can mitigate the risk of investing in film is to pool their money with other investors in an equity fund. Equity film funds all have their own investment criteria regarding the type of film in which they are willing to invest, based on the budget, content, format of the film and credentials of the production company and key crew. For example, Limelight Media in the UK has a fund that invests in projects with large sales potential. "The people behind this are a private equity fund, so they're not doing this in order to lose money," says Chris Hunt, managing partner, Limelight Media; "the minimum they will lend is £250,000 ... which means the sales expectation needs to be somewhere around a million, so this is not for small one-off projects."

One type of fund that UK investors can invest their money in is the Enterprise Investment Scheme (EIS), which is a specialized scheme that offers a range of tax reliefs to investors who invest in qualifying high-risk trades (of which film production is one). Benefits to the investor include income tax relief, inheritance tax relief and capital gains tax relief. If someone invests the maximum £500,000 allowed, once all the various tax reliefs and credits have been applied, the most the investor will lose if the film flops is £130,000. There are strict rules governing EIS, for example, 80 percent of money raised by the sale of shares in the scheme must be spent within twelve months, and the remainder 20 percent spent in the following twelve months, making an EIS funding suitable only for projects that are able to go into immediate production.

The EIS has traditionally been used to fund fiction feature films, but in 2011 a new documentary EIS was launched by the Documentary Company in London. It focuses on funding documentary films about politics, nature and the environment or music, and a film must also have international appeal. The first film to be funded through the documentary EIS was *From the Ashes*, a film about the thrilling 1981 cricket season when England thrashed Australia. In order to receive funding through this particular documentary EIS, filmmakers must have a demonstrable commercial and creative track record (James Erskine, director of *From the Ashes*, has a long track record as a TV producer/director and directed feature documentary *One Night in Turin*). Sheryl Crown, managing director of the Documentary Company, says she is looking for projects that will deliver a 120 percent return on investment. "I can't justify this to our investors if it looks like we're never going to make our money back, however passionate we might feel ... but we are compassionate at heart," she says.

In the USA, New York-based Impact Partners are a "fund and advisory service for investors and philanthropists who seek to promote social change through film." They've been involved in financing more than twenty-five documentary films, such as the Emmy-winning *The Ghosts of Abu Ghraib* and Academy Award winner *The Cove*. "Impact Partners are interesting because they have a group of investors who are interested in social issues, but they are also making money back, because it's an investment not a grant," says filmmaker Hugh Hartford. "By going down the investment route you can get 100 percent of your budget before the film is finished but you have sold a portion of your film so you, the filmmaker, will make less money once the film is finished."

In France, a micro-investment platform Touscoprod invites the general public to invest ten Euros or more in a "co-production share" of a film, which earns the investor a share of any eventual profits for a period of three years. Rainer Hoffmann and Anne Linsel's *Dancing Dreams*, a documentary about the choreography of Pina Bausch, raised 11,451€ and Lucy Walker's Oscar-nominated *Waste Land* raised 6,201€ via Touscoprod.

Needless to say, because of the legal complexities of equity funding and loans it's essential that you get someone with professional expertise in this area to help you. "There's a complicated set of rules about what you can and cannot do, and if you don't get it right the whole financial structure could fall," warned Andrew Baker, founder of Rights.TV. LA entertainment lawyer Peter Levitan urges tracking down expert advice for guidance if considering equity investment for your project "Most entertainment attorneys are not particularly well versed in that area so filmmakers seeking equity investors should be sure to find an entertainment attorney who is also experienced in dealing with securities law," he says. A financing of this type usually constitutes a "securities offering," which is subject to the often complex securities laws in the country where prospective investors are solicited. In the US there are certain exemptions available from the onerous requirements for "public offerings" that an experienced attorney with expertise in this area can help with. These exemptions "typically involve limiting the number of investors, the amount being raised, and the wealth or financial sophistication of the investors," says Peter. "To set up a public securities offering is extremely complicated, burdensome and expensive—in the region of $100,000 in legal fees if you use a major firm."

He also warns that "**IT IS GENERALLY ILLEGAL IN THE US TO SOLICIT FOR INVESTORS IN A PUBLIC FORUM SUCH AS THE INTERNET** [he insisted this be put in bold caps] without going through the prohibitive cost and rigor of qualifying as a public offering. In fact, doing so generally prevents the financing from qualifying for one of the exemptions as a 'private placement.' I've noticed that on a lot of social media, especially on LinkedIn, filmmakers are soliciting for investors." It was even reported in an internet forum that some filmmakers were caught soliciting for investors on eBay, offering "units of membership" (the equivalent of shares in a corporation—for which investors would receive a share of the film profits commensurate with their investment) via the "Buy It Now" button. The listings were promptly removed once eBay found out what was happening. "In the US this is absolutely illegal if the offering has not been qualified and registered as a public securities offering," says Peter, "I used to post comments in LinkedIn's film industry related groups, warning that trawling for investors online is a blatant violation of US federal and state securities laws but most people seemed to be ignoring me and proceeding anyway. They may be figuring that no one is going to know, but they don't seem to be aware that the SEC (US Securities and Exchange Commission), and state securities agencies actually have things called computers and they know how to find people. There have in fact been a number of convictions and decrees obtained against people violating securities laws, committing securities fraud, or selling unregistered securities in connection with film financings." There are similar restrictions and regulations in Europe and elsewhere. To avoid falling foul of the law, you should only approach people with whom you have a pre-existing business relationship or reach out to potential investors privately and individually. There is also often a set limit to the number of people you can approach for investment in this way. Double-check with a legal advisor regarding the specific securities regulations in force in your country.

Pitching to Equity Investors and Banks

Both equity investors and banks will want to see that the film or program already has a good proportion of the budget in place, preferably from sources that don't require repaying, such as TV commissions, presales and grants. Therefore investors and banks normally come onboard late in the funding process.

An investor starts getting a share of the profits once all the production costs have been paid and any production loans have been repaid. But what happens if, as often happens, there is no profit? "There will be one or more disappointed and disgruntled investors who will turn around and sue you," warns Peter Levitan. "A former student of mine ended up at a law firm that represented producers defending these lawsuits. One critical way to mitigate and lessen that risk is to make every conceivable disclosure, to both your potential and actual investors, of absolutely everything that can go wrong, no matter how obvious it seems.

"Risk disclosure is very important, and you'd be surprised at the level of detail that is required," he says. "It sounds obvious but it's necessary to caution investors that there is a strong likelihood that there will be other films like yours in the marketplace place at the same time, and that the film will be competing with other activities for people's leisure time and leisure dollars, etc. A plaintiff's attorney will find all sorts of things that you didn't say, but should have, or that you did say that were misleading. The most important thing when dealing with potential investors is to not give them the usual happy talk, or rosy optimistic projections—'Look at how much a particular hit picture such as Blair Witch Project or Paranormal Activity made; we have the same elements, etc.'—suggesting that there is some likelihood or reasonable expectation that your project is going to be just as successful," says Peter. "One recent calculation was that perhaps 99.5 percent of independent projects, especially lower-budget independent projects, never get any distribution, are never seen by anyone and therefore never generate any revenue. Investors need to know that the overall likelihood is that they're not going to recoup their investment, let alone see a profit. Independent filmmakers are very wary that this will discourage people, but the fact is that the prospective investors who are discouraged by that are investors you don't want because they are unrealistic. You want somebody who is knowledgeable and invests in things like oil wells and racehorse syndicates and other high-risk ventures, because they understand the risk and can afford the loss."

You need water-tight contracts in place to protect yourself against lawsuits. "Experienced attorneys have form documents that they've developed for their own use, such as private placement memorandums or prospectuses that they have vetted and that will, as much as is possible, discourage and defend against an investor lawsuit," says Peter Levitan. If you want to cover your back, he also cautions against taking boilerplate contracts directly from the internet. "Many independent filmmakers think that they can find a self-help tool, take documents from all over the place on the internet and get started, and only bring an attorney in when it's 'necessary,' but what invariably happens is that they've already committed a series of missteps and were poorly advised, so it costs them even more to have the attorney unwind everything they did, try to fix it and then redo everything correctly the way it should have been done the first time." Obviously legal advice costs, but if you've factored it into your budget right from the start an unexpected legal bill won't suddenly deplete your funds and possibly halt production.

Some investors will also want to see a business plan. While an attorney, distributor or media rights specialist can draw up a formal business plan for you, you still have to supply them with all the relevant information, much of which can be adapted from the prep work you've already done on your proposal, budget, finance plan and schedule.

Business Plan Outline

If you prepare a draft business plan before approaching a lawyer, you'll be better able to answer their questions and the process of drawing up all the correct documentation will be quicker, and cheaper. There's no need to be put off writing a business plan by the apparent dryness of the process: it's a just sales document written to enthuse the reader—just like your written TV proposal—presented in a format that businesspeople recognize. Brian Finch, author of *How to Write a Business Plan*, recommends thinking of a business plan like a story with a beginning, middle and end:

1. The Scene—company background and key crew, market;
2. The Story—the synopsis of the project and why it deserves to be made;
3. The Stakes—what finance is needed, the risks and the rewards.

"It is important," he says, "to remember the plot, the descriptive bits (background or scene setting) and the characters. Your plans and background are essential but so are the people who will carry it all out. Some people get the balance wrong and write endlessly about the market or about themselves or about the history of the business. Remember to balance your story and don't bore your reader." As in a TV proposal, your writing should convey how exciting your proposed project is without resorting to hyperbole.

A business plan generally contains the following elements:

1. **Executive Summary**—This section repeats—more concisely—the information in the rest of the business plan and, for that reason, is usually written last. It's equivalent to the first paragraph of your written TV proposal, but concentrates on the business elements of the project rather than the story. It's the Who, What,

Why, How, When of your business plan, including the amount of money already raised and the amount being sought and what is being offered in return.

2. **Company Background**—In many instances it is legally and financially beneficial for a filmmaker to form their own company (an entertainment lawyer can advise), or an independent filmmaker can team up with an established production company who will "house" or "umbrella" a film project. This section of the business plan contains information on the history, mission statement and track record of the production company, along with biographies of key staff working on the project, including executive producer, producer/line producer, director, editor, cinematographer etc. The biographies should highlight high-profile projects and any awards won alongside critics' reviews/press coverage/column inches on previous projects.

3. **Synopsis of the Project**—An outline of the format, story and characters and why this is a film rather than a book or photo-essay. Describe how the film is constructed, why it's being made now, where it's shot and how far along in the production process you are. Also say what you need to do to finish it and when you hope to complete production.

4. **Industry Overview**—While specialist banking divisions will be familiar with the industry, private investors might be drawn toward the bright lights but not understand how the industry actually works. This is the section to explain the TV landscape and how films and TV programs are financed and distributed via TV, DVD, theatrical, VOD etc. Remember to avoid industry jargon and explain all terms clearly.

5. **Audience/Market Analysis/Distribution Plan**— What is the intended market— in terms of both viewers and buyers—for your film and how do you intend to reach them? A domestic TV commission and international sales? Festival run and theatrical release? Do you have a distributor onboard? If so, how does your film fit into their catalogue and what is their track record? What competing films are on the market and why is yours unique? While there are a lot of business data on the box office returns of movies (boxofficemojo.com, boxoffice.com, the-numbers.com), it's much harder to accurately predict which documentaries will be successful and as it's a much smaller market data are harder to come by. You could unearth figures for films in a similar genre to give some idea of what the film could possibly make (but remember to err on the side of caution to avoid misleading potential investors). Other data you could use to support your proposal include:

a. Audience figures/share in domestic market for previous films/programs in the same subject area. For example, here are the viewing figures for *End of the Line*, a feature documentary about over-fishing of the oceans:

End of the Line	(to September 2010)
UK TV transmission (aggregated audience—both More4 and Channel 4 showed one première and one repeat)	1.2 million
Newspaper DVD giveaway	70,000
Community screenings	10,000
Cinema (average audience for social issue theatrical documentaries like this and others such as *Black Gold* and *Burma VJ*)	9,000
DVD sales	2,763
Festival screenings	1,000

b. Size of online community involvement, e.g. Facebook fans or crowdfunding investors
c. Celebrity involvement
d. Newsworthiness (controversy might appeal to or repel investors)
e. Size of fanbase for specialist films such as music documentaries
f. Details of funding already in place, preferably from a well-respected institution or source
g. Book sales for a documentary film based on a book
h. Evidence of book rights secured/celebrities onboard
i. Back-end possibilities—DVD, book, games, etc.
j. Territories sold/available

Finance Plan

A finance plan is a list of actual and anticipated funding sources—broadcasters (commissions/co-production/presales), distribution advances, brand funding, film grants, private equity investors etc. (For an example, refer back to *Dino Stampede* in Part I.) This section could also include a cash flow plan (when the money will be received and spent), sales projections for various territories (which a distributor can provide) and recoupment schedule (the order in which the various investors will be repaid). Certain investors will insist on taking the first recoupment position and there can be a lot of negotiation and renegotiation as more investors come onboard. A recoupment schedule might look something like this in order of the debts that must be repaid (every lender and investor will be keen to recoup first, so the actual order of recoupment will differ on each production depending on what was negotiated and contracted with each party):

1. Distributor's commission
2. Distribution advance repayment
3. Equity repayment to investors
4. Deferred Producer's fees
5. Profit

Once your legal advisor has put together your business plan, sometimes called an Information Memorandum (which provides prospective investors with information about a project, usually used in financing that involves a syndicate), it can be sent to prospective investors, with a letter (also drawn up by a legal advisor) that makes clear that the plan is confidential, does not in itself form a contract and that the recipient should do due diligence and seek legal advice before entering into any agreement.

Having said all that, the preparation of a business plan may turn out to be something of a hoop-jumping exercise, as "experienced entertainment investors often completely disregard the business plans submitted to them by those seeking funds, knowing that the meticulously prepared historical data and performance projections contained in such presentations are unreliable indicia for making their investment decisions," says Peter Levitan. For example, Impact Partners just ask for:

- Written treatment
- Budget—overall budget and a list of all the money raised so far, along with the outstanding amount left to be raised
- Trailer or rough cut
- Submission release form

"But a well-prepared and well-researched business plan is still essential, even to such investors," says Peter Levitan, "to show them that you know what's expected, you've done your homework, and you're a responsible, knowledgeable professional."

If a prospective investor is interested in your project you'll be invited to meet with them. The purpose of this meeting is for you to reassure the investor that you and your team are competent and that your project has real commercial potential, and to answer any questions they have. Be honest about the risks and potential downsides of the project as an experienced investor will know that no investment is without risk, and suggesting your project is risk-free suggests you are inexperienced and therefore not a good investment risk.

There is an excellent section on handing negotiations in *The Film Finance Handbook—How to Fund Your Film* by Adam P. Davies and N. Wistreich, which can be summarized thus:

1. Take someone with you to the negotiation to take notes and offer support.
2. Dress appropriately: bankers and financiers expect something smarter than jeans and sneakers.
3. Know the market—do your research so you know what the "going rates" are for what you are negotiating.
4. Know your deal breaker—what's the lowest you will go to before walking away? Keep this in mind throughout negotiations and stick to it to avoid making a regretful decision under pressure.
5. Know what you want out of a deal—rights, credits, profit share, fees and length of contract. Work out what your best-case scenario and bottom line are— where you walk away from negotiations—and work within these parameters.
6. Aim for a win-win position—everyone wants to walk away from a negotiation feeling like they've "won." Davies and Wistreich suggest starting negotiating at a figure 10–20 percent more than your ideal figure so you have some leeway to give some ground to the other person. This kind of give-and-take negotiation allows you to start building a longer-term relationship, which might be more beneficial than striking a hard bargain with someone who will never want to do business with you again. At the start of your career it's likely you will need to concede more in negotiation, but once you have built you reputation you can use that to leverage better deals.
7. Resist accepting the first offer you're given and try to negotiate up if the other person shows their hand first.

8. Stay calm and be polite otherwise you will look unprofessional.

9. Don't rush into a decision. Taking time to consider the offer means you can take advice on any parts of the deal you don't understand.

10. Keep a paper trail—take detailed notes (or ask a colleague do it while you concentrate on the conversation). Confirm what was discussed and what next steps have been agreed.

11. Once you've agreed a deal don't try to backtrack if you subsequently feel you could have got a better outcome. Learn from the experience and your next deal should be a better one.

If someone is interested in investing in your project get back in touch with your legal advisor to get a contract drawn up. No one is an investor in the project unless they have actually transferred the money into the bank account associated with your project, so keep pitching and meeting other potential investors.

Advantages of Bank Loan and Equity Investors

1. They are able to come in and fill the final gap in your budget that allows you to go into production.

2. They might also bring other benefits such as business expertise.

Disadvantages

1. Bridging loans and gap financing come with high interest charges and fees

2. Equity investors take some ownership in your project and therefore share any profits with you.

3. Investors are only likely to invest their money in film projects in countries where government taxation policies make it as, or more, attractive than other forms of investment.

4. It's likely that a documentary producer will attempt to presell a documentary into several territories in order to raise some of their budget, but as producer Rachel Wexler points out, "there's a down side to that because the more you presell, the more you are giving away the rights and so your investors might not get their money back," because there won't be any rights left to sell once the film is complete.

5. It's easy to fall foul of the law when dealing with investments. Take professional legal advice if considering accepting money from investors.

6. **Investors might sue you** if they don't get the return they had hoped for.

Next Steps

1. Construct a draft business plan
2. Start a database with the names of any personal contacts you have with wealthy individuals who might be interested in investing in a film like yours— think about who you know professionally, personally, and through crew and friends' contacts.

Jargon Buster

Term	Meaning
Bridging Loan/ Finance	A short-term loan. Used when a production is financed but the anticipated funds won't arrive until after a production needs to start shooting.
EIS	Enterprise Investment Scheme. UK scheme that provides investors with a series of tax reliefs in exchange for investing in high-risk qualifying trades, e.g. film production.
Equity	Ownership. Once all the debts in a program or film have been repaid, people who hold equity in the project share any subsequent income from sales in proportion to the amount of equity they hold, e.g. 60/40.
Gap/Deficit Finance	A loan (from a bank or distributor) that fills in the gap between the money raised and the actual budget needed to make a film (usually the final 10–20 percent). The loan is repaid out of future sales.
Gross Profit	Amount of money received from sales before expenses, e.g. distribution fees, have been deducted.
High Net Worth Individual	Very wealthy person with financial assets of more than $1m (excluding their home). An Ultra High Net Worth Individual has a disposable income of more than $20m. Exact definition varies from country to country.

Information
Memorandum
A legal document that provides private potential investors with detailed information on a business, including its risks. Might also be called an offering memorandum or private placement memorandum (PPM).

Net Profit
Income from sales after all loans have been repaid and all expenses, such as distribution fees, have been deducted.

Prospectus
A legal document that is used to outline the risks, prospects and terms of publicly traded bonds or stocks (and therefore not applicable to us).

Return on
Investment (ROI)
Profit expressed as a percentage of the total sum invested.

Securities
Stocks, bonds or other types of document that indicate ownership.

Further Reading and Resources

Filmmakers and Financing, Business Plans for Independents by Louise Levison – Accessible and comprehensive guide to writing an indie film business plan from the author of the business plan for the *Blair Witch Project.* Features interviews with equity investors.

Ignite—Factual Development Initiative that provides interest development loans of $5K to $30K and helps with contracts, business affairs and distribution to projects with confirmed broadcaster interest. They may also make an equity investment into the project.
http://www.ignitedevelopment.com/

Impact Partners—A company that matches investors with filmmakers who are making documentaries that have the potential to have a social impact.
http://www.impactpartnersfilm.com/

Enterprise Investment Scheme—An explanation of the EIS from HM Revenue & Customs.
http://www.hmrc.gov.uk/eis/index.htm

Lawyers.com—Directory of a million peer- and client-rated lawyers worldwide that can be searched by area of expertise.
http://www.lawyers.com/find-a-lawyer.html

Reelgrok—Comprehensive resource of inexpensive (from $5) downloadable sample business plans, budget and other documentation relating to film and television.
.http://www.reelgrok.com/documents.cfm

The Biz: The Basic Business, Legal and Financial Aspects of the Film Industry by Shuyler M. Moore—A comprehensive guide to financial and legal issues related to the film industry (US focused).

The Documentary Company—An Enterprise Investment Scheme specializing in feature documentaries.
http://www.documentarycompany.com/

The Film Finance Handbook—How to Fund Your Film by Adam P. Davies and Nicol Wistreich—A comprehensive and readable guide to all types of film finance, which is full of useful resources worldwide.

Touscoprod—A French all-or-nothing microinvestment platform—people pay at least ten Euros in exchange for a "co-production share" in the project, and get a share of the eventual profits from the box office, DVD and VOD sales for three years after the film's release. Fees: Co-producers are paid 80–90 percent of the profit for three years; Touscoprod keeps 10–20 percent.
http://www.touscoprod.com/

5 Government—Compliance-driven Box Tickers

Government funding is best suited to TV production companies with:

- A big factual, specialist factual, reality series or documentary with international appeal
- A good creative reason for your show to be partly shot in another country
- Good connections with foreign production companies
- A high level of comfort when working with a foreign co-production partner
- A TV commission in your home territory

> " Nina's Heavenly Delights *(the worst film that I or anyone else has produced) was given £250,000 by the Film Council via Scottish Screen, not because it was a good story—far from it—but because it was about Asian lesbians making curry in Glasgow ... It was a critical and commercial flop, but no matter; we ticked the boxes.*
>
> —Chris Atkins* (producer/director of *Starsuckers*, *Taking Liberties*)

TV channels fund your production because they want the exclusive right to transmit your program; distributors give you an advance in exchange for the right to sell your program (and a fat distribution fee); brands fund a program in order to promote their products; rich people invest in the expectation they will get a cut of the profits and banks lend money in return for a steep interest repayment.

*Despite being funded for "the worst film" he ever produced, Chris Atkins failed to get funding from the UK Film Council for *Taking Liberties*, a BAFTA-nominated documentary about the loss of civil liberties in Britain. Go figure.

Everybody wants something in return. Another form of funding is available from funders who want nothing except for you to spend money in their local economy.

We are now entering the realm of what's known as "soft money." The clever—and dogged—producer can get as much as 35 percent of their budget from soft money sources. The advantage of soft money is that it doesn't need to be repaid; the more a production budget is funded with soft money, the sooner the film can pay off any debts—such as loans and deferments—and you can start to make money from sales of the finished film. Soft money sources include:

- **Regional grants**—funding given to promote filmmaking (and therefore the local economy) in a certain geographical area; the money is usually paid upfront and doesn't have to be paid back.
- **Rebates**—either a cash rebate, in which a percentage of the money spent on production is refunded, or a tax rebate, in which a proportion of income tax or VAT is refunded. The rebate is calculated against the amount of money spent and therefore isn't issued until after the film has been made.

In order to secure a grant or rebate the production must meet certain criteria. For example, some funding is available only to theatrical documentaries, or projects that have a minimum budget of $1million. Other schemes require that there is confirmed TV channel interest, an international presale or a distributor advance in place. Applying for such money requires filling in lot paperwork (and possibly a foreign accountant), which might not be worth the headache for many small-scale productions.

There are also risks associated with dealing with government sources of funding, in that they are subject to flux and change. Regional film funds come and go as their funding is approved or withdrawn and changes to tax regulations, currency and political fluctuations can all threaten the availability of soft money. For many years, the UK had a number of regional screen agencies (Screen West Midlands, East Midlands Media, Northern Film & Media, Vision & Media, Screen Yorkshire, Screen South and Film London) that provided funding and other production support to filmmakers working in their respective local areas. However, a change in government in 2010 saw all of the various agencies restructured into one, Creative England (centered around three hubs: Creative North, Manchester; Creative Central, Birmingham and Creative South, Bristol), which created a huge amount of uncertainty about future funding activities.

As tax incentives are highly complex and different in every country, you should investigate the specific incentives that apply in your own country.

International Co-production Treaties

We've already encountered one type of co-production financing—an arrangement whereby two or more international TV channels share the cost of funding a program. But producers of high-end documentaries are increasingly using another kind of co-production, known as a "treaty co-production" or "official co-production." These are government initiatives aimed at boosting a local economy by attracting business and dollars in the form of film and TV production activities. They do this by offering various production incentives.

In simple terms, if a production undertakes a specified amount of its production in a certain country, or employs a certain percentage of local crew or spends a set proportion of the budget in that country, it will be entitled to benefits in the form of national and regional tax credits, or other government subsidies. For a production to qualify it is usually necessary to team up with a production company in a country that has signed a co-production treaty with your country. Partnering with a foreign production company brings its own benefits. For example:

- They can help deal with the vast amount of paperwork that must be completed for a treaty co-production.
- You can share their local market knowledge and contacts to secure a broadcast commission in that country.

Canada has a well-established international co-production program and has treaties agreed with fifty-five countries. In 1998 they produced seventy-seven official co-productions, twenty-eight with French producers and nineteen with UK producers. Once the broadcast license fee from a Canadian channel has been added to the various public-funding initiatives, it's possible to raise up to 50 percent of the total budget simply by joining forces with a Canadian production company.

The European Convention on Cinematographic Co-Productions offers a similar scheme, in which producers making their films in more than one European country gain access to various government subsidies in those countries.

Every treaty agreement offers different benefits and incentives, and you can only partner with a foreign production company in a country that has a treaty agreement with yours. For example:

Australia	Singapore	Spain	UK
has treaty co-production agreements with:			
Canada	Australia	Argentina	Australia
China	Canada	Austria	Canada
Germany	China	Brazil	France
Ireland	Korea	Canada	India
Israel	New Zealand	Chile	Jamaica
Italy		Cuba	New Zealand
Singapore		France	South Africa
United Kingdom		Germany	
		Italy	Treaties in
		Morocco	negotiation:
		Mexico	China
		Portugal	Israel
			Morocco
			Palestine

It's important to find a production company in the partner treaty country that has the same vision and working style as you, in order to make the process as painless as possible. "Like any marriage, make sure you're discussing your finances, make sure you're choosing partners you respect and admire, and you have the same creative integrities," said Tanya Kelen, CEO of Kelen Content in Toronto. You also need to work out who is taking the editorial and financial lead on the project. "There are majority and minority partners," explains Jenn Kuzmyk Ruch, VP Factual, Cream Productions in Toronto. "Sometimes it can be 50/50, sometimes it can be an 80/20, depending on where the spend is, where the money comes from, who did the legwork to develop and pitch it, who originated the idea; it also it depends on which stage it is at when the co-producer is brought on. Let's say a UK producer comes to us and they have almost all the financing and they would like to have a Canadian partner to fill in the budget gap—if we think it's a great project and we think it will work for the channels we work with, then we will come in. The key there is that the British producer should already have funding out of the UK."

Every treaty has its own rules. According to Peter Levitan, "Most of these treaties require the 'junior' (less involved) co-producer to contribute at least 30 percent to the production (in terms of financing and key elements such as script, cast, other key personnel, locations and services), and the 'senior' (leading) co-producer to contribute no more than 70 percent. In some instances, the floor and ceiling are 40 percent and 60 percent, respectively. A few bilateral treaties also permit there to be three official co-producers." The treaties work on a points system, whereby a set number of points is awarded to various elements of the production, such as the nationality of the director, location of post-production activities etc., and to qualify the production must achieve a certain number of points. This kind of points system will be familiar to anyone who has applied for an Australian visa.

Because of the legal complexities of treaty co-productions they are "only worth the legal gymnastics if you're doing a very high-end documentary series," said Australian producer Stuart Menzies, who co-produced *Darwin's Brave New World* with Ferns Productions, a production company based in Canada.

A provisional application for an international co-production must be made at least four weeks before filming starts, and the application is completed after production has finished. It can cost an estimated $15,000–$30,000 in legal fees to ensure all the paperwork is in order. Once production of the film or program has been finished, a local accountant needs to confirm that the production spent a certain amount of money on goods and services in the region before the rebate is issued. The obvious disadvantage is that rebate money is not released to the producer until after the production and all the accounting has been completed and audited, so the money comes too late to fund production. The advantage to producers is that they can access other loans and grants on the strength of the promise of co-production treaty money.

CASE STUDY
The Great Sperm Race

Dan Chambers, Company Director, Blink Films, London

"*The Great Sperm Race* was a big-budget science documentary that followed the journey of sperm racing to reach an egg, but we scaled it up to human size, so we had hundreds of people dressed as sperm running through spectacular mountain valleys. There was no way one broadcaster could cover all the funds for it. We pitched it to Channel 4 and we knew that the absolute maximum they would come on for was £200,000 or £300,000 and we needed several times that to make it.

"The Wellcome Trust have an annual TV bursary fund and we applied for the full amount of £200,000. We had two or three meetings and did lots of pitching and they funded some development to establish that the film had proper scientific credibility. We hired a good science researcher to produce a paper that explained who the scientists were and what they were saying. They eventually agreed to give us £200,000.

"Around the same time Discovery Canada came onboard. Discovery Canada either pre-buy for a low contribution, or if they are coming in with more serious money it has to be a treaty co-production because it allows them to tap into extra funds. They have something called the CMF (Canada Media Fund) that they are able to draw on if it's a UK–Canada treaty co-production. But a treaty co-production also comes with strings attached because the money from Discovery Canada had to be spent by a Canadian production company. There is also a points system where one has to make sure that there are enough creative personnel at the Canadian end to qualify. For instance, I think the editor and musicians and various other people had to be Canadian in order for us to make it eligible for this co-production treaty. We approached Cream Productions in Toronto, and they came on as co-production partner. Because Canada is set up with all sorts of tax break provisions, it means that the local indie is able to then recoup lots of money that would normally be paid in corporation tax into their budget, so that can all be factored in to the budget at the Canadian end. A distributor put up an advance to cover the rest of the budget.

"We shot all the big drama sequences in Canada and did everything else in the UK."

Regional and Pan-regional Funds

Some regions have schemes in place that encourage cross-border productions. For example, MEDIA is a funding initiative aimed at established European production companies. Application for MEDIA funding is through a central office in Brussels, but each participating country has their own office (variously called the MEDIA Service, Desk, or Antenna), which offers advice and support to producers seeking funding. Grants of 10,000–60,000 Euros (up to 50 percent of the development budget) can be awarded for a single project, but it must either be paid back to MEDIA from the production budget, or rolled over into the development of the production company's next project. Norma Percy, producer of *The Death of Yugoslavia*, raises a quarter of her money via the MEDIA route for her high-end documentaries. "Brook Lapping is increasingly looking to a multitude of smaller Scandinavian countries and Benelux to chip in small amounts, which are then matched by the European Union Media Fund," she told *Broadcast*. "So, you get the Danes, the Dutch and the Belgians giving you a small amount, and if you get enough out of them, they [MEDIA] give you something really significant."

The MEDIA TV Broadcasting Fund has a rolling deadline with two open applications a year, but the submission procedure is strict and requires materials to be set out in a specific way. "You need to be very clear about their rules and regulations," says producer Leigh Gibson, who has experience of applying for MEDIA funding through their TV Broadcasting Fund. For example, "The letter needs to have a date on it, be on headed paper and specify what the broadcaster contribution *will* be rather than *might* be; the wording is really important. It's worth stressing that you have got to be really serious about applying for MEDIA funding, because it is a full-time job, for about three or four months. Their application forms require a huge amount of information and more materials than many other funding applications," she warns. "The TV Broadcasting fund requires letters of interest from key broadcasters that you have onboard, showing it has international appeal. MEDIA is a European funding body so their main priority is interest from European broadcasters—that's where their money comes from—so the European territories are probably the most important, and the smaller European territories are even more important: Latvia, Lithuania, Eastern European territories." Check the MEDIA website in your country for the latest applications guidelines.

There are a growing number of Asian organizations that are keen to partner with Western producers. For example, China Imagica is a joint venture between the State Council Information Office (SCIO) in China and Discovery Communications in the USA, which started with the funding of two specials, *China's Man Made Marvels: Ancient Beijing* and *Man Made Marvels: Rebuilding Sichuan*, for broadcast on Discovery Channel. The Media Development Authority (MDA) in Singapore has helped fund *Asia's Wild Treasures* (for NDR Hamburg and ARTE France and Germany) and *Monumental Challenge* (History Channel UK).

Local Funds

In the USA, most states offer filmmakers incentives of some description—rebates, grants or tax credits—to persuade them to film and undertake other production activities in their state. Elsewhere, local screen agencies often have funds they can grant to productions that are made in, or have some other connection to, the area they serve. Their motivation is the same as that of governments in treaty co-productions in that they want to encourage production activities (and therefore the spending of money) in their particular region. For example, in Germany, the Berlin-Brandenburg Film Commission and the North Rhine-Westfalen Film Fund offer interest-free loans to encourage filming in their particular regions.

Screen agencies tend to get involved later in the funding process once you have already secured some funding from broadcasters, and they are unlikely to contribute a large amount of money to your budget. Having said that, New South Wales Film and Television Office (FTO) and SBS in Australia jointly commissioned and funded nine half-hour character-driven observational documentary programs as part of the *Secrets and Lives* strand.

Besides money there are various advantages in getting to know the people at your local screen agency or the one in the area in which you intend to film. Their knowledge of the funding landscape can throw up some unusual solutions to your funding issues. When *Sons of Cuba* was chosen to open the Full Frame Festival in the USA the filmmakers couldn't afford to attend the première. Someone at "Screen South had heard that the Department of Trade and Industry (DTI) had some money and she knew we were trying desperately trying to raise the funds to go to the Full Frame Festival," says documentary producer Francine Heywood, "so she put us in touch. They had some funds available and gave us a travel bursary. As a result of this we also found out about the DTI's scheme called Passport to Export." This was aimed at helping traditional businesses win overseas trade, so the filmmakers "put a product spin on it" and the DTI gave them some money that they used to attend the International Rome Festival where *Sons of Cuba* won the Best Documentary award, create sales materials and find sales agents.

If you think creatively you might also be able access other sorts of regional funding. For one UK series, *A Brush with Britain* (10 x 30', Discovery Real Time and Discovery Travel and Living), in which an artist traveled to British beauty spots to paint a watercolor, Orion TV managed to raise most of the budget from DFS, a furniture retailer. Then they persuaded a number of local councils, such as Scottish Borders Council, County Kent and One North East, to put in some money in return for featuring their local beauty spots. Executive producer Bob Whittaker said of the deal, "Every indie out there has to start thinking laterally about who would benefit from the programs that they create. We had never pieced together funding in this way before, but it's a game of survival right now and you have to diversify."

Locating your production in a region that is keen to encourage filmmakers can have some unusual benefits. Hugo Blick, director of BBC2 drama *The Shadow Line*, told an audience at BAFTA how they shot the series in the Isle of Man. "One night scene was hampered by the glow from the airport lights, so we asked if they could switch them off. To our surprise, they duly obliged –as long as they were back on by 10 p.m. as a plane was coming in." While thinking creatively can help you locate new sources of funding, don't be tempted to get creative with the accounting. In 2011, a filmmaker was sentenced to ten years in prison in the USA for inflating the budgets of two films in order to secure state tax credits.

Advantages of Government Funding

1. Government funding is usually regarded as "soft money," which doesn't need to be repaid.
2. With the right production partners and careful structuring of the production to take advantage of international incentives a large proportion of the budget can be sourced via government incentives and rebates.
3. Collaboration with a foreign co-producer gives access to different skills, local knowledge and international broadcasters.

Disadvantages

1. There is a lot of administration, and it can be challenging to comply with all the regulations.
2. Creative decisions might be made based on co-production treaty requirements, rather than on what's best for the project.
3. There are added costs, not least of legal and accounting services, as well as co-producer fees and the cost of producing foreign-language versions.

4. The money often comes in the form of a rebate against money spent, therefore it's necessary to find another source of funding to cash flow the actual production.

Next Steps

1. Assess whether it would make sense editorially for you to produce your show or film in a different country.
2. Research countries that have co-production treaties with yours.
3. Research the rules and regulations around co-production treaty productions in the host country and your own.
4. Research production companies that might be good co-production partners i.e. they have experience of handling a treaty co-production and have experience in programs similar to yours.
5. Get good specialist advice from legal and tax advisors.

Jargon Buster

Term	Meaning
Hard Money	Financing that comes at a cost and must be repaid with added interest and/or fees, e.g. bridging loans, distribution advances.
International Co-production	An international production involving two or more companies in different countries. If the production meets specific criteria set out in the official co-production treaty between the two countries, it is acknowledged as a national production in each of the partnering countries and benefits from a range of financial incentives such as government subsidies. Also known as an official co-production or a treaty co-production.
Rebate	Money refunded after payment, such as a tax rebate. Can also mean discount.
Soft Money	Production funding that doesn't need to be paid back, e.g. grants presales or donations. (Sometimes soft money does have to be repaid if there is a future profit; terms are usually favorable, e.g. at a low or no interest rate.)

Tax Relief   A reduction in the amount of tax payable under certain circumstances.

Treaty   An agreement under international law.

Further Reading and Resources

Association of Film Commissioners International—Directory of film commissions around the world, with a handy clickable map.
http://www.afci.org/browse/find.php

Creative England—A new UK agency that replaces the Screen Agencies. It facilitates access to finance and provides specialist support to the creative industries.
http://www.creativeengland.co.uk

MEDIA European Union program that supports feature films, television, documentaries, animation and new media. Each country has its own office, known as a "Desk," "Antenna" or "MEDIA Service."
http://ec.europa.eu/culture/media/

Media Development Authority, Singapore—An organization that aims to attract foreign investment into Singapore to encourage economic growth and a dynamic media industry.
http://www.smf.sg/SingaporeMediaCity/Pages/MediaInitiatives.aspx

Screen International's Global Guide to Soft Money—A guide to the key tax incentives in nineteen territories around the world, including the UK, USA, Canada, Australia, Germany, Ireland, New Zealand and South Africa.
http://softmoney.screendaily.com/

Telefilm Canada—Comprehensive information on international co-production treaties. Also has a handy directory of Canadian production companies who have participated in an international co-production in the last five years.
General information: http://www.telefilm.gc.ca/en/co-productions/co-productions
Co-production company directory: http://www.telefilm.gc.ca/en/co-productions/co-production-directory

The Film Finance Handbook—How to Fund Your Film by Adam P. Davies and N. Wistreich—Includes a comprehensive list of international incentives in more than fifty countries.

UK Department for Culture, Media and Sport—An explanation and guide to current UK co-production treaties.
http://www.culture.gov.uk/what_we_do/creative_industries/4112.aspx #agreements

6 Issue-driven Funders— Guilt Trippers and Global Reformers

Issue-driven funding is best suited to independent documentary filmmakers and TV producers with:

- A subject, characters or themes related to the environment, conservation, human rights or any other subject for which there is a nonprofit organization or foundation
- A film intended for theatrical, DVD, festival and/or internet release
- A need for development funding
- A need for help with distribution and marketing activities (from nonprofits and CSR departments)
- The backing of a fiscal sponsor (for US nonprofit funding)
- A film that has been rejected by all potential TV broadcasters (e.g. Channel 4 BRITDOC Foundation was specifically set up to help fund films that haven't been able to secure a TV commission)

> *The financial side of making documentary films is not where my interest lies. Making a documentary takes far too much time and effort to be wasted on anything other than a project you are passionately interested in.*
>
> —Barry Hampe (writer/filmmaker)

In 2009, *The End of the Line*, a feature documentary that highlighted the over-fishing of the oceans, became the poster child for brand-supported documentaries. The filmmakers' agenda was to increase the consumer demand for sustainable fish—and thereby protect endangered fish species from over-fishing—by influencing public opinion on the issue. The film was credited by the Channel 4 BRITDOC Foundation, one of its early funders, as "a tipping point in corporate policy." It prompted British companies, such as sandwich chain Prêt à Manger and Whiskas cat food, to source their fish from sustainable sources. A little over one million people saw the film, but 4.7 million were aware of it and the press coverage was calculated to have a PR value of more than £4million.

The film's £1million budget was co-funded by a range of nonprofit organizations including Fledgling Fund, Oceana, Marviva, the Oak Foundation, WWF, the Clore Foundation, the Weston Foundation, the Waitt Family Foundation, the Marine Conservation Society, AD Charitable Trust, GD Charitable Trust. Of all the funding partners only the Channel 4 BRITDOC Foundation, whose staff are experienced filmmakers, had any editorial input and Jess Search, chief executive of the Channel 4 BRITDOC Foundation, acted as one of the executive producers on the film. Waitrose supermarket joined once the film had been completed and provided marketing money to promote the cinematic release of the documentary, alongside in-store promotion of the film. However, the filmmakers only agreed to Waitrose's support after examining the supermarket's sustainable fish policy, and requesting that they remove swordfish from their shelves. Waitrose's association with the film resulted in a 15 percent increase in sales of sustainably sourced fish in their stores.

The film had impact elsewhere too. Celebrity chef Jamie Oliver removed all references to bluefin tuna from his recipe books and restaurant menus (the film shows him recommending the endangered species in a TV program). And as the ripples continued, Channel 4 capitalized on the "noise" around the film by commissioning *The Big Fish Fight* in January, 2011, which was a season of programming that harnessed Jamie Oliver and three other celebrity chefs to explore the issues around over-fishing and champion the need for sustainably sourced fish; celebrity involvement guaranteed a big audience and Channel 4 basked in the reflected glory of being further associated with a hot-button issue. Twenty percent of the program's viewers visited its website, where 640,000 people signed a petition against unethical fishing practices; 40,000 people followed the program on Twitter and 200,000 joined a·campaign on Facebook.

Waitrose's involvement in *The End of the Line* was confined to promoting the film, but issue-based documentary makers are increasingly turning to brands to help them develop, fund or distribute their films. A brand's association with a good cause brings a number of benefits:

- The brand is seen to be giving something back to the community, which is good for a brand's image, conscience and staff morale
- Nonprofit organizations with an interest in the issues raised in a film benefit from increased awareness of their cause, through screenings and associated marketing of the film
- And in turn, filmmakers, can harness the marketing might of a national or global brand that will help them get their film's message out to a broad audience

Thus a virtuous circle is created. As Waitrose's involvement in *The End of the Line* wasn't within the film itself but in the activities around the film, the producers avoided accusations of having their message hijacked by a corporation (and indeed, by making Waitrose remove swordfish from their stores, the filmmakers ensured the store adhered to the film's agenda), and they benefited from the supermarket's promotional activities around the film.

The film was also supported by a number of nonprofit organizations that shared the film's conservation agenda. Issue-driven nonprofit organizations are similar in many ways to brands in that they are master marketers and culti-vate strong brand identities In order to promote their chosen cause, and both nonprofits and brands have started to see the benefit of partnering with film-makers. However, this blending of commercial and agenda-led interests with issue-driven documentaries causes anxiety about the editorial independence or otherwise of these documentaries. Morgan Spurlock's exploration of branding in documentaries was a tongue-in-cheek stunt, but many documentary makers are wrestling with the ethics of accepting funding from brands versus not being able to make a film that raises awareness of an important issue. Ross Cairns, who directed a surfing documentary, *Powers of Three*, which was funded by Relentless, a Coca-Cola-owned energy drink, said, "There are two ways to approach branded content—you can put the brand in it or you can let the brand surround it. We take the latter view, rather than corrupting the content," thereby neatly differentiating between the type of brand funding explored in a previous chapter (where the product is overtly present in, and promoted through, a TV program) to the type of funding we're talking about in this chapter (where an issue takes center screen and any product or brand involvement remains discreet or invisible to the audience). Funding discussed in this chapter may be given as "in-kind" help with marketing and outreach rather than hard cash and documentaries made in this way are often referred to as brand "supported."

Types of Issue-driven Funders

There are three main types of organizations that might fund an issue-driven documentary: corporate social responsibility (CSR) departments of brands, nonprofit/charity organizations and issue-driven grant foundations.

Brands with a Conscience

There's a growing trend toward brands wanting to support (and to be seen to support) community social action, environmental or social justice work. In the UK, the Co-operative supermarket, an ethical brand with a strong social conscience, is directly involved in funding the production and distribution of documentaries that chime with its social agenda. It sponsored screenings of *Burma VJ*, and partly funded *The Vanishing of the Bees*, and even supports a fund, the Tipping Point Film Fund, which funds films that explore issues around trade in developing countries. The Co-operative discovered that audiences at its sponsored screenings are interested in finding out about its other campaigns too. This accidental cross-marketing "works for us in a way that promotes our whole social goals agenda, not just this one campaign. That was quite surprising," noted Co-operative marketing director Patrick Allen. And of course, as the supermarket stocks sustainable fish and Fairtrade products, it can also benefit from raised awareness of the brand, driving like-minded consumers into its stores.

Global sports brand Puma has a number of funds to help documentary makers make social issue films. The Puma Catalyst Fund aims to fund development of forty documentary films annually to a maximum of 5,000 Euros each. The fund launched in September 2010, and in the first round they received 400 applications for ten grants. The motivation for setting up the funds was to allow the brand to contribute to "a world that is more peaceful, safer, sustainable and more creative," according to chief creative officer Jochen Zeitz, who said, "businesses have to transform themselves from a capitalistic model to an eco-capitalistic model."

Elizabeth Radshaw, director of the Hot Docs Forum and Market in Toronto, says brand-facilitated or -supported documentaries work best when, "both the content creator and the corporation or brand have shared values in getting a story across. The more I talk with agencies and organizations, especially brands, they love the idea so much, they want to be associated with a shared value set and get to know their consumer in a much more genuine way."

Nonprofit Organizations

Another type of issue-driven funder is the nonprofit organization, that is one that uses its income to support its goals rather than distribute any surplus to shareholders or owners. Charities, NGOs (non-governmental organizations) and foundations are forms of nonprofit organizations. Nonprofits generally work with filmmakers in one of two ways:

1. By directly commissioning or sponsoring a film as part of a campaign to help them spread a specific message.
2. By collaborating on an independent filmmaker's project at the distribution and marketing stage to help the filmmaker reach an interested audience.

In the first instance, a nonprofit organization might commission (or employ in-house) a filmmaker to make films that highlight the organization's chosen issue as part of a media-savvy communications strategy. In this instance the filmmaker is working as a gun-for-hire to make a film that is editorially controlled by the organization to tell the story they want to tell (and in this they are not much different from corporate videos funded by companies that want to present a certain message). The filmmaker is employed by the nonprofit and is therefore not independent. That's pretty straightforward.

There are also independent filmmakers who want to raise awareness of an issue but also to retain editorial independence. In this instance the filmmaker would probably choose to fund their documentary through alternative means (perhaps a mix of film funds, TV presales, crowdfunding and credit cards), without the input of any kind of agenda-driven organization. This is particularly important if the filmmaker has ambitions for TV transmission, as many broadcasters will reject a film that might be deemed to be editorially biased in favor of one of the funding organizations. In other words, accepting production money from an issue-driven organization can disqualify you from receiving TV funding or distribution. This is particularly true for public broadcasters. Canada's CBC, for one, won't consider funding films on controversial subjects that already have funding in place from issue-driven funders. Professor Klaus Stanjek, at the Konrad Wolf Potsdam-Babelsberg Film and Television University (HFF), Germany, told *DOX* magazine that even where the only input of an organization is to provide access to subjects or experts, it "can become an indirect editorial influence that needs to be avoided to sustain a documentary's credibility." As a filmmaker, "if you take your journalism seriously, you ought to promote independent views," says BBC *Storyville* Editor Nick Fraser. "I don't have problems with campaigns at all but they should be independent campaigns. If they're funded by an organization they become something different." Which is also fairly straightforward.

It starts to get complicated, and you are likely to run into trouble, if you try to combine the two models—agenda-driven/nonprofit commissioned vs. independent filmmaker—in the same production, as happened in the case of *Your Mommy Kills Animals*, a documentary about the animal liberation movement. In 2005, the president of a public affairs company that managed a number of nonprofit organizations, including one that opposed the agenda of animal rights group PETA (People for the Ethical Treatment of Animals), invested $300,000 in the production (this represented the full cost of the expected budget, plus he ended up paying a further $10,000 to cover extra filming costs). In return for funding the documentary he wanted to recoup his money in a priority position, receive a $60,000 profit on his investment and have the exclusive right to promote the film. The original treatment described a narrative that was based around a critical examination of the work of PETA, but the director subsequently decided to focus instead on the story of the trials of six members of the Stop Huntingdon Animal Cruelty campaign, who were brought to trial and convicted of conspiracy to commit "animal enterprise terrorism." Instead of a critique of PETA, approximately 80 percent of the film presented the animal rights activists "as champions of free speech, and thus in a positive light." In the documentary world it's accepted that the proposed story might change once filming commences; access may change, outside events can have an impact on the logistics of filming, or the narrative might take an unexpected, and more interesting turn. Whatever happens, the independent documentary maker is free to follow whichever narrative they choose. However, someone who has funded a documentary film precisely because it supports their specific viewpoint is unlikely to be happy if presented with a very different version of a film to the one in which they thought they had invested; even more so when they are the sole funder. In this particular case, the investor, upset that the director had disregarded his "recommended changes" to the film, sued for breach of contract and fraud. He "was awarded $360,000 in damages for breach of contract and $10,000 for the fraud claim." He lost an appeal to retain exclusive promotion and distribution rights in the film.

Filmmakers in North America have long inhabited a funding landscape that forces filmmakers to turn to nonprofits for funding. Pat Aufderheide, Director of the Center for Social Media at the American University, acknowledges that the nonprofit sponsorship of documentaries is "a kind of Wild West, but I think that bothers Americans less because we have lived in a world of sponsored and hybrid films. We don't have government funding for film—with a few significant exceptions—so independent filmmakers have, since the field was born, been working with sponsored projects, that is they work with entities and make films with an advocacy or marketing message."

The editorial issues involved in the direct funding of documentaries by nonprofit organizations, alongside the fact that films are expensive to produce, mean it usually makes better sense for a charity to support a film, at the distribution and marketing stage once all the filming has been completed. This has a number of benefits, not least of which the film is editorially independent and the charity can see the rough-cut or finished film before committing their support. The nonprofit also benefits from being associated with an authentic filmmaker-driven message, which is much more powerful than a puff piece.

Whatever their level of input, nonprofits are interested in getting a return on their investment. "Nonprofits have a particular message to put out and they measure that in terms of dollars raised and members added," says Pat Aufderheide, "so they are not any different from Proctor and Gamble in their strategic objective, they just have a different thing that they are selling". And just as brands see the funding of TV programs as a small part of their marketing mix, nonprofits have a range of tools at their disposal and a documentary film isn't necessarily the best way to get their message out. "They are not interested in promoting filmmaking: if it's cheaper and more effective to go with Twitter than making a documentary then they will go with that," says Pat Aufderheide. Their target audience "don't necessarily have an hour and a half to watch a film in a theatre; on TV there's no easy place for them to click to join a petition; you can't capture their email address for future contact." In comparison, social media offer a much better platform on which a nonprofit can interact with the public. In the future, filmmakers who want to change the world through long-form documentary might become redundant, suggests Pat. "People who want to effect social change will use film, when they do, strategically within a social media environment, for instance with shorter documentaries, compelling short stories in fictional or docudrama formats, and interactive features ... those people who have donned the mantle of the good guy because they work on important social issues in long-form media, may find themselves in a difficult position because their work is not as useful as it used to be."

In the meantime, a number of new initiatives aim to bring nonprofits and filmmakers together. For example, Channel 4's BRITDOC Foundation runs an open round-table forum in London, New York, San Francisco and at Silverdocs Documentary Festival in Washington DC, in which nonprofits, brands, advertising agencies and government organizations are invited to hear pitches from filmmakers making social justice films in the hope that they will be able to help with outreach and distribution. Films that have found support in this way include:

- *Calvet*—a biopic about troubled French artist Jean Marc Calvet
- *Hell & Back Again*—the story of a US Marine battalion during a tour of Afghanistan
- *Guilty Pleasures*—a documentary about the global appeal of Mills & Boon romance novels
- *Chosen*—the story of three men who were sexually abused by their teachers
- *Afghan Star*—an exploration of a new Afghanistan as seen through the lens of a TV talent show

Foundations

A foundation (sometimes known as a charitable foundation or private foundation) grants money to other organizations in support of work that the foundation wants to promote. According to the Foundation Center there are approximately 100,000 corporate donors and private and government grantmaking foundations in the USA. Some of these foundations are big names, such as the Ford Foundation and the MacArthur Foundation; others are small family-administered funds. Some are used to making grants to filmmakers and others are not. "We identified that filmmakers really understood about foundations and funds, but there were foundations and funds that didn't know our language and didn't really know how to deal with the documentary community," says Elizabeth Radshaw of Hot Docs in Toronto. In response, organizations such as Hot Docs and BRITDOC are working hard to bridge the culture gap by inviting foundations to open days that explain what types of film are suitable for foundation funding and how the documentary funding and production process works.

When working with funders that aren't familiar with film production, there can be misunderstandings and assumptions on the part of the funder that could cause a rift or breakdown in the relationship. For example they might fail to understand that the production schedule might change, which could cause them internal problems when planning their campaigning activities. In the case of *End of the Line* there were eleven foundation funding partners in addition to the TV channel, More4, and several others, such as Greenpeace who weren't funders but did commit to performing outreach and lobbying support. That's a lot of people to keep in the loop when you are also trying to keep on top of a shooting schedule and complicated budget; it's not surprising that some of those partners might feel a little neglected during the production process. To avoid inadvertently upsetting valuable partners, factor regular updates into your production schedule so communication doesn't get pushed off the bottom of the priority list.

Every foundation has different funding and application criteria. For example, the MarViva Foundation is interested in marine conservation, so it would be pointless to fill in a grant application for a film that didn't specifically address that issue. Competition is fierce for the large US foundation grants, such as the MacArthur Foundation, Ford Foundation and the National Science Foundation, but getting a smaller foundation onboard first can help draw their attention to your application. You can research each one via their website and by talking to other filmmakers.

Foundations are likely to be most receptive to filmmakers living and working in the country in which the foundation is based, as it's easier to maintain a working relationship and there's less anxiety about perceived or real cultural differences that could cause communication difficulties. Debra Zimmerman, Executive Director of Women Make Movies, has worked with international filmmakers, and discovered they often "have very little or no experience in putting together proposals for US foundations. They wrote wonderfully, but in some of the sections they don't quite understand what is being asked of them, particularly in terms of outreach and the questions that American foundations ask about diversity and representation—the identity politics questions that are much more important in the US than in other Western countries."

The advantage of foundation funding is that foundations are generally happy to let a filmmaker make the film without interference as long as the film's subject matter is as originally pitched. They usually don't require the grant to be repaid; nor will they require a share in the rights. However, there are some strings. Foundations typically require some kind of report once the film is complete (or annually if it's a long-running project), along with a credit at the end of the film and on any press and publicity materials.

Do You Need a Fiscal Sponsor?

A fiscal sponsor is a nonprofit organization that can receive and administer funds on behalf of individual filmmakers. In the USA, the law prevents many private foundations from giving money to individuals; they have to give money to a nonprofit—also known as a 501(c)(3)—organization. "There are many different organizations that provide fiscal sponsorship," says Debra Zimmerman; "it doesn't need to be a film organization, it can be any charity. If you are making a film about homelessness, for example, it could be an organization like Coalition for the Homeless, but it must be a US-based organization." However, she advises filmmakers to work with fiscal sponsors who specialize in filmmaking, like Women Make Movies, "because there could be real problems in there not being clarity in who's actually getting the grant. The homelessness organization might think that they are getting money to make a film and can control the content of the film; but the reality is that the fiscal sponsor is only an administrator of the funds and has only to ensure that the money will be spent in a way congruent with the aims of the person giving the money. The filmmaker should have full control of the content, and there should be a contract that makes that clear." The fiscal sponsor will provide proof of their tax-exempt status to the filmmaker that can be included with foundation grant applications. If the grant application is successful, the money is paid into the fiscal sponsor's bank account and then released to the filmmaker (minus an administration fee of around 5–8 percent).

Fiscal sponsorship is mainly of interest to US-based filmmakers. It is possible for international producers to apply for foundation grants through a fiscal sponsor, but tax laws make it more complicated. In Part III, Debra Zimmerman explains how to apply for fiscal sponsorship and how it works in more detail.

How to Pitch to Issue-driven Funders

1. **Identify the issue**—Certain types of documentary subjects naturally lend themselves to grant funding or outreach support from a nonprofit organization: films about the environment or human rights issues are obvious frontrunners. "My personal opinion is that the personal is always political in some way," says filmmaker Jilann Spitzmiller, "so you can always find ways that a film reflects a social issue. Even if it's a purely entertaining film, I think there are still underlying themes that you can bring out." For example, Jilann tackles the

problem of the aging population in her documentary, *Still Dreaming* (working title). "It's about some retired actors who are in their seventies and eighties and they stage *A Midsummer Night's Dream*. It was deeply compelling to watch them in the process of putting on this play, but for writing grants we've really had to brainstorm the social issues underpinning it. There are some underlying themes that we are exploring that will make the film deeper and richer, such as the way we treat the aging population, but our original impetus was the totally unique and compelling characters."

2. **Map an outreach strategy**—While nonprofits and foundations are interested in a documentary's narrative, what they really want to know is how this film is going to help them achieve their aims of changing the world in some way. When dealing with this type of funder, you have to talk in terms of "outreach" rather than distribution, which means being able to explain how you are going to get people to watch your film. Work out:

- Who is your film aimed at?
- How are you going to reach them i.e. on what platform?
- What's your outreach campaign?
- What evidence do you have that you can get distribution? For example, have you had other films in distribution or have your films been transmitted on television?

If you are making your film purely because you are passionate about an issue, then you might be happy to take on the long-term commitment of managing an ongoing outreach campaign, but if you are a filmmaker who wants to make films on lots of different subjects you can find your time so consumed by press requests and general campaign management duties that it can damage your ability to progress your filmmaking career. Fortunately there are experts you can call on to help you manage your outreach. Active Voice and Participant Media ran a year-long campaign for *Food, Inc.*, that involved thirty community screenings and panel discussions in low-income neighborhoods in the USA; identification of public health issues such as school meals and food labeling; information guides written in Spanish and English; a peer learning network, newsletter, blog and user-generated content.

Sample Outreach Plan

Donor Unknown

Donor Unknown is a challenging, thought-provoking and compelling film for television and cinema, and a film rich in issues for a contemporary audience. We believe the film has an extraordinary power to reach diverse audiences and stimulate exciting discussion and debate. The Wellcome Trust, the UK foundation committed to opening up discussion of ethical issues arising from bio-medical science, has awarded us a grant to create an outreach programme to support the film, including a dedicated website; a media campaign; a social networking presence; a programme of screenings, Q&As, seminars and debates; and a DVD with extras.

The Outreach Screenings with Q&As will run from March–June 2011, and after each screening, director Jerry Rothwell, producers Hilary Durman and Al Morrow, plus special expert guests will be there to answer questions and join in the discussion. We will draw our expert guests from clinicians in the field, academics and researchers, plus key organisations working in donor conception and assisted reproduction like the National Gamete Donation Trust, the Donor Conception Network, the Progress Trust, UK Donorlink, Nuffield BioEthics, the British Fertility Society, and the HFEA.

The Outreach Programme will:

- Encourage audiences to explore their sense of identity, and the way that factors such as genetics, family, friends, influences, experiences, roles, history and culture shape that identity;
- Stimulate debate on the ethics of sperm and egg donation;
- Explore some of the contemporary developments in reproductive medicine and technology, and some of the ethical issues they raise for society today and in the future.

There are so many issues to discuss. For example:

- Who is really the parent—the donor of the genetic material or the person who brings up the child?
- How important are genetics in knowing who we are?

- Should the parents of donor-conceived children be legally obliged to tell them about their genetic origins?
- When is the best time to tell children about their origins?
- Should donors remain anonymous?
- What are the risks of consanguinity [kinship] where donors are used to create children in multiple families?
- Should couples be allowed to choose the characteristics of their donor? (e.g. hair colour, eye colour, musical ability?)
- How are we shaping evolution if we heavily screen men and women as donors and only select "desirable" characteristics?
- Should donors have rights to say who can or cannot use their donations?
- What do we know about the impact of donor-assisted conception on the donor's partners, parents or children?

As well as a programme of cinema screenings with Q&As, discussions and television broadcast, we are creating a specially developed DIY package of the film plus briefing notes on the issues so that schools, colleges, film clubs and all kinds of networks can hold their own special screenings and discussions. We hope that in the UK our partners in this will be Good Screenings and Film Club UK. Our Donor Unknown website has two interlinked parts, one focusing on the film, press, screenings and the film-making context, the other an interactive site: home for creative contributions about the wider issues raised through the film, and for discussion and debate about science and ethics.

Our consultant for the Donor Unknown Outreach is Dr Allan Pacey, Senior Lecturer at the University of Sheffield School of Medicine. He is also the Head of Andrology for Sheffield Teaching Hospitals where he directs the Andrology Service overseeing diagnostic semen analysis, and the sperm banking facility. Allan has been involved in the recruitment of sperm donors since 1992. His research investigates many aspects of human infertility and he has published over fifty papers and book chapters. He is a lecturer and broadcaster whose recent television programmes include *The Great Sperm Race* (2009), *The Truth About Food* (2007), *Make Me a Baby* (2007) and *Lab Rats* (2004). For more information about *Donor Unknown*, go to **www.donorunknown. com** and **www.facebook.con/donorunknown**

3. **Identify appropriate nonprofits**—Major libraries keep directories of foundations and other grantmakers. The Foundation Center has directories and other resources available at its branches in Washington DC, New York City, San Francisco, Cleveland and Atlanta as well as online at www.fdcenter.org.

   It's good to think laterally and spread your net as wide as possible, but your final shortlist of potential issue-driven funders should only include those that:

   ● Have a proven interest in your film's subject or theme;
   ● Will make grants to people/projects in the geographic area in which you live or where your film is set;
   ● Have already funded film projects.

   In *Grant Seeking for Storytellers*, Cheryl Clarke recommends that a list of between six and twenty-four funders is optimal.

4. **Draw up a grant application strategy and schedule**—Those foundations that are a good fit with your project and with whom you have a pre-existing relationship should take priority. Next, consider whether it's better to spend your time approaching fewer, bigger grants rather than a number of small grants that might not yield much return on the amount of time you have to invest in preparing each grant proposal. Put your shortlisted funds in order of their application deadlines and factor some grant-writing time into your diary. Other factors to take into account include:

   ● **Where you are in your production cycle**—there's no point applying for finishing funds when you have yet to secure development or production funding. CSR departments of brands and foundations are your best bet for development and production funding. Nonprofits are often best left to the end of the cycle, where they can provide distribution and marketing support.

   ● **The type of application form**—some funds are easier to apply for than others; experienced grant writers say it can take up to three weeks of full-time work to fill in some application forms. For those foundations that require only a simple letter of inquiry, it's worth sending those first so they can be working their way through the system while you work on more complex applications.

   ● **The type of supporting evidence required**—some grants require a letter of interest from a broadcaster or proof of tax exemption from your fiscal sponsor. Request those documents well in advance of any grant deadlines so you have them at hand when you are ready to send off your applications.

5. **Identify amount of grant or type of support to be requested**—Some grants are more generous than others. Find out their upper and lower limits, as well as the value of the average grant awarded. It can help your case to request an amount that sits comfortably within their award range. Grant writer Cheryl Clarke advises that the rule of thumb "is not to be too aggressive with a first-time proposal submission. Ask for an amount in the middle of the range. It may even be a wise strategy to go in a little lower. Once ... [you have] established a relationship with a grantmaker, it is easier to engage in a dialogue with that funder about increasing the amount requested in a renewal application."

   An application that specifies exactly what the money will be used for, e.g. an animator for six weeks, two flights to Colorado to film contributors, or three weeks of editing time, reassures the funding body that their money will be put to good use. If the foundation is not used to giving money to documentaries and doesn't understand the production process, be especially careful to explain everything clearly and avoid jargon that a grant reader might find alienating.

6. **Fill in the grant application**—It's reported that 5–10 percent of issue-driven grant applications receive funding (which sounds discouraging, but it compares favorably to TV proposal submissions of which it's estimated there's a commission rate of between 1–10 percent. For the big film funds the success rate is typically 1–2 percent), so your application must be impeccable. Make sure you understand and follow the guidelines any deviation from the requested word count or omission of information gives them a valid reason to reject your application. If you have questions after reading the FAQ on their website, call the organization to ask for clarification. For some grants, speaking to a member of staff is a prerequisite of application. Grant officers can often advise and help guide your application and talking to staff is a good way to start building a relationship with a funder.

   A typical grant proposal is approximately five to ten pages long. Applications might be made via paper or electronic submission. The main challenge for filmmakers is that non-film foundations are likely to have application forms that aren't specifically tailored to a film project, making it difficult to know exactly how to present your information. The key thing to remember is that issue-driven funders are more interested in their issue than they are in your film, so highlight all the ways in which your film is relevant to their issue and how your film could help them fulfill their remit or achieve their goals.

The good news is that good storytelling, which is after all a filmmaker's stock in trade, is integral to a good grant proposal. Frances Phillips, a senior program officer at a foundation that usually receives funding requests from nonprofits, describes how a good proposal features "heroes (and many, many nonprofits and their leaders are truly heroic), conflicts (the challenges of addressing society's most pressing problems), and inspiration (the visions those organizations maintain in their work)," all of which are key parts of a good social justice film. Depending on your particular project, the hero might be one of your characters, or you as filmmaker if you are exposing an injustice; conflicts might be between the characters in your film or it might illustrate the conflict between man and nature. Your film should inspire emotion and ideally spur the audience into action of some sort—donating money to a cause, signing a petition, changing their shopping habits etc.

A typical application is likely to include the following elements in addition to all the information that goes into a traditional TV proposal or treatment (how to fill in a general film grant application is discussed in more detail in the next chapter):

- **A hook to introduce the problem tackled by your film**—
    - A shocking statistic related to your film's subject, issue or theme
    - A tantalizing question about the issue that the film will set out to explore
    - A compelling quote about the issue from an expert or character in your film
- **Context**—why the issue highlighted in your film is important, what's at stake and how your film will help to tackle the problem by raising awareness, influencing public opinion or changing behavior
- **Relevance**—how your film is relevant to the funding body to which you are applying, in terms of issue tackled, geographical location, religious, cultural or ethnic make-up of the characters/crew etc.
- **Statement of authority**—why you are qualified to explore this issue in a film—your personal connection or other motivation, and evidence that you are well informed about the issue you are addressing. Keep it relevant: a foundation concerned with the human rights of women in the Congo is unlikely to be impressed by your long track record on *Big Fat Gypsy Weddings*.
- **Mission/Goals/Objectives**—what kind of change do you hope to achieve with your film? In grant funding terms, a goal is usually understood as a big

overall long-term aim. An objective is more short-term and is measurable within a specific timescale. For example, the filmmakers behind *The End of the Line* had the goal of halting the over-fishing of endangered species. Their objective was "to use the film as a strategic tool to raise politicians' awareness of over-fishing and lobby for tougher regulatory policy in the UK and internationally, as well as an expansion of marine reserves." The result?

○ In the same year the film premièred it was screened at the Conservative and Labour political party conferences

○ Prime Minister Gordon Brown's wife, Sarah, held a screening at Downing Street

○ The Fisheries Minister told a newspaper that he was boycotting Nobu restaurant in protest at the restaurant refusing to remove endangered bluefin tuna from the menu

They didn't manage to change regulatory policy, but they certainly raised politicians' awareness of the problem. Other measurable objectives related to raising awareness about an issue might include TV audience figures, signatures on a petition, column inches in the press, Facebook fans, celebrity involvement etc. Your objectives need to be reasonable and achievable.

● **Method**—this is the section where you get to talk about your film—the narrative, approach, characters, crew, distribution plan plus any multiplatform content such as a website or social media campaign—and how all those elements will help you achieve your (and the funder's) stated objectives.

● **Finance plan**—outline of other funding secured, applied for or to be applied for. Demonstrate how you will be able to find enough money to complete the film.

● **Competition**—other films or media that have covered the same issue and why yours is different/complementary—in its approach, tone, intended audience etc.

● **Evaluation**—how and when you will measure the success of your film in achieving your stated objectives.

● **Summary**— this might be the only section of your document that an assessor reads before deciding whether to reject or progress your application. This section is typically restricted to 100–250 words and you need to include all the key points from the rest of your proposal.

● **Citations**—to back up your quoted facts or statistics.

In each section, aim to be as specific as you can, giving concrete evidence rather than vague assertions. Some grant foundations insist on a rigorously academic approach—with citations and footnotes to back up your statistics and statements of fact. Wikipedia is not a credible source of information for your grant application (although Wikipedia's footnotes might allow you to track down suitable primary sources of information).

Other foundations respond more to a more emotional approach. According to Cheryl Clarke, "smaller family foundations and corporate giving programs are receptive to anecdotes and client stories." These funders tend to "give from their hearts." Large institutional funders are not as favorable, for they tend to "give from their heads ... In my experience, grantmakers in the San Francisco Bay Area are more receptive to anecdotes and client stories, whereas grantmakers in other regions are not. The lesson here is: know your funder."

Throughout your application, keep asking yourself how funding your film will help the funder achieve their objectives rather than how their funding will help you make your film.

Every time you write a new grant application you must tweak it to fit each funder's specific criteria. For example, when UK filmmaker Dan Edelstyn was making *How to Re-Establish a Vodka Empire*, a film about his Jewish grandmother's flight from Ukraine to Belfast, he emphasized the fact that it was a story about a Jewish family when pitching it to Jewish foundations. However, when pitching to advertising agencies that might help him with pro bono marketing, he emphasized the part of the story in which he attempts to turn around the fortunes of the village from which his grandmother fled by inventing a new vodka brand to bring new business into the village distillery. It's the same film, but each funder was interested in a different part of the story.

Grant Application Housekeeping Tips

a. Once you have written your first grant application, save it as a master so you can use it as template for subsequent applications (save each one with a different name).

b. It's useful to have a back-up copy, as some electronic submission systems don't save your work and a computer crash can be catastrophic if you lose your work.

c. If you are submitting a paper application check the specified format—single- or double-spaced and what, if any, supporting documents are required. Be sure to include them with your application.

d. It is a nuisance for the reader to have to remove binders or staples, so a simple paper clip is best.

e. Make sure your pages are numbered, and it helps to have your contact details in the footer, in case the top page or covering letter goes astray.

f. Keep a record of the date you submit an application, and any follow-up correspondence, including any rejections.

g. If your application is rejected, ask for feedback and whether it's worth you applying in the next funding round. Some filmmakers have been successful on the third, fourth or fifth application.

Letter of Inquiry

Some foundations prefer to receive a preliminary inquiry before inviting a full grant application and most corporate funders are likely to respond to a letter in the first instance. This letter is a short one- to three-page overview of your project and an explanation of why it is a good fit with the funder's goals.

Advantages of Issue-driven Funding

1. If your film has a message that aligns with that of a nonprofit they can help you get the word out about your film via their newsletter and screenings.

2. A brand's CSR department can leverage the marketing might of a brand to advertise your film on packaging, in-store, to their staff and customers.

3. The money is "soft" and doesn't need to be paid back, the funder doesn't have an equity stake in your film.

Disadvantages

1. A film with nonprofit funding might have its editorial independence questioned.

2. Many broadcasters won't transmit a film that has been funded by a nonprofit organization.

3. Funding may come as "in-kind" support rather than cash, which doesn't help with the production budget.

4. Getting a nonprofit on board requires an extensive outreach program, which is a long-term (and time-consuming) commitment, when you want to get on with your next project.

5. You might end up making several versions of your film to satisfy different funders and multiple platforms, which increases the cost of the film.

6. Funders might harbor unrealistic expectations of a TV transmission or Sundance screening.

Next Steps

1. Brainstorm the themes of your film.
2. Plan your outreach and distribution strategy.
3. Start a database of foundations, including contact details, funding criteria and range of grants they offer, organized by their application deadline dates.
4. Research films that have a similar subject/issue to yours and find out if they had foundation or nonprofit funding.
5. Consult the nonprofit and foundation databases. Identify potential foundations that have an interest in the issues explored in your film:
   a. Locally/regionally
   b. Nationally
   c. Internationally
6. Find out if your shortlisted foundations have previously funded films; contact the filmmakers to see if they would be willing to share their experience of working with the funder.
7. Identify the average size of grants awarded by key foundations and grants that have an interest in your subject.
8. Brainstorm whether you, your friends, family or anyone on your crew have contacts at brands, nonprofits or foundations who can make personal introductions.

Jargon Buster

Term	Meaning
Brand Associated	Describes the way in which a brand helps with the production of a film through funding, outreach, marketing, distribution and other activities, that isn't primarily motivated by selling the brand's product. The brand's association with a documentary film instead enhances their reputation as an ethical, socially responsible company. Also known as brand facilitated or brand supported.
Charity	A type of nonprofit organization with philanthropic aims that serve the common good.

CSR	Corporate social responsibility. Refers to company activities that are designed to encourage socially responsible behavior that has a positive impact on the environment, the community or its employees and customers.
Fiscal Sponsorship	Many grantmaking foundations can't grant money to individuals, they have to give money to a nonprofit organization; a fiscal sponsor acts as a nonprofit "umbrella" and can receive charitable grants and tax-deductible donations on behalf of filmmakers in exchange for a small administration fee.
NGO	Non-governmental organization. An organization that operates independently from a government and usually has some kind of social agenda.
Nonprofit	An organization that uses any profits it generates to further the goals of the nonprofit. Also known as not-for-profit or charity.
Outreach	Refers to the ways in which a nonprofit engages and educates the public about their work or cause.
Third Sector	A term used to describe voluntary or nonprofit organizations as opposed to the public sector (government) and private sector (business).

Further Reading and Resources

Active Voice—A San Francisco-based organization that works with filmmakers to develop outreach strategies.
http://www.activevoice.net/

An Inconvenient Truth: Beyond the Box Office—Academic research paper that explores whether a financial value can be placed on the impact of socially conscious documentaries.
http://site.britdoc.org/pages/983/view

"Assessing Creative Media's Social Impact"—An excellent paper from the Fledgling Fund about how a film's impact can be measured and examples of various documentary film outreach campaigns.
http://www.the fledglingfund.org/impact/

Charity Navigator—A searchable database of 5,500 charities in the USA, which rates the financial health of the organizations listed.
www.charitynavigator.org

Fiscal Sponsors:
- Arts Engine—http://www.artsengine.net/fs
- Artspire—http://www.artspire.org/artists.aspx
- Center for Independent Documentary—http://documentaries.org/fiscal-sponsorship/
- Creative Activist Program—http://www.creativevisions.org/capp/about.html
- Documentary Educational Resources—http://www.der.org/services/fiscal-sponsor/
- Fractured Atlas—http://www.fracturedatlas.org/site/fiscal/
- From the Heart Productions—www.fromtheheartproductions.com
- International Documentary Association—http://www.documentary.org/content/fiscal-sponsorship
- San Francisco Film Society—http://www.sffs.org/Filmmaker-Services/Project-Development-and-Fiscal-Sponsorship.aspx
- Women Make Movies—http://www.wmm.com/filmmakers/fiscal_sponsorship.shtml

Ford Foundation—The JustFilms initiative funds documentaries that focus on "courageous people confronting difficult issues."
http://www.fordfoundation.org/issues/freedom-of-expression/justfilms/for-grant-seekers

Foundation Center Directory Online—Directory of more than 100,000 US grant foundations and corporate donors.
http://fconline.foundationcenter.org/

GrantCraft—A joint project between the Foundation Center and the European Foundation Center aimed at increasing the knowledge and improving the practice of grantmaking and philanthropy.
www.GrantCraft.org

Grantmakers in Film + Electronic Media—An association and database that matches media creators with funders.
http://media.gfem.org

GuideStar UK—A database of registered charities in England and Wales, searchable by location, size and grantmaking policy.
http://www.guidestar.org.uk/guidestaruk.aspx

Latin America Donor Index—Database of foundations, NGOs and other grantmakers in Latin America.
www.lacdonors.org/about

MacArthur Documentary Film Grants—Offers grants of $100,000–$200,000 to documentaries that address under-reported and social issue topics.
http://www.macfound.org/site/c.lkLXJ8MQKrH/b.943279/k.C2BD/General_Grantmaking_Media_Grantmaking_Guidelines.htm

NOZAsearch—A database that lists the donation history of corporations, foundations and individuals in North America. Subscription-based service, but foundations can be researched for free.
https://www.nozasearch.com/nonprofit-grants.asp

Outreach Extensions—A US-based outreach consultancy that plans and implements customized campaigns around media projects.
http://www.outreachextensions.com/

Participant Media—A US company that designs outreach campaigns that encourage people to get involved via screenings, educational curriculums, classes, house parties, seminars and action kits. They've worked on *The Cove*, *Waiting for Superman*, *Food Inc.* and *Countdown to Zero*.
http://www.participantmedia.com

Shaking the Money Tree: The Art of Getting Grants and Donations for Film and Video Projects by Morrie Warshawski—A guide to grantwriting for film projects.

The Prenups: What Filmakers and Funders Should Talk About Before Tying the Knot—A downloadable guide to making a filmmake–nonprofit relationship work based on candid interviews and observations.
http://www.theprenups.org/

Waiting for Superman: Entertainment Evaluation—A study into the impact of the documentary on the public perception of the public school system in the USA, and whether people were inspired to take action.
http://harmony-institute.org/cases/waiting-for-"superman"/

WANGO—Worldwide NGO directory
http://www.wango.org/resources.aspx?section=ngodir

7 Knowledge-driven Funders—Scholars and Educators

Knowledge-driven funding is best suited to TV producers or independent filmmakers with:

- A film with a subject, characters or themes related to science health/medicine, natural history, art, history or religion
- A need for development money
- The desire to add academic credibility to your proposal
- A narrative that would benefit from access to an institution or its experts

> *To talk about learning in Factual [TV] is to be trapped in a commissioning mentality. Television is about going out into the world and telling stories about it.*
>
> —Adam Curtis (Filmmaker, *The Power of Nightmares*)

If nonprofits want to counter the ills of the world by opening people's hearts (and wallets) via documentary film, there are other institutions that hope to change the world by opening people's minds. These funders are less interested in the medium of the message and so the filmmaker is likely to be competing for funds with theater and community groups, experimental artists, scientists and festival organizers. The main funders in this category are universities, governments and knowledge-driven grant foundations.

Universities

History of the World (BBC1, 2012), is an eight-part series that features "dramatic reconstruction, computer graphics and gripping storytelling to reveal the events, conflicts and characters that have shaped our destiny." In the series, presenter Andrew Marr reveals the major turning points in history. He explains "the significance of each key moment and how it shaped our world [while standing on] … the very spot where it happened. From Cleopatra's encounter with an asp and Marco Polo's journey along the Silk Road to China to the arrest of Marie Antoinette and the firing of a bullet in Sarajevo in 1914, this will be the definitive account of human civilization." Dramatic reconstruction, computer graphics and international filming are all expensive, so it's inevitable that this series would need to be a co-production, but what makes it unusual is that one of the funding partners is a university, the Open University in the UK. (The other funders were BBC1, Discovery Channel and a distributor, BBC Worldwide.)

The Open University (OU) offers students the opportunity to study for a part-time degree via distance learning. From the early 1970s the Open University broadcast a range of TV programs that delivered course-related programs to "students, insomniacs, night workers, early risers in all forms of people from feverish babies keeping mothers awake, to the elderly for whom the blue-grey glow of the box is a companion." Eventually they built up an "archive of scripts for the tens of thousands of OU course-related programs ever made," which measured ninety-two meters (the same length as a soccer pitch).

Recently Open University has moved away from making its own programs, and has instead, in a formal co-commissioning partnership with the BBC, helped to fund programs on primetime television, such as *History of the World*. As well as funding, the OU helps program makers by providing academic consultants. Jana Bennett, the then Director of BBC Vision (the in-house production department), remarked that it was partnerships such as this that allowed the corporation to maintain "the BBC's reputation for the most ambitious and creative landmark factual programming and [for] providing exceptional value for license fee payers." While the BBC gets to share the cost of commissioning high-quality programs, the OU raises its profile and benefits from the skilled storytelling of experienced primetime TV producers to make programs that complement its curriculum: a win-win situation.

Other programs the OU has helped to fund include:

- *The Barristers* (BBC2, 4 x 60')—a behind-the-scenes series about the British legal system
- *Sectioned* (BBC4, 1 x 60')—an award-winning documentary about mental health
- *The Search for Life: The Drake Equation* (BBC4, 1 x 60')—a documentary exploring the possibility of extra-terrestrial life
- *Coast* (BBC2, 8 x 60')—a team of presenters explore the geography, flora and fauna and social history of the British Isles
- *Theo's Adventure Capitalists* (BBC2, 3 x 60')—one of the *Dragons' Den* entrepreneurs explores what it takes for British businesses to survive in India, Brazil and Vietnam

The Open University now works with other broadcasters and independent producers through its Open Media Unit, which gives OU funding to the wider TV community.

Other universities are waking up to the possibilities of collaboration too. In Belgium, the University of Leuven partnered with producers at a TV channel to put together a series that set out to select and train the first Belgian women's bobsled team and get them into the Olympics.

CASE STUDY
Bobsled Operation Vancouver
(13 x 30' + 1 x 60')

Niels Janssen—VRT, Belgium

"I am the editor-in-chief for a public broadcaster, the biggest network in Belgium. We have two networks: Eén, which has 30–35 percent of the market, and a smaller channel, Canvas, for documentaries and news programs.

"For the past three years I've been working on a documentary series called *Bobsled Operation Vancouver*. It began with a wild idea in a brainstorm—to begin the first Belgian female bobsled team in history and, with the help of science, get them to the Winter Olympic Games in Vancouver, in only two-and-a-half years' time. It ended with a thirteen-part sports/science series, TV-hype and a real Olympic team.

"We had a small production budget of approximately $80,000 an episode: enough to make a science documentary but not enough to begin a bobsled team. It costs 250,000€ to run a bobsled team for one season; that's for buying and transporting the sled, paying the athletes, hotel accommodation and competition fees. We also wanted to take girls who had never seen a bobsled and give them top trainers, and top scientific facilities where they can be trained and tested, so we started to look for partners in the world of science, universities, sports and business. The thing was to find the right people, and get those people so excited by craziness of the idea that they would say OK.

"Because we are a public network we cannot do advertising or get sponsorship, so we had to get them to participate in the story without giving us money. We found a businessman who said, 'OK, if you are willing to make a documentary series, I will manage the bobsled team.' Next we went to the University of Leuven and told them about the idea and that we didn't have any money to pay for the training and testing facilities. Because I work for Canvas, which is a serious channel, they could identify with our network, which has lot of credibility. They thought it was a mad idea—we don't have any mountains and we don't have any snow—but they were excited by it and saw that if we succeeded they could be identified with a successful project. So with us doing the media coverage, the business guy doing the sports management and the university looking after the science, we had the ideal combination to make the puzzle click.

"We began with sixty-nine girls and ended up with three girls who qualified for the Olympics, where they came fourteenth out of twenty-one sleds. The team still exists now but we aren't following them any more.

"It was a unique partnership between television, university and a company that everyone thought would be impossible, but step-by-step we managed to do it."

Government Departments

Knowledge-driven funding can sometimes be found from government departments. The Canadian Navy was one of the partners (alongside Channel 4, Smithsonian Networks, History Channel Canada and National Geographic Channel

International) in *Atlantic Convoys: The War at Sea*, a co-production between Darlow Smithson in the UK and Cream Productions in Canada. When Professor Bekir Karlığa of Bahçeşehir University in Istanbul, Turkey wanted to tell a less Eurocentric story of global civilization he came up with the idea for a TV series, *River Flowing Westward/A Story of Global Civilization*, and asked London-based Lion Television to produce it. The Promotion Fund of the Prime Ministry in Turkey provided funding along with TRT (Turkish Radio and Television), BBC, PBS and History Channel. The Promotion Fund was set up by the Turkish government to fund projects that promote art, language, culture and tourist attractions, and they are clearly open to working with foreign producers.

While universities have a clear motivation to increase knowledge and learning, governments are more likely to be concerned about promoting good health and citizenship through education. "Much government communication is about behaviour change, encouraging people to start doing something good or stop doing something bad. In recent years [UK] Government departments have funded a number of television series to promote awareness of its policy agenda in the areas of, for example, healthy eating, tobacco control, advice for small business and the study of foreign languages," said David Seers, Director of Content at the UK Government's Central Office of Information (COI).* "With the availability of sponsorship, spot advertising, branded content and product placement, the opportunities for a broadcast presence for government messages are wide."

Some of the programs funded by the British government include:

- *Border Force* (Sky 1, 8 x 60')—Home Office (£400,000)
- *Business Inspector* (Channel 5, 4 x 60')—HMRC (Her Majesty's Revenue and Customs)
- *Beat: Life on the Street* (ITV1)—Home Office (£400,000)
- *Debutantes* (Channel 4/T4/Bebo)—Transport for London

Not all these government-funded productions were without problems: in 2009, Ofcom judged that *Beat: Life on the Street* had shown the police officers in an "overwhelmingly positive light" and had not made it clear enough to viewers that the show was funded by the Home Office. The previous year it was reported that Sky handed back £40,000 to the Home Office to ensure *Border Force* was "wholly independent." The British government concluded that funding of TV programs

*In June 2011 it was announced that the COI would be closing as part of a restructuring process.

"stands a better chance of success when the policy area is clearly defined as health, safety and welfare. It would be difficult to argue that spin is at play in a programme about blood donation."

David Seers went on to note that in an age of austerity, "where funding is available, government will expect to cut deals that give it a return on its investment. In future there will be more reliance on partnership models so producers should be thinking about what government can offer in addition to money. Access to real human drama or physical estate, for example, that can attract the attention of the commissioners."

Knowledge-driven Grant Foundations

Another potentially rich (and less controversial) source of knowledge-driven funding comes from grant foundations. Each one works in a different way and has its own area of interest and eligibility criteria. Some are small family-run foundations, others are huge institutions that have several different programs running concurrently, but they all have a desire to spread knowledge and so are likely to be of most interest to you if you have an idea for a documentary or series about history, science, religion or the arts. Many of these grants are not specifically aimed at filmmakers, so the greatest challenge is to unravel exactly what the institution is looking for in the projects it funds and how you can present your film project to match their remit.

Some institutions, however, are very media-savvy, with ex-TV producers in charge of their film funds. In 2011, the Howard Hughes Medical Institute in Maryland, USA, announced a new $60million documentary fund. (The institute has previously funded the NOVA *scienceNOW* series and science news reporting, both on PBS.) Michael Rosenfeld, who is a former president of National Geographic Television, was appointed to oversee the fund. His stated ambition was to fund programs that make "complicated science clear, entertaining, and fun." One way of working out if there is a good fit between your film and a funder is to find out what they've funded in the past (or wish they had funded). Michael Rosenfeld has said that he is particularly proud of having produced *Strange Days on Planet Earth*, an Edward Norton-hosted conservation series; *The Human Family Tree*, about population genetics; and *Six Degrees Could Change the World*, about climate science. You'd be well advised to have watched those programs and understood what makes them appealing before pitching to him for funding.

Tom Ziessen runs the grant program at the Wellcome Trust in London, which promotes the public understanding of science through a number of grants, including:

- **Broadcast Development Awards**—grants that help production companies develop their more off-the-wall ideas—the type of ideas that TV commissioners might not be willing to take a risk on in their earliest stages. The Broadcast Development Awards are "about pushing boundaries through innovative approaches and also about getting science into slots that are not commissioned by science commissioners," says Tom. Programs that have received funding from the Broadcast Development Awards, and gone on to win a TV commission include:
  - ◯ *The Forgotten Fallen* (BBC4), a drama about a doctor's attempts to protect the citizens of Manchester, England from the Spanish 'flu epidemic in 1918.
  - ◯ *23 Week Babies—The Price of Life* (BBC2), a documentary that explored the ethical dilemmas of doctors looking after babies born four months early.
  - ◯ *Too Fast to Be a Woman? The Story of Caster Semenya* (BBC2), the story of a South African athlete whose running career was thrown into doubt when her gender was questioned.
- **People Awards**—which offers grants up to £30,000—can fund any type of activity that promotes engagement with biomedical science among the general public. Filmmakers "are competing in quite an odd market because they are up against all kinds of different stuff," says Tom. For example, the Wellcome Trust has previously funded a touring play about the menopause called *The Tide Tables*; an online competition called "I'm a Scientist Get Me Out of Here," in which children voted for their favorite scientists until there was a winner; and an adult comedy show that explored the mathematics of public health. TV programs that have received funding from the People Awards include:
  - ◯ *Dream School* (Channel 4), a Jamie Oliver-fronted project that set out to inspire school dropouts with lessons from well-known academics and professionals at the top of their respective fields.
  - ◯ The online element of *The Operation: Surgery Live* (Channel 4), a live brain operation on Channel 4, in which viewers could use Twitter to ask the patient questions during the operation.

Some knowledge-driven funders are happy to be hands-off, but those with a more academic remit are likely to take a more hands-on approach. When the

Wellcome Trust was considering funding Blink Films' *The Great Sperm Race*, they wanted reassurance that the science would be solid. "We saw and commented on the script in multiple versions and commented on the rough-cuts," says Tom Ziessen. "We paid for an executive producer to act on our behalf to make sure the science was accurately represented and our Broadcast Manager was also an executive producer on the film." Tom also insisted the script went to peer review before production started and also reviewed the scripts throughout the production process (not always the case, but this was a particularly expensive and high-profile project). The scripts were returned with comments after a couple of weeks—this kind of input would have had to be built into the schedule and might end up costing a production money if filming is delayed while waiting for sign-off on a script. This needs to be discussed at the start of the project and expectations on both sides voiced and agreed to avoid frustrating delays and deteriorating relationships as the production rolls on.

One advantage of working with a university or an organization such as the Wellcome Trust or the Howard Hughes Medical Institute is that they can give you access to experts and recommend good interviewees, and any potential contributors will feel reassured by the involvement of a venerable institution. In addition, notes Sean Carroll, vice president for science education at the HHMI, there are editorial benefits to partnering with a knowledge funder because "we have our ear a little closer to the rail of emerging stories in biology or biomedicine because we are in that world," so you might get access to a breaking story before anyone else.

How to Pitch to Knowledge-driven Funders

The first port of call should be the foundation's website to check the eligibility criteria of their funds, deadlines and method of submission. Some funds require broadcaster interest before they will consider an application; others will come onboard sooner to give a project the credibility needed to persuade a TV broadcaster to commit. The producers of *The Great Sperm Race* had secured conditional interest from TV broadcasters who would fully commit only once all the funding partners were in place. In this instance, the Wellcome Trust provided the final piece of the funding jigsaw, which triggered firm commitments from Channel 4 and Discovery Canada.

According to Tom Ziessen, TV producers often fail to pitch their project properly.

The people who approach the Wellcome Trust for a Broadcast Development Award "don't necessarily understand that we need a very clear road map of how we go from funding to commission," says Tom. "Quite often they just want to talk about the story, but we can't just have that if we are going to fund it. We want to know what the development plan is, how they're going to be working with their experts in order to produce their taster tape, which channel and slot they are aiming for, etc. Another way people sometimes fail is by applying for a grant for a project with a presenter that nobody's ever heard of, and without providing any evidence that they might be any good. If an idea hinges on the talent, it would be crazy to throw £10,000 behind something without knowing if the talent was any good or not." He advises putting a minute's worth of footage on Vimeo and including a link in the application so he can see how the talent works onscreen. A producer applying to the People Awards for production funding "would need a clear distribution plan" as part of their pitch, says Tom.

Each application must be tailored to the specific interests of each organization "A big project can be presented in lots of different ways," points out Hugh Hartford, director of *Ping Pong*. "The Wellcome Trust is all about public engagement in biomedical issues, so I made sure that all of the ways the film covers biomedical issues were highlighted in the application." A word of warning: don't mislead your funders by pretending your film is something it's not, as you will end up having some very difficult conversations in the edit. Not only that, you also risk destroying relationships on which you might be reliant for the funding of future projects.

It's possible you might be required to go through several different written application rounds as your proposal progresses through the organization, or you might be invited in to give a verbal pitch. Either way, you need to be very clear by this stage what your film or series is about. A personal bugbear of Tom Ziessen is "people who come across as wishy-washy and can't explain their ideas—it doesn't mean they are 'creative,' it just means they can't explain their ideas and they are unlikely to be able to explain their ideas on film any better than they can in words." You might make your pitch directly to the person who has the authority to grant you money (if you are talking to a small family-run foundation) or you might have to pitch to a liaison officer who then pitches it up through various layers of management within the organization, which makes it doubly important that you get your idea across in a way that enthuses them and is clear enough for them to pitch to other people in their organization. "I remember the first time [the producers] came in to talk about *The Great Sperm Race* and the first time we talked about *Surgery Live*—as a result of each of those meetings I thought I really, really want this to happen," says Tom.

Once you've submitted your application form you need to follow it up, but keep any inquiries brief. "If someone sends a short email I can quickly respond to, they are more likely to get a response than if they send a 500-word one, because I'll just look at that and think I'll deal with that later," says Tom Ziessen. Don't pester them with repeated requests for updates. The consensus seems to be that producers should email a couple of lines only when they have something new to report on their project. That serves to jog the funder's memory about your project and also demonstrates that you are making progress, which might prompt them to invite you to reapply.

Sample Grant Application: *Here's Johnny**

Producer: Kat Mansoor

Organization: Animal Monday

Period for which support is sought: 18 months

Proposed start date: January 2006

Summary of proposed activity (250 words maximum)

Multiple Sclerosis is a disease generally associated with the old, infirm and wheelchair-bound. *Here's Johnny* is a documentary that looks at the disease from a fresh and original perspective—through the eyes of a maverick comic book artist Johnny "Deadstock" Hicklenton. Johnny was diagnosed with MS four years ago, when he was just thirty years old, sending his flourishing career into disarray.

We started filming his progress a year after diagnosis and have been following the developments in his life ever since. Previously renowned for his powerful images of "Judge Dredd," his creative output is now increasingly preoccupied with the frailties of the human form; as his own body has begun to change and deteriorate, his emphasis has changed from the exterior

---

*NB: This application is for a grant from an award that will also fund art, exhibition and performance projects. Because the application form isn't specifically directed at filmmakers it requires the applicant to insert the information where it seems most appropriate. The actual format of the application form has been edited to save space.

contours of the muscular body to the twisted, contorted yet beautiful vulnerability of the broken body.

Here's Johnny aims to present Multiple Sclerosis through the eyes, words and images of one of the most inspiring artists of his generation. The film will explain the science behind the disease through hand-drawn images and animation, making it an innovative and visually compelling educational too. Johnny is *not* your stereotypical MS sufferer—provocative, funny and insightful, Johnny has had to rely on his character to resist the ravages of his illness. For Johnny, to draw is to live. *Here's Johnny* aims to document this amazing man's journey.

Is this or a related application currently being submitted elsewhere? No

Details of the proposed activity

Proposed Activity Summary

The proposed activity involves the making of an hour-long documentary entitled *Here's Johnny*, the objectives of which are two-fold:

The first objective concerns the educational aspect of the documentary. By presenting the subject in an interesting and innovative way, we intend to give the subject of Multiple Sclerosis a fresh perspective in terms of style and content, making it more palatable for "hard to access" audience groups (e.g. 18–30 year olds).

The second objective concerns the contemporary debate, which surrounds MS, and the ethical and social implications concerning its treatments. Using Johnny's case as an example, the documentary will explore the range of therapies, historical and contemporary, which are available, and the wide range of risks they involve. Since being diagnosed Johnny has had to make harsh choices about which treatments will offer him relief, but not hinder his life. Johnny's poignant and honest examination of this little-known disease will initiate interesting debate about how we treat the disabled and challenge our perceptions of such disabilities.

Education

Contemporary education issues surrounding Multiple Sclerosis are complicated. The disease itself has several "types" some of which can remit for long periods. MS is a disease which affects 85,000 people in the UK, most of whom are women, and its public image is still commonly associated with wheelchair users and the elderly. Most people are diagnosed in their late twenties/early thirties and it is therefore extremely important to reach this core audience of people who often know the least about the condition.

While various medications are used to battle against the debilitating aspects of the disease, there is no actual cure against its effects and much biomedical research has gone into finding solutions. As medical science has improved, MS has become more manageable for many sufferers; however the strength of the treatments used often means severe side effects, which affect quality of life (e.g. sexual dysfunction, mental illness, incontinence). Palliative care needs to be tailored to the individual, but many people are afraid, through fear or ignorance, of challenging their doctors and ensuring they get the most effective treatment. This is best illustrated when juxtaposing contemporary medical problems (in the diagnosis and treatment of MS) with the social implications that this places on the person living with MS (e.g. when choosing a medication how do you balance the trade-off between the pain relief and the side effects of the drug? Should Johnny take something that will make walking even more difficult for him, just so he can feel less pain?)

Contexual

We started filming Johnny three years ago, when he started taking Beta-interferon and was weakening from its side effects. The drug had begun to affect the personal and social aspects of his life to such a point that he decided he "preferred the pain" to the effects of Beta-interferon—slurred speech, loss of libido, dry pallid skin, greying hair. Since being diagnosed, Johnny's physical condition has deteriorated to the point where he cannot walk without crutches, and has limited feeling in his legs. He has learnt a great deal about MS and its treatments and, over three years, has tried and tested many types of medication, from prescribed to alternative, most of which we have documented. At present he is stabilized on his current medication (in the form of strong pain relief) but is considering trying GOAT therapy which is about to start as a trial and which has, in some cases, radically altered the development of the disease in some of the patients who have taken it.

Programme

Set over three years, *Here's Johnny* intends to be a self-reflexive documentary charting Johnny's personal journey while living with the disease, by retrospectively showing where he has come from and also showing his current condition and his ongoing search for the most suitable treatments. Using evidence from medical experts, the audience will see how MS attacks the central nervous system, and the programme will examine the extreme effects of the disease in a visual yet scientific manner. In direct opposition to the traditionally prescriptive ways of relating science, *Here's Johnny* will use the dark comic-book style that Johnny is famous for, incorporating animation and hand-drawn graphics to convey the medical information and push the story forward. Split screens using Johnny's drawings from the past few years will also be used to visually support what is being said onscreen by the interviewees. By using contemporary graphics in this way, the programme will show how Johnny's style and subject has changed as the effects of MS have become more profound.

The documentary will feature interviews with Johnny's MS nurse, neurologist and the following key medical practitioners who will explain how MS affects the body:

Professsor Alastair Compston (PhD, FRCP) is Professor of Neurology at the University of Cambridge. His principal interests are the genetics and neurobiology of demyelinating disease, particularly Multiple Sclerosis, and he leads the Multiple Sclerosis Genetics group within the University Neurology Unit, based at Addenbrooke's Hospital.

Nick Rawlins is Professor of Behavioural Neuroscience at Fellow of University College, Oxford. His research interests include: anxiety, pain; memory storage and its failure; schizophrenia; and neurodegenerative disease.

Proposed Plan

We propose to begin filming *Here's Johnny* again in the winter, following his progress as his MS gets worse and he spends more time at the doctors and with his neurologist. We hope to shoot through to the summer 2006.

Once the production process is fully underway, we will enlist the work of a key animator and a graphics person to begin working on the MS explanations in the style that Johnny dictates through his "key frame" drawings. This will be done in accordance with contemporary medical knowledge.

On completion of the core production in the summer, we aim to spend six to eight weeks editing the project, while merging the core footage with the animation and graphics.

We aim to cut a trailer for promotion/marketing purposes and it is at this point that we will contact both British and international broadcasters and distributors. We will also enter the film into the festivals and competitions mentioned.

Audience

Here's Johnny will be a new type of documentary. It is primarily a science programme; however, it will be the first of its kind to relate science in a comic-book style. We hope that it will be broadcast and have had tentative feedback from Discovery, Monster Distributes, late-night Channel 4, and the Community Channel, as a possible means and outlet. Audience numbers are hard to predict, and would largely depend on the broadcast slot that the programme received. Despite this, Johnny has a committed fanbase from his fame within the comic-book industry, and we are confident that any programme featuring him would ensure a core niche audience. Through Monster Distributes there is real scope for an international sale of the programme and we can confirm interest from them in the programme. Other outlets will be high-profile festivals UK, European and International. *Here's Johnny* crosses over many genres including science, arts, animation and disability. Other outlets could be for places of education. The Multiple Sclerosis Society have resource centres all over the country and this could be a useful tool for people diagnosed with the disease.

Experience

Please provide brief details of the relevant experience that you or your organization have in undertaking activities of a similar nature to that proposed.

Animal Monday is an independent television production company whose chief aim is to provide engaging, original films and documentaries for television networks and other commercial interests.

Using an innovative and stylized mix of mediums including Digital Video, CGI, Cel by Cel Animation and Photography, Animal Monday are committed to producing challenging, creative programmes that address key social issues.

We have been in operation for three years and specialize in topics related to disabilities and social issues. Credits include:

● *Retrograde—Life without Memory*, broadcast 2003, ITV—a programme about the difficulties of living with Retrograde Amnesia.

● *Pakistani–Israeli Diplomacy*, broadcast 2004—a programme about President Musharraf's recent comments regarding Pakistan's re-evaluations of its diplomatic stance with Israel. Interviews included Shimon Peres (Nobel Laureate, Chairman of the Labour Party), Ambassador Zvi Gaby (Ministry of Foreign Affairs) and Itamar Rabinovich (ex-Israeli Ambassador to the US). The programme reinforced the need, and desire, for peace within the region.

Animal Monday also make educational videos about autism and complex disabilities for local government organizations. This is a scheme that educates both professionals and communities about individual autistic cases.

Evaluation
Please indicate how you intend to:
a) Measure the effectiveness of the activity
Here's Johnny is a programme that has the potential to reach a huge range/number of people. Measuring effectiveness, therefore, partly relies on assessing the numbers reached, which can be evaluated by a statistical evaluation.

Because MS affects hundreds of thousands of people (sufferers and their families) there is a clear need for widespread education and the programme would raise awareness about the prevalence of the disease. Quite how much effect the programme would have in terms of increased donations to MS-related charities and organizations would, however, be hard, if not impossible, to gauge.

b) Use any learning gained from undertaking the activity

We intend to use this activity as a springboard for making more cross-genre programmes, which move away from pigeonholing disabled people as "one-dimensional characters." We are interested in better understanding how to pitch and produce such specialized programming while maintaining broad audience interest. *Here's Johnny* hopes to be a groundbreaking programme, in that it breaks away from traditionally formatted "Science" programming to create a more accessible, more engaging, cross-format style. The film will be entertaining as well as educative, and insightful as well as interesting.

Financial details of support requested

Total project cost:	£29,900
Total amount sought:	£26,000

Pre-production Costs

Production co-ordinator x 2 weeks	£1,000
Camera/Soundman x 2 weeks	£1,000
Producer x 3 weeks	£1,800

Core Production Costs

Cameraman x 5 weeks	£2,500
Soundman x 5 weeks	£2,500
Camera and Sound Equipment	£1,500
(Specialist equipment: tracker, DSR570)	
Producer/Director x 5 weeks	£3,600

Post-production Costs

Editor x 6 weeks	£3,000
Key Animator x 6 weeks	£3,000
Graphics x 4 weeks	£2,000
Producer/Director x 6 weeks	£3,600

Facilities Hire

Offline Edit Suite x 4 weeks	£1,200
Online Edit Suite with support x 1 week	£1,800

<u>Additional</u>

Composer x 1 week	£500
Post-production sound x 2 days	£300
Materials (tape stock/stills)	£200
Insurance	£350
Travel	£250
Marketing/Publicity	£400
TOTAL	£29,900

Justification for costs

Please detail and justify all requests for costs itemized

Within the filmmaking process there are three main sections that require attention: Pre-production, Production and Post-production.

We have completed the Pre-production stage with revenue accrued from other projects. We are now looking for money to help with the realization of the project as its technical/artistic requirements are demanding and require the employment of specialists.

The Production costs are relatively low, because the desired "artistic merit," which include the inclusion of high-resolution art and animation, are Post-production elements. All core-staff pricing, such as "camera-person" and "sound engineer" have been modelled on BECTU rates for professional media staff. We intend to subcontract this work to media professionals with a contract which is payable by the "job" with a calculation of time being made beforehand.

The Producer/Director has been costed for the whole project as they are the most accountable for making the project consistent in its narrative and aesthetic structure. We believe that the Post-production part of the project will be the most demanding, as it requires a lot of interplay between the footage and the graphics. Time will need to be spent on the exact structures of the piece so that every graphic fits into the comic-book image and cohesion is made between all of the sections. We are planning on using a "split-screen" format, which is time-consuming but integral to the narrative flow piece.

It is also important to cut a trailer of the project so that we can take it to the Documentary markets (MIPDOC) and send it to our contacts to ensure the best possible exposure is ascertained to ensure its saleability.

Commercial exploitation
Is the proposed activity likely to lead to any patentable or commercially exploitable results?
There is a high chance of it being seen locally, regionally, nationally and perhaps internationally. We have interest in the programme from a distributor and feel confident that broadcasters will be interested in its acquisition once complete. We are also keen to show it at the major festivals as well as the "disability"- and "science"-related specialist festivals.

We are keen for this project to inform, educate and inspire people, including those within the MS community. We hope that MS centres nationally will hold a copy of the film.

Summary for the Wellcome Trust website (100 words maximum)
In the event that your application is successful a summary of your project will feature on the Wellcome Trust website and for other publishing purposes.
Here's Johnny focuses on the life and work of graphic artist Johnny "Deadstock" Hicklenton. Renowned for his contribution to various legendary comics (*2000AD/Dark Horse/Judge Dredd*) Johnny was diagnosed with Multiple Sclerosis in 2000. Drawing has always been the most important aspect of Johnny's life, and the film will use his drawings to graphically illustrate how MS affected his life—and therefore his art—for Johnny to draw is to live. Spanning over four years, the film follows Johnny on his journey as he tries to balance the demands of his life with the effects of MS.

Advantages of Knowledge-driven Funding

1. Knowledge driven funding is generally "soft" money that doesn't need to be paid back.
2. A knowledge funder might be able to help with access to experts or institutions.
3. Knowledge funders might come onboard early in the fundraising process, which will add credibility and reassure other funders that there is an appetite for your film or program.

4. Knowledge funders are often more willing than other funders to take a risk on projects that are hybrid or experimental.

Disadvantages

1. A funder that funds all kinds of projects, such as art and performance, may not understand the production process of a film and therefore have unrealistic expectations.
2. Being funded by an institution that has limited understanding of the TV industry might give you false expectations of the quality and saleability of your project.
3. Funding may come as "in-kind" support rather than cash, which doesn't help with the production budget.

Next Steps

1. Identify all the knowledge-driven themes in your film.
2. Identify potential foundations that have an interest in the issues explored in your film:
   a. Locally/regionally
   b. Nationally
   c. Internationally
3. Find out if your shortlisted foundations have previously funded films; if you can, contact the filmmakers to see if they will share their experience of working with the funder.
4. Identify the average size of grants awarded by key foundations that have an interest in your subject.
5. Draw up an application schedule.

Jargon Buster

Term	Meaning
Blue Chip	Term used to describe high-budget, high-quality programming of the kind produced by veteran and award-winning program makers. Most usually applied to internationally co-produced natural history, science or history programming that has the potential to generate revenue from DVD, book and other merchandise sales.

Foundation	A type of nonprofit organization that supports other organizations through grants and donations. Might also be known as a charitable foundation. Might be associated with a large organization or, in the case of a private foundation, administered by a family or individual.
Public Engagement	The way in which experts, such as academics and other specialists, attempt to understand and better interact with the general public.
Public Service Broadcaster	TV broadcaster or channel that has a remit to transmit programming that is for the wider public good, rather than for commercial purposes. Public service broadcasters might be financed by government, public donations or a license fee paid by the general public. Typically there is a obligation to broadcast a certain amount of news, children's and religious programming.

Further Reading and Resources

Foundation Center Directory Online—Directory of more than 100,000 US grant foundations and corporate donors.
http://fconline.foundationcenter.org/

Grantmakers in Film + Electronic Media—An association and database that matches media creators with funders.
http://media.gfem.org

Howard Hughes Medical Institute Documentary Fund—A $60million documentary fund that aims to "extend HHMI's science education outreach to the global television audience." The fund will cover programs on all aspects of science, including biology, astronomy and paleontology.
http://www.hhmi.org/

National Endowment for the Humanities—Development (up to $75,000) and production grants ($100,000–$800,000) for films that explore humanities themes

such as ethics, history and religion. Several downloadable examples of successful grant applications (PDF) can be downloaded from the website.
http://www.neh.gov/grants/guidelines/AmMediaMakers_production.html

NOZAsearch—A database that lists the donation history of corporations, foundations and individuals in North America. Subscription-based service, but foundations can be researched for free.
https://www.nozasearch.com/nonprofit-grants.asp

The Open University—Funds a variety of factual programming and, since 2011, has funded programs for a variety of broadcasters and worked with a range of producers via the Open Media Unit Based in Milton Keynes, UK.
http://www.open.ac.uk/

Wellcome Trust Broadcast Development Award—A development grant of up to £10,000 for films that explore biomedical themes and are aimed at TV broadcast in the UK.
http://www.wellcome.ac.uk/Funding/Public-engagement/Funding-schemes/Broadcast-Development-Awards/index.htm

Wellcome Trust People Award—A grant of up to £30,000 for films that explore biomedical themes and encourage public engagement in science.
http://www.wellcome.ac.uk/Funding/Public-engagement/Funding-schemes/People-Awards/index.htm

WorldView Broadcast Media Scheme—A number of funds aimed at UK filmmakers making films that promote understanding of the developing world and have broadcast potential.
http://worldview.cba.org.uk

8 Film Funds—Movie-making Mentors

Film funds are best suited to independent documentary filmmakers with:

- An idea for a one-off TV or feature-length documentary
- The need for development, production, completion or distribution funding
- A film that has a strong narrative and you can tell it with flair
- A character-driven documentary
- No agenda to change the world
- The ability to articulate your idea in an application form so it comes alive visually
- A documentary film that has international appeal (or domestic appeal if applying to a local fund)

> *Some filmmakers say they want to send a message and I tell them that Mr. Warner said, 'If you want to send a message go to Western Union.' If you want to make a film, tell me a story.*
>
> —Carole Lee Dean

Glance at the awards listings—*The Cove, Erasing David, Burma VJ, End of the Line*—and you might be forgiven for thinking that the only documentaries being funded these days are those with a serious society-changing agenda. But what if you want to make a film on a subject that doesn't have a commercial, knowledge- or issue-driven agenda? Fortunately there many film funds that are interested in documentary as an art form (sometimes known as "creative documentary") and just want to encourage filmmakers to make films, regardless of subject. For example, Cinereach funds films that "favor story over message, character over agenda, and complexity over duality." While film funds are more filmmaker-focused than issue- focused, there is often some crossover with the knowledge- and issue-driven funders. For instance Sundance Documentary Fund is also interested in the social issue aspects of film, in addition to looking for strong characters and storylines.

Whatever the subject of your documentary, it's likely that your finance plan will include funding from a least one of these general film funds, many of which have a relationship with a TV broadcaster or film festival. Some have one fund, others several funds with different criteria. Funding might be awarded as a grant or as a no-interest loan; some funds are specifically for development, others for production; and some funds offer completion funding to get a film through post-production. It is common for there to be several stages to the application process, each one demanding ever more detailed information.

Competition for the well-known film funds is fierce and documentaries often compete with narrative (fiction) feature films, and with applications from filmmakers around the world. For example:

- The Gucci Tribeca Documentary Fund received applications from more than 450 filmmakers in thirty-eight countries, including Egypt, Korea, Mongolia, Namibia, Palestine and Slovakia for its 2011 grant cycle
- Cinereach received more than 1,000 letters of inquiry for their winter 2011 grant cycle.
- Jilann Spitzmiller applied to ITVS five times before being awarded funding for *Shakespeare Behind Bars* (which went on to win the Grand Jury Prize at Sundance).

What Are the Odds of Getting Funding?

One filmmaker reported having applied to, and been rejected from, ITVS Open Call (five times), LINCS (twice), and the POV Diversity Fund even though almost every application made it through to the final phase. So what are the odds of success?

Fund	Application deadline	Grant size	Typical no. of applicants	Percentage successful
Cinereach	Summer and winter	$5,000–$50,000	1,000	1–2 percent
IDFA Jan Vrijman Fund	January and May	Development: up to 5,000 Euros Post/Production: up to 17,500 Euros	N/A	Approx. 45 projects a year
ITVS International Call	December	$10,000–$150,000	1,600	1–2 percent
ITVS Open Call	January and August	$25,000–$300,000	1,800	1–2 percent
MacArthur Foundation	June and December	$100,000–$200,000	N/A	8–12 projects a year
Sundance Documentary Fund	Spring and autumn	Development: up to $20,000 Post/Production: up to $50,000	1,400–2,000	1–3 percent

As you can see from the table, the chances of being successful in an application to one of the big funds are slim. Of the more than 1,800 applications ITVS Open Call received in 2010, fewer than ninety were awarded funds. However there can be tangential benefits to filling out an application form even if you aren't successful. "I'm applying to ITVS because I need the deadline pressure to get anything done and it will force me to come up with a better synopsis—as well as discover what the film I'm making is really about!" Laura Paglin wrote on the D-Word forum, "I really, really, hate these ITVS applications—but they do help—even the very annoying critiques." ITVS used to offer feedback to all unsuccessful applicants, but this service has been cut back and feedback is offered only to those who reach the later stages of the application process. They are, however, expanding their website (itvs.org) to provide online tools to help filmmakers strengthen and refine their proposals.

Another downside to film foundation funding is the amount of paperwork involved. "ITVS in America want cost reports, the contract is enormous, and they need a lot of input, so it's a huge undertaking," says Rachel Wexler. "Their remit is wonderful because they want to get films about the wider world on American television, but it is a lot of work. If you are going for a fund like ITVS you have to be really organized and professional about it and ensure you have an adequate business infrastructure; a good lawyer and accountant are essential." If you are applying only for a small amount, the time in administration costs might not be worth it. For example, you might want to apply for a grant of $10,000, says Rachel, "but if it takes you three weeks to write the application and then you have to cost report every month, and you need to hire an accountant, you might consider it's not going to be a worthwhile use of your resources to apply for that particular fund."

While the odds are against you for the well-known foundations, securing the early support of a smaller fund helps you catch their eye. It's tempting to jump in and apply for the first grant you come across in the rush to procure some money, but it's worth a more considered approach. "The more time you spend researching the funding sources, the more successful you are going to be," says filmmaker Jilann Spitzmiller. "When we wrote our first application, we were just so enthralled with our idea we weren't really paying attention to what the funder was looking for. Granting organizations work really hard to articulate their mission, but I think that the written word only goes so far. Look at their written mission, but also look at what they've funded in the last few years and then read between the lines. They are going to fund a few things outside of their mission, just because they are extraordinary, one-of-a-kind projects, but most of the time you are going to see trends in what they are funding." Jilann recommends going back over the past few years to really get a feel for a funder; view the trailers or watch the full films, so you really understand where your film fits in.

How to Apply for a Film Fund Grant

Once you've researched all the potential grants available to you, it's a good idea to try to build a relationship with someone at the foundation, by phone (by asking a sensible question that isn't answered on their website) or in person, if possible. This is more achievable with film-focused foundations as many are run by, or associated with, the various documentary film festivals around the world. Attending a festival before you submit your application could give you the opportunity to hear the fund managers talking about their work during a panel session, or you might bump into them in the bar, which allows you to strike up a casual conversation and establish a personal connection before you approach them for money.

You can go back to your original one-sheet proposal and treatment, and adapt it for your film fund application. One of the biggest complaints that TV commissioners and film foundations have is that filmmakers pitch the issue or the research instead of the story. So if you've been pitching to issue-driven funders, take a step back and recalibrate your project in your mind; push the issue to one side (if there is one) and instead imagine how the film will play out on the screen. What will the audience see? What is the beginning, middle and end of the narrative? Who are the characters and how do they interrelate? What obstacles do they need to overcome? Where's the physical or emotional jeopardy?

Typically you'll be asked to include the following information (*How to Re-Establish a Vodka Empire* extracts are used to illustrate):

Outline of the Project
- **Title** e.g. *How to Re-establish a Vodka Empire*
- **Logline**—a one-sentence summary of your film, e.g. "A vodka-fuelled journey into the heart of the Russian Revolution"
- **Synopsis**—a two- or three-paragraph summary of the story and how it will be told

"This feature-length film is about three of the great events of the twentieth century: the Bolshevik Revolution, the Holocaust and the collapse of Communism. It is told through the story of the filmmaker Dan Edelstyn, whose Jewish grandmother fled the Bolshevik Revolution as a twenty-year-old, to end up in turbulent Belfast in the early 1920s. Dan, discovering her diaries a few years ago, decides to investigate her life. He discovers that most of the remaining members of his family died at the hands of the Nazis in Kiev, but the family vodka factory still exists—tottering on the edge of bankruptcy. To save it—and the village on which it depends—he decides to import its high-quality vodka to the UK. The film will interweave Dan's attempts to get the business going, with his historical investigation into the history of his family—including his father, who became an eminent cancer specialist in Northern Ireland. This is a film about identity, belonging, cultural integration and the Jewish experience of the twentieth century, told with wit, insight and a gripping unfolding narrative."

- **Narrative Summary** (might also be called a treatment)—two or three pages that explain the story from beginning to end, that includes:
  - An introduction to the characters—who are they? How do they relate to each other? What is their journey through the film? Where's the conflict, drama and tension likely to occur?
  - An outline of the narrative highlighting the stakes and obstacles faced by the characters
  - Theme—this is the thing that will make your film relatable to audiences in different parts of the world, such as an underdog story, triumph over adversity, David vs. Goliath etc.
  - An explanation of the approach—how the film will be structured, shot and edited. Do you use fly-on-the-wall filming? Archive? Talking-head interviews? Undercover filming? What's the shooting/editing style?
  - Audience takeaways—why will people want to see the film? What will they learn by watching it?

How to Re-establish a Vodka Empire weaves together a multitude of themes in two overarching time frames. In the first strand we meet film director Dan Edelstyn in the present day and follow his story as he attempts to trace and reconnect with his Jewish Ukrainian routes.

Edelstyn, who was three when his father died, grew up in a non-Jewish household in Northern Ireland. Before discovering his dead grandmother's memoir he was only remotely aware of this side of his heritage, but the snippets he did hear led to the harbouring of a long-term childhood fantasy of "returning" to reclaim lost riches and set things right. Grandmother Maroussia Zorokovich's story stands out from the predominant experience of east European Jewry in and around the First World War. Voicing the experiences of a highly educated cosmopolitan Jew, it contrasts with the dominant narratives of the Shtetl, and the Jew as the downtrodden victim, and represents a rare social stratum inhabited by a merchant Jewish family fully integrated with the aristocracy of the day, living in the romantic tradition of nineteenth-century European landed gentry, oblivious to the imminent collapse of that world. As an adult, this world discovered through his grandmother's manuscript acted as a powerful call to action for Dan to enact the long-held desire for return. The ensuing adventure explores and reveals the inner feelings connected to this heritage in an open and brutally frank manner.

The other time frame is that of Grandmother Maroussia's experiences of becoming a young woman during the prolonged throes of the 1917 Russian Revolution, her activities during the ensuing civil war (part of a dance troupe enlisted to keep up the morale of the beleaguered white army) and turbulent journey out of Ukraine, across Europe and into exile. After a harsh period of adaptation, she died young in Belfast, Northern Ireland to be buried a Catholic on the Falls Road. With adventurous style, the film interweaves present-day documentary, rare archive footage and animation. This animation is an important device to bring the writings and experiences of Dan's grandmother to life as a dark fairytale, recounting the stream of events in the lives of the family and the flight to safety and an unknown and unwelcoming Britain.

Lo-fi, subjective and surreal, the animations have a potent ability to shed light on history with vivid emotion. Within the film's structure Dan Edelstyn and his grandmother Maroussia Zorokovich are constantly on parallel journeys—she by cart from Kiev to the little town of Dubouviazovka—he arriving there by plane, train and decrepit Lada. While she waits in trepidation for immigration papers to be stamped he sits, out of his depth in a language and culture he doesn't understand, awaiting a decision for vodka export to be approved by the distillery boss. Their stories intertwine in what is both a kaleidoscopic journey into the heart of the Russian Revolution experienced by a young Jewish girl and the experience of a young film director who has gone in search of the past—a past that very quickly has more influence on his present and future than first expected ...

Dan's discovery of the spirits distillery which once belonged to his great-grandfather, mixed with witnessing the poverty of his ancestral village, creates a potent cocktail in his overactive mind—and before long he's hatched a plan to try and save the village and to reconnect his family to the place. Dan's impulsive notion of rebranding the vodka created in the village seems simple at first but rapidly descends into a white-knuckle ride into a cut-throat alcohol business by a naïve filmmaker. The deeper he gets and the worse it all becomes, the more the viewer becomes ensconced in this strange and unique story. Dan's need to reconnect is costing him dear, but he is determined to see his way through and to bring the vodka into the UK—in the process connecting himself to the village and villagers and connecting them to the same place his grandparents were forced to go so long ago—the new world of opportunity.

In this film past and present are not so much woven as welded together, reinvigorating history and experiencing the present in the light of what has gone before.

● **Director's Statement**—why are you making this film? Why you? Why now? If this isn't explicitly asked for, you should try to weave this in somewhere.

DIRECTOR'S STATEMENT

This film was only made because it's still impossible to build real time machines (as far as I know). I discovered my grandmother's journals in the attic of the family home and was immediately whisked away into a world full of atmosphere, drama and cataclysmic events unfolding in rapid succession against a decor of chandeliers, ballrooms and elegant drawing rooms soon to be destroyed. This world, in Ukraine before the Bolshevik Revolution, was populated by increasingly desperate dashing French officers, swooning young women in the first throes of adulthood, and among this mêlée were my relatives—chief of these Maroussia Zorokovich, writer, dancer, painter and romantic. I determined to resurrect the life and times which exerted such a powerful influence over me, and in doing so have created a sort of time-travelling vehicle reconnecting me to my roots and happening upon the family's vodka empire—still (just) in business. But I needed an engineer and partner on the adventure—and I didn't have to look far. My wife Hilary Powell is an artist and created powerful visions of Maroussia's world based on her writings.

The film thus combines three narrative techniques—the authentic documentary action of me trying to re-establish a vodka empire, the investigation of my family's history—set against the great historical events of the twentieth century—and the re-creation of the world and life of Maroussia. In doing this I discovered the truth about my past, but have also unwittingly stumbled on my future.

- **Context**—How your film's subject fits into a wider social narrative—why is it relevant today?

Business is a hot topic; it's been made sexy by such TV stories as *Willie's Wonky Chocolate Factory* [on Channel 4] and the hit format *The Apprentice*. This story trumps the lot, however, with its back-story of the Russian Revolution, the whole thing coming to life out of a manuscript discovered in a slumbering old suitcase in the attic of my mum's house. This film taps into the verve for business stories—but also the massive interest in roots and family history. It also paints a unique picture of Ukraine just as it begins to look towards integrating with Europe.

- **Evidence of Your Credibility** as a filmmaker/production company.
  - Filmography
  - Broadcast transmissions
  - Audience figures of previous programs
  - Awards
  - Letters of support from key industry figures
- **Brief Biographies** of other key members of your production team and their credentials—this is particularly important if you are a new or emerging

filmmaker. "You don't need all the people onboard, but the more solid your creative team is, the more credible your whole project will be," says Jilann Spitzmiller.

Dan Edelstyn, Director

Dan Edelstyn graduated in 1999 with a degree in history and French from UCL and the Sorbonne Paris IV. After an early journalistic career, his love of cinema soon led him to start making films. In 2001 he established Optimistic Productions—understanding "optimism as a creative energy expressing commitment to social principles." He produced and directed "Subverting the City"—*4 x 3 Minute Wonders* (Channel 4, 2005) exploring alternative negotiations of urban space, leading to commissions for Five and Current TV and a stint producing commercials. *How to Re-establish a Vodka Empire* is his debut feature film.

Hilary Powell, Producer and Artist

Hilary Powell is an artist with a track record of producing ambitious multi-media events and films. Since making "The Games" (2007) staging a DIY Olympics with the sites/communities of the future 2012 park, she has led an active cultural programme in its fringe-lands. The project "Pudding Mill River: Purveyors of Sporting Spirits and Foodstuffs" involves gathering and marketing the last wild harvest (sloe gin vintages) of this "zone" creating viral "behind-the-scenes" videos of pseudo-scientific production and multi-media breakfasts/events with LIFT, Home Live Art, V&A and CABE. She is now based at the Bartlett School of Architecture, UCL developing the miniature theatrical construction skills seen in this film through an AHRC Fellowship in the Creative and Performing Arts building animated pop up books that examine processes of urban collapse and demolition with a series of large-scale film projects and pop-up works in derelict urban sites in production.

- **Location**—Where the film will be shot and/or the nationality of your crew (an international crew might give you access to funding in two or more countries)
- **Length of Film**—expressed in minutes
- **Target Audience**—in terms of sex, geographical location, age and interests
- **Distribution Plan**—how are you going to tell people about your film, and how

are they going to see it? Theatrical release? Terrestrial TV broadcast? DVD? Video on Demand? Who are your existing or anticipated distribution partners?

- **Budget** (full or summary), amount of funding sought and what it will be used for. Make sure your budget is realistic—neither too high nor too low—and takes into account any worldwide clearance costs for music and archive if you intend to have international distribution
- **Overview of the Filming/Delivery Schedule** and how far you are into production

While the funder wants to know about the nuts and bolts of your project, the budget, schedule and crew and so on, they also need to be drawn into the narrative. "When you are writing a grant you have to remember that film is a visual medium and you can't just write about the idea or the issue, you have to use descriptive, evocative and emotional storytelling," says Jilann Spitzmiller. "You have to write a grant as you would a story in some sections; your aim is to captivate the reader just as you would do in a short story or a novel, you have to paint the picture, because they are sitting there looking at stacks and stacks of applications and they want to go to lunch, or they are bored or tired, and you have to grab them with your writing. That means describing certain shots, and the light and how things look and feel and smell, and describing some scenes that you've shot, really articulating character goals and obstacles—what is at stake for the characters—because that is what hooks us. Make sure too that all the different sections of the grant speak to each other and that it is cohesive, that you are not writing in one style in one section and then being really dry in another." Jilann does this wonderfully in her application to ITVS Open Call for her documentary *Shakespeare Behind Bars* (which you can read at the end of this chapter).

Carole Lee Dean, who manages the Roy W. Dean Film and Video Grants, an independent US grant foundation, reads more than 500 applications every year. The synopsis is the most important part of the application she says, because it's "a way of categorizing and separating one type of film from another. If your synopsis is dynamic and is strategically placed on your application, it will remain active in the sponsor's mind." She also recommends using some photos to enliven the application—stills from the film or of you, the filmmaker, in action on location.

Although film foundations are primarily concerned with the narrative of your film, some funds are aimed at underserved groups, such as Native American or Hispanic filmmakers. If that's the case be sure to make explicit why your project is a good match for their fund.

Before you submit your proposal, check your spelling and grammar, and make sure that you have fully answered all the questions—with the information in the most appropriate categories—and that you haven't left any sections blank. "If the writing or the presentation of the proposal is sloppy, then that also reflects on how you go about doing something," says Jilann Spitzmiller, who has also acted as a grant reader. "I know how meticulous you need to be in getting a film finished to the very end, so if I see a slapdash application, then I think you are not taking the film seriously. When I have fifty other ideas on my desk, and those filmmakers have really crossed every 'T', I'm going to put more stock in their commitment."

What to Do if Your Application is Rejected

If your application fails at the first attempt don't give up. "If you are not accumulating several rejections a month, you are not doing your job," notes Carole Lee Dean; "even the best grant writers end up with far more rejections than they do grants. Here are some things you can do to if you get rejected by a funder:

1. **Don't get mad, get philosophical**—However wounded you might feel by a rejection don't take it personally and definitely don't fire back an angry email. There are dozens of reasons why your application might be turned down, not least because funds have a limited amount of money, and can't possibly fund every proposal that lands in their inbox. "In addition you have to remember that for many grants, there will be a different initial readers group for each new round of the grant," says Jilann Spitzmiller, "so you have to imagine that those people are looking at things subjectively in terms of what ideas they like, and although they are supposed to be objective, there is really no way of getting around the fact that people are going to go to bat for certain things, so ultimately it is sometimes about getting into the right readers' group."

2. **Ask for feedback**—Find out if the funder will give you feedback so you can see where you could improve your application (not all funders offer this service).

3. **Bring in the big guns**—Foundations tend to fund (just as TV commissioners tend to commission) people whom they've already funded. Consider collaborating with an executive producer who has successfully secured film foundation funding in the past (preferably from the fund(s) to which you are applying).

4. **Get help from a successful grantee**—Not all filmmakers can write good proposals, and not all good writers can write successful grant applications

(and not all successful grant applicants can make a compelling film ... but that's another discussion). If your applications are repeatedly rejected, ask someone who has some experience of grant funding to give you some honest, constructive feedback.

5. **Throw money at the problem**—If you are really stuck (or too busy filming to concentrate on writing), you can hire grant writers for around $50–$150 per hour (via word-of-mouth or recommendation in one of the many documentary forums), but it's worth remembering that while they can produce a compelling, elegantly written document they can't do so without you having worked out exactly what the story is, who the characters are etc.

6. **Apply again**—Despite the answer being "no" this time, it might be "yes" next time, especially if your project has moved on. Funders like to feel that they are contributing to serious projects with committed filmmakers, and that's easier to demonstrate when you can show that the project has progressed and that you have secured money from elsewhere since your last application. Everyone likes to back a winner. Repeated applications also ensure your name becomes familiar and that's the first step of building a relationship with them.

Sample Grant Application

Shakespeare Behind Bars *

OPEN CALL 2004 PHASE III

Applicant Name: Hank Rogerson and Jilann Spitzmiller
Applicant Contact Information: Philomath Films

Length of Show: 56.40
Format: DV CAM 16 x 9
Amount Requested from ITVS: $249,776
Total Cost of Program (Cash Only): $426,900

* This text is taken from a real-life proposal that was successful in obtaining funding from ITVS Open Call 2004 Phase III, kindly provided by Jilann Spitzmiller and Hank Rogerson of Philomath Films. The film is well into production at the time of application and this application represents the final stage of a three-stage application process. The original document has been edited due to space constraints, but demonstrates all the elements included in the original proposal.

Brief Summary of Proposed Program

Shakespeare Behind Bars is a documentary about a diverse all-male Shakespeare company working within the confines of a Kentucky prison. The film follows this unlikely acting troupe for one year, as they rehearse and perform Shakespeare's last play, *The Tempest*. The men in the troupe have committed the most heinous crimes and are now often faced with reliving those crimes on stage. They use this process as part of their rehabilitation, and staging *The Tempest* allows them to explore the themes of Forgiveness, Isolation and Transformation.

Synopsis

Shakespeare Behind Bars is a documentary in post-production about a diverse all-male Shakespeare company working within the confines of the US prison system. The film follows twenty inmates for one year as they rehearse and perform a full production of a Shakespeare play at the Luther Luckett Correctional Complex in LaGrange, Kentucky. Five of these men are followed in-depth. In this prison atmosphere, theater is changing their lives, as the words of Shakespeare act as a catalyst for these inmates to examine their past with remarkable candor. They are all individuals who have committed the most heinous crimes, and are now confronting and performing those crimes on stage. In this process, we see these unlikely men testing the power of truth, change, and forgiveness.

Treatment

The film *Shakespeare Behind Bars* opens on two men in a wide golden field learning a speech from *The Tempest*. The camera begins to close in as they work on the piece, bringing passion to the famous line, "We are such stuff as dreams are made on ..." As their energy builds, the camera pulls further and further back to reveal the larger picture—these men are behind many barriers of barbed wire and metal. An armed guard watches them through binoculars from a tower nearby. But for a moment in time, these two inmates are transported from the bars of the prison to the place where creativity and dreams reside. [See WIP* tape, start]

*Work in Progress, also know as demo—which might be a rough-cut of the film or a selection of scenes that demonstrate the look and feel of the film as well as introducing characters and showcasing parts of the narrative.

Shakespeare Behind Bars, the film, is about this journey—how the words of Shakespeare act as a vehicle to transport this group of incarcerated men to a potentially better place in their hearts and minds. In this unusual prison theater program, they have the support and encouragement needed in order to examine their darkest selves, and to shed light on how they might find healing and redemption.

The film is structured around the creative journey of one year in the life of this group that calls themselves "Shakespeare Behind Bars". This is their seventh year, and the troupe will be performing *The Tempest*, Shakespeare's last play. Combining several genres, *The Tempest* has elements of romance, tragedy and comedy. The play focuses on Forgiveness as the main theme, and also explores the ideas of Isolation, Nature vs. Nurture, and the Father–Daughter Relationship. The inmates will cast themselves according to their own crimes, backgrounds and what they are willing to take on emotionally. They will work intensely with volunteer director Curt Tofteland. Curt is part director, part therapist, part mentor, part father to these men. Whenever they can, the inmates rehearse on their own during Curt's absence. And just as in Shakespeare's day, men play all the female roles.

The film begins in Fall at the start of rehearsals as the men cast themselves, and progresses as they rehearse and develop their characters throughout the year. The viewer is a fly-on-the-wall at cast read-throughs where the men grapple with the text, and have intense one-on-one discussions with Curt, who constantly pushes them to find their personal experience within each part. The film will focus on certain key, pivotal scenes of *The Tempest* and revisit them in both rehearsal and performance footage. Through the actors' journeys, viewers will vicariously examine and understand the timeless language, characters and themes of Shakespeare, which can sometimes seem daunting to audiences.

At the heart of the film are the conflicts that the men struggle with inside themselves. As the year progresses, the parallels between themselves and their characters is enlightening and sometimes uncanny. Our audience will first be introduced to these men simply as actors. Their past acts will be revealed gradually over the course of the film to build dramatic tension. Each interview will go deeper into the reason why they committed their crime, their feelings about their actions, where they are emotionally in the current moment, and how the words of Shakespeare are helping them to process these complicated issues. (See character descriptions below.)

Shakespeare Behind Bars will not glorify these men or excuse their crimes, but rather attempt to take a more humane look at them. The objective of *Shakespeare Behind Bars* is to give audiences a close-up, visceral experience—a unique look at prisons and the incarcerated. To go beyond political rhetoric about crime and the need for more prisons. To shed light on a program that costs the taxpayer nothing, and to profile dedicated individuals who are tackling the shortcomings of the American prison system.

By following these men through this creative process, the film explores the universal themes of redemption, transformation and forgiveness. It will raise questions for the viewer such as: Should we rehabilitate criminals? How does art transform the human conscience? Who deserves forgiveness? The inmates' interviews address these probing questions and provide revealing answers. Because of the unlikely setting of the prison, these themes and issues are given a fresh, new angle, and will provide a broad and varied appeal for many communities across the US.

The Context

The statistics on the US prison system are jarring, and title cards interspersed throughout the film will help put this particular prison program in context. Since 1980, the prison population in America has quadrupled, while the violent crime rate has stayed about the same. Today more than 60 percent of those in prison are there for non-violent crimes, and in the past twenty years social programs for education, drug rehabilitation, job training, Head Start, affordable housing, and legal aid have been cut to help fund 700 new prisons nationwide. At the current rate, by 2020, approximately 60 percent of black males between the ages of 18–34 will be behind bars; 12 million people will be incarcerated nationwide.

Also adding insight will be the prison's progressive and genial warden, Larry Chandler (see WIP, 04:30). He personally believes in trying to rehabilitate prisoners in a political climate that is largely about throwing away the key. He talks about how politics dictate the way in which the prison system is run, and how this interferes with effective reform. "I guess I'm just a warden who hates prisons," he laughs. "More than anything, the day they come in, you ought to be preparing them for the day they leave." Statistics support his view, as 97 percent of the Luther Luckett population will be released to walk the streets again. Warden Chandler runs a reform-minded institution, which concentrates on education in hopes of making the inmates better members of society. The Shakespeare Behind Bars Program is part of the overall attempt by Luther Luckett to reform its population through education, therapy and job training, and new members of the Shakespeare Program must have a clean prison record, and be sponsored into the group by a veteran member. Since the program began in 1995, of the twenty inmates who have participated in the Shakespeare company and then been released, only two have returned to jail. This 10 percent recidivism is far below the national average of 41 percent. This information will be presented on title cards.

The Characters

The characters in *Shakespeare Behind Bars* are not your ordinary, stereotypical prisoners. These guys are "the best of the best," or so they say at Luther Luckett. Luther Luckett is the most rehabilitatively focused prison in the Kentucky system. It has the most educational and therapeutic programs, and prisoners are expected to partake, or they get transferred to a prison with less to offer. And within the general population at Luther Luckett, one has to have a clean record to join the Shakespeare group. As a result, at first glance, most of the men in this program do not seem to be hardened criminals. But their past actions all have a deep darkness that haunts them.

Leonard Ford (Caucasian) says that he and the group are "ready to go" with the new season after their summer hiatus. "We're all people trying to achieve something unique for ourselves and take advantage of this process," he says as we see him and the others playing theater games (see WIP, 10:00). He underscores that this is no ordinary acting troupe—that they will most likely have to deal with someone getting sent to solitary confinement or getting transferred, and will have to recast roles midstream. Leonard is the intellectual of the group, and his work in rehearsals and his interviews provide the film with thought-provoking moments from a philosophical mind behind bars with plenty of time to contemplate.

Leonard believes that Shakespeare Behind Bars is subversive—"It subverts society's desire to separate me from humanity." In 1995, Leonard was married with four kids and working as a computer programmer. He was highly respected in his church community and even ran for the office of Mayor. Today, he is serving a fifty-year sentence for sexual abuse of minors. At the start of the film, after seven years in prison, he evades questions about his crime. But Leonard says he looks forward to working on *The Tempest* and its theme of isolation—it takes place on a deserted island—and playing the role of the villain, Antonio. "He's a villain who does not get what he deserves, and that's unique." In years past, Leonard has always played the villain, and although he tried to avoid doing so this year; he ended up with the role when another cast member got transferred in the first week of rehearsals.

Over the course of the film, Leonard's role of the villain takes on literal meaning within the walls of Luther Luckett. "I pray to God it doesn't get much lower than this," says Leonard in January, dressed in a green jump suit, his hands shackled (see WIP, 33:50) "Antonio is fun to play, but not one to mimic in real life." In an ironic self-fulfilling prophecy, Leonard has become the cast member sent to "the Hole," or solitary confinement. "A prison within a prison." On day twenty-one of a ninety-day stint in the Hole (for allegedly messing with the prison's computer system), he is a stark example of the effectiveness of isolation. He appears shell-shocked and his interview is raw. For the first time, Leonard admits to his crime of sexually abusing seven girls. He has spent a lot of time in the Hole rehearsing his lines to blank walls, and thinking about mercy. As he makes his bed, washes his hands, eats his lunch alone, we hear a cacophony of delirious inmates shouting obscenities at each other from their solitary cells. "It seems that those who need mercy the most are those who deserve it the least." Even though he has been rehearsing in solitary, Leonard will never get the chance to play the role of Antonio. Two weeks later he is shipped to another prison in Kentucky. "Antonio" has to be recast, and ultimately, this new actor, Rick Sherroan, also gets thrown in the Hole just days before the performances. The group must recruit a new inmate who has no acting experience but who admirably learns blocking and lines in only four days.

Sammie Byron (African American/Hispanic) is a leader and mentor in the group, and has been in the Shakespeare program for seven years. This year, as he prepares for possible parole in August, he will take a smaller role in the play and will help coach less experienced members of the troupe. At the beginning of the rehearsal process, he performs the famous St Crispin's speech from *Henry V* to inspire the new guys (see WIP, 13:00). Sammie is a survivor of physical and sexual abuse who had created a seemingly stable adult life with a wife and a successful business. He threw it all away, however when he strangled his mistress almost twenty years ago. He is now serving his twentieth year of a life sentence. As one of the original members of the program, Sammie feels Shakespeare has been a vehicle for him and the guys. "In rehearsals we deal with our own personal pains and what it is we need to change our behavior ... it changes lives. It's changed me." Sammie tells us that while playing Othello two years ago, he experienced a breakthrough when forced to strangle Desdemona, his wife, onstage. (Stills from the production will help illustrate this event.) In reliving his crime, he was able to examine the reasons it occurred and then began taking steps to change himself through therapy, and job training at the prison. *The Tempest* provides Sammie with an opportunity to further explore forgiving himself, as he works toward his parole hearing a few months after the performance of the play.

Over the course of the film, we see Sammie preparing to be set free after twenty years in prison, while at the same time coping with the fact that he may never get out. "My emotional state—that's what worries me most about getting out," he says. "'Cause I don't want to make the same mistakes I made in the past." Although Sammie is nervous about leaving prison, everyone else in the group is confident that he will make parole and do well in the transition to life on the outside. They look to him as a mentor, not only regarding Shakespeare, but also as someone who has truly grown and changed in prison.

[... Original proposal continues with three character portraits of Hal Cobb, "Red" Harriford and Richard Hughes (removed due to space limitations).]

Curt Tofteland is a lifetime Shakespeare actor and director who has been coming to Luther Luckett to work with adult male inmates in the Shakespeare Behind Bars Program since 1995. The film will touch upon Curt's journey as a person coming from the outside, trying to help repair lives devastated by acts of self-destruction. Although he works with professional actors most of the year, he says that working with this group of inmates is far more rewarding because of their courage and dedication. Curt also thinks Shakespeare would have appreciated this motley acting company of convicts. "People in the theater back in Elizabethan times were thought of as pickpockets, thieves, rapists and murderers." Curt believes in seeing these men for who they are today, not for who they were, and not as defined solely by the crime they have committed. For Curt, his key direction for these guys is: "Tell the truth."

Dramatic Structure

The film will follow a three-act structure and will largely play out like a character piece. What supplies much of the dramatic tension will be the pace at which information is revealed about each of our characters. We will learn about each main character's crime at different points in the film, beginning with Sammie in Act One, followed by Leonard, Richard and Red in Act Two, and finally Hal in Act Three. As the viewer gets to know them as actors, they will begin to wonder what these seemingly charming and interesting men could possibly have done. Then, as the viewer learns about each dark past, they will have to wrestle with the conflicts presented by appearance versus truth, character versus action, past versus present, vengeance versus forgiveness. As Prospero learns to forgive those who wronged him in the play, the viewer will go on the same journey, deciding whether or not to forgive these felons in the film.

Act One of the film will set up our main characters and their inner conflicts, as well as the external conflicts they are dealing with, such as going up for parole after twenty years in prison, in Sammie Byron's case, or trying to reconcile with family, as with Hal Cobb. It will lay out the main themes of *The Tempest*, and give a clear idea of how the Shakespeare program is run and directed by Curt. For the viewer, the text of the Shakespeare becomes more accessible, as we see Curt breaking it down, and the guys beginning to learn and understand it. We'll get a solid sense of place at Luther Luckett, as the film crew was allowed unfettered access to daily life in the prison. And as rehearsals begin to take off, we will see how the words and characters of Shakespeare are beginning to open the men up, exposing emotions and issues that need to be resolved.

Act Two will provide for further character development as rehearsals progress, and as interviews deepen. In this act, more of prison life is shown as a backdrop to these interview sequences—such as inmates receiving their daily meds, doing laundry, in the cafeteria chow line, or seeing their families during the weekly visiting hours. In rehearsals, a general sense of ennui has taken hold as the guys are at different levels of commitment with the play, and the performances seem a long way off. Key events of this act will be Leonard getting thrown in the Hole and Richard's epiphany.

Act Two continues to build toward the performances, and the tension and nerves in the group are starting to rise, as evident in vérité scenes in rehearsal. Sammie steps back as the group's leader in order to let someone else take charge, but at this point they are a "ship without a captain." Both in rehearsals and on the yard, guys are critical of each other, and arguing as their egos clash. Some of these men are learning to use communication skills for the first time, and understanding how to take and give criticism, as well as how to work in a group. As Red says, "This is what you get when you put together a cast of convicts. It ain't Mary Poppins theater." This is illustrated perfectly when the cast loses their Antonio once again, as Rick gets thrown in the Hole for selling drugs. In a humorous scene that breaks some of the tension, we see the men, about twenty this time, rehearsing on the recreation yard without Curt's supervision. They choreograph the play's banquet scene into a free-form break-dancing sequence, and create a rap song from Shakespeare's text.

Act Three. Finally, May arrives and it's performance time (see WIP, 1 hr). With two cameras catching all the action, we see Sammie speaking his lines to the wall, Hal and Red holding hands, Richard checking entrances and exits with the "new" Antonio, Ray and Curt shouting orders to anyone who will listen. The men huddle up and with a "1-2-3 Shakespeare!" the play begins. The first performance is for the prison population and will briefly cover parts of some scenes from the first half of *The Tempest*. These will be scenes that are already familiar to the viewer, since we can recognize them form the rehearsal process (such as the scene where Red connected with this character, Miranda, for the first time.] This performance footage will be intercut with audience cutaways and backstage footage, such as the guys coming backstage to apologize to each other for missing lines, or high-fiving another cast member for a job well done.

The rest of *The Tempest* will be briefly covered in footage from the second performance, which is done for friends and family. Once again, key scenes and lines will be highlighted, such as Prospero's line "The rarer act is in virtue/than in vengeance." [See WIP 1 hr. 09 min.] These moments will also be intercut with backstage shots—Hal adjusting Red's costumes, Sammie looking out at his family. The play comes to a close and the men have an opportunity to speak to their families. For Hal, none of his family comes, but a former member of his church shows up to support him. Sammie is overcome with grief, unsure whether this is his last play at Luther Luckett. The energy is high, the emotions are deep, but the moment is brief, as the men must get back to their dorms to be counted. In a slow dissolve sequence, we see the men exit the visiting room for a final time as the lights go out.

Epilogue: It is the Fall of 2003, and Sammie Byron did not get parole in August. He was given six more years. But in a bizarre turn of events, he will be getting out of Luther Luckett for a short period of time, as he and the inmates are going "on tour" with *The Tempest* [see WIP, 1 hr. 10 min.] Transporting prisoners is an enormous security risk, so the men will be shackled and wearing orange jumpsuits as they are given the opportunity to see the outside. A familiar face rejoins the cast as Leonard Ford has come back to Luther Luckett, and for the first time he will not play a villain. He will replace one of the fairies.

The second prison they visit is a woman's prison, where the reception is electric. The women get charged up by the performance, and it's Gospel meets Shakespeare. It's a high note after a year of soul searching and hard work. The Epilogue will be used to tie up story arcs and with title cards over footage. Over the course of the year and the film, we will see men changed—enriched, challenged, awakened, and fulfilled. In a time of ever-shrinking funding for the arts, this documentary demonstrates to general public television audiences the universal idea that a creative process offers everyone the opportunity to change.

Shakespeare Behind Bars on public television

Public television and this program will be a perfect match-up for several reasons. This film will raise vital issues regarding the role of rehabilitation in the criminal justice and US prison system—issues that deserve more public discourse and consideration as we continue as a society to put more and more people behind bars as a "solution" to crime. As prisons become severely overcrowded and more privatized into commercial operations, the questions regarding how much rehabilitation should exist and what works deserve further examination. In addition, the film raises the larger questions of the relevance of art in society, and whether or not the arts can be a path to growth and a source of healing.

Public television, and specifically the participation of ITVS, affords a project such as this an important element of public outreach, which will result in viable public dialogue on these issues. This film would not have the same impact on a commercial channel. A public television broadcast offers far greater opportunities to promote follow-up discussion groups, both in communities and on the world wide web. For these reasons, the filmmakers would like this film to be accessible to the widest possible audience, not just those are able to subscribe to pay TV.

Communities who will benefit from this program

This film will appeal to and serve citizens in a wide range of disciplines, such as those interested in public policy; the criminal justice system; the arts; theatre; education; and psychology. These categories touch people in all geographical and cultural corners of the US; in addition, prison issues are relevant in any community, due to the prevalence of prisons nationwide. In terms of racial and social communities, the cast of characters in the film is quite diverse, but their stories are universal in nature. In addition, anyone who is interested in the psychological healing process—whether to address grief, anger, or abuse, among other issues—can draw inspiration from this film. This film also has a valuable educational aspect, potentially demystifying Shakespeare for viewers.

Most specifically, this film can inspire dialogue for the incarcerated, as well as those working with or who are touched by the criminal justice system, including victims and law enforcement. This Shakespeare program can serve as a model to others who would like to explore healing through the arts. And the focus on incarcerated men gives voice to people who have been largely forgotten by society. Convicts are often stereotyped, stigmatized and disenfranchised even though they may be striving to change, or have successfully put their past behind them.

Filmmaker's relationship to subject/community

Director Hank Rogerson has been an actor for over ten years and has been involved in Shakespeare and other theatre programs throughout his career. While directing the film, he was able to understand the inmates' journeys as actors, and could bring light to those internal processes of discovery that happen when studying a part. For example, Hank asked Red about playing the role of fifteen-year-old Miranda, and how he would physicalize their part. He asked Red, "How would a fifteen-year-old girl stand?" It's something that Red hasn't thought of yet, and the moment is poignant and revealing as Red envisions the delicateness and innocence of the body language of his character (see WIP, 18:00).

Shooting format, style, approach

Shakespeare Behind Bars is shot in 16x9 on DV cam, in a cinema vérité style—straightforward and intimate, revealing the emotional journeys that the inmates are taking. Complete access within the prison itself has yielded a variety of footage of life inside the wire and will provide for textured montages of prison life. We filmed our main characters in a wide variety of activities, in order to avoid too many "talking heads," and this vérité footage will be woven together with interview clips.

Transitions between scenes will consist of anonymous, close-up shots of prison life, which convey the tedium and repetition of daily life. And the film will use the visual theme of reflection—in mirrors, windows or puddles—to underscore the inmates' own process of self-reflection in the Shakespeare program. The film will have some titles to give background on the inmates, the prison, and the prison system in the US. The film's opening theme song will be a polished version of a rap called "Honor" that the inmates created using text from *The Tempest* (see WIP, 1 hr. 08 min). The soundtrack will have ensemble instrumental music, as well as rap and hip hop themes, echoing the music created by the inmates for the play. The sound design will incorporate the natural sounds of prison—steel doors, PA calls for count, crickets mixing with the electric buzz of floodlights.

The editing will reflect the moods of the scenes themselves, whether it is a heated scene in rehearsal, or a slow scene of a man praying in his cell. We will also experiment with the convention of Time, using slow motion, freeze frame and time-lapse.

Length considerations

In cutting this film to 56:40 for public television, we may find that five characters is too many to follow. At this point, however, we cannot say which of the five we would be eliminating. This will be revealed through the editing process.

Relevance of sample work and work in progress tapes previously completed sample work (archival at ITVS)

Homeland—A presentation of ITVS

Homeland is a documentary film about four Lakota Indian families on the Pine Ridge Reservation in South Dakota. Shot over three years, the film reveals both the vibrancy of the Lakota culture and the hardships of contemporary reservation life.

Length:	56:40
Format:	16mm
Budget:	$315,171
Date completed:	November 1999

Hank Rogerson and Jilann Spitzmiller—co-producers, directors, editors
Shana Hagan—director of photography

Homeland's relevance to this proposal is an example of our cinema vérité documentary style (in collaboration with DP Shana Hagan). This style and approach to the subjects of our films lends itself to showing changes in the men in *Shakespeare Behind Bars*, as well as allowing the process of transformation to unfold naturally. We used this observational approach in our sample work, *Homeland*, and were provided with access to a culture that can be distrusting toward the media and outsiders. We used this style again in *Shakespeare Behind Bars* to provide a look inside the gates, and into the hearts and minds of people who are struggling with personal and psychological transformation.

Work-in-progress: *Shakespeare Behind Bars*
The work-in-progress tape that we are submitting is meant to introduce funders to the who, what, where and when of this film's subject. The entire tape is approximately 1 hours 15 minutes in length and is cued to the start.

The first 22 minutes is a clipreel for the project, and shows scenes of the beginning of the rehearsal process for *The Tempest*, and introduces the viewer to the main characters. Included are some vérité scenes in rehearsal and interview clips woven together with prison life visuals. The inmates' crimes are stated in title cards, but in the final version their crimes will be revealed in the prisoner's own words, in interview clips. In addition, it also gives a sense of place and a feeling for the Shakespeare Behind Bars Program at Luther Luckett. Although it may seem like the beginning of a film, this clipreel is not necessarily intended to be the final opening of the film.

At approximately 22 minutes on the WIP tape "Selected Scenes" begins. These scenes are rougher than what is on the clipreel section, and include some key rehearsal scenes, Richard talking about his epiphany, Hal's confession to his crime, and Leonard in solitary confinement.

In addition, at approximately 1 hour on the WIP tape are some performance selects, including footage of the men on their "Tempest Tour" at a woman's prison.

Where would you say you are at in the Production of the Progam ...
Production
  Early Production
  Midway through Production
  End of Production
Post-production
  Beginning Editing
  Assembly
  Rough Cut
  Fine Cut

Shot to date

In hours, indicate how much footage you have shot to date?   160 HOURS

How many hours do you estimate left to shoot?   NONE

What percentage of the way through Production would you
estimate that you are?   FINISHED WITH PRODUCTION

Timeline

Please provide a timeline for the Project (be realistic):

	DATE (MONTH)	YEAR
Completion of Production	September	03
Preparation for Editing	November 03—March	04
Begin Editing	April	04
Assembly	June	04
Rough Cut	end of July	04
Rough Cut #2	September	04
Fine Cut	October	04
Final Delivery	December	04

Description of Production to date [...]

Advantages of Film Funds

1. Film grants are "soft" money that doesn't need to be paid back
2. They value the craft of filmmaking and don't necessarily need to see that you have another agenda
3. They understand filmmaking
4. They fund one-off documentaries
5. There are funds for all stages in the production process—development, production, completion and distribution
6. Many funds are open to filmmakers from anywhere in the world
7. Many funds cater to a specific demographic of filmmaker—based on gender, geographic location, experience or ethnicity, for example—that could give you an advantage
8. They send representatives to the main film festivals so you have a chance of meeting with international funders in your home territory.

Disadvantages

1. Competition for the larger funds is fierce and may take several applications before you are successful
2. There is a lot of paperwork to complete
3. Some of the funds are only open to certain demographics—gender, geographic location, experience or ethnicity, which reduces your options
4. The film funds are so oversubscribed that they have little time to develop personal relationships with filmmakers or to offer constructive feedback

Next Steps

1. Identify film funds:
   a. Locally/regionally
   b. Nationally
   c. Internationally
2. Find out whether they have funded films similar to yours in terms of narrative, point of view, location or approach
3. Research submission criteria and make a list of materials you need to assemble for each application
4. Draw up a schedule of submission deadlines

Jargon Buster

Term	Meaning
Creative Documentary	Term used to describe a documentary film as an art form; one in which the director is an artist with a unique vision expressed through originality and innovation. They are subjective rather than objective. Examples include *Bombay Beach*, *The Power of Nightmares* and *Senna*.
Director's Statement	In which the filmmaker explains what inspired them to make their film; their personal connection to the subject of their film; and the reason why the story deserves to be told.
Narrative Feature	Fiction feature film.

Treatment   An extended description/outline of a film's narrative that tells the story from start to finish, explains the look and feel of the film and introduces the main characters. Typically five to ten pages in length.

Further Reading and Resources

Cinereach—Offers a comprehensive list of film funds
http://www.cinereach.org/grants/resources/funding-support

Documentors—Lots of useful resources for filmmakers including a funder database, with plans for a vendor database (for grant writers etc.) and Doc Talks, a series in which funders are interviewed about their application processes
http://www.documentaryhowto.com/

Hot Docs-Blue Ice Film Documentary Fund—Grants given to filmmakers working in African countries
http://www.hotdocs.ca

ITVS (Independent Television Service)—Funds programs aimed at public television in the USA. ITVS funding comes in the form of "co-production investment in the program," rather than a grant. There are several funds:

- Open Call (completion funding)
- International Call (production/post-production funds)
- LINCS (match funds partnerships between independent producers and public television stations)
- Diversity Development Fund (research and development funding for producers of color)
- Commissioned Funding (ongoing submissions process for projects that fall outside the remits of ITVS's other funds, such as documentary series)

http://www.itvs.org/funding

Jan Vrijman Fund—Gives grants and advisory support to filmmakers from the developing world
http://www.idfa.nl/industrymarkets-funding/vrijman-fund.aspx

SFFS (San Francisco Film Society) Documentary Film Fund—A number of grants for feature-length documentaries in post-production. Emphasis is on innovation, intriguing characters and strong storytelling
sffs.org/Filmmaker-Services/Grants-and-Prizes

Shaw Media-Hot Docs Development Fund—Offers grants and no-interest loans to Canadian independent filmmakers
http://www.hotdocs.ca/shawmedia

Sundance Documentary Fund—Development, production and post-production grants awarded to filmmakers making documentaries on contemporary social issues that have global relevance
http://www.sundance.org/programs/documentary-fund/

The Art of Film Funding: Alternative Financing Concepts by Carole Lee Dean—an accessible guide to applying for film grants from an experienced grantor

The Lynn and Jules Kroll Fund for Jewish Documentary Film (LJK)—Funds documentaries that focus on aspects of Jewish life, culture and history
http://jewishculture.org/film/

TFI Documentary Fund—In association with HBO, this fund films character-driven documentaries. There are three funds:

- TFI/HBO Documentary Screen Test Fellowship—$50,000 to an emerging film-maker making their first feature-length film
- TFI/HBO House I Live In—$25,000 completion funds to a film focused on a filmmaker's personal story
- TFI/HBO Outside Looking In—$25,000 to a character-driven film that takes the audience in to a different world

http://www.tribecafilminstitute.org/filmmakers/tfi_documentary/

TFI Latin America Media Arts Fund—Gives grant to filmmakers living or working in Central and South America or Mexico
http://www.tribecafilminstitute.org/filmmakers/latin_fund/

9 Crowdfunding—Couch Producers and Micro-patrons

Crowdfunding is best suited to independent filmmakers with:

- Little or no previous filmmaking experience
- Few or no industry contacts
- A track record, a recognizable name and an established fanbase/subscriber list
- A noncommercial one-off documentary (rather than a commercial TV format)
- A film with a subject that appeals to a niche audience who are passionately engaged and active online
- A film about a band or performer, a social issue, or about a subject that has a cult following
- A large following on social media—via your blog, newsletter, Twitter, Facebook etc.
- The time to devote to setting up a campaign, with incentives, updates and fulfilling pledges
- The need to raise less than $20,000
- The need to raise money within three months
- A desire to keep all the rights in your film
- The time-management skills to juggle filmmaking with running an active blog, Facebook page and Twitter account

> *Learning the hard way ... doing things cheaply is very expensive.*
>
> —Erik Proulx (Director, *Lemonade Detroit*)

What if you could—even with little or no filmmaking experience—raise money quickly, without having to worry about paying anyone back, changing the world, editorial interference or sharing any profits? Welcome to the exciting new world of crowdfunding.

- Jennifer Fox asked the general public to donate money to her document-ary film, *My Reincarnation*. In return she offered various rewards such as a signed postcard from the director, a yoga DVD or a limited-edition print. She hoped to raise $50,000 but actually raised $150,456 from 518 backers in ninety days.
- Gary Huswit raised $118,505 from 1,814 backers (with an original goal of $85,000) for his film *Urbanized*, a documentary about the design of cities. Before he'd completed the film he'd already presold 211 DVDs, forty-one Blu-Ray copies and 764 digital downloads of the film. He told Indiewire, "For any filmmaker that has an audience and has made a few films, I don't understand why they're not on Kickstarter," he says. "It's totally the direction documentary funding should be headed."

As he went on to point out, it's not just Kickstarter that is helping filmmakers fund their projects.

- Internet Celebrities, two bloggers and a director who make satirical short films that expose "economic, political and culinary" injustice, in New York invite people to join them as "producers" by donating small amounts of money via their website http://internetscelebrities.com so they can make their films (and eat): $20 earns the donor a Producer credit or for $100 or more you will get an Executive Producer credit. Some of their funders have, unprompted, put money into several Internets Celebrities projects. The advantage for the filmmakers is that they don't have to deal with sponsors or TV channel executives and can get on with having fun making their films.
- Erik Proulx is funding his feature documentary, *Lemonade Detroit*, by selling individual frames of his film to donors, for $1 a frame or $24 a second. In return they get a Producer credit on the end of the film and on IMDB. For $7,200 or more you get an Executive Producer credit, a specially designed movie poster, a video clip and a VIP invitation to a red-carpet event in Detroit.

Crowdfunding platforms have revolutionized the funding process by allowing the general public to donate small amounts of money—from as little as $1—to help fund creative projects such as films, music albums and tech innovations that they deem worthy of support, so crowdfunding supplies you with two things: hard cash and proof that there is an audience keen to see the finished product.

Other advantages include avoiding having to pitch to TV executives, retaining all the rights in your film and not having to pay interest fees on expensive loans. However, even this type of funding doesn't come without cost; crowdfunding, if done properly—and it must be done properly if you are to be successful (and stay within the law)—necessitates a huge amount of investment in terms of time and, inevitably, you still have to spend money to raise money.

Individual Donors

Before we get on to crowdfunding proper, it's worth spending a little time considering individual donors who perhaps might be regarded as the forerunners of crowdfunding. According to Peter Savage, managing director of Azule Finance, the simplest way to fund your budget is to ask your family and friends. This assumes that you are from a wealthy family, but in the UK "typical creatives now come from the most affluent 25 percent of families," he says. Depressing if you aren't from one of those families, but handy if you are.

If you aren't lucky enough to have millionaires in the family, you could cultivate some. When Nina Gilden Seavey was raising money for *The Ballad of the Bering Strait*, a documentary about a Russian country and western band, she cold called Russian oil magnates to ask for money. After a lot of rejection she found a tycoon willing to strike a deal with her: if she could arrange for the band to perform at his birthday party he would make a donation. She did and he kept his promise.

How to Pitch to Individual Donors

The time-honored tradition of asking for money from a rich benefactor is to write a begging letter. But the rich, as newly minted lottery winners find out to their financial and emotional cost, are regularly on the receiving end of pleas for money from all kinds of worthy, and not so worthy, causes. Charles Asprey, an art collector and publisher, constantly receives letters pleading for financial support, but he complains, "It's kind of boring. Instead, make a virtue out of the difficult situation you are in and ask me to commission a piece of music, publish an unpublished novelist or plan a pleasure garden. I'd be much more likely to say yes."

The most personal way to pitch is face-to-face. This can be engineered by mining your contacts book and throwing a fundraising party at which you can present your pitch. Franny Armstrong raised the first £17,500 for *The Age of Stupid* at such an event where she invited thirty-five people to give her £500 each (although she admitted that having to ask for money made her feel sick). Fundraising parties are a much more familiar concept in the USA and both Carole Lee Dean (*The Art of Film Funding*) and Morrie Warshawski (*The Fundraising Houseparty*) have written in detail about how to throw a successful fundraiser. Warshawski claims that, if you do it right, about 70 percent of people will give money at a fundraising party. He estimates it takes five or six weeks of preparation and you can expect to raise $3,000–$10,000 on the night. But however well you prepare, things might not go to plan, as Jilann Spitzmiller's cautionary tale demonstrates:

We met a celebrity at a dinner party; he had just been in one of the highest-grossing Academy Award-winning films of all time, so he was flying high. He had always wanted to get into producing and was so enamored of our project that he offered to help. He thought we should raise money by holding a big, splashy benefit. We thought that sounded great because he has this great address book; we really thought the gates of Hollywood were going to open ...

We organized this incredible benefit, which took us a couple of months of really intense work. Right before the invitations were due to be printed, he said, "I just got a gig in Africa and I'm going to be gone for several months so I'm not going to be here for the benefit—I think you need to put on the invitations that I'm hosting it but I'm not going to be here." Oh my god, our hearts just fell!

A couple of celebrities did come to our beautiful benefit, but it was mostly our friends. It cost us $4,000 to put on the event. At the end of the night we counted our money ... and we had $4,029. So from this big Hollywood benefit we had raised just $29, which was pretty disappointing. I would caution people to be very wary of celebrity interest and avoid throwing big events. Keep it very simple.

One thing that is easy to overlook in the excitement of party planning is working out how you are going to accept money on the night. If you have a fiscal sponsor they might loan you a credit card machine, or you can have your laptop set up with a PayPal or payment page where you can capture donors' details before they leave.

Not all personal donations need be solicited at a specially run event, as you may be able to make use of serendipity. One filmmaker got chatting to a man while waiting to pay for her groceries and told him that she was making a film about Greece; it turned out that his family was from Greece and after swapping cards and a phone call he agreed to donate $5,000 to her film. Make the most of every situation by having two-minute "elevator" pitch prepared that explains the narrative of your film, its status and what you need to finish making it. Have some business cards with an evocative still taken from your rushes, the address of your film's website and your contact details. If you are in the USA your donor can get a tax exemption on their donation by giving you money via your fiscal sponsor (if you have one), so add your fiscal sponsor's details too. When you secure a donation from someone you'll need to send a letter of receipt and any information they might need for their tax return.

Crowdfunding

Online crowdfunding platforms are relatively new: IndieGoGo was launched in January 2008, and Sheffield Doc/Fest held their first crowdfunding pitch session in 2010. However crowdfunding is not a new concept. In 1885 Joseph Pulitzer launched a six-month newspaper campaign to raise money to finish building a plinth in New York Harbor in time for the Statue of Liberty's arrival from France. In five months the general public donated cash, often $1 or less per person, raising around $100,000 from more than 120,000 people.

The first filmmakers to crowdfund their films had to build their own website to market their film and attract funders, and there were some notable successes:

- In 2006, Robert Greenwald raised $385,000 in ten days for his documentary *Iraq for Sale*. That impressive feat was possible only because he already had a substantial following and subscriber list of 170,000 people. He sent out a request for individual donations of $50 and 3,000 people responded; a few generous donors gave between $82,000 and $100,000 each.
- Franny Armstrong successfully raised £450,000 for *The Age of Stupid* via the film's own website.
- By August 2011, Nirvan Mullick's *1 Second Film* had raised over $327,000

from more than 13,000 people including Spike Jonze, Samuel L. Jackson and Stephen Colbert, who paid upwards of $1 in return for a producer credit. The finished film will be one second of animation followed by one hour of credits accompanied by a "making of" documentary. Any profits from the film will be donated to the Global Fund for Women.

Legally, it's important to be clear about the terms of any request for money. What we are talking about in this chapter is the donation (not investment) of small amounts of money to a noncommercial project by ordinary individuals. A donation (either from a private individual, or via a crowdfunding platform), like a donation to a nonprofit charity, gives the donor nothing in return except for a warm, fuzzy feeling. A legitimate crowdfunding campaign is one in which donors *do not* share in any profits and "a filmmaker who does encounter commercial success and generates a profit may not share any of that profit with bona fide donors, or the financing becomes a 'security' since it now constitutes profit-sharing," says entertainment lawyer Peter Levitan. Franny Armstrong ran into trouble when she invited people to buy "shares" in her film in return for a donation. Her lawyer said, "It's the most innovative film financing scheme I've seen in twenty-five years. But it's totally illegal." Donations and investments are two completely different things in the eyes of the law; donors do not share in any profits whereas investors most definitely do. However, "It's possible to have both a crowdfund component for a portion of the production budget, and equity investors for another portion, but the two must be kept separate in terms of advertising, marketing, solicitation and operation," says Peter Levitan. *The Age of Stupid* was eventually funded via a hybrid crowdfunding and investment model such as this.

If you have a bona fide noncommercial project there are dozens of specialized crowdfunding platforms available to guide you through the crowdfunding process with fully integrated platforms that allow you to build, launch and market your campaign, as well as collect money and keep a record of donors. Two, Kickstarter and IndieGoGo, dominate, but there are many other crowdfunding platforms around the world, with more springing up all the time. Some concentrate on funding music or technology, others cater to a broad spectrum of projects; some are territory-specific, others global. Indiegogo, for example, is in more than 159 countries and has seen more than 23,000 campaigns conducted via its platform.

According to Danae Ringelmann, IndieGoGo's co-founder and COO, crowdfunding has several benefits:

1. **Money**—crowdfunding raises money towards your production budget at a time when you most need it
2. **Market validation**—proving that there is an interested audience out there. (Although Tom Ziessen at the Wellcome Trust said he wouldn't necessarily take crowdfunding success as proof of future audience, particularly when done through a global platform, because what it "doesn't tell you is whether there is an interest in the idea where we want the interest to be—our funding is about getting stuff shown in the UK.")
3. **Marketing**—drawing attention to your film so that the potential audience is engaged and eager to see the film on completion
4. **Fan participation**—allowing people to feel as though they are part of the creative process
5. **Psychological boost**—if people respond well to your fundraising campaign it can inject some much-needed energy at a time in the production process when energy and motivation might be at a low point

It's inevitable that the biggest advocates for crowdfunding are those who run the crowdfunding platforms, especially as some projects have exceeded all expectations:

Documentary	Amount Raised (Goal)	
IndieGoGo (global)		
Anyone Can Play Guitar	$32,569	($30,000)
Not Dead Yet: The Story of Jason Becker	$26,136	($20,000)
The Bully Project	$25,580	($25,000)
Out on a Limb	$15,635	($12,000)
100 Yen: The Japanese Arcade Experience	$14,848	($9,000)
Hava Nagila (1st campaign)	$13,834	($12,000)
Hava Nagila (2nd campaign)	$3,000	($10,000)
Kickstarter (US residents only)		
Minecraft: The Story of Mojang	$210,297	($150,000)
My Reincarnation	$150,456	($50,000)
Urbanized: A Documentary Film	$118,505	($85,000)

Finding Vivian Maier	$105,042	($20,000)
The Pirate Bay—Away From Keyboard	$51,424	($25,000)
The Banjo Project	$46,000	($25,000)

Others, like lawyer Peter Levitan, are more cautious about the potential benefits. "I'm hearing from a lot of filmmakers that they are disappointed" with the results, he says. "Even if they are just trying to raise a portion of their production financing package from crowdfunding, I'm hearing that they are not reaching their target amount that they were hoping for and that they need." One report on Rockethub. org painted a particularly bleak picture:

● More than 65 percent of unsuccessful campaigns raise not even one single dollar
● More than 95 percent of unsuccessful campaigns fail to reach 10 percent of their funding goal
● 99 percent of unsuccessful campaigns fail to reach 15 percent of their fund-raising goal

It's been reported that only 44 percent of Kickstarter projects receive funding (Kickstarter works on an all-or-nothing model—if you don't reach your target you don't get any of the money that's been pledged). Peter Broderick, President of Paradigm Consulting, and distribution expert, warns that the failure of a crowd-funding campaign should be taken seriously. "If you do crowdfunding and you get no response, that might be a sign of things to come and maybe [you should] think about doing another project."

The good news is that documentaries tend to be more successful at raising money through crowdfunding than fiction features or shorts, although as of November 2010, of the ten most successful projects on Kickstarter only one was a documentary film, *The Pirate Bay*, which raised just over $51,000. The better news is that, at the time of writing, eight months later, at least four documentaries have smashed that record.

Crowdfunding can put a significant amount of money in your bank account within a couple of months but it's not an easy fix. A successful crowdfunding campaign takes a huge amount of time and commitment in the run-up to, during and after the campaign. A lack of communication and failure to deliver promised perks will seriously harm a campaign (and any future campaigns). John Trigonis, who raised more than $6,000 for a fiction short, describes crowdfunding as "the first full-time job I'd ever had because it was an everyday thing ... constant updates, not canned responses, every tweet was slightly different, and Facebook updates were slightly different from tweets, we were human about it ... every time I got a donation I would shoot them a thank-you email ... one of my perks at $10 was that I would write a poem in their name ... it was personal, I was giving a piece of me and people love that."

You should also seriously consider what happens in the event that you are unable to complete your project. Crowdfunding sites tend to be a little coy about this—if you look really closely at their terms and conditions there's generally a clause that states that donations are non-refundable and that the project owner is obliged to complete the project. However, there's some confusion among film-makers about whether crowdsourced funds have to be returned if a film isn't completed and there's little clarity about this on crowdfunding websites (or if there is, it's well hidden). One producer tackled this head on by issuing a list of FAQs in which they stated that crowdfunded donations wouldn't be spent until the film had been fully financed and was therefore guaranteed to be completed. If the film wasn't finished by a specified date all the money raised through crowd-funding would be donated to a charity that supported issues similar to those featured in the film. In other words, donors wouldn't get their money back, but in the event that the film was not completed the filmmaker was completely transparent about what would happen to their donation, which seems like a sensible approach to take.

This chapter's section on how to pitch is by far the longest in the book, and for good reason: crowdfunding is not, by any stretch of the imagination, a passive way of raising money.

Is Crowdfunding Right for You?

It's wise to take a step back at this point, before you pour too much energy into planning a crowdfunding campaign, to see if you have what it takes to be successful. Crowdfunding requires you, the filmmaker, to be much more visible to, and interactive with, the audience than other types of funding, which may make you feel uncomfortable if you are not used to promoting yourself.

Key elements for crowdfunding success include:

- **A subject that has a ready-made passionate and engaged audience**—"If you are the only person in the entire world that cares about ballpoint pens, for example," says Danae Ringelmann, "and you cannot find anyone else in the world who cares about ballpoint pens then maybe you shouldn't be making a documentary about ballpoint pens because there is no audience for it." Documentaries that focus on music or environmental issues, on the other hand, are more likely to find an already interested and committed fanbase or community.

- **Social media savvy**—if you are uncomfortable using social media, don't already have a large following social media and don't have time to commit to building an online presence, it is unlikely that you will raise much money through a crowdfunding campaign. An article on RocketHub concluded that most projects fail "because people post projects then expect 'the internet' to take over." If you don't already have a Twitter or Facebook following, blog or subscriber list it is possible to build one, but it takes time. As a guide, TVMole.com, a website that collates TV industry information relating to the development, funding and pitching of factual/reality TV programs and documentaries, was launched in January 2009. Over two-and-a-half years it grew by word-of-mouth to approximately 1,200 subscribers and 18,000 visitors per month (and continues to grow month on month). In that time 4,200 posts (on average more than thirty posts per week) were published. That's a lot of hours of work, especially when you add the amount of time spent responding to comments, emails and requests for information. Twitter provides a less labour-intensive way to find and engage an audience, but it still takes time and effort to tweet regularly, find and build an audience of followers, engage with and respond to people.

- **Creativity across a range of media**—crowdfunding requires the filmmaker to offer a range of unique incentives, which requires lateral thinking and sometimes the creative skill to create imaginative perks, such as poems or drawings.

Plan a Crowdfunding Campaign

A haphazard approach to your crowdfunding campaign is likely to leave you overwhelmed and disappointed with the results. As crowdfunding becomes more mainstream, the funders are becoming increasingly discerning about the projects they back, so you need a clear strategy. Lewis Winter, who is, to date, Kickstarter's most prolific backer (he has supported 170 projects, one-third of which were documentaries), looks for a number of things in a campaign:

- "First and foremost, I'm pulled in by an idea that interests me. The quicker and clearer the heart of the project is communicated, the more likely that is to happen.
- "Second, I'm looking at the project creator themself. How well they understand their idea, how passionate about it they are, if they've set themself an achievable goal; things like that. Basically … how likely is this to go anywhere if it's funded?
- "Third, I look for a reward I'm interested in. That affects the amount I pledge, but if the first two things are there I might just pledge a little bit to help the project anyway. None of these are deal breakers though. If I like an idea, *or* a project creator, *or* a reward enough any one of those things could get me to back a project."

Work through each of these steps logically and you'll build a solid campaign that has a much higher chance of success (and on which you can build future campaigns). But first, you must chose your crowdfunding platform.

Choose a Crowdfunding Platform

Spend some time reading the FAQs of different crowdfunding sites, reading their blogs and articles on crowdfunding to get a sense of best practice and the level of customer support offered by each plaftorm. Each platform has its own pros and cons, and no one platform is right for every project. There are a number of things to consider when choosing a crowdfunding platform:

1. **Type of projects featured**—if a site concentrates on music projects it won't be the best place to try to raise money for your film about war crimes. However, if your documentary focuses on a cult band it could be an option as you won't be competing for attention with hundreds of other film projects.
2. **Average amount of money raised per project.**
3. **Funding model**—some, like IndieGoGo, give you the amount of money pledged, even if you don't reach your stated goal; others, like Kickstarter, only collect money from donors if you reach your goal.

4. **Number of visitors** to the site and how easy it is for the casual browser to find projects like yours.

5. **Amount of customer support** offered to fundraisers.

6. **Marketing**—the ease with which supporters can share your campaign via buttons, widgets and embedding tools.

7. **Territories covered**—does it have national or global reach? For example, Kickstarter requires a US address and bank account; IndieGoGo is global.

8. **Fees charged**—you are usually charged a percentage of the money raised. If the platform processes payments via a third party, such as Amazon, they will charge a fee too.

9. **Fiscal sponsorship integration**—some platforms, such as IndieGoGo, can transfer your funds via a fiscal sponsor (in which case you pay only the fiscal sponsor's fees). According to Danae Ringelmann, campaigns that have fiscal sponsorship integrated tend to raise higher amounts, which might be due to a higher level of preparedness and engagement on the part of the filmmakers, or it could be that rich donors are able to tax deduct their donations if they give money via fiscal sponsor and are therefore inclined to donate more.

Set a Funding Goal

Your first consideration when setting your crowdfunding target is obviously how much money you actually need to make your film. Next, consider whether you can raise this in one campaign or whether it would be better to split it into smaller chunks and run several campaigns. To get a guide for what is realistic, research how much comparable projects have raised on your chosen platform. This is particularly important when using a platform like Kickstarter where you don't receive any money if your goal isn't reached.

Aymar Jean Christian tracked 100 Kickstarter campaigns for web series and discovered that 62 percent of projects failed. On average, unsuccessful projects managed to raise only 9 percent of their funding goal. Peter Broderick recommends choosing a conservative amount that you are confident you can reach, and suggests starting with a goal of $5,000–$15,000 and running repeat campaigns to raise further funds. On IndieGoGo the average individual donation across all campaign categories is around $80.

Break your budget down into specific items and choose something that can become the focus of your campaign. It's easier for donors to relate to the cost of a named award-winning editor for twelve weeks than simply asking them to put money in for "post-production."

Set a Time Limit

The ideal campaign is long enough to give you enough time to reach all your potential donors, and short enough that you maintain a sense of urgency and don't lose momentum. On IndieGoGo, the optimum amount of time seems to be between sixty and seventy days (with campaigns of that length raising 141 percent more money than campaigns of other durations).

Write the Campaign Copy

You can use your TV proposal as a starting point for your web copy, as it should be suitable brief and snappy, but adapt it to include more of your personality and to make it interesting and accessible to the general audience. Read other people's campaign pitches and work out which ones are the most compelling and why—think about how different types of pitches make you feel or react emotionally, and most importantly, whether they make you want to donate. It's particularly important to remember that you are not *selling* your project (although you are); rather you are trying to engage in an authentic way with like-minded people. It needs to introduce:

● You and why you are making this film
● An overview of the film
● An introduction to your characters and the obstacles they face
● A clear call to action, e.g. Help me pay this award-winning editor to craft the film

Create Perks

When a potential donor reads your crowdfunding page they are usually encouraged to donate money in return of one of several perks; the more money they donate the greater the level of perk they receive. At its simplest they might be offered a handwritten thank-you note and an end credit for donating $1, a DVD of the finished film for $25, or a private screening for their friends and family for $1,000. However, as crowdfunding becomes more popular, filmmakers have to be more creative to make their project stand out. For example, if you donated $5,000 to Roberta Grossman's film *Hava Nagila* she would "include a photo of your family singing the song, with the traditional chair dance, in the film." On the *How to Re-Establish a Vodka Empire* website you can sign up to the Zorokovich 1917 Vodka Club for £50; in return you receive a bottle of Zorokovich vodka, tickets to the première and your name in the end credits. The things that are most likely to stand out are those that are "very unique and specific to the project that you can't get anywhere else in the world," says Danae Ringelmann. A signed DVD is better than an unsigned one. A handwritten thank-you note is better than an emailed thank you.

Create some low-value perks too, but allow donors to donate more money than the value of each individual perk as some people might be willing to donate at a higher level but don't want to receive the higher-level perk. A wide range of price points also ensures there is something for every budget.

Decide how many units of each perk you can provide—both in terms of how many you have available, or can realistically produce, and also to introduce an element of scarcity, and therefore desirability. Make sure the rewards won't cost more to buy and ship than the amount being donated.

Here are some examples of existing perks on Kickstarter and IndieGoGo to get you going:

- A thank you in the credit roll
- Access to exclusive behind-the-scenes footage and updates
- A personalized postcard from the film's location
- A pamphlet with practical tips for preparing for an emergency
- A DVD of the finished film
- A packet of coffee beans
- A copy of a love letter never sent
- A personalized haiku
- Private live chat with the filmmakers
- An invitation to the première and Q&A
- A year's supply of honey
- Gift voucher for a feminist sex shop
- Hand-knitted key chain
- The film's director singing a song on your voicemail
- A box of Girl Scout Cookies
- The design for a puppet you can make at home
- Ten swing dance lessons

- A massage
- A custom-made suit
- A ticket to Burning Man festival
- A guided tour of the director's hometown
- A CD of the soundtrack
- A Gibson Melody Maker Dual Pickup guitar
- A download of the sound of flirting elephants
- A stylish hat as worn in the film
- A personalized video message from each of the crew
- A short documentary about your family made by the crew
- A signed original print based on images in the film
- Limited-edition poster
- Original storyboards
- A visit to the edit suite
- Three-course dinner with the director
- A personal screening at the donor's home
- A one-day workshop with the director
- An executive producer credit

Make a Pitch Video

When putting together a pitch tape for TV executives you are showcasing the access, the characters and setting up some conflict or a question that will be resolved in the finished program. For grant foundation officers you are also demonstrating your filmmaking and storytelling skills. For a crowdfunding pitch video you need to do all of these things but it requires a different approach. Partly because you don't want to post your best footage online (which might jeopardize future distribution deals), but also because you are not so much selling your project, as selling yourself.

Fernanda Rossi, author of *Trailer Mechanics*, describes a crowdfunding trailer as "a movie preview crossed with a public service announcement or politician's campaign" where the filmmaker is "in the film and they say, 'I am doing this, this is what matters, and this is why I am doing this film.'" And that means getting in front of the camera. "A great pitch clip is something that is really personal," says Danae Ringelmann. "It showcases not only what you are doing, but who is behind the campaign, why are you doing it, its impact on the world. People need to watch your clip and say, "Wow, how can I not get involved in this thing?""

Therese Shecter made a successful trailer to raise post-production funds for her documentary *How to Lose Your Virginity*, by inter-cutting footage from her film with shots of her speaking to camera. She had a goal of $10,000 and raised $13,000.

For many filmmakers, being in front of the camera is highly intimidating. Robin Sloan, a writer who raised almost $14,000 (target: $3,500) for a book project, says all you need to do is "tell us *who* you are, *why* you're doing what you're doing, and how you *feel* about the whole thing." He recommends writing a short script and then recording it several times in front of the camera, letting it evolve as you become more comfortable. You can then choose the best takes to use in the final video. Make sure the first thirty seconds grabs the viewer's attention otherwise they will click on to the next campaign and you'll lose your potential funder. If you can't shoot anything yet you can use a montage of photographs or audio, a technique Samantha Farinella used to great effect in her pitch video for *Hoonah's Heroes*. RocketHub have identified five things that make a video pitch successful:

1. **Tangibility**—the project becomes real through association with a real person who can be seen and heard explaining their film
2. **Credibility**—the filmmaker demonstrates their passion and expert knowledge by talking about the project
3. **Engagement**—the storytelling, surprising information or sense of humor pull people in and make them want to find out more
4. **Dynamism**—new videos can be added as the campaign progresses. For example, Jilann Spitzmiller regularly added new character profiles, photographs and video clips for her film *Still Dreaming*
5. **Shareability**—a witty, engaging or emotional video will encourage people to link to it, embed it and talk about it—all things that will help you reach more potential funders

Engage with Potential Donors

In a typical campaign, the first donors are the filmmaker's family and friends. If you have already made a number of films and have a name in the industry, you are likely to have a core group of fans and followers whom you can invite to contribute. Or the subject of your film might come with their own fans. The producers of *Wish Me Away*, a documentary about Chely Wright, the first openly gay country music star in the USA, raised $22,120 in the first couple of weeks of their campaign simply by emailing her fans. A good crowdfunding platform will provide a range of social media tools, such as share buttons and widgets that donors can use to tweet, email and otherwise spread the message to their own friends and followers, setting up a marketing cascade. This obviously assumes you have a solid group of social media savvy friends who are willing to support you.

If you don't yet have a following, spend a few months working on your Twitter following and Facebook presence so that a) you will have a big enough group of people to reach out to, and b) the first communication they have from you isn't a request for money.

Research key bloggers who might be interested in your film and send them information before and during your campaign, perhaps offering an interview or a guest post in return for being featured on their blog. Don't confine yourself to film bloggers, think laterally about who the audience might be for your film, and reach out to specialist bloggers. "A good example is *100 Yen*," says Danae Ringelmann, "which is a documentary about the Japanese video arcade experience—a subject that people are passionate about, so this campaign raised almost $15,000, they only needed $12,000 to finish the film, and they pretty much raised all their money from getting two write-ups in two online gamer geek magazines that most people have never heard of, but people who do read them are the avid gamer geeks who are the people who would want to see the documentary made about their experience. Crowdfunding is all about going to the people who are passionate about the topic you are covering and letting them get involved." Similarly, a reader contacted maritime blog, gCaptain, which has 20,000 readers, to tell them about a Kickstarter campaign for *Stolen Seas: The Untold Story Behind Modern Day Piracy*. The film raised $15,750, approximately 50 percent of which was donated in the six days after the story was posted on gCaptain.

You'll have a much better chance of a response if you've already got a relationship with the people you approach—perhaps you've been a long-standing contributor to their forums or have left (sensible not spammy) comments on a number of their posts. Keep any email requests to bloggers and editors friendly and personable. You're unlikely to get a response if they think you are just pushing a product, so work out what's in it for them to feature your project on their site. Give some thought to your all your friends, acquaintances and colleagues past and present and work out who might be motivated to donate to or promote your project to their networks.

I've contributed to a number of crowdfunding campaigns and each time I had a different motivation (none of them to do with the actual film):

- *A Summer Rain*—I'd taken director Ela Their's excellent screenwriting class. She operates a "pay what you can" system and as I was unemployed when I took her class I paid the minimum amount. When she was raising money to make her first feature I wanted to offer her some financial support in return for her previous generosity.

- *The Age of Stupid*—I wanted to use some text from director Franny Armstrong's blog in my book *Greenlit*. She granted me permission to use it in return for a donation to her film.

- *How to Re-Establish a Vodka Empire*—I had interviewed director Dan Edelstyn for *Greenlit,* and so when he offered the chance to join his "Vodka Club," which came with a free bottle of vodka in return for a donation of £50, I was happy to oblige.

- *Red Robin*—the first feature of an ex-BBC NYC colleague. I happened to be on Facebook when he was launching the campaign and he messaged me to ask if I would tweet about it. I did and also donated to the campaign.

- *Strange Powers: Stephin Merritt and the Magnetic Fields*—I had done a small amount of editing on the film and had worked with one of the directors (although not directly); I donated some money to secure a DVD copy of the film for my library.

- *Porches*—filmmaker Tatiana Bacchus was a stranger who had been actively promoting *Greenlit* on Twitter, and we'd struck up a Twitter friendship. When she launched her campaign I wanted to pay back some of the goodwill and made a donation (unfortunately she didn't reach her funding goal on Kickstarter and so she didn't get any money).

The one thing that links all those examples is that I had some kind of prior relationship (however tenuous) with the person who was asking for money. Some people might donate because they have some kind of connection to the subject of your film, or to one of the contributors or crew. Others might donate in hope of getting hired: "I've just donated, and I'm an editor ..."

Schedule and Launch the Campaign

Draw up a schedule that covers the length of your campaign and plot out when you are going to send out updates and requests. Make sure that you factor in how much of your time it's going to take and that you can comfortably sustain it for the length of the campaign. "You could be working on it every day if you wanted to," says Danae Ringelmann. "We don't necessarily encourage that, but what I recommend is to take one day a week and make it your Fan Friday or something like that. Have a dedicated time to write blogs and updates, reach out to bloggers and influencers and post updates. A great way to mitigate the time you spend is to get a great college intern involved. Typically young film students know everything about Facebook and Twitter, but don't necessarily know how to make great films; filmmakers know about how to make great films, but are not necessarily as comfortable or savvy on Facebook or Twitter, so it's a great trade-off as you can teach them how to make a film, and a young intern can come and help them with a crowdfunding campaign."

You need your friends and family to donate early to validate your campaign. Just as people prefer to eat in busy restaurants because it provides social proof of the quality of the food, people prefer to donate to films that other people have funded. However, if you have a rich uncle who is willing to give a big donation, it might be worth keeping them back until the end of your campaign so they can come in at the last minute to make up any shortfall between the amount raised and your goal (this is particularly important if your crowdfunding platform will pay out only if you reach your goal).

You are most likely to see a lot of traffic at the beginning and right at the end of the campaign, with a dip in contributions in the middle of the campaign. Plan to post some exciting new information, updates or new perks in those slow middle weeks, both to give you something to do to stave off the inevitable sense of despondency if money isn't coming in as fast as you'd hoped, and to renew interest and inject some momentum.

On IndieGoGo, the most successful campaigns post more than eleven updates over the course of their campaign (raising 137 percent more than campaigns that send fewer updates). However, it can be wearying for early supporters (and I speak from experience) to keep receiving increasingly desperate pleas for more money. If I've already contributed as much as I can afford, have posted your campaign to my Facebook and LinkedIn pages and also tweeted about it I'm not going to harass my friends by sending them constant requests for help. However, you can get around this by scheduling a series of interesting facts, short articles or links to stories in the news related to the subject of your film. Producers of *The Bully Project* shared news stories related to bullying and in doing so positioned themselves as experts in the field; this attracts press attention and gives the filmmakers greater credibility, which in turn makes people feel more inclined to support their project. Whereas the usual filmmaking adage is "show don't tell," in crowdfunding it is "share don't sell."

Another way to raise the stakes and create a sense of urgency is to find a foundation, brand or other potential donor who will match fund the amount donated on a certain date or over the course of a week. Such a promise gives you something concrete to tweet, email and post about and is likely to be shared by others who get caught up in the excitement of a ticking clock. As the final deadline approaches you can ratchet up the tension and tell people how close you are to reaching your goal.

Make sure that you link to your crowdfunding campaign from as many places as you can—your blog, Facebook page, Twitter profile, email signature—create as many points of entry to your campaign as possible. Encourage everyone else involved in the film, crew and contributors (if appropriate) to do the same. Once you are getting the message out, listen and respond to the reaction (if there is one). When JetBlue airline started trying to engage its customers it discovered that "chatty posts and customer service assistance tended to generate a lot of replies and new followers. Press releases and announcements were met with silence." Find a voice that works for you, and don't be afraid to tweak it as you refine what works and what doesn't.

Advantages of Crowdfunding

1. You don't give up any equity (ownership) in your project
2. You have complete editorial control—you don't have a broadcaster or other funder to take into consideration
3. You can raise money relatively quickly
4. You can repeat the process as many times as you like to cover different parts of the budget
5. You are also building an audience for the finished film

Disadvantages

1. Thinking up rewards and executing them takes mental energy and physical effort, not to mention time and possibly money
2. Funding fatigue can set in if you don't reach out to enough people—your friends and family might start avoiding you
3. You are entering into a relationship with hundreds (or potentially thousands) of people and need to manage their expectations and deliver on your promises

4. Depending on the crowdfunding platform you choose you might get no money at all

Next Steps

1. Make a list of all rich relatives, friends and acquaintances
2. Make a list of niche groups who might be fans of the subject of your film
3. Identify key online forums and bloggers who might support your project
4. Set up a website or Facebook fan page and start adding material
5. Set up a newsletter so you can start building a mailing list; commit to sending out useful information or other news at regular intervals
6. Set up a Twitter account and start using it to interact with like-minded people
7. Make a list of potential incentives for several levels of donation
8. Make a budget—in terms of time and money—that it will take to fulfill the pledges
9. Make a trailer, preferably featuring you/the filmmaker
10. Select a suitable crowdfunding platform, taking into account suitability of the platform, funding model (all-or-nothing or keep what you raise) and fees
    Questions to ask:
    - Do you have to be resident in a certain country to post a project on the site?
    - Is it an all-or-nothing funding model?
    - How much are the fees? If you are successful? If you fail to raise your goal?
    - Is a global or local reach more useful to you?
    - Is the site relevant for your type of project?
    - How much traffic does the site get?
    - What is the success rate of funding similar projects?
    - How much support is there from crowdfunding platform back office team?
    - Is there an application or invitation process before you can submit your project?
    - What happens to the money if the project is funded but you are unable to make the film?
11. Decide how much money you want to raise
12. Set a time limit for your campaign

Jargon Buster

Term	Meaning
Crowdfunding	Refers to the way in which film (and other) projects can be financed through lots of small donations from many ordinary people, who can donate from as little as $1.
Crowd sourcing	Uses the knowledge and wisdom of crowds on social networks to source information or ideas.
Donation	A gift of money.
Noncommercial Project	A project is not being made for commercial gain and is not anticipated to make money.
Perk	Something that is offered to someone in exchange for a donation to a crowdfunded project. Also called incentives or privileges. They can be simple or elaborate, and a project typically has a different perk for each level of donation.

Further Reading and Resources

Crowdfunding General

Crowdsourcing—Comprehensive site dedicated to crowdsourcing and crowd-funding. Includes a directory of more than 1,000 crowdsourcing sites, which can be searched using country, language, type of input required (knowledge, funding etc.)
http://www.crowdsourcing.org/directory project.

Digital Bootcamp Wiki—Crowdsourced information on crowdfunding, festivals, distribution and social media for filmmakers
http://digitalbootcamp.wikispaces.com/

How to Crowdfund Your Film—A comprehensive guide to crowdfunding from the producers of *The Age of Stupid*
http://www.spannerfilms.net/crowd_funding

Revolution in the Mailbox, Revised Edition and *How to Write Successful Fundraising Letters,* by Mal Warwick, Jossey Bass (2011)

The Fundraising Houseparty: How to Party with a Purpose and Raise Money for Your Cause by Morrie Warshawski. Available from twww.warshawski.com

The Mercifully Brief, Real-World Guide to Raising $1,000 Gifts by Mail, by Mal Warwick, Emerson & Church (2005)

Campaign Building

Trailer Mechanics by Fenanda Rossi, Magafilms (2012)—A guide to making documentary trailers that will help raise funding. Also helps you work out *why* you are making your film, so you can articulate your passion for your project to potential funders

How to Make a Great Video—Simple guide to making a crowdfunding video
http://www.sponsume.com/how-shoot-yourself-camera

Creator's Guide to Video—How to make a compelling crowdfunding pitch video from Robin Solan, whose *Robin Writes a Book* project raised almost $14,000 (with a goal of $3,500)
http://blog.kickstarter.com/post/173046259/creators-guide-to-video

Lulu—A print-on-demand publishing platform that allows you to turn photographs or a production diary into a printed book, ebook or calendar that could be used as a reward
http://www.lulu.com

PickFu—Fast instant feedback on questions that have two options e.g. web copy or documentary title. Five dollars buys a focus group of fifty people who give their opinion on your two options
http://pickfu.com/

Online Marketing

Create A Successful Website: Easy Do It Yourself Steps To Online Success by Paula Wynne, Lean Marketing Press (2010)

Movie Sparx—A specialist film marketing platform where you can create a website for your film, upload a trailer, promote it via social networking and email, sell merchandise and get donations
http://moviesparx.com/how

OpenWiFiSpots—A worldwide list (although mainly focused on the USA) of free wi-fi hot spots, which could be useful for keeping your crowdfunders up to date when you are on location
http://www.openwifispots.com

Ten Twitter Tools—Twitter tools to help target potential followers
http://sixrevisions.com/tools/10-new-twitter-tools-that-will-make-your-life-easier/

Crowdfunding Platforms

New crowdfunding sites are launching all the time so this list is by no means comprehensive. Comments on crowdfunding blogs are good places to pick up information on new crowdfunding platforms. All sites are subject to changes in their terms and conditions, so read their sites thoroughly before making any decisions.

Chip In—A global money collection website that allows people to donate to your project via PayPal. Provides widgets that you can add to your website and social networking sites
Fees: Usual PayPal fees
Time frame: up to 365 days
Fiscal sponsorship: not available
www.Chipin.com

IndieGoGo—Global platform where you can keep any funds raised. No submission/approval process. Fiscal sponsorship is available through Fractured Atlas and San Francisco Film Society
Fees: 4 percent on successful project; 9 percent if you don't meet your goal. Also need to factor in PayPal fees of 2–3 percent
Time frame: up to 120 days
www.IndieGoGo.com

Invested.In—Global platform that offers investors services, special offers or products (not money) in return for investment in a project. Investors can take their money out of a project before it reaches its goal
Fees: 3 percent for withdrawal
Time frame: unlimited
http://www.invested.in

Kickstarter—All-or-nothing funding platform open to residents of the USA (funding can come from anywhere in the world). Projects must be submitted and approved before the campaign can start
Fees: 5 percent for successful projects + processing fee for Amazon.com payments. No fee for unsuccessful projects
Time frame: up to ninety days
www.kickstarter.com

Kiss Kiss Bank Bank—French crowdfunding platform with an all-or-nothing funding model
Fee: 10 percent
Time frame: up to ninety days
http://www.kisskissbankbank.com/

Movere—Brazilian all-or-nothing crowdfunding site
Fees: Approximately 12 percent for successful projects
Time frame: thirty to sixty days
http://www.movere.me

Pozible—Australian all-or-nothing crowdfunding platform. Projects must be invited by Pozible employees (via a submission form on their website), or previous successful project owners
Fees: 5–7.5 percent for successful projects + credit/debit card transaction fees
Time frame: up to ninety days
http://www.pozible.com

Rockethub—Global platform
Fees: 8 percent for successful project; no fee for an unsuccessful campaign
Time frame: Open
www.Rockethub.com

Sponsume—European platform that sells project "vouchers" that can be exchanged for rewards. The site is planning to launch in the USA
Fees: No fees
Time frame: Open (but nine months is suggested)
http://www.sponsume.com/

10

Beg, Borrow, and Negotiate—Local Heroes and Hopefuls

Begging, borrowing and negotiating is best suited to independent filmmakers with:

- A non-commercial project
- A self-funded project
- A low-budget project
- Few or no industry contacts
- Lots of contacts in the corporate and business world
- The ability to offer everyone who contributed to the film a credit and a DVD of the finished film for their showreel
- The desire to develop creative filmmaking skills without the editorial constraints of working on a commercial project
- A strong sense of ethics, e.g. you will give crew a share of any subsequent profits if they contribute their labor for free or deferred payment
- No other options
- Chutzpah

> *We're living in a moment of tremendous change, and the industry is spitting out filmmakers every day, and can't afford them in the first place ... It's like the Wild West in some ways. It's the gold rush without the remuneration!*
>
> —Lucy Walker (Director, *Waste Land*)

It's likely that at some point in your career you will find it impossible to raise money from traditional sources such as TV channels, distributors or funds because you are just starting out and don't have a track record with which to reassure funders, or because you are making a passion project for which there is little or no commercial interest. When Ricki Stern was trying to raise funding for *Joan Rivers: A Piece of Work*, she kept getting knocked back by TV executives who said, "We love Joan but she's not our demographic" (broadcasters tend to chase the demographic that most pleases the advertisers—those aged between eighteen and forty-five years old). Ricki has her own production company, Break Thru Films, so ended up funding the film from profits from her other projects, with 50 percent of the crew working on deferred payments for their labor. If you find yourself in this position you are in good company; even renowned filmmakers have had to resort to low- to no-budget filmmaking techniques.

What's important, whatever type of funding you seek, is to have some kind of fallback plan in place if the funding doesn't fall into place immediately (which it won't). "Be very strategic in advance about how you are going to support yourself," advises filmmaker Lindsey Dryden. "Be realistic about the length of time it will take, and give yourself time for development, pitching and fundraising, and work out how you are going to support yourself financially during that process. I've had to cobble together bits and pieces of freelance work since I stopped working full-time in TV production—I'm used to doing that now and I like it—but at the beginning it was quite difficult to do six jobs at once."

Cut the Budget

The simplest thing to do if your funding doesn't match your budget is to cut your budget to match the funding you have in place (or are likely to get). And having a small budget doesn't mean that your film won't be noticed; the controversial documentary *Catfish* became a festival favorite, but it was shot for just $2,000, which paid for HD cameras and plane tickets, and cost around $30,000 in total to make.

There are a number of ways to reduce costs:

1. **Shorten the shooting and post-production schedule**—which reduces the number of weeks you need to hire crew, kit and facilities. There is a temptation to set off and shoot whatever you find when making an observational or

vérité film, but this increases the amount of time you'll have to spend in the edit (which is expensive). A period of research before you set off can help you identify key events around which you can build your film within a limited timeframe. This doesn't mean that you have to shoot in six weeks rather than six months, just that you might have to limit the number of days within those six months and spread them out, or take a break between shooting and editing to give yourself time to raise, or save the money you need to complete it.

2. **Reduce the crew**—you might decide to self-shoot or edit rather than hire crew. This could be a false economy if your skills aren't up to standard, and shooting and editing on your own can mean that you won't have the necessary objectivity in the edit to recognize and tease out the best narrative.

3. **Save on travel costs**—use budget hotels and airlines where possible; limit the number of locations you visit; stay on the couches of friends and family.

4. **Cut down on expensive shots**—do you really need a helicopter shot?

5. **Rethink the use of archive, music and graphics**—some commercial music is extremely expensive to clear for worldwide use. Assess whether you can use stock music or hire a composer to do it more cost-effectively. Archive footage can also be prohibitively expensive, as *Senna* director Asif Kapadia discovered: "When I was asked to do the film the budget had been put together in a more conventional documentary way," he told reporters, "so there was forty minutes of interviews, talking heads, and forty minutes of Bernie [Ecclestone]'s archive." But he wanted to tell the story of racing driver Ayrton Senna entirely though archive, so he "cut this film which was seven hours of archive! Now, every minute over forty was something like £30,000 or something crazy. So, we were like £5 million over budget! I was accused of doing everything I could to get fired!" Think about cutting the amount of archive you need to use, negotiate a better deal or find a different way of telling the story. You might be able find a talented up-and-coming graphics artist who will do your graphics for a good rate. Try asking for recommendations at colleges and universities. The BBC managed to make several CGI-heavy documentary series, such as the BAFTA-nominated *Seven Wonders of the Industrial World* and *Hiroshima* using the visual effects skills of an ex-student of West Surrey Collage of Art and Design, England; he was affordable because he was working out of his bedroom. Fast forward several years and Gareth Edwards was the writer/director/cinematographer/production designer/VFX artist of the multi-award-winning

sci-fi feature film *Monsters*. Hiring a graphics house outside of expensive cities such as London and New York is another way to reduce costs.

Going through the budget line by line is useful exercise because it forces you to really examine your narrative and work out what is essential, and what doesn't need to be shot.

Work as a Gun-for-Hire on Commercial Projects

Many people work day jobs and make their films on the side, or alternate between working paying gigs and working on their own project. This is a situation mid-career filmmakers increasingly find themselves in, as broadcaster budgets drop and slots get squeezed. Producers and directors with a few years' experience might not have the heavyweight reputation to secure a TV commission, but are able to find short well-paying jobs on music videos and commercials that pay enough for them to live on with enough left over for them to spend on their own project. This obviously requires a steady stream of jobs, and a documentary project that can be picked up and dropped at regular intervals. However, the advantage is that you are not pawning the family silver or maxing out your credit cards.

When Chris Atkins was making *Star Suckers*, an exposé about how tabloid newspapers print untrue stories about celebrities, he worked a series of highly paid commercial jobs to fund the film, as no one else would fund him. He negotiated a deferred payment to the post-production house and went £200,000 in debt. When the story broke that he and his team had sold fake celebrity stories to the tabloid press he was able to sell the film to More4 and secured theatrical distribution.

Music video director Alma Har'el had trouble getting funding for her first feature film, *Bombay Beach*. She told reporters, "I tried to get financing for the movie but nobody would give me money and everybody thought it was a bit of a joke—that it sounded really interesting and cool but they didn't want to put any money on it. Ironically the film would have been an "issue" film in someone else's hands and so might have been able to find support from issue-driven foundations or nonprofits. The film's got it all: a kid medicated with Ritalin, racism, blackmail, death, poverty. But instead of a hand-wringing documentary that asks the audience to feel pity or "take action," it's a beautifully shot lyrical film that combines observational scenes and choreographed dance sequences that are full of humanity and hope. No one who has seen the film would argue it wasn't worthy of funding, but creative or hybrid documentaries often struggle to find a place in a funding world that is driven by genres and commercial logic.

Pay for It Yourself

Investing some of your own money might be the only way to get your project off the ground. Chris Hedegus and D. A. Pennebaker couldn't get funding for their observational documentary about a prestigious French pastry competition, *Kings of Pastry*. The organizers, the Meilleurs Ouvriers de France, had never granted anyone permission to film the competition, and so potential funders were unwilling to commit to a project that didn't have secured access. The filmmakers used their own money to fly to France and managed to get permission to film the day before the competition started. Once they had shot the key scenes, complete with all the tension and drama of a high-profile contest, they were able to get funding from the BBC and European TV channels.

Indeed, "one of the oldest showbiz traditions for first-time filmmakers is to max out your credit cards and hit up your family and friends," says Peter Levitan, "and that's about as cost-free as you can get except for the interest you pay on your credit card, which is of course enormous." It also relies on you having a good enough credit rating to persuade banks to issue you with credit cards in the first place. But there's a limit to how much you can borrow and the debt could be with you for many, many years if you can afford to pay off only the minimum amount each month. Tim Hetherington and Sebastian Junger funded their $700K Oscar-nominated documentary *Restrepo*, about a year in the life of a US platoon stationed in Afghanistan, by maxing out their credit cards and doing a deal with Gold Crest Post-production, who agreed to do the post-production for a deferred payment.

One way of lessening the load on your credit card is to see if there are any lifestyle changes you can make that will save or bring in more money. Can you rent out your spare bedroom or sell off your unused books or clothes?

Think Laterally

If you have self-shooting and editing skills, it is possible to buy reasonably priced camera and sound kit and editing software relatively inexpensively, and make your film or program without having to find any funding at all. *Tarnation*, an award-winning documentary that used twenty years of family archive, was originally edited using iMovie, a free editing software for Mac computers, and was made for just $218 (although it cost a further $400,000 to make a theatrical version). It went on to make almost $600,000.

New York-based filmmaker Samantha Farinella had a passion for film when she left film school, but quickly learned that it wasn't a good way to make a living, so worked as a hotel concierge for several years. Her friend, Alix Olson, a spoken-word artist and comedian, persuaded her to become her tour manager. Once on the road they decided to start filming their adventures, which became a ninety-minute documentary, *Left Lane*. "I bought a camera with my own money that cost about $4,000 with microphone and everything. I love to shoot and direct, and I know how to edit, but I don't have the speed or the talent to actually edit, so I usually hire an editor, which in turn costs money. My mother gave me a $15,000 inheritance from my grandfather that was supposed to be for grad school. I put that in and Alix also kicked in $15,000 and we made the film for $30,000. I have a friend who owns a post-production house, so we edited there for six months and they only charged us $10,000, which is dirt cheap." Samantha decided to enter the film into the festival circuit, starting with the New York Gay and Lesbian Film Festival. "Luckily, it won the audience award for best feature film and after that an avalanche of festivals wanted it, so it was just great. It went into another fifty festivals; we were flown out to New Zealand for Q&As and we were flown to Ireland for the Galway Film Festival. The film won eight awards. It was great, we were living the high life, it was awesome."

Shed Simove, a stand-up comedian (and ex-TV producer) took a different—and highly ingenious—route to get his show on TV. After leaving his job as commissioning editor for *Big Brother*, he started creating novelty gifts such as "Credit Crunch Breakfast Cereal," "Martin Loofah King" scrub mitt, "Clitoris Allsorts" candy and a book titled *What Every Man Thinks About Apart from Sex* (which as you might expect consisted entirely of blank pages. More unexpectedly, it shot to number forty-four on the Amazon chart.)

I was doing my stand-up routine, which is a mixture of my life and techniques for being creative involving my novelty products. A guy came up to me and he said, "Shed, I manage all the night-time slots that you see on the Shopping Channel and I think we should sell your products on television." Now, I've been interested in shopping channels for years and I've always thought they were a wonderful segment of television in their purity and honesty and the science of selling is fascinating. So I said, "Tell me more ..." He told me that these days there are various infomercial slots sold on different channels that are specifically designated for selling a product or service, and because of the diversification on the channels these days, you can pick up some of these slots very cheaply.

I was excited by this, but you have to jump through a few hoops in order to get on, you can't just broadcast content like you can on the internet, you have to go through Clearcast, the [UK's advertising] regulator. I had to create a transcript of what I wanted to say—plus there are certain rules about the top and tail of the infomercial, in which you have to say clearly that this is a paid presentation—and then you have to fill a half-hour slot or however much time you buy. The price of the slot depends on the time of day and how many people have watched that channel in the past. I managed to pick up some slots for hundreds of pounds rather than a normal advert slot, which would cost tens of thousands. It took maybe three months to [to get on air] as opposed to getting a TV show, which is more like eighteen months to two years. There are strict rules about shopping television, just as there are strict rules on normal television ... on shopping television you have to sell something, your content can't be just entertainment, you have to actively sell a product or service.

People ask me, "Why not just put it straight on YouTube?" Because television is a different medium, there is something about "as seen on TV" and there's something more exciting about being able to tell your followers, tune in tonight and set your PVR for 1 a.m. and see me on television. Television still plays a large part in many people's lives, and it's in the corner of the room, for a bit longer at least. Of course in future, YouTube will probably be in the corner of the room and big, but for now, it's still a differentiator.

Can I tell you that my infomercial sold loads and loads of products? No, it didn't. But it did give me a spike on my website and selling is all about eyeballs, and then it's about converting those eyeballs. My infomercial was a small experiment, but the fact is that I was able to get on television way, way quicker, and with far fewer barriers to entry than the traditional route.

Forget TV: Go Online

The big problem with pitching ideas to TV and other funders is that you always have to appeal to their specific agenda, and you need a track record to secure a commission. Until relatively recently, you had no other choice if you wanted your show to be seen by more people than just your friends and family. "Because of the limited amount of terrestrial channels it's tough to get on television, but it's much easier to go on YouTube and get potentially millions of viewers," says Shed. "The great thing about TV, if you have a commission, you then have the clout of the channel behind you, which shouldn't be underestimated. But there are other outlets out there for you to reach an audience without anyone telling you 'No,' which for me is wonderfully empowering and important."

Once your project is complete you can upload it online and attract an audience, just as you would in the more traditional TV space. In fact some projects have been just as, if not more, successful in the online space as they would have been on a traditional terrestrial or cable channel. *Epic Meal Time*, a food show on YouTube, has more than 600,000 subscribers and averages 2 million views per episode. (In July 2011, an episode of a cooking show, *Rick Stein's Spain*, got 2.3 million viewers on BBC2.)

Sally Bee, cookery-book author and ex-TV producer, decided to make her own web-based cooking show after failing to find funding from TV commissioners for the program she wanted to make. She'd self-published her first book before it was picked up by a publisher, and it was her publisher at HarperCollins who suggested she should take a similar tack with her TV show. "So, in this climate, I have decided, again, that I need to put my money, or rather my energy, where my mouth is," said Sally. "I see an internet show as the perfect solution as it allows me the freedom to explore my creative ideas further and see if they work in practice." As Sally is the show's host, she's roped in her husband as director and hired an editor. "In reality, production costs are low and I don't have to adhere to the strict advertising laws enforced in television. I hope to prove a viewership, and secure funding for the show through sponsorship," she says. "It feels great to be in control of my own destiny and embark on a project at a time and in a place that suits me and my other commitments."

Royston Crabaugh, an ex-NBC News producer, created a short-form reality series on YouTube. *Rap Rinse Repeat*, which was launched in September 2010, focuses on stylist Christopher Gamper and his gossipy salon clients in New York. In June 2011, Royston pitched the series to TV executives at NATPE's PitchCon conference in Los Angeles and got some initial interest from several cable channels, including TLC and Bravo. "If you don't have a big agent but have ideas for a show, PitchCon can help you meet actual decision makers at cable and broadcast networks," said Royston.

Even if you don't manage to catch the eye of a broadcaster, some people who have become stars on YouTube are making more than $40,000 a year through ads linked to their videos via the YouTube Partners program. Emily Kim gave up her job at a nonprofit when her Korean cookery show became a hit on YouTube. She now makes roughly the same amount as she did in her day job, and has invested her earnings in increasing the production values of her show.

Get Businesses to Donate Props, Locations and Equipment

When Luke Seomore and Joseph Bull were making *Isolation*, a documentary about the problems British soldiers face when they come home from war, they managed to get free equipment from the suppliers they'd worked with on music videos and commercials, as the companies liked having an association with the documentary. Their usual hire company also gave them £5,000 of kit in return for equity in the film. Their colorist and sound engineer worked on the film overnight using the same equipment they used in their day job, saving them even more money.

If you need to approach people cold (rather than calling in favors from colleagues), think about what is in it for them. For example, kit manufacturers might want someone to test a new camera in the field and therefore be able to give it you (or at least loan it) for free. It also helps to know your film's intended demographic so that can be part of your pitch to airlines, hotels or other businesses. The more upscale your audience, the more attractive they're likely to be to high-end brands.

When advertising executive Erik Proulx was laid off from his job in New York in the recession he decided to make a film about how other people in the advertising world were coping with the loss of their jobs. He put out a call for interviewees on Twitter and set in train a chain of events that led to him being able to make his 30' film entirely through donations and goodwill:

Erik asked for interviewees on Twitter

Seventy-five people responded

Picture Park, a production company in Boston, offered to film the interviews

Someone from Sony Pictures sent Erik the name of someone at a rental company who would loan cameras

A few of Erik's friends asked Virgin America via Twitter whether they would contribute free tickets

Within two hours Virgin America offered to fly the crew from Boston to Los Angeles

A journalist noticed the tweets and contacted Erik to ask if she could write an article about the film for *Fast Company*

Lemonade Movie was researched, staffed, produced and publicized through donations, contacts and volunteers found via Twitter.

Francine Heywood, a UK producer, has also been able to get money and equipment donated. "Asda gave us some money for a short film and that was done very quickly; Europcar have given us vans for our shoots in the past, also very quickly through personal connections." But even if you don't have existing connections, Francine says you can still ask. "I would start as high up as I can, so if I can find out the name of the CEO or marketing director's PA. That would be a good place to start. You tell them the story in such a way that they can see that they are helping young filmmakers and there's benefit to them in terms of getting their name attached."

If you are getting things for free, you are likely to lose some control over your shoot, says indie filmmaker Jarod Warren, because if you are relying on other people's goodwill you have to work around them. "If I need three days in one person's location, the first thing I determine is how can I shoot there without disrupting their business. So you have to organize your schedule around that, which requires a lot of forward thinking and good time management because you have to maneuver your schedule around other people's needs. What would normally be a three-day shoot in one location might get divvied up between three days over two weeks, so you need to make sure the continuity remains the same. You also need to have back-up plans, so you can say, OK we lost this location today, but we are going to move to this other location and shoot that."

Another option is the Roy W. Dean Grant, which provides goods and services rather than money. The winner of a grant receives a range of benefits, such as:

- $1,000 off the cost of a trailer edited by a famous trailor editor
- 50 percent of a consultation with a distribution specialist
- 30 percent discount off lighting services
- Three life coaching sessions
- $1,000 of voiceover services
- Photography to the value of $500
- Movie Magic Budgeting software
- 25 percent discount on legal fees

Or you could get your kit for free (or at least cheaply) by making it. For example, you can make a DIY steadycam for $14 by following the instructions on MicroFilmaker.com.* They also have DIY instructions for:

- A $10 PVC Fig Rig Camera Stabilizer
- Build your own matte box
- How to build a $100 crane
- How to build a gimble steadycam
- Make your own rollerblade dolly
- Build your own shoulder mount

Ask Post-production Facilities to Defer Payment

Parthenon, a producer and distributor, also owns facility and graphics houses and they will sometimes trade use of those facilities. It's likely that a facilities house will want a share in the equity in return for providing free post-production.

*www.microfilmmaker.com/tipstrick/Issue1/steadycam.html.

Ask the Crew to Defer Payment

In a deferment arrangement, the crew (including the producer) agree to postpone the receipt of some or all of the payment for their work and to receive the rest when more money is raised (and there's no guarantee that it will), so it's a high-risk strategy for the crew. Think about what else you could offer to sweeten the deal.

Find Crew Who Will Work for Free

Another way of slashing your budget is to get other people to work on your film for free. When David Bond was making *Erasing David*, a film that explored issues around privacy and civil liberties in the UK, he asked the crews he usually uses to make his corporate videos to make the trailer. He often hires the same kit and crew so he was able to persuade them to work for free as a favor, but he stressed that it's better to ask people with whom you have a reciprocal relationship of some sort, and not to expect strangers to work for free.

The Edit Center in New York offers filmmakers free rough-cut editing through its six-week Final Cut Pro editing course (for which the students pay a course fee). Selected films are put through the class and have twelve or so editors of varying levels of skill working on different sequences. "It's really great for first- or second-time filmmakers who have limited funds, which often happens when you get to the end of the project. When you get to post production, oftentimes your budget has been spent," says director of education, Rachel Mills. "It's completely free to the filmmakers." The students learn to edit on real-world films (many of which go on to win awards at Sundance and other prestigious festivals) so the Edit Center presents a win-win situation for both students and filmmakers.

However, when you are asking people to work for free, with no prospect of anything in return (such as training), you are stepping into murky ethical territory. Someone made the point, during a lively panel discussion on the subject at an industry event, that raising the budget is an integral part of the production process and you shouldn't hire a crew on a professional production until you have raised enough money to pay them properly. The feeling from part of the audience (which was split on the subject), was that some unscrupulous filmmakers used the excuse of a low budget as a lazy way to avoid fundraising, while maximizing their own potential for making money out of the project at the back end. An editor in New York described having to beg their trust-fund-supported director for (repeatedly late) payments because he couldn't afford to pay his rent; the director wasn't being deliberately unkind, he just didn't comprehend that, for some people, money is a matter of day-to-day survival.

Eric Glatt has worked on both paid and unpaid projects. "I worked as an unpaid intern on a documentary film that went to the Tribeca Film Festival and it was interesting that when the term of the unpaid internship was over the director kept me on, but rather than pay, offered to bump up the credit. So the director was still benefiting from unpaid labor, and a novice like me got something better by staying on longer term. But then I worked as a paid PA for a short documentary film that won an Oscar, and that director was very insistent about paying people for their work as a matter of principle. She is probably the only person I've ever met with that attitude in this practice." Understandably he's against the exploitative nature of the business. "I know that filmmaking is perhaps the most collaborative art form there is; it's almost impossible to make a film entirely all by yourself, like you could with painting or sculpture or music. Also, it's very expensive and a lot of people who are just starting out need to establish their artistic voice and don't have a lot of funds, so they rely on favors. I get it. But there are postings for people to work for free on network TV shows and studio pictures. That's just outrageous. One of the things that keeps that structure in place is the fact that if I don't accept that unpaid internship somebody else will. There are plenty of upper-middle-class kids who can afford, because of their parents' generosity, to work for free for six months. But other people don't have that luxury. Because some people are willing to undermine even basic minimum wage laws, it undermines the sustainability of a whole segment of the labor force and it puts a lot of negative pressure on wages."

BECTU, the UK's film and TV union, tackled this issue in a debate with Shooting People, which led to them drawing up some guidelines (*Guidelines for New Filmmakers—Make Your Film: Keep Your Friends*, available from http://www.bectu.org.uk) to help filmmakers differentiate between a project that is a genuine creative collaboration (which people are happy to work on for the joy or experience of it, rather than for any kind of financial recompense) and those on which producers cynically exploit free labor on a commercial project. They point out that even if you are making a non-commercial voluntary project you still have legal obligations regarding health and safety, must make sure you have appropriate production insurance and pay out-of-pocket expenses to your crew. If there is any commercial intent, i.e. you intend to sell and distribute your film, then you are running a commercial business with all the legal responsibilities (including as an employer) that entails. If in any doubt, take advice.

How to Pitch to Businesses and Individuals

In a situation where you are asking for something—products, services or labor—it has to be a deal that is beneficial for everyone. You know what you want out of the deal, but work out what the other party might be happy to get out of the negotiation. It might be to have their business's name or logo on the end credits, or to have your crew wear their branded baseball caps on location or receive an invitation for all their staff to attend a VIP screening. Small businesses often respond better to requests for freebies. "I absolutely prefer going to private businesses," says Jarod Warren. "Small businesses need to get their name everywhere, so what better than to get their name on a film? When the film releases and people watch the credits they will see the special thanks and so they start generating business."

When pitching to a business it's likely you'll have to sell your film face-to-face (in the case of a local business) or over the phone, so practice making your pitch short and relevant to the person whom you are approaching. Does your film speak directly to their customers in some way? Or is it concerned with an issue that is of relevance locally? Or might the company be in need of some good PR? If you are approaching a larger corporation they will consider whether the subject of your film is something they want their brand to be aligned with, and might ask you to send some footage. "It's not just about salesmanship, it's about honesty," says Jarod. But it's not a job for wallflowers: "You need to be a go-getter, you have to be willing to engage with people you have never met before, because if you just go mumbling along, you are not going to get anybody's support for anything." If you aren't the most confident sweet-talker on your team, delegate the job to someone else.

Advantages of Begging, Borrowing and Negotiating

1. You have complete editorial control—you don't have a broadcaster or other funder to take into consideration
2. You will get a response to your requests relatively quickly
3. You can repeat the process as many times as you like to cover different parts of the budget

Disadvantages

1. You are at the mercy of people who might not follow through on promises of help or donations of equipment
2. Crew might want equity in the project in return for their labor
3. You risk souring relations with colleagues and friends if they feel that you took unfair advantage of them
4. Your film might have poor production values

Next Steps

1. Make a list of friends and family who might be willing and able to help or donate locations or props
2. Identify local businesses that might be willing to donate something in return for an end credit or other publicity. For instance, a sandwich shop might feed the crew, a printer might provide posters and flyers or a local car hire company might provide a van
3. Identify national or international corporations that might be willing to help out, e.g. airlines and hotels
4. Work out what you need from each potential donor and what you can offer in return
5. Start making some approaches. Don't get discouraged if the first few people you ask say no

Jargon Buster

Term	Meaning
Deferred Payment	An arrangement in which it is agreed that crew (including the producer) or post-production facilities house will accept a delayed payment of part or all of their fee, in order to allow the film to be made on a lower budget. They are paid the money owed to them out of income from sales of the finished film (if there are any).
In-kind	A type of non-monetary donation of goods or services.
Intern	A short-term paid or unpaid position in which someone works with the intent of gaining experience in a certain field. All countries (and some US states) have their own regulations regarding the

use of unpaid interns. Formal internships run in conjunction with universities might offer an academic credit; most interns will be hopeful that their internship will lead to a long-term paid position.

Work Experience   UK equivalent of intern. Intended to be a way of undergoing on-the-job learning and training, therefore a person undergoing work experience shouldn't undertake work that would ordinarily be carried out by a paid member of crew. National Minimum Wage Regulations might apply to individuals on work experience placement depending on the nature of their duties.

Further Reading and Resources

'Guidance for New Filmmakers—Make Your Film: Keep Your Friends'—BECTU Union guidelines for setting up an unincorporated association in order to clarify your film's status as a non-commercial voluntary project
http://www.bectu.org.uk/advice-resources/library/955

MicroFilmmaker Magazine—Dozens of articles on making no-budget films, including instructions for making your own equipment
http://microfilmmaker.com

Money Saving Expert—UK site detailing the best 0 percent credit card deals, discounts and vouchers for meals, hotels and travel
http://www.moneysavingexpert.com

NATPE Pitch Con—Annual event in January that matches people with ideas with development executives for one-on-one pitch meetings in Miami Beach. The site also has tips on pitching ideas
http://www.pitchcon.org/

New York Women in Film and Television—Offer in-kind post-production completion grants (for an online and/or sound mix session) to films produced and directed by women in New York
http://www.nywift.org

The Angry Filmmaker Survival Guide: Part One—Making the Extreme No Budget Film by Kelley Baker, Booksurge Llc (2009)—No-holds-barred guide to independent filmmaking from Gus Van Sant's sound designer. He directed (among others) a fiction feature in eighteen days on a budget of $6,000. There are lots of other resources—"Cool Crap to Own"—on his website
http://www.angryfilmmaker.com

The Big Art/Little Debt Plan: Balancing Risk and Responsibility While Making Great Films by Ester B. Robinson—A five-step plan for getting your film made if you don't have a trust fund, *Filmmaker Magazine*, Winter 2010
http://www.filmmakermagazine.com/issues/winter2010/successful-filmmaker.php

The Edit Center—An edit facility in New York that trains people to use Final Cut Pro. As a (narrative/fiction or documentary) filmmaker, you can have your rushes turned into a "rough" rough-cut for free. Films that have gone through the center include *Winter's Bone, Frozen River, Hot Coffee, Garbage Dreams* and *Strange Powers: Stephin Merritt and the Magnetic Fields*. See the interview with the Edit Center's Director of Education, Rachel Mills, in Part III, for more details of how the scheme works
http://www.theeditcenter.com

The Roy W. Dean Grant—Provides three grants per year of goods and services for films with budgets of less than $500,000 that are "unique and make a contribution to society." You can apply from anywhere in the world, but must film in Los Angeles or New York in order to take advantage of the grant
http://www.fromtheheartproductions.com

PART III:
The Reality

Tales from the Frontlines of Film Finance: The Players and Producers

> *Networking is really important, because you realize that the people who don't have a track record and don't have any contacts, where do they go?*
>
> —Leigh Gibson (Producer, *The Boy Mir*)

Players

Véronique Bernard
President, Iliad Entertainment, New York City
www.iliadentertainment.com
@verobernard

Iliad Entertainment helps producers develop their non-fiction TV ideas for the international market and sources co-production and presales money from international broadcasters.

"We mainly represent non-fiction television projects, and we do it in four ways:

1. We help American production companies who need international co-pro money and don't really know where to start;
2. We sell American producers' projects to US broadcasters where we have the relationships and they don't;
3. We represent international content that we bring into the US;
4. We sell projects from international producers to channels all around the world.

"Producers can come from any country and the buyers can come from any country. We work quite a lot with Asia and there are a lot of opportunities for non-Asian producers to get co-production partners in Asia. There are also lots of very interesting producers coming out of Asia with product and content that has international legs, especially food and travel programs that aren't too culturally specific.

"Our decision to take something on or not is based on whether we think we can sell it to our extensive network of contacts in the market. I would say it takes six months to sell a show, realistically. If you can get the whole budget from one broadcaster, then bingo! But if you need to negotiate between a number of different parties, then it takes longer.

"Things that would make the project exciting are unique characters, unique access, or unique expertise in the subject matter that gives an insight into a particular world. Those are the three ingredients: if you have one of those ingredients it's good, if you have two it's even better and if you have three, then that's a winning trifecta. The concept itself is not enough on its own, in fact the idea is probably about the fourth thing you look at because people have ideas all the time.

"We also consider the person who's bringing the project. What's their personal connection to it? There has to be some passion there between the producer and their particular idea. I've had people pitching me who say, 'Oh, I don't want to make it, I just want to sell it and make some money,' and I think, hmm, I don't think so. There's got to be a reason why it's *you*, as a producer, with *this* idea. We have to go in and not only sell the idea but sell the producer. Now if you don't have a lot of experience that's fine, because we can partner you with more experienced people, but you must bring something to the table, and that starts with your connection to the project. If it's something you feel really passionate about, and it's your unique insight, it makes sense that you are attached to the project.

"Life's too short to work with difficult producers. The beauty of working for yourself is that you can pick and choose who you work with, you don't have to do it just to do it; I prefer the idea of a partnership. We are a small boutique, only working with say fifty projects, and so we want to have the personal touch with each one. There is no idea that is so good that you are prepared to sacrifice a good working relationship with a channel. What would be warning flags? Producers who don't listen, producers who don't seem to have a realistic grasp of the industry or the market generally, or who are just not in touch with reality. That happens a lot.

"Our business model is that we make the bulk of our income when we sell something. We charge a flat fee upfront and we really help producers develop their idea to get it to the pitch stage. Once we sell something, we take a percentage of the budget that we raise. So say we are working with an Australian production company that already has an Australian broadcaster onboard, we will take a percentage on the funding we bring by getting a US partner, a European partner or whoever. So if we bring in 40 percent of the overall budget, we take a percentage cut of that.

"I like to get in as early as possible because then there is still time to develop the project and show it off at its best in terms of the co-production partners we might approach. So early is better. But I have taken projects on at any stage throughout development, pre-production, production and post-, as long as they are not completed, finished shows. I am not a sales agent. I am interested in something where money still needs to be raised in order to complete it and that's where I can be helpful.

"Sometimes I stay on the project as executive producer. The payment for that is a line in the budget and is agreed upfront as part of the production agreement. Sometimes the broadcaster requests that because they know me and feel comfortable that I know how to deliver. That's particularly true when I'm pitching a project from an international producer or somebody they don't know. Alternatively, the producer might suggest it because they feel that I know that market better than they do and that I can provide that guidance."

What do producers need to know about international co-productions?
"There is a language issue, so if you are working in an English-speaking company it helps to work with another English-speaking company. And culturally, different ways of storytelling work better in some countries than others. For example, Australian work translates really well in the US, the UK and Canada. But I've done US co-productions with both France and Germany so it depends on the subject matter. Some subjects are more suited to large international co-pros and some are more suited to specific countries. Docuseries and docusoaps don't easily translate in the international market, but history or science programs tend to have broader international appeal.

"Every production is a co-production really because even if it's just you and one broadcaster it's already a co-production; you aren't just going off and making whatever you want to make, there's a huge editorial dialogue going on all the way through. For an international co-production it just multiplies, so instead of having one buyer you might have two or three. All the broadcasters have to be in agreement over major issues like style and storytelling and content, so that should be discussed early on. What it means in practice is that you have more masters to please, so I can liaise between all those different partners, making sure that everything is smooth in terms of production, because you don't want to have to end up making three or four different versions (unless you've agreed to do that upfront). Anything that has to be specifically produced for one of the partners significantly increases the budget and we have to work out how you are going to pay for that."

How best to pitch to you?

"We ask for something in writing first, because time is short and I don't really want to take a meeting if I already know from a paragraph that something isn't going to work for us. In a good written pitch you need to get across what the program is in the opening paragraph: the format, the genre etc. A great logline is good, and if there isn't one I will try and create one. A logline is basically a one-line description that encapsulates the essence of the show, and sells it in a positive way, shows it off at its best: what would be the line that describes the show in the TV guide? Something that's going to make the audience want to watch, and in a few words tells them what this show is about, so they can decide whether it's the kind of show they like. It's a very American thing to do, and it's been going on in the industry since the beginning of Hollywood.

"Another thing that helps—and there's disagreement in the industry on this— but I think that it helps if you can refer to a couple of existing shows as models. You can say it's 'this show meets that show,' but try not to use overused ones. There was a period when everything was '*Mythbusters* meets ...,' or '*Queer Eye* meets ...,' and they were done to death. Think about successful shows that your show is reminiscent of, and then point out how it's different, the new twist.

"The written pitch should be short. A one-pager or a two-pager at most to begin with: if you can't get us to understand what your show is in one or two pages, then there is something wrong with it.

"Tape is key, and we always encourage people to make one. These days, with the equipment that's available, no one is looking for a polished Hollywood production in a sizzle reel, but you should be able to translate the winning elements of your show into some kind of visual tape. We don't invest in sizzle reels, they are on the producer's dime; you don't have to spend tens of thousands of dollars, but it is still going to cost. If it's a producer who can't afford to do that then we will try to pair them up with a production company that would be interested in then producing the show with them, and maybe they would be able to invest in creating a sizzle reel. These days a sizzle isn't presented on tape, it's not even on a DVD—you can just send a link."

How do you pitch to broadcasters?

"We pitch the idea *and* the producer, the whole package. We see the broadcasters face-to-face at least twice a year or more; we might wait until one of these face-to-face meetings, or just shoot an email saying, 'Hi, we have this show, what do you think, are you interested in seeing it?' Since we tend to work with people that we've known for a long time we can do that. We don't have to have a formal meeting every six months where we come in with our fifteen pitches or anything like that, so it's a bit more proactive and on a rolling basis."

What if the producer/director is inexperienced?

"Production companies take pitches all the time from up-and-coming or emerging producers who understand that they are not going to get a meeting at a network without being partnered with an agent or an established production company. We would broker that deal and bring the partners together in a way that the person who brought the idea will be involved in the production. If the idea comes from somebody who has less experience, they are not going to be series producer on that production, but you can always attach them and bring on a showrunner who has experience of doing that particular type of show. We would never want the producer who had come up with the idea and brought it to us to lose their involvement with the show, so we make sure that is in the contract. The risk is that the originating producer loses complete control, but you lose that anyway when you are working with a broadcaster because they are calling the shots."

Are producers involved in the pitch to the broadcasters?

"Sometimes, but not often. A lot of producers aren't able to be at the big markets so that's why we go and pitch on their behalf. But if we feel that having the producer in the room is going to enhance the selling of the show—if they have technical expertise, for example—then they are going to be able to answer certain questions much better than we can; in that case we would bring them along to talk to the broadcaster."

What mistakes do people make when pitching their projects to you?

1. "Assuming that content that is of interest in their own territory will be of interest internationally. Broadcasting is really local and broadcasters are looking for local stories. So in order for something to appeal internationally, it needs to have something that is going to make it of interest in another territory.

2. A lot of producers think that they can sell their project internationally before they have sold it in their own territory. We can take projects out internationally before they have a local buyer, but you really want to have that local partner onboard because a UK or French broadcaster isn't going to commission an Australian or American producer to make a show just for them: they have producers within their own borders with whom they have existing relationships that they prefer to go to.

3. Likewise, people think they can sell a format before it's been produced in their own territory. A format on a paper is just that—a format doesn't exist until it's been produced, so it's not something you can sell internationally.

4. Some producers are not prepared to adapt their project to a co-producer's needs. Which is not to say you have to sell your soul, but you have to prepared to be a little bit flexible."

Elizabeth Radshaw

Director of the Hot Docs Forum and Market, Hot Docs Canadian International Documentary Festival, Toronto
www.hotdocs.ca
@hotdocs

Elizabeth Radshaw has run the industry and market events at the Hot Docs festival in Toronto since 2008. One of the main events is a two-day public pitching forum where selected filmmakers pitch their films to a panel of broadcasters in the hope of securing co-production funding.

"The goal of Hot Docs Forum is to find funding and support for original and unique international content. Over fifteen years ago, the big international pitching forums like Hot Docs and IDFA (International Documentary Film Festival Amsterdam) were set up to facilitate international co-production at a time when broadcasters had less interaction with each other. They were great opportunity for:

- filmmakers to present their work in front of ten or fifteen broadcasters
- individual broadcasters to identify projects they were interested in
- broadcasters to build relationships with other broadcasters, which helped them to co-opt each other to complete the financing for projects they wanted to get off the ground
- launching new and emerging production companies

"The forums were originally intended to finance auteur documentary, not factual TV series, but the industry has evolved. Recently the big forums like IDFA and Hot Docs have had to struggle with a shift in the market and the shift in financing structures. Year in, year out, there are fewer slots for documentaries on television and lower license fees. This year, the majority of the proposals were from established production companies because they are not getting money from their traditional funding sources. My belief about who might be a market partner is also becoming broader.

"We work with the producers of selected projects via weekly Skype/phone calls in the weeks leading up to the festival; we do our best to be a sounding board for their story ideas and financing strategies, and offer feedback on pitch technique and trailers. We introduce the filmmakers to potential buyers and have them build up a relationship ahead of time before they all sit at the table and have to pitch in front of an audience. Some film foundations are a constant presence at the forum and they sit alongside specially invited broadcasters and brands.

"We also help educate filmmakers in the audience about what makes a great pitch. Most of the time individuals around the table are quite candid about their opinions of the work. My favorite reactions are when a commissioner can say, 'Look, there's no place on my channel for this, my controller's going to kill me, but this project means x, y and z to me and I want to be a part of it so I'm going to find a way ...,' and so you start to understand where commissioners can support work, which could be critical for when you are pitching your own work.

"Some of the pitched projects collapse—and that can happen for any number of reasons—but I know of many producers who have gotten other projects on their slate commissioned because of the meetings they took at the forum. That's pretty amazing."

Won't ideas get stolen when pitched in such a public forum?

"That will always happen, even if you are not in a public forum. But I can't tell you how many projects I've seen repeated: sometimes even the same characters are pitched! Frankly, there are only so many stories in this world and filmmakers need to get over that. The most important thing is that filmmakers have an exclusive access with their contributor(s) and offer something unique in their telling of the story."

How can I get a place in the forum?

"Read the rules and fill out the form properly. Not doing so is the biggest reason why people get disqualified. We are flexible, but you've got to understand what we are trying to achieve—projects need to be strong and international in scope, with well thought-through audience engagement, interactive and distribution strategies."

Mark Starowicz

Executive Director, Documentary Programming, Canadian Broadcasting Company, Toronto

www.cbc.ca

CBC is Canada's public service network. Mark Starowicz, who heads up their documentary department, explains how a complicated co-production can be made to work from a channel's perspective.

"We have both an in-house production section and an independent commissioning section: we are quite unusual that way. We have two strands, *Doc Zone* and *The Nature of Things*, a science strand, and both strands commission pograms from independent producers.

"When we commission a documentary in Canada, our commissioning essentially triggers access to independent documentary funds that allow you to finance 80 percent of your documentary. We won't pay you 80 percent of the budget: we pay you about 35 percent and then pretty much all of the other financing, such as provincial incentives, falls into place. The rest of the budget can be raised from a second window broadcaster in Canada and an offshore customer. We also do 50/50 co-productions with foreign partners where we split the bill.

"We had a co-production for a program called *China Rises*, which is a case of a good collaboration between networks. A lot of the best ideas aren't necessarily proposals written on paper, they come up in the bar, when meeting people; a lot of them are about commissioning people getting together and saying, 'It would be great to do something on this.' So, that's what happened. We had a serendipitous meeting with the *New York Times*, which had a television channel and a partnership with Discovery. We hit it off, brainstorming ideas about China and what should be done and this and that. We proposed the idea of a four-hour, four-part documentary on the reawakening in China, both the light side and the dark side of it. Each episode follows about six characters; you see China through those individuals' stories.

"We brought in our colleagues at France 5, ZDF in Germany, and S4C in Wales, and each one had specific needs, so it was obvious we would need four directors. The Welsh were happy to produce the Welsh-language version of it, so basically the other four participants would each produce one of the hours. We appointed one hands-on executive producer, who would run those four directors and we agreed that they had to be approved by everybody. So that was a case where five parties—four networks plus the *New York Times*—split the bill equally.

"The *New York Times* then picked an independent producer they had the most confidence in, and ZDF picked the German producer, S4C hired an independent to do the Welsh version and we had an in-house person do ours. It was a mixture of in-house and independent and different languages. It sounds like a formula for a disaster but it worked spectacularly well.

"It worked because we brainstormed regularly by conference call through the entire concept and development stage. We needed to agree on some things before the cement set, such as the graphics style, how the interviews were framed etc., so we had to come up with a cinematic bible. We outlined what we wanted in each episode and came up with several very detailed pages. We spoke every five or six weeks through production to make sure that we were all still going the same way; there were arguments but they were contained and we settled everything. The different producers assisted each other too, which helped with efficiencies. So someone who was shooting in Guangzhou in southern China would shoot stuff for somebody on another episode who couldn't afford to go to Guangzhou because they were working in northern China.

"I think what often happens with these co-productions is that you get excited about a well-written proposal, and you commission something, but then you don't see the person again for about six months, and you get something back that isn't quite the meal that you thought you ordered. If three broadcasters have commissioned one independent to make something, sometimes three people end up not getting the meals that they thought they'd ordered. That happens because the independent producer is working on his own and the story evolves into something different than he set out to make, but there's been no communication with the channel. That's when you get that horrible feeling in your stomach in the rough-cut.

"An existing relationship between channels is an enormous advantage in a co-production. If I know that I am going to end up giving notes on a rough-cut with someone I've worked with before, let's say my opposite number at ZDF or somebody I know at the BBC, then that's a great comfort level. It's much more difficult with a broadcaster you've never worked with before, or whose editing and pacing style or audience is enormously different. If, however, you have put in 40 percent and you are working with a familiar channel that has put in 40 percent and a third broadcaster, who you don't know, has put in 20 percent of the financing, that's less worrying.

"As an independent producer you are just lucky to get a sale, so if you've landed a sale at Channel 4, say, it's not a bad strategy to find out which channel they normally co-produce with and see if you can get them to climb onboard. You could even ask your Channel 4 commissioner if they will call their contact at the other channel to make the introduction."

Carl Hall

CEO, Parthenon Entertainment, London
www.parthenonentertainment.com

Carl Hall runs a hybrid distribution and production company that specializes in specialist factual—science, history and natural history—and children's programming. He explains how distributors buy and sell TV programs at the major TV markets such as MIPTV and MIPDOC.

"I became a distributor because I didn't want anybody else to be selling the programs I'd made. I wanted a boutique that was about finding the right customers for little gems, not selling fodder.

"There are probably forty people in the world who control factual programming on TV; they are the gatekeepers for all programs and they travel to the big markets. To get a meeting with those people, you need more than one project, because they don't have time to have 400 small one-off meetings. A channel executive can have one meeting with a distributor and see thirty projects in less than half an hour at the markets. Between markets we also travel to see the international channels because there's nothing like sitting in a buyer's office. We become sub-commissioners in a way, because we know what channels want for the next season, and so we can act as a filter and hunt things down for them. When we go to the markets we have a combined acquisitions, development and sales role, so we are both pitching and being pitched to; it is funny how you can switch on and off between the two.

"Charming producers can do really well at the markets, and this is where producers can miss a trick sometimes. You can tell who the really good producers are because the sales team is more than happy to take them along to a meeting in Cannes and introduce them as the producer of the program they are trying to sell. The buyer is sitting in a darkened room for days, never going anywhere, so if a producer can come along and tell a story of how they got bitten by a lion in Africa, that's a sale.

"We need to have a certain rate of financial return, so we do business plans for each program and the sales team are measured against what they say they are going to deliver. For example, if they've promised they will deliver sales in the US but they don't, we could be in a lot of trouble at the end of the year, so someone else in the sales team has to over-deliver to make up the loss. There is a lot of internal pressure.

"We sign up programs for a set number of years. When you sell transmission rights to a broadcaster it's normally for an exclusive seven-year license, so the distributor needs longer than that to exploit all the other rights. We'd probably want a minimum of ten years on a bigger project because there is always a new channel launching that is keen for more content. DVD still accounts for approximately 20 percent of our turnover and DVD rights now have merged with VOD, so downloads have also become quite lucrative."

What's a distribution advance?

"A distribution advance is a figure based on the sales projection and the needs of the project and can come in several forms:

- Deficit finance (top-up funding)—if you've sold your show to Channel 5, but you still need to find the final 20 percent, we can give you 20 percent of your budget. We will then sell the program to other territories outside the UK until we've recouped our money, and then any money that comes in after that goes to you, minus our commission.
- Cash flow—in a presale, a channel agrees to buy the program but they don't pay anything until the finished program is actually delivered to them. So you know the money is coming, but you don't actually receive it in time to finance the production phase. So an advance these days is more likely to be an upfront payment that cash flows the actual production and is usually paid on agreed milestones.
- Advance against future sales—if it's for a finished program (an acquisition) the advance is a one-off payment that is a percentage of the projected sales that the distributor expects to make.

"Being a distributor used to be the best job in the world; we could just top up the last 20 percent of the budget and get all rights worldwide. Now we have to help the program get made, and can end up funding and cash flowing the whole program. Out of that we get a distribution fee, but we might get some of the back end as well depending on the amount of risk we take. Top-up funding is not so interesting to distributors anymore, because it's not worth it, so many programs fall over because they can't close the last 20 percent of the budget. When you think that production fees are about 10–15 percent it means that producers are forced to say, 'I won't make any money, I'll just make the program and then make the money on the next one,' and subsequently they go bust a couple of months later.

"The thing about a distribution advance is that it shows goodwill, because the distributor is on the hook with you and will be working hard to recoup that money. As they are financially invested in your program they are unlikely to pull the plug on it if the going gets a bit tough. If they have no financial investment they can experience a bit of malaise when the market goes cold and stop selling it as enthusiastically as they might."

How else can a distributor help me to finance my project?

"Parthenon also own facility and graphics houses. Post-production and graphics often makes up 25–30 percent of the budget, so we can often do the post-production in exchange for getting the distribution rights. If we take over post-production for the final 20 percent of the budget the advantage is that you've probably got only two other co-producers [broadcasters] on the production with only one of them driving the editorial (as opposed to having to deal with three or more broadcasters that all want something unique if you've sourced 100 percent of your budget through co-production deals).

"Another common scenario is that a US broadcaster wants a host in the program but the rest of the world don't. We'll put in the extra money to shoot some wraparounds to make a hostless version."

Are there any other advantages to working with a distributor?

"Being a small independent production company now is much harder than ten years ago and lot of producers just don't have the business nous. Say you make one £500,000 sixty-minute film (which is a huge budget), the production fee is likely to be 10–15 percent, so you are making about £75,000. That doesn't seem like that much when you can be a line producer earning £50,000 without any of the aggravations by working for somebody else. So unless you can reach a critical mass of five or six commissions a year, it becomes very marginal as a business. By partnering with a distributor, you can still work as an indie, but we take care of the business side of things.

"For example, we have a whole team that just looks after the deliverables. We have six people working for us fact-checking and looking after delivery of National Geographic programs alone. You also get legal input free of charge as part of the distributor service, because we have to check everything out to make sure we are not in breach of all the underlying rights. There's also the risk of breaching holdback windows (where a TV channel has exclusive transmission rights for a certain period of time). So, for example, if you've sold your film to an airline for its in-flight entertainment system, you don't want the top executive of a channel with which you've done an exclusive deal to take a flight somewhere and say, 'I've just bought that program, what's it doing on this airline?' Sometimes when individual producers have sold some of their own rights we've had to approach a broadcaster and say, 'Sorry about this, could you go nonexclusive in the following territories, because this guy's done this deal ...'

"Sadly, the other thing we have to do now that we never had to do before is to make the broadcasters pay up. They always used to be really good payers, but now they're absolutely terrible. Sometimes we have to get heavy and recall rights if they don't pay on time.

"You could get a loan from a bank rather than take money from a distributor, but your program is no good as collateral so you have to put something more tangible up like your house, your car, or your granny ... and guarantee it. That's all they are interested in. Distributors can go to the bank themselves and pass on the money to the producer, because we can borrow against the value of our library, assets, buildings and everything we own, not on your individual show. The same goes for E&O (errors and omission) insurance, which can cost you £3,000–£4,000 just for a one-hour show. We distributors all have blanket policies that cost tens of thousands of pounds, so we can save you a lot of incidental costs.

"You could go to a bigger indie and ask them to warehouse you (provide the production back-up to reassure TV commissioners and other buyers), but if they are working on margins of 10–15 percent, then there's not a lot of money to split, and you might end up with just 5 percent. If you work with a distributor you keep your own 10 percent production fee and are learning how to do it for yourself next time."

What does it cost to have a distributor?
"Distribution fees range from 20–30 percent; producers think it's a rip-off, but to hire a stand at an industry market is about £20,000, so you'd have to do about £80,000–£100,000 worth of sales just to pay for the stand, let alone your travel and the overpriced food and drinks. If we fly to the USA specially to pitch a show, that's also covered in our overheads. That's why running a distributor is such an expensive thing and I don't feel bad about charging for all of that.

"Some producers don't want to spend the fee and decide to do their own distribution, but then they find out how much they have to do, and all their lovely profit margin is eaten up by the cost of travel, legal fees, marketing and man hours."

How can I find a good distributor?
"Some people on the lower end of the distribution business will take anything, so you could have your show in their catalogue alongside porn. At the upper

end, distributors are very selective about what they will take. Buyers go to certain distributors because they know they are getting a certain quality and don't have to worry about whether all the rights are cleared, for example. So the point of securing a good distributor is to give your show some gravitas and have your program associated with a group of high-quality shows.

"You want to make sure that there is a good match between your program and the shows the distributor already represents. Some distributors specialize, for example in lifestyle programming; Passion TV do a lot of distribution to women's channels in the US and their niche is very much what the commercial broadcasters want. If you have a show called *Botox Disasters*, for example, you would be mad to put it in with a more traditional catalogue. Some distributors concentrate on topical programs that only have a shelf life of two or three years. At Parthenon Entertainment, our specialty is in bigger-budget programs that don't date. If great ideas come along that just don't fit our criteria we pass them on to other distributors who might be interested.

"The bigger the distributor, the more careful you need to be. Some of the really big ones have 10,000 programs in their libraries, so there's a risk your program will get lost in the catalogue. The smaller distributors are more likely to milk the back catalogue; they will approach all the major broadcasters for the preliminary sales, then four or five years later they will sell to the cable satellite channels, and then work down through VOD and so on.

"Your relationship with a distributor is all about trust. the distributor has to love your program as much as you love your program. I also advise you to find a distributor who enjoys a good laugh, because it's a serious world out there unfortunately."

What mistakes do producers make when trying to find a distribution partner?

"Be honest about where you have pitched your idea before. The problem with producers is they do something I call blanket bombing; they go to festivals and they pitch everybody. If you think of any other business you'd be mad to give away your trade secrets, but a couple of drinks at the conference bar and suddenly you are having off-the-cuff discussions with broadcasters. But these people aren't robots—if they have heard an idea, albeit at 4 a.m. in the bar, they've heard it. So when the producer fails to sell their show at the market, they think they can come home and get us to sell it for them, but it's too late, it's already been shopped. STOP, THINK, before you pitch.

"We don't take something on for just a couple of territories, there has to be a good reason to do it. So it may be that the producer has sold all the TV rights, but worldwide video rights are still available, or there's something else attractive about it such as a niche that we want to get into."

Chantal Rickards

Head of Programming/Branded Content, MEC, London
www.mecglobal.com

Chantal Rickards started her career in TV production programs such as Through the Keyhole, Masterchef *and* Countdown. *She then helped to set up UKTV Food channel, ran the Carlton Food Network and later became a commissioning executive for UKTV Style, UKTV Food and UKTV Garden while at the BBC. She currently works for media agency MEC acting as an intermediary between brands, TV channels and producers.*

"I look after branded content across Europe, the Middle East and Africa, for the clients on the books of MEC, which is part of WPP, the world's largest advertising and media group. Our biggest domestic clients are people such as Lloyds Banking Group, Nintendo, Specsavers, Sony Ericsson, and Orange; internationally, we look after Visa, Xerox, Bacardi and Colgate Palmolive, among others. When MEC decided to get into branded content they deliberately employed people who had a TV production background because they wanted to be able to offer brands best-in-class talent with a specific expertise in this area.

"I can take a brief from anywhere. Sometimes ideas come in from TV channels who have an idea they love and want to find out if there are any brands which might want to fund it. Other times a producer will come to us with an idea that they think might work for a brand. Or an idea can come to me from a brand or from the internal communications team here at the agency who are trying to solve a problem for a client. It can happen any which way, basically.

"An idea from a brand often doesn't work, because they don't know what makes a program idea viable, they don't necessarily understand the different channels and won't know the idea's been done before. So sometimes brands will give you ideas that are naïve, not because they are stupid, but because their level of knowledge and understanding is not the same as people in the TV industry.

Brands and TV people also speak two completely different languages, which is why we sit in the middle as translators.

"If an idea that comes from a brand is good enough I would probably go straight to a channel, bounce it off them and if they like it ask them if they have a preferred production company they like to work with; if not, I will suggest some producers. When I worked at a TV channel, I worked with and commissioned production companies, so I've got a pretty good knowledge of who the best producers are for a particular project. The other reason that I would want to go to the best in class is because the channels will know those people and will trust them, so it is in my interest to go to production companies who have strong channel relationships and a good track record in whatever their field of expertise is."

What makes a brand want to fund a TV program?

"What brands are trying to achieve changes all the time. When a brand advertises to people it could be to tell them about the existence of a new brand; it could be to launch a new version of an established brand; it could be to try and shift perception of a brand; or they might want to put across a friendlier, warmer human face to counter some kind of ill-will towards the brand. There are many reasons for using branded content as it can solve many marketing problems in lots of ways. Branded content also has many touch points: TV, web, social media, books etc.

"When considering a TV idea, the brand first looks at what kind of audience it wants. Your program idea might be the most fantastic idea on the planet, but if it doesn't appeal to consumers that a company wants to attract—women aged over forty-five in the case of a chocolate manufacturer, for the sake of argument—it doesn't work for that brand. So the program idea has to work for the target audience first. Then you have to find a target channel, so in the example of chocolate to women over forty-five you'd probably look at a daytime audience. And of course the program idea has got to work for the broadcaster's schedule too. Channels have to balance programs across the day and finding a suitable slot at the right time in the right place can be tricky."

What types of programs are unsuitable for brand funding?

"Unless a partnership feels appropriate a brand simply won't put their money behind it. And if the program idea contains any negativity then the chances are a brand will walk away. For example, they wouldn't want to fund war documentaries because they wouldn't want to attach themselves to something that is dark and gloomy.

"International television projects tend to be difficult because an idea doesn't always translate from one side of the world to the other, so a Ukrainian TV program probably won't work for the Japanese because of their cultural differences. For example, if SPAR, a supermarket brand, wanted to get the idea across that it is convenient to pick up a few extra grocery items at your local SPAR mini-market in the UK, that idea wouldn't work for China or South Africa because SPAR shops in those countries are super-scale hypermarkets. On the other hand, *How Clean Is Your House* might work for a cleaning brand in many territories, as a format like that will travel well. The drawback is that the marketing for global brands is handled locally in each individual country; there are very few brands that are trying to say the same thing across the world."

How do you pitch an idea to a brand?

"Producers generally just bring a treatment, a couple of pages, which is the kind of thing that they are putting in front of television commissioners all the time. I can see whether a show will work as it stands and I have a good idea whether a commissioner is likely to take it up or not. So when I pitch it into a brand client I will say, 'This is the basic television treatment, this is the company behind it,' and then I tell them about the other things that we can do around this television property that will resonate with their audience.

"I also show them examples of how other branded content has worked, explain my background, and demonstrate how the agency has achieved results for clients in particular way, by offering up examples that resonate with the brand; case histories are incredibly important.

What are the pitfalls of working with a brand?

1. "Be realistic about your timescale because if you think you are going to get an instant answer from a brand you won't—you'll be lucky to get the go-ahead in under three months.
2. Be prepared to take on a lot of new information.
3. Having brand money attached to something feels a little like having another commissioner at the table.
4. Leave your prejudices behind. Don't just assume that a brand will browbeat

the producer to get their own way because—as long as there is someone like me sitting in the middle—that doesn't happen. But you do have to be prepared to see brands in a different light and be accepting of different levels of involvement. It's all about collaboration at the end of the day—if everybody collaborates then it's a very easy process."

Tom Ziessen
Public Engagement Advisor, People and Broadcast Grants, Wellcome Trust, London
www.wellcome.ac.uk/Funding/Public-engagement
@tomziessen

The Wellcome Trust is a global charitable foundation that aims to improve human and animal health through biomedical research. Tom Ziessen's remit is to increase the public engagement and understanding of biomedical science. He oversees a number of grants: the Broadcast Development Awards, the Broadcast Awards and the People Awards.

"The Wellcome Trust is a charity. We have an endowment of around £14 billion and of that we spend about £600 million a year on research around the world. A very small fraction of that is spent on public engagement of science and of that only a small amount on broadcast projects. We probably spend around £750,000 on broadcast a year through the:

- Broadcast Development Awards—we spend £200,000 per annum on funding program development (up to £10,000 for each project).
- People Awards—we give £30,000 to five or six projects every year; we can fund any kind of project including exhibitions and plays as well as film and TV projects.
- Broadcast Awards—this is a larger pot of money from which we can fund projects, but it's by invitation only; people can't apply. Producers have to come to talk to us about their ideas and we invite selected people to come in and present their project to a committee.

"Broadcast Development Award money is given as a grant; we get nothing back. People can keep any profits they make as long as it's still being used to promote the product, and engage people with the science. For the very large awards some money does, in theory, come back to us. We get something like 15 percent after the distributor has taken their share, but we haven't yet got any money back; if we did it would probably be a small amount. *Here's Johnny* sold in a lot of different territories, but prior to it being sold the production company had barely enough money to make the film, so they need to be paid before we would even consider taking any money back.

"We've been funding broadcast projects for a long time, but in the beginning we didn't really know the market very well; we funded some great films like *Here's Johnny*, but we were also funding very expensive films that were essentially going nowhere. It's only in the last four or five years that we've started to be far more strategic. We started attending industry events such as Sheffield Doc/Fest and the Edinburgh TV Festival to try to get a better understanding of the landscape. We try to stay in touch with who's looking for what by reading the trade magazines, and having meetings. I see the commissioning editor for science at Channel 4 on a fairly regular basis, for example. We are always trying to guess what commissioners might want."

What type of films does the Wellcome Trust fund?

"We commissioned some research, which said that people got most of their science information from television. There is already lots of science on television— on BBC1, BBC2, BBC4 and Channel 4—but we also want to reach the audience on channels where there isn't currently much science, such as ITV1. Our remit is to get the science where the audiences are, but where the science currently isn't.

"For the Broadcast Development Awards we aren't interested in developing ideas that are aimed at the festival circuit: we want films that are going to get a commission on terrestrial TV. We are allowed to fund development for anyone.

"For the People Awards, almost without exception, those projects already have a commission or they might be classed as conditional on commission (we are not allowed to fund production costs for BBC programs because they can't accept money for productions that doesn't come in the form of co-production money from other broadcasters or the Open University). We do sometimes fund films that have no broadcast finance in place—in these cases we need a convincing distribution plan and route to audience. We don't often fully fund a film."

What kind of people pitch to you?

"We get everyone from very experienced production companies such as Windfall, through to people who've got some experience making films for organizations but have never had anything broadcast and also some first-timers.

"For our Broadcast Development funding, we almost always need to see an experienced executive producer onboard, because otherwise the idea won't get in front of a commissioner. It massively boosts your confidence as a funder to see a known name attached to a project.

"We can take more of a risk on people who haven't got very much experience for our People Awards. For example, *Here's Johnny* had a little bit of money from BRITDOC and we gave them some money from the People Awards. It took a while for the production company, Animal Monday, to get the film broadcast on TV, but now it's been shown all over [and has won two prestigious Grierson Awards]."

What advice do you have for people pitching to you?

"My top tip is that the film has to be about more than just an interesting piece of science. It has to be a story. People often just list a whole bunch of interesting facts. It needs to have a clear audience and people who would want to watch it. It can't be something that you just want to do.

"Applications are often very vague regarding which channels the film is aimed at. Even at the earliest stage, we need the filmmaker to say, 'This is an idea for such-and-such a slot on this channel, this is what the commissioner is looking for ...,' to show they know the TV landscape. We completely understand if the project changes direction, or a stated commissioner says no, and so they have to pitch it to another channel, but you do need to start off with a sensible plan. Clarity is important.

"For the Broadcast Development award, we don't want to see the full budget. We just want to see how the £10,000 award will be broken down, e.g. one writer/producer for a number of weeks to research the proposal.

"If you have had money from us before and have done a good job you are more likely to get money from us again. If you've a done a bad job, then you need to demonstrate that you've learnt from what went wrong."

How involved are in the films you fund?

"With Broadcast Development funding, we have no control over the project; we're just saying, 'This is an interesting idea, run with it.' We know that when it gets in front of a commissioner they are going to take it in whatever direction they think best. But by giving filmmakers time develop their project and think about how the science might work within it, when they take it to a commissioner they have a better chance of being able to convince them that the science is integral to the film.

"As the awards go up in value, we get more hands-on. We can't make editorial decisions about what the final outcome might be, but we do make a lot of suggestions. We sometimes go to rough-cuts at the filmmaker's invitation. There are some people who are very, very nice but they want a bit of handholding and are in touch all the time; we sometimes have difficulty managing filmmakers' expectations of when it is, and isn't, appropriate to ask for help."

Are there advantages in partnering with the Wellcome Trust, beyond the funding?
"If you want to get scientists onboard and be taken seriously by them it can help that we've said, 'Yes, we think this is a good idea.' We can help match filmmakers with scientists, and we can do that before a grant is given. There's a separate team which works on supporting science researchers and train them to take part in public engagement, so they can tell TV producers which of them are engaging speakers.

"Our involvement can also help with getting commissioners interested, because we've funded a lot of films that have ended up winning awards. We also have drama consultants and we are looking at other things we can offer filmmakers, such as occasional legal advice, for example."

How do you judge that your involvement in a film has been successful?
"TV audience numbers are a key part of measuring success for us. But if a film was on ITV1 at primetime and got the lowest ratings of anything on at that time, it would still be a success because a film with science in it made it on to ITV1. Other things we look at are the amount and accuracy of science in a film, the amount of press coverage, and whether people are talking about the program.

"We funded development on a documentary about the athlete Caster Semenya. It was a really interesting film and it had some good science in it, but it never really answered the question of why she may, or may not, be female, and didn't discuss sex chromosomes. Despite that, I think that film was a success in that it was commissioned by Current Affairs, so success and failure can be part of the same thing."

Debra Zimmerman

Executive Director, Women Make Movies, New York City
www.wmm.com

Women Make Movies is an organization that provides fiscal sponsorship, production support, distribution and seminars to women filmmakers.

"There are lots of film organizations that provide fiscal sponsorship, and Women Make Movies is one of them. We actually call the program the Production Assistance Program, because it's not just fiscal sponsorship; we also offer filmmakers consultations on their proposals, make suggestions of where they might want to go for funding, advise on budgets and look at their rough-cuts—we don't just act as a conduit for the funds.

"The unknown truth is that the majority of money our filmmakers raise—something like $3million a year—comes from individuals. It could be from a fundraiser, where a filmmaker holds an auction or asks them to donate to an online campaign. Each of our projects has a place on the Women Make Movies website where anybody can make a donation to the film. This online process for contribution is the same thing that Kickstarter does, the difference is that Kickstarter is not a tax-exempt entity and so people can't claim a tax deduction against their donation."

How does someone apply to get fiscal sponsorship from Women Make Movies?
"We view the applications and base our decisions on:

- the quality of the project
- whether or not we think that the filmmaker has the experience or energy to actually raise the money that they need to make the film
- whether we think there are funders that will be interested in funding the project

The filmmaker also needs to send us a sample [demo or taster tape] that they've done—oftentimes with their own funding. A sample is very similar to what you might see at the film festival pitching forums. It's anything from two to ten minutes long and it gives you an idea of what the film is going to look like. It could be interviews with key subjects or it could be the very beginning of the film; it shows the style of the film and that the filmmaker has the access and capability to make the film. If it's not a good sample we are not going to be able to support it. In a way, we see Women Make Movies as the first hoop that you have to jump through, because if we don't think a film is viable, a funder is not going to think it's viable.

"We give feedback on unsuccessful applications. We recently got a letter from somebody saying how helpful the feedback was—we explained why we didn't accept their film into the program—and they felt like it was really valid, constructive criticism that will help them in putting together their next proposal. It's definitely more difficult for first-time filmmakers, because they may have a really good idea but know nothing about the fundraising process. But if we think it's a really viable project oftentimes we will recommend that they take some of our workshops in proposal writing and fundraising."

What are the main reasons that you turn down requests for fiscal sponsorship?
"Sometimes we have to turn down first-time filmmakers who don't have enough experience and have not put together a team of people that can back them up— they don't have any advisors, or an experienced producer or editor. Sometimes they haven't budgeted properly and that tells us that they don't know what they are doing. Sometimes another film has recently been made on the same subject and they are not aware of it and so haven't done their research.

"The other main reason is that we just don't think that there are appropriate funders. In order to get funded for a project from grantmaking foundations, it generally has to be a social issue film or it has to be a subject that has the support of a community where there are going to be enough individual donors to help fund it."

Once a filmmaker has a fiscal sponsor, what's the next step?
"When a filmmaker applies for a grant they normally include a copy of our tax-exemption form with their proposal, to let the funder know that we are the fiscal sponsor. The funder then sends us a letter saying this person has been awarded a grant. We oftentimes have to sign a grant agreement saying that we will accept the funds and reassure the funder that they will get a report on how those funds will be spent; they then send us a check and we deposit it in a bank account. We have a separate account for each film that we sponsor and we notify the filmmaker that the funds have come through. The filmmaker can then request the

money against current or planned expenses and we cut them a check for that amount less our 5 percent fee. The reason why filmmakers might not take the full amount is because as long as it stays in the Women Make Movies bank account the money is not taxed; but once they've received the money, if they don't spend it within that calendar year they have to pay tax on the money they've received from us. The same is true if they spend the money on salary. We report all monies spent on salaries to the IRS—whether it is for crew or the producer/director. Some fiscal sponsors just cut the check as soon as they get the money, and they send a tax form at the end of the year and the filmmaker has to pay tax on it no matter what. So another part of the service we provide is to help filmmakers decrease their tax liability.

"If the grant is for development, it's not that big a deal if the film doesn't actually get made—the grant closes with a report saying that the money was spent in development. If the filmmaker gets the money to finish the film and they don't finish the film that can present a real problem, but it doesn't happen very often."

Do you work with international filmmakers?
"Fiscal sponsorship has been very much an American way of raising money, but one of the things that has been interesting for us is that international filmmakers have recently become more aware of it. Most programs are not open to international filmmakers because of the tax laws. If we give money to a filmmaker and they spend it on their salary we need to withhold tax according to the treaty agreement that the US has with their particular country, which makes it really complicated, so we can't really get involved in that. We have started to invite international filmmakers—on a very selective basis—to work with us, but there needs to be an agreement that the money will be spent outside of the USA."

Rachel Mills
Director of Education, the Edit Center, New York City
www.theeditcenter.com
@TheEditCenter

The Edit Center was founded by award-winning editor and producer Alan Oxman (Hot Coffee, Control Room, Unzipped) as a place where aspiring editors could learn to use Final Cut Pro. The students work on real-life narrative and documentary films, many of which go on to win awards.

"I was introduced to the Edit Center in 2006. I was a fledgling editor and I came here to take the six-week Final Cut Pro class. The owner, Alan Oxman, is an editor, post-production supervisor and producer. We believe that the best way to learn how to edit, both technically and aesthetically, is to work on real projects so we partner with filmmakers who put their films through our six-week program. Students get to edit real footage and the filmmaker receives a (very) rough-cut of their film at the end of the course, which is completely free to the filmmakers.

"It's great for filmmakers who have limited funds: documentary makers usually have no money to begin with, and when they get to post- it's almost guaranteed that they've got no money. But they come to us because they need help with the narrative to get to the rough-cut stage or need to find an editor or an assistant editor. It's mainly word-of-mouth—a lot of the filmmakers have had a film go through an Edit Center class before, and Edit Center alumni also submit their own films. The filmmakers are usually New York-based; I don't get many submissions from overseas, but we are definitely open to international submissions.

"Recently we had a film called *Hot Coffee*, which is a documentary by Susan Saladoff about tort reform in the USA. She was a first-time filmmaker, and we thought the film would be great for the class because the material was really interesting, although it is a little heavy on talking heads. Susan was a go-getter and really understood the process. After the class we recommended she work with editor Cindy Lee, who also edited *No End in Sight*. The film went on to Sundance and Hot Docs and was picked up and premièred by HBO in 2011.

"We don't take every film. Alan and I pick films that we are interested in, made by filmmakers we like. Not every film that goes through the class is going to win the Grand Jury Prize at Sundance and not every film is even going to see the light of day. On the other hand, some films that I've turned down have gone on to do great things."

What is the submission process for a filmmaker?

"People call me up. I can be on the phone to a filmmaker upwards of thirty minutes because they have got to a point in the filmmaking process where they don't know what to do, and a lot of times that's when they stumble upon us and seek guidance. A lot of times I feel like I'm a therapist.

"As I talk to them, I figure out if their film could possibly work for the class. The first step would be for them to send a link to a trailer of some kind—maybe a grant submission trailer—or any kind of treatment or synopsis; anything that will give me a quick idea of their project. I'm looking for an interesting project with a filmmaker who really does need our help, and who understands the process of the class—I don't want people to think they are going to come out with a finished film. I'm also looking for a good balance for footage for the class—we a variety of vérité, B-roll and interviews.

"Then I ask the filmmaker to bring in their drive with all their footage on it. I sit down with them to quickly go through the footage to get an idea of their project and their level of organization. If they are happy to leave it with me overnight, I watch more to get a good sense of their shooting style, coverage and if they have enough hours of footage. We have an average of twelve students per class, so if there is only twenty hours of footage it won't work for us, even if it's the best footage in the world."

What happens if a project is accepted?

"We have to rely on the documentary filmmakers to organize the rushes in a way that works for the class (it's a much simpler process for narrative films since we have the script to work from and don't have to rely so much on the filmmaker to prep the footage). So if the filmmaker has 200 hours of footage, they have to have an idea of what the story is, who the main characters are and what happens in the film. They have to organize the footage in such a way that each student is receiving a sequence that contains raw footage of interview, vérité and B-roll. Just having to organize the footage for the class is extremely beneficial to the filmmaker. We've just had a film that was shot over ten years and had more than 200 hours of footage: to have the filmmaker sit down and look through that footage connect with that footage again really gets them thinking about their film, the story they want to tell and how they are going to tell it. We need the filmmaker to give us twenty scenes that range from ninety-minutes to four hours of raw footage. So right there we need eighty hours of footage. We probably can't get through all the scenes that the filmmaker provides, so we ask the filmmaker which scenes they most want to see cut.

"Each of those raw footage sequences is assigned to a student and the filmmaker comes in to introduce the film to the class. They give a general overview and talk about any difficulties with the footage or story and explain any of the things they really want to emphasize in the film. It gives the students the chance to ask any questions they may have.

"The instructors—who are all working editors, and change from class to class—teach the students. They are a great asset to the filmmaker because, in a way, the instructors end up acting as supervising editors. The students work on their scenes for two-and-a-half weeks, during which the instructors regularly offer constructive criticism. The filmmaker also gives each student notes. A lot of times, this is the first time the filmmaker has seen actual scenes cut together. When you have twelve to fourteen students each working on one tiny section of your film it's actually really great because they are not overwhelmed by the overall amount of footage and they are giving it all their concentration. The filmmaker comes back and watches each scene again, and offers more feedback.

"At the end of the class, the instructors string together a rough-cut from the scenes the students have worked on. The rough-cut that comes out of the class won't be a finished film, but it's going to be something they can work from.

"The filmmaker gets a DVD rough-cut of the film and also all of the students' project files that they can reconnect to their own media. They can use any of the cut scenes they like in the finished film, or they can choose not to use any of them. The only requirement is that each student can have the scenes they worked on for their personal reel, and that all the students' names are listed in the final credit roll under 'Additional Editing Provided by the Edit Center.'"

What are the advantages of putting a film through the Edit Center besides free editing?

"Filmmakers come to the class at different stages in production. Maybe they're unhappy with a rough-cut they've already done; or perhaps they are looking for a new perspective because they're too close to the material; sometimes the film's been on a shelf for three years and finding us prompts them to bring it out again. They might already have an editor onboard who is watching the footage at the same time the students are working on it. Although we get them at different stages we treat them all the same: as if the footage has never been edited before.

"Filmmakers get different things from the experience. If, for example, they have 200 hours of footage, a student who works with ninety minutes of that footage for two-and-a-half weeks can find shots that the director didn't know were there. When you have hundreds of hours of rushes you can no longer see the forest for the trees, so it's a good opportunity for filmmakers to stop and be without their rushes for a certain amount of time and that breathing space gives them a jumpstart to get through to the next phase of their edit.

"Geoff Richman [*Sicko, The Cove, Murderball*], who is one of the best editors in the world in my opinion, teaches here once or twice a year. It's great for the students to have Geoff as a teacher, but it's really great for the filmmakers to have Geoff Richman as a supervising editor. Maybe you can't afford to hire Geoff Richman, but he is there every day looking at your footage in the classroom.

"A lot of the films that go through the Edit Center end up using someone we recommend to edit the final film. That might be an editor who is making $2,000 a week, or someone who's been assisting but wants to work on a feature, and is maybe willing to work for $500 a week. We also have workspace here and if we think that the filmmaker will benefit from it we will rent our editing systems out at a very reasonable price, but we don't do that for everyone."

Producers

Rachel Wexler
Executive Producer, Bungalow Town Productions, England
www.bungalow-town.com

Rachel Wexler has produced a number of award winning films, including The English Surgeon *and* Guilty Pleasures. *She explains the role of a producer and what makes a film attractive to a producer.*

"In my twenties I did lots of freelance production managing on dozens of documentaries, and so I've never been frightened of the finance side of things. I started at the bottom and it took me a long time to become a producer, but I don't regret any of that because if I have to do a quick budget I just know the process so well. People can think it's much more complex than it is if they haven't done it before, so if they get asked by a broadcaster to come up with a finance plan, a budget and a cash flow, they think it all sounds terrifying, but when you've done it a few times you realize it's quite simple. I think that some people who come into producing at a high level, or from the researcher side, they lose out on that grounding. I'd really recommend people knowing production inside out to be a producer.

"I very much wanted to be a producer. I was lucky because I was working with small companies—Seventh Art and at ZEF Productions—so I could push a bit and I was given the opportunity to help raise money. I moved from a production manager role into a line producer role/co-producer role and from there I learned to talk to broadcasters, presell films, and go to the markets—IDFA in Amsterdam, Hot Docs in Toronto and Sheffield Doc/Fest. Terrifying as it was being chucked in at the deep end, I just turned up, gritted my teeth, smiled and tried to get meetings ... and got turned down. I went back again and again; and there were six years of that. It was hard, so I don't recommend it, because it's scary and daunting, and it's emotionally draining, but I was driven and I found it very exciting to learn that stuff, because it was a whole new area.

"Then in 2004, my partner Jez [Lewis] and I set up Bungalow Town Productions. We were both at a certain point in our careers where we thought it would be great to make films independently as a company, so we set up Bungalow Town to house our first project, which was *Philip and His Seven Wives*, directed by Marc Isaacs. That was a really good one to start with because I'd had a chat with Nick Fraser [at the BBC] and he told me he admired Marc's films and he'd love to work with him. I had worked with Marc on his first film, *Lift*, and we were very keen to work together again. So that sowed the seed to look for projects specifically for Nick and BBC *Storyville*, with Marc at the helm.

"It took about six months before I found the story of *Philip and His Seven Wives*, which is about a British man living in a seaside town with seven women. One of his wives had been banished and she was my cleaning lady. She came to clean my house and we got chatting, and because I'm a really nosy person, that's how we found our first project. Marc Isaacs came to visit the family with me and then we went to see Nick and he was immediately really excited about the project. It was amazing to have *Storyville* onboard, but that only gave us a very modest BBC4 budget. I had enough experience and contacts at that point from working with Phil Grabsky and Luke Holland on their international feature documentaries to know I should start looking for international finance to boost the budget.

"At first all I got was a small presale from YLE in Finland, and a little bit of money from TV2 in Denmark. Once we had a ten-minute teaser we started to get interest from Sundance Channel in the USA, but it took until we had a completed film to turn it into a deal. That's the thing that people don't always realize, they think it's going to take a few weeks, but sometimes it can take two years to actually turn broadcast interest into a sale. I decided to continue to keep in touch with all the other broadcasters who had shown an interest, to show them a rough-cut and then send them the finished film. It's very hard to get anyone to come onboard early, especially the Americans; they often wait until rough-cut. Why would they want to come onboard any earlier if they don't have to? They just say, 'I'll buy it when it's finished, when it's a quarter or half the price of a commission.' So we learned to cut our cloth to make the film. We raised about 75 percent of the budget during making the film, so we had a fairly healthy budget, but unless I've got a full budget, I never stop talking to broadcasters.

"It is a really useful thing to continue those relationships. Once you've put in a huge amount of work making a film, you've got all that knowledge and contacts, so in the end we did our own sales for the first few years—I think I sold *Philip and His Seven Wives* to twelve broadcasters, which was hard work, but it really paid off. That is money in the bank, rather than handing the film off to somebody else to distribute for a fee. I also learned a lot about acquisitions and we got it into various festivals, where the film did well. If you are doing your own sales, it's continual; you just keep going, you don't give up. But you do get fatigued, and also I do think if you bang on the door too many times people can get annoyed with you. I only usually go back to people when I've got news to tell them or something positive to say, so I'll go back to them and say 'I'm just updating you ....' You have to go with your instincts, I think.

"I am involved in the editorial, I think it's impossible not to be, but a lot of it is down to your relationship with the filmmaker. Marc Isaacs will often generate an idea, a thought, a general inkling of what he might want to do and we will talk, talk, talk—I'm a sounding board for him, which I really enjoy. I go to all the meetings, and we discuss ideas and we find a route through. I don't know how I couldn't be involved in the editorial really, it's integral.

"We're often going for a British subject that has the potential to get full, or nearly full funding from one broadcaster—it's lovely if you can do that—but with the understanding that it might not then have an international life; it's for a British audience predominantly. Most of our films do tend to go much further afield, even though they are British subjects. Marc Isaacs is an auteur and in Europe he's really popular. His films do well in festivals and they sell well internationally, because even though they might be about a British subject they are all universal. *All White in Barking* [a documentary about an area of Britain with a high immigrant population] did very well internationally, for example.

"When considering which funders to approach you are thinking about your rights: the back end, like the rights in each territory, the television rights, theatrical rights, DVD rights. Your package of rights is like the family silver and you should only really give out rights when it's worth it. You need to retain as much of the ownership of the project as possible, because that's your profit.

"On one project you might think it will appeal to the USA and UK, so you go for two large pots of money and find two funders who will work together. That can work beautifully because then you've got the rest of the world rights to sell, but on the downside you have given up two very big territories to do that.

"So when I'm looking at a film I'm thinking how much money can I raise whilst giving away as little as possible. But some funders add a lot of cachet and added value, so if BBC *Storyville* or More 4 *True Stories* come onboard in the UK, it can help open doors internationally because they've given it a big tick of approval.

"If I look at a project and think it's very commercial and will sell well, I can seek equity finance for it. Equity investors own a percentage of the back end of the project forever. You get all different kinds of investors. You can go to a more traditional film finance company and they look at the risk and the costs, the director (they are unlikely to put money into a first-time director), the whole package. They want to know whether you have a good track record, and whether they will get their money back. If you want to compete with something like *Man on Wire*, that's the way to go. The beauty of that is that you then have your theatrical window and you don't have to go begging to a broadcaster to let you show your film theatrically.

"If a TV channel has given you money for a film they usually want to transmit it as soon as possible, they don't want to wait eighteen months until it's had its cinema run. If you are commissioned by a large UK or US broadcaster then they are likely to want to have the première, so they don't tend to like to do theatrical films. But if they can see the potential of theatrical and they think it could potentially enhance their broadcast they might go for it. For certain films the US broadcasters like to go for the Oscar, but a film can't be shown on television before a certain cut-off point if it's going to be eligible for an Oscar nomination; the film has to have at least a week-long theatrical run in New York and a week-long run in LA to qualify. A lot of filmmakers will be keen to go for an Oscar, but it costs a lot of money and very few will get on to the shortlist. However, a broadcaster might say, 'OK we'll hold off on our broadcast and we will allow you theatrical because we think this film could get nominated.' On the other hand, some broadcasters, like POV in America, the PBS strand, they are very supportive of theatrical, because they see it as potentially good for them.

"What I sometimes do is mix investment money with broadcast money and grant money all in the same project. That's hard to do, but it can be done. I've seen people get into a real muddle because they have a £200,000 budget and sign a contract for £40,000 and then they get stuck and can't find any more funding, and that's going to happen more and more. You do hear horror stories. I'd say do your research, know who you are getting into bed with and you really have to know what their expectations are.

"If you want a career as a producer, I think being really honest and straight up, enthusiastic and passionate goes a long way. It's not just about getting the money at all costs, because actually it's a very small industry, and people will always notice if you don't deliver and they will find it hard to trust you again. If you are a director, build your craft; if you are a producer, build your contacts and be a mensch, do what you say you are going to do. Be personable, and don't get all chippy when people can't give you money, don't blame people. Try to remember that it's a long, long road we are on, and sometimes it takes six meetings before someone will trust you enough to give you money. It might be your sixth project, but eventually, you'll get there. There are some funders that still haven't funded my films, but I think that's just another challenge: maybe one day I'll have exactly what they want and it will all come together. My feeling is that some people just get focused on making one film and they think they've got to make or break it in one film and so will promise the world to everybody, but they'll piss people off if they take money almost under false pretences. The biggest compliment I ever had was when a broadcaster came over to me at a festival and said, 'Rachel, you deliver what you say you are going to deliver and you just keep delivering'. And I realized that's what really matters as a producer."

Tom Roberts
Independent Executive Producer/Director, London

Elephant is a £4million feature film set around a village in Assam, India. Its director discusses the challenges of pitching and funding a film that doesn't fit into a neat genre and explains the motivations of different kinds of funders.

"My latest film, a feature documentary, is about elephant—human conflict in Assam. A village is troubled by the depredations of a wild herd that is led by an elephant that exhibits abnormal behavior. The herd is stressed because it is in constant conflict. We are filming the events observationally, from within the herd. The crew will be on the back of domesticated elephants that have been trained to be with wild elephants, so we can look out towards the villagers from the perspective of the elephants. We'll be filming them for fifteen months to pick out the elephant characters and story threads that support the narrative of my film.

"There's also the human element delivered through the villagers. Their whole livelihood, the success of their families, maybe even the life and death of some of their children, is contingent upon whether the herd comes into their village or eats their crop. One of the villagers loves elephants and believes he has a religious connection to them through the god Ganesh. This man travels across India seeking a Brahmin who will come and protect the village from further attacks by the elephants.

"But the film is neither a social documentary nor a natural history documentary; it's about the conflict between mankind and nature. The emotional journey within the film will create sympathy in the audience for the elephant, and then shift that sympathy to the villager and then back to the elephants, in order to re-create the conflict. The whole purpose of the film is to deliver a powerful emotional experience to the audience; it's meant to drive an audience to tears. It will be a different kind of experience than the David Attenborough type of natural history program. It will be a truly cinematic experience.

"This film certainly doesn't fit a particular genre and one of the most difficult things you can do is to try to get a non-genre film off the ground. I've never been interested in slavishly following somebody else's creative dictat nor the limitations imposed by rigid adherence to schedules or pre-conceived styles, and so consequently I've always been interested in cross-genre stuff.

"Many commissioning editors have a very narrow idea of what the audience wants from social action films like Michael Moore etc. When I come along and talk about moving an audience in the profound, deep way that a novel might do, or a great feature film might do, whilst using factual elements, they say, 'Well, we don't really do it like that.' And that's because they have very narrow limitations in terms of their own thinking, often lacking in imagination. They say they want new ideas and they want originality, but most people are terrified of new things, even commissioning editors. They will talk to you until they are blue in the face about originality, and then you give them a new idea and their first reaction is, 'But that's entirely new, untested! Oh my god! What are we going to do with that?' One of the exceptions, of course, is Nick Fraser of BBC *Storyville*, and I am very lucky to be working with him.

"So there's always a tremendous dilemma in pitching. You obviously want to sell your film and need to think very carefully about how you approach it. How can you get them to step outside their own narrow perspective? At the same time, if you mislead people, if you make them think the film is something other than what it is, then you are going to be found out at some point, possibly even before the money arrives. My films are founded on integrity and truth, so how can I justify being dishonest with people who are going to make my film possible? The trick is to inspire them with your film; it's all about presenting a new idea without engaging their fears and without giving them a false image.

"To finance a film, what you really need to do is find a really good producer. In television a lot of people are producer/directors, but that's really about shooting out in the field, it's not really about raising money. A great producer is someone who has knowledge, experience and contacts in areas that you don't, combined with wisdom and judgment. He is someone who can be inspired by you but at the same time can also challenge and question you. You need to work together in a close partnership.

"Luckily I've found James Mitchell, who used to own and run Little Bird, a feature film company, and has produced a lot of *Storyvilles*. James now has another company called Soho Moon. James is the opposite from me in a lot of respects. I love coming back from the mud and mosquito-ridden jungles of Assam with sunburn and a bit of diarrhea: James's feet never leave concrete! What James does is think through the funding methodology.

"The best way to understand film finance, I think, is to look at what the funding purpose is. So you have broadcasters, who will give you money because they want a film to broadcast, you have the national film councils, like the BFI, the German or Irish national film funds etc. that want to encourage cinema, help creative people and build the industry. Then you have the regional film funds. Here there are two models: those that want to develop talent in their region, like the Welsh fund, for example, and those that are trying to promote general economic development and want film production to be a part of it.

"Then there are equity funders who just want to make a profit. There are broadly two types of equity funders. There are those who want an interesting experience, want to be stimulated and rub shoulders with filmmakers. They generally demand less onerous financial terms. Then you have the more straightforward equity funds, which put in money to make money. There are also many kinds of ways in which they can recover their money, other than through profit, via tax benefits and other complicated mechanisms. A further kind of equity funder is one who believes in and supports the aims of the project. There are many wealthy or famous people who have an interest in the welfare of elephants and we are talking to them about whether they can put money in or help bring other funders onboard—other people who care about wildlife conservation. So they might say, 'I'll give you 10 percent of your budget because I want to see this film made and I want to make my money back if the film makes a profit, but I don't require really demanding terms.' Or he might initially demand big terms, but you then work out that he is really interested in animal conservation, so you use that in the negotiations.

"It's highly complex, whenever you try to sell a project. You don't just want money, you need partners. A partner is someone who isn't just signing a contract, a partner is someone who says, 'We'll make a phone call for you,' or 'I think you should call this person in that territory,' or 'I've just been to this festival and I met this person from Italy and they are interested, why don't you give them a call?' Partners are trying to help you and you need a lot of those people throughout the process. We are in touch with a company in New York which was involved in *The Cove* and they fell head over heels in love with the project. They said, 'We have an equity funder and they'll be in touch.' They got excited and made a phone call, and that's what you want. So there is an equity funder in the States who is quite interested and could put in a lot of money; he won't come in until we have other funding, but when we do, he might come in with a significant portion of the budget.

"To sum up, the complication of funding is that all money has a cost. Basically when you look at money you have to ask: what do they want in return? To support the film industry, the creative process, or do they want a film to broadcast or sell, or just to turn a profit? Is it hard or soft money? Soft money is what you start with—MEDIA development money, for instance [which doesn't necessarily have to be paid back]—in order to initiate the project. MEDIA are trying to help people get their projects off the ground so they accept a certain amount of loss in the process. Gradually, as you build up your budget, the money gets harder—regional funds, national film funds, broadcasters, distributors, finally equity funding. Equity money comes in last because they are not going to fund you from the beginning, they are going to fund you when you need your last 20 percent, when they can ask for terms that are beneficial to them and you are going to take it.

"BBC *Storyville* is keen on original work and takes brave chances, so it's often an early funder of development. I have a legal obligation to bring the project, once I have got it funded, back to them, but it's an early contract and I could renegotiate with them. I can offer them various options, like taking it to BBC Films or other cinema outlets, which still means we can bring it to *Storyville*, but it would already have been released in the cinema. So it's all about negotiation and things are never finally resolved until the very end—so you need a top producer, with experience, who can negotiate very effectively."

Jenn Kuzmyk Ruch
Vice President Factual, Cream Productions, Toronto
www.creamproductions.ca

Jenn Kuzmyk Ruch oversees both the creative and financial aspects of development for Cream Productions' factual programming. The company produces everything from lifestyle formats to reality series, docusoaps and big CGI specials, and regularly co-produces series and blue-chip specials with UK and European partners.

"When we are financing we know what it's going to cost to produce something and our goal is to get that money together using as few sources as possible. It's not just about bringing the money in; it's about bringing in the right partners. If you are co-producing a program everybody has creative input and you have multiple sets of notes, possibly with several versions of the program to deliver, but it costs more to do multiple versions so you have to make sure that's built into the budget.

"We never turn down a good idea, but we are not going to develop something if there is no market for it. If you have a relationship with someone at a particular channel you go there, and if you don't have a good relationship there you build one. You set up phone calls, go to the market events and do the legwork to build a relationship. Obviously it's easier when you are working for a company that has a good reputation and you've have had hits on other channels, because they will listen to you.

"Don't go to a broadcaster without a pitch if you haven't worked with them before. The worst thing is to go to a meeting and ask them what kind of things they are looking for and then just say, 'Thank you, goodbye.' You want to have something in your pocket that you think is great, because that's the impression you are leaving them with. That said, when you go to industry events, you certainly meet people and it's great to do some networking, and to be able to say, 'I'd like to develop something for you, and when I have something I'll come and talk to you.'

"If a producer doesn't have the right track record the broadcaster will say, 'I like your idea but I don't think you have the ability to execute' and the broadcaster will often suggest they team up with a good production company that can help them to put financing together. Cream is the production company that a lot of independent producers in that situation will come to.

"Because we are a Canadian company, we most often try to get a Canadian broadcaster in first. Sometimes we can source all of the financing from our Canadian broadcast partner—that's still possible. We can also access Canadian tax credits, and other funding such as the Canadian Media Fund. If there's a little gap a distributor might come in for an advance. That puts us in a great position because we can share in the rights and sell it around the world. The worst thing in the world is when you have most of your financing, but you have a gap and you just can't fill it, and you can't make your project; that's heartbreaking. It's doesn't happen to us very often, luckily.

"When we are putting together a more expensive, multi-territory financed show, we know who our broadcast targets are. If you have a great project and you've got a good relationship with a commissioning editor, it doesn't matter where they are. We've worked with partners in Germany and France, but it's mostly the UK and the US. We get to know people by going to MIP, Realscreen, the World Science Congress and Hot Docs. It's about relationships.

"When we've already produced for a channel we know what they want and we also know the ballpark of what they can give per hour, so we figure that into our plan. Broadcasters always want more for less: license fees are going down but they want more rights. It's up to the independent producer to navigate all that and give them what they want within their budgetary constraints; but you'd better be sure that you can deliver what you are promising on the budget that you create. That's the big thing.

"We've done lots of official treaty co-productions with the UK. Canada has official co-production agreements with many different countries. A treaty co-production allows you to work with a producer in another country and bring multiple partners into the financing. In order to take advantage of tax credit funding and the Canadian Media Fund the production has to be qualified as Canadian. So a treaty co-production allows us to work with other partners but also gives it that stamp of being a Canadian show. As a Canadian producer we normally bring a good proportion of the budget out of Canada—the majority of the budget in many cases.

"There's a creative reason to do co-productions too; so if a Canadian company can do live-action stuff but they need a partner to do the animation then they could go and find a company who can do that portion of it. Maybe some of the writers come from one country and the director comes from another one; post-production is done in one country but all the shooting is done in another; the host comes from one country and everything else is done by the other—it just needs to work and to be representative of what each partner brings financially. When you are into production everybody has an interest and if you have an issue everybody needs to know what is going on, so you need to set up regular multi-partner conference calls.

"You have to make sure when you are putting partnerships together that it is going to work in terms of the relationship. Some relationships are better than others. We've all done co-productions that were an absolute pleasure and we've all done ones that were more difficult, but hopefully in the end you forget all the pain—it's like giving birth! Once you've done a lot of partnerships, your company gets to be comfortable with certain partners and we've co-produced multiple times with some partners."

Lucy Stylianou
Managing Director, Furnace, London
www.furnacetv.com

Furnace is an independent production company that makes specialist factual TV programs for an international market. When they had the idea of making Terror Attack Mumbai, *a film about the role of technology such as Facebook, GPS and email in the Mumbai terrorist attacks, it made sense for it to be a treaty co-production with Australia.*

"We were talking to Channel 4 as the terrorist attacks in Mumbai were happening; we thought that once the attacks were over, it would be a good idea to tell the story from the survivors' perspective, and we got immediate interest from them.

"We have an existing co-production relationship with Electric Pictures in Australia, so we developed *Terror Attack Mumbai* jointly with them and they sold it to ABC in Australia. In order to access Australian tax credits and regional and federal funding the production money had to be spent in Australia, and a large proportion of the creative team had to be Australian. So the entire production team was Australian, with the exception of me, one of the lawyers, one of the executive producers and an assistant producer. We produced four versions: a UK version, an Australian version, an American version and an international version (although the Australian and American versions were almost identical).

"We needed to bring in a certain amount of money from overseas too, so we brought in Lilla Hurst of LillaVision. Lilla's a sales agent and co-production executive. We told her we had Channel 4 and the Australians onboard and that we needed to make sales to the USA and the rest of world. She made a sale to *Secrets of the Dead* strand in the USA and also to Discovery Asia, and later we also sold it to CBC Newsworld in Canada, which is a digital channel. We paid her a commission on the sales that she generated.

"The advantage of using a company like Lilla's is that it saves time. It is incredibly difficult and time-consuming to find the right people to sell to, and there might be lots of people you want to sell to but you don't have a relationship with. Someone like Lilla already has those relationships in place. Also, if Lilla is representing a project, it represents a certain quality threshold, a level of experience and expertise, and that instantly opens doors to you in terms of financing.

"You do have to factor the cost of the agent's commission into the budget, so once we knew how much money had been raised from the license fees realized by Lilla's presales we calculated what the commission was going to be and added it into the budget as another cost. It's slightly more expensive to do it this way, but I think what you have to pay out is more than compensated for by an agent's ability to open doors and bring in those critical foreign sales.

"I have a number of tips for people doing co-productions:

1. Try really, really hard to get confirmed interest in your home territory. If you have a home broadcaster who is really interested in the project, then you can go to the rest of the world and it immediately gives you a leg up.

2. Be first. There were a lot of Mumbai films going around at the time, but ours and Dan Reed's film, *Terror in Mumbai*, were the two that got off the starting blocks first.

3. Use a co-production agent. I really can't recommend that highly enough.

4. Go to the international markets. If you've got a project to sell into the US, for example, then it is a very good idea to go to RealScreen in Washington DC (or if you've got a sales agent your agent should go).

5. Beware of exchange rates and bank charges. For example, if you have made a big sale to the US and a big proportion of your budget is in dollars, you want to make sure that you spend as much of that money as possible in dollars. You should have a US dollar bank account at the very least. The cost of money on a co-production is huge, because each payment from an overseas broadcaster, will be subject to charges from your bank. Furthermore, if you have to convert any of that money into sterling, you could lose on the exchange rate. When you are working out what the exchange rate is on your budget you need to be quite canny about how you calculate it and then you fix your budget at that exchange rate. Discovery US are good because they will agree an exchange rate with you for the sterling costs in your budget, and you know you are going to get paid in sterling and it's fine. But not all US broadcasters will do that, they will pay you in dollars and that's expensive.

6. Know how many versions you will have to make—it can be a nightmare. We had one film, *Churchill's Darkest Decisions*, which we sold to Channel 4 and National Geographic in the UK, PBS in the USA, ABC in Australia and ZDF in Germany; that's an awful lot of broadcasters. In the end, National Geographic and ZDF and ABC in Australia all took the same version as Channel 4, so we only had to make three versions: the Channel 4 version, a separate version for PBS in the USA, and then we had to make an international version for our distributor, which was basically the Channel 4 version rendered seamless [without ad breaks] with a separate music and effects track [to allow for foreign-language dubbing].

7. Understand the difference between a co-production and a presale/buy. If a channel is investing as a co-producer rather than a pre-buy, it's a really important distinction. A co-producer has editorial rights in their own version of a project and you get more money upfront. In a pre-buy it is a lower level of investment: they just take the finished program as it is. Then if they want to version it for themselves, by putting in commercial breaks or whatever, they can."

Sarah Cunliffe
Managing Director/Executive Producer, Big Wave Productions, West Sussex, England
www.bigwavetv.com

Big Wave specializes in wildlife, science and adventure programming for an international market, particularly the BBC and Channel 5 in the UK and Discovery, National Geographic and Animal Planet in the USA.

"A lot of our productions are wildlife shows, which are quite observational and require a lot of time in the field, so I know right from the start that we will need co-production money. The simplest thing is to deal with one broadcaster but with budgets decreasing that's increasingly unusual these days.

"I pitch to all the channels synchronously, just one paragraph by email, or ring them up and say, 'I've got this idea, what do you think?' You have to be able to articulate your idea in one paragraph. I've generally found broadcasters are good at feeding back very quickly about whether they like an idea or not. I don't think commissioning editors want to see anyone doing huge amounts of work on something that is going to go nowhere. If there is interest from a broadcaster, we write a proposal and often make a promo tape. In the US market, or if there is onscreen talent involved in the program, a three- or four-minute promo is essential and we usually fund it ourselves. In its simplest form, I might just ask someone to record themselves on their mobile phone and send me the clip. If we need something more elaborate, we might source some archive footage to create something that will give the broadcaster a feel for the project.

"Pitching is more problematic if you are trying to forge a new relationship with a broadcaster that doesn't know you. It's not easy; it's quite tough out there at the moment, you just have to keep banging on their door.

"My dream scenario is to have one or two co-producers, usually in the UK and/or America, and then bring in a distributor. Recently we've been working with BBC Worldwide but we've worked with others. BBCWW essentially takes the rest of world rights (ROW) and if your project sells well you get some money back, which is critical if you are to survive in the indie sector. Depending on the project, distributors will often invest in the project upfront. When we did *Animal Heroes* for Channel 5 and Animal Planet the investment was 5 percent from Big Wave, 40 percent each from Channel 5 and Animal Planet, and BBCWW took ROW for 15 percent. The distributor recoups their investment from sales and gets a distribution fee and expenses of some 20–30 percent. That's a model that has worked well for us; we have recouped our investment and it is in profit. An even better model is to fund the whole deficit yourself. You then keep ROW and sell to the individual countries, but it takes a lot of time and effort to go to all the markets such as MIPCOM.

"When a distributor has invested in a program, they will expect to recoup their investment in first position from any sales they make. If we, as a production company, have also invested then we would expect to share that first position recoupment. This is not always easy to agree. I think the distributors earn quite a lot for what they do, but having them handle the worldwide sales allows us to carry on finding and developing more new programs, so I don't think that is really a downside.

"My top tips for successful co-productions would be:

1. Be utterly clear what your potential co-producers' program output is—the number of people who aren't clear about that is extraordinary.
2. Keep the lines of communication open and frank; if your co-producers are giving you money it's good practice to keep them in the loop—and will serve you well for future collaborations.
3. The American market has different needs to the UK market and that has to be respected. You have to take both sides into account; I wouldn't say make compromises, but you have to be aware that you are making a program for two different audiences.
4. It's a pain if your co-production channel really doesn't like your presenter and you have to do a presenterless version—they are very different beasts. Try to make sure you have a program and talent that appeals to all parties from the start."

Leigh Gibson

Independent Feature Documentary Producer, Brighton, West Sussex, England
@leighgibsonf

Leigh Gibson specializes in finding funding for feature-length documentaries. The project she's spent most time on is The Boy Mir: Ten Years in Afghanistan. *She joined the project in 2005, and the film transmitted on More 4 (and internationally) in 2011, following its theatrical release. She explains what makes a project attractive to a producer and offers some excellent fundraising tips.*

"I'm a freelance producer, I work mainly with Seventh Art productions who are a well-known production company based in Brighton. I've worked for them for about eight years, but I also work with other directors to help raise finance and develop projects. I've quite a varied career and I was involved in the production side for a long time before I took on the financing and broadcast sales of projects—it was a natural progression. Feature-length documentaries are my specialty; I have worked with TV series but mainly in production rather than fundraising.

"When I'm considering a potential new project I look at the story and the characters first, above and beyond a director's history or track record, and regardless of whether they have made a film before. Then I think about whether this film could reach an international audience. Films that have international themes running through them—love, childhood, war, for example—and human stories generally have the ability to reach an international audience. Films that deal with local issues, or are related to a specific country, are sometimes more problematic. Historical documentaries can work for an international audience, but it depends on the structure of the film and how it is presented. If you have incredible archive footage and exclusive access, something that is unique, then that would rate quite highly.

"If you have a written proposal, it would then be a case of trying to find some development money from broadcasters. If the filmmaker is British then I would go straight to a UK broadcaster first. It is the obvious route in terms of interest, but international broadcasters also like to see that you have your home territory onboard first. If there isn't any interest from a broadcaster, which is quite likely because it's very tough to get development money, then there are various other funding organizations.

"A possible place to start is CBA [Commonwealth Broadcasting Association] Worldview Broadcast Media Scheme. They provide travel bursaries to enable research or filming trips and that's useful because the key thing in development is getting footage to show to potential funders. Worldview provides travel bursaries of around £5,000–£10,000 for filmmakers who have got international stories or stories in the developing world. You do, however, require a letter of interest from a UK broadcaster in order to access those funds. It's often very tough to get a letter of interest from a UK broadcaster; generally it's not something that they like to give out unless they are very convinced that it is a project that they will take, but there are producers out there who can get them if the project is strong enough.

"A lot of the funding organizations need to see that you have a passion for this type of filmmaking and they may request a screener of your previous work. If it's wildly different from what you are proposing it may be problematic.

"If you haven't got a track record, there are quite a few funds that you can still apply for. For people who are making feature-length documentaries about international stories, Cinereach are a good option. Cinereach provide funding at all stages of production, development, production and post-production. If this is your first film you could align yourself with an executive producer at an established production company and the application can come from them. This puts some experience and reputation behind your project.

"I'd aim to put together a taster tape to convey the key characters and the style of filmmaking. It's not good enough to show just one scene of your characters with one interview, it needs to show that there is some narrative development. It also shouldn't give so much away that the broadcaster or funder thinks they've seen all there is to see.

"So once you've got a taster, and you've got something to show, then it's time to try to get broadcasters onboard. Fantastic ways of doing that can be directly through your producer but also attending markets, so somewhere like Sheffield Doc/Fest where they have the Meet Market, for example. Having a taster makes you one step higher up the ladder to everybody else; it gives you that leverage to show your characters to the financiers whilst meeting them face-to-face. Quite a few markets, like IDFA, have pitching forums where you have to be pre-selected, but if you do get through that process then you have twenty or thirty broadcasters at your feet and the opportunity to sell them your program. In the documentary world I believe it's all about getting the opportunity.

"I have also pitched at the MIPDoc Co-production Challenge, which happens every year. It's actually a pitching competition, so that's slightly different, because the judges are ultimately judging you on how you pitch. I recommend you go along and watch people pitching in that situation, not only to see how well people get on, but how they fail as well. There is a lot of critique afterwards.

"People fail in pitching by telling people about the project as if they are reading a proposal. A pitch isn't a proposal, it's a performance; it's an opportunity to demonstrate the potential of the project, showing your style and the way in which you can develop that project. You can show your taster alongside the pitch, but the words you use need to give as much insight as possible into the characters and your passion for your subject.

"After the pitch itself, you get the broadcasters around the table expressing interest or not. You may find that the whole room decides that they all love the project and you come away feeling really elated, thinking all your problems are solved. Then you come home and the money's still not in your account. In any market you will never walk away with a signed contract or money in your account, it doesn't happen like that; you get your face known and meet people, but you have to work very hard afterwards to maintain those relationships and it's as much about this part of the process that makes the sale as the pitch itself. As in any business, people want to work with people they get on with and you can do that only if you meet with people regularly and create a rapport and relationship with them. So it's all about chasing those people, reminding them of the pitch and keeping the communication going and giving them more information as soon as you have it. You can't afford to lose momentum."

Peter Lamberti

CEO, Aquavision TV Productions, South Africa
www.aquavision.co.za

Aquavision are natural history specialists, making blue-chip wildlife films. For Peter Lamberti, making a taster tape is an essential part of the fundraising process, and keeping your overheads low is the key to long-term survival.

"We specialize in wildlife films that show new or remarkable behavior, which are often referred to as 'wow' shots. We start the process by doing the research and finding stories—when I'm making one movie I'm always looking for my next idea—and then I go and spend a couple of months filming to get those 'wow' shots. For example, I was making a film on baboons in the Luangwa Valley and while I was there I filmed some lion—crocodile interaction on a carcass. I did a little bit more research and I found out that this was happening fairly regularly, so I finished the first film and I went back up there specifically to look for interaction between lions and crocodiles. I looked for carcasses in the river or next to the river, and staked them out; eventually I got the mother of all fights between crocodiles and lions.

"Once I've got some key shots I cut a sizzle reel, write up a proposal, do my budget and then I go and sell it. I've found that that way works really well. If you try to sell something on paper, people are always worried about the risk involved. There're all sorts of things that can happen in the time it takes you to raise your budget—there are no guarantees that the lion pride that was exhibiting some kind of remarkable behavior will still be there or behaving in that way when you go back in a year or a year-and-a-half's time when you get your money—there might have been a pride takeover, for example.

"I do a fairly detailed budget: you need to determine how many days you are going to film, what your accommodation is going to cost, what your vehicle will cost, what your camera kit will cost you, who the crew are, how many days in post, what's in the budget for music, what's in the budget for stock footage and all that kind of stuff.

"It takes a few months after the greenlight to actually receive the money, because you have to go through the budget and iron out any discrepancies. The channel wants to make sure that you have allocated enough for graphics or haven't allocated too much on camera hire etc. Then you've got to agree to a production schedule. Once all that is done and all your deliverables are agreed, then they issue a contract and depending on how many clauses there are, it can take up to several months before the contract is signed. Normally 25 percent is released on contract signing and the rest at milestones, normally on the delivery of rough-cut, delivery of fine-cut, and then final delivery. For a rule of thumb you would get 25 percent at each stage, but it varies.

"Then I would approach a second broadcaster, usually via a distributor. They would use the same sizzler reel and proposal to get other broadcasters onboard who will come in with reasonable chunks of money to make up the budget. We normally have two or three co-production partners. Discovery, Animal Planet and National Geographic are our key partners.

"We go international straight away because what the domestic South African television market can afford is pretty insignificant, it doesn't really warrant going there. There are incentives, but they require an international co-production. If you have an international co-production partner onboard, the Department of Trade and Industry [here in South Africa] will give you a percentage of your funding. If the majority of the copyright stays in South Africa, you use a South African director and you've got an international distribution plan they will sometimes kick in 20 or 30 percent of your budget.

"We've co-produced with most of the major broadcasters at one stage or another. On one production we had NHK, Animal Planet and ZDF all at once and that was quite interesting, but that was all done through the distributor, Off the Fence, so they oversaw and channeled the creative input from the broadcasters, so we didn't get pulled from one end to the other by conflicting requests from different channel executives. We normally supply the same cut to everybody. I've found that a channel like NDR in Germany prefers a slower, more traditional cut, whereas countries like America and the UK like a faster, pacier type of cut; NHK in Japan like something a lot slower and very often you have got to supply them with a lot of raw footage and they will recut the film themselves.

"I use one of three distribution companies: Off the Fence, Parthenon Entertainment or National Geographic Television International. They look at the pitch and decide if this is a film that they can sell. They will indicate that they want to distribute it and sometimes they will put up a distribution advance, which can also help your budget. That advance will tie you into a distribution agreement that will lock them in as the distributor for anything between ten and twenty years. You provide them with the film, they sell it, deduct their expenses and then give you your royalties.

"There are a number of markets where you can go to meet the distributors, like Wildscreen in Bristol, Jackson Hole in Wyoming or Wild Talk Africa in South Africa. You can go there to meet the distributors, pitch your ideas and get representation. Some distributors will fully finance you, take your idea, make the presales for you and get the finance that you need; for doing all of that they will take a slice of the back end as well as a distribution fee. The distribution fee is standard, between 25–30 percent, that's the fee that the distributor will make for selling your film. When they raise the production finance as well, they could take a further 30 percent, so they could be taking about 50 percent ownership of your film, but as they have financed it, it's a reasonable business model.

"Most distributors will want to take the whole world, not many will take only a portion of the market. What I normally do is carve out our own market, which is Africa, and give the distributor the rest of world.

"Raising finance for the first time is definitely the most challenging. I would say marry rich! We managed to survive because we started small. We're in a big office block now, but I worked from home when I started. I never hired a camera, I bought my own cameras. I kept my overheads as lean as possible, because when you do make money you've got to be able to put away enough to see you through the hard times. That's the big trick: so many people, they make money and spend the money as it comes in, buying new equipment. Then their next idea is not accepted and the next idea after that is not accepted and then they run out of money and they can't carry on. I've always kept ownership of copyright and I've always had that royalty trickling in, which helps you through the difficult times. I think that's really the only way you can make it.

"The 10 percent production fee is standard, but if you think about what you go through to make a movie, nobody in their right mind would ever do it for the 10 percent financial gain. The way to make it pay is to own your cameras, so you earn money on your cameras, own your edit suite so you earn money on your edit suite, and put your overhead into a building that you own. You charge against the camera and edit suite because you have to pay them off, but once you've done that you start making a bit of money off them. That's the only way to make the industry work."

Jonathan Goodman Levitt
Independent Filmmaker and Producer at Changeworx, New York City

Follow the Leader: Young, American and Right is the first film in a series about different aspects of American leadership (www.followtheleaderfilm.com). It's a coming-of-age story about three teenage boys who want to be president of the USA; the film follows them for three years as they face crossroads in their own lives at a critical time in the country's political history. With a release date set for 2012, the year of President Barack Obama's re-election campaign, the documentary was designed to provoke intelligent political discourse in the run-up to the election. The film's director describes the difficulties he encountered when unforeseen circumstances busted the budget.

"My last film, [the Grierson-nominated] *Sunny Intervals and Showers*, was self-funded through other work, savings and credit cards, though I did have a Fulbright Scholarship that funded much of the shoot. I was lucky to sell *Sunny Intervals* to BBC *Storyville* after a festival run. We were one of the first (along with Franny Armstrong's *McLibel*) self-funded UK films on BBC. The film was acquired by a TV distributor, sold in several smaller territories including Scandinavian countries, and sold well educationally. It became a 'calling card' that opened doors to meetings with many people I'd always wanted to talk with about being involved in my next film.

"I wanted to make a film that explored what being an American patriot means for tomorrow's generation, by following three characters over multiple years as they became adults and their political views crystallized. It's almost unthinkable to fund that kind of film through broadcasters, but it was clear to me that to have any chance at all I would require a great trailer or 'sizzle reel.' I did a year of research and a couple of months' shooting at some youth leadership programs in the US in the hope of recording some bombastic, sexy footage that would sell it, even though the film I was pitching was always intended to be a lot more nuanced.

"Using that early material—the idea and footage of the characters—I began talking with broadcasters I had met before at events such as Sheffield Doc/Fest and IDFA, and the project also was accepted into the 2007 Discovery Campus development scheme (now called Documentary Campus Masterschool), which put it on the radar of several more potential broadcast partners. By late 2007— albeit over a year after starting to film—we had presales agreed with VPRO and SVT. In the UK, we also had the unlikely situation where the BBC and Channel 4 were both seriously interested. The BBC was more interested in a fully funded series, but approval all the way up the commissioning structure was uncertain, and at a minimum would take months to get signed off. Channel 4 offered a generous presale (for a one-off), as well as a flexible slot length, schedule and contract, so I went with Channel 4.

"In practice, it took nearly a year to actually get the contract through the system. Broadcasters are really set up to deal with big production companies, and their terms—how much money is paid at different points in the production process, holdback windows and so on—can be problematic for small, truly independent producers. When the paperwork finally gets to the people who are dealing with the actual contracts, people who have had no involvement in the original negotiations, they add in a lot of other clauses, which aren't workable. You then have to go back and say 'No, that's not what was agreed,' and as the filmmaker you end up looking like an asshole. And when you've already been self-financing for months or years, the length of time it can take for contracts and even individual invoices to be processed can itself cause continuing problems. It can be easier to deal with smaller channels because there is less bureaucracy, which means things can happen more quickly. But that said, they have far less money, which obviously translates to less ability to help you guarantee you can actually make the film. At broadcasters where the commissioners do everything themselves, there's also much less incentive to deal with small producers—especially international producers—at all, given how overworked they are.

"Making this film at a time of great flux in the industry, and also over multiple years, threw up numerous problems too. It's actually plain to see why broadcasters prefer films with short schedules by local people with whom they've worked before. I'm now on my fourth commissioning editor at our main broadcaster, and each one has had different ideas of what the film 'is.' One insisted that we continue working with a problematic crew member; another had a somewhat different idea of what the film should be, which necessitated months of editing in a different direction (which cost us significantly, even though we were allowed later to return to the original focus); and during crucial months of the shoot, we were without any commissioner at all. Beyond that, because it simply wouldn't have made sense to end a film about politically ambitious youths at the start of what was shaping up to be the most exciting year in American politics in a generation [2008], we were essentially forced to double the length of the shoot. Understandably, nobody was prepared to pay more, so the budget got stretched to the point where Changeworx (our company) became by far the majority investor in the film. At a certain point, the actual budget for many films just becomes a joke on paper—the actual amount of cash raised is small compared to the in-kind contributions of the crew.

"There were also some disagreements about when the film would be delivered and broadcast. But we eventually agreed to a new schedule that allowed us more time to both finish the film properly and raise enough money from new partners to be able to do so. The disagreements themselves delayed the film for at least another year, during which time the fate of the film and our company hung in the balance. As a filmmaker, you always wind up looking like the bad guy in any situation where you can't deliver by a contractual deadline (which is often difficult to determine in advance on an observational film), and the circumstances that caused the delay almost don't matter.

"There might have been less pressure on us and easier access to more funding had we been making this film at a different time. But the shift in the industry from mid-2007 to early-2009 was tremendous. Broadcasters were feeling the brunt of the global recession, and channels were coming in later for less money, if they were coming in prior to completion at all. The recession really exacerbated changes that were already happening globally; and economic problems in many countries that have traditionally been the biggest backers of documentaries threatened many broadcasters' budgets. It was difficult for commissioners at those channels to protect investment in small documentaries like ours.

"Effectively, producers had to shoulder more risk in order to get their films to rough-cut stage, when the film could be 'seen' and considered a much lower risk for broadcasters. It's somewhat ridiculous to think that you can only make 'presales' shortly before the film is actually completed—but that's often the reality now for films that rely on execution rather than celebrity or current affairs angles. On this film, having a current affairs angle was actually somewhat of a complication: The rise of American conservatives in 2010 was generally helpful because it reinforced one of the film's themes and gave broadcasters the hook they needed; but some were disappointed that it wasn't simply an exposé of the so-called Tea Party.

"As of early 2011, we had broadcasts scheduled for 2012 on Channel 4, DR, SVT and NRK, with others pending. And we had a number of highly respected television distributors eager to represent it. It is ironic that many filmmakers are often in truly weak positions—completely leveraged financially, exhausted at the end of a long shoot or edit, forced to cancel even basic necessities like health insurance—and yet at the same time are forced to both exude strength and make decisions about all-important partnerships and contracts that really will impact our future 'recoveries,' financially and otherwise.

"Distributors were also particularly enthusiastic to have the film because we're doing two versions from the outset—a feature-length and a fifty-eight-minute version for territories without a longer slot. If you want to sell to TV, and you haven't just made one of the biggest critical and audience successes in recent times, you are creating problems for yourself if you don't have a short TV version. Mostly in America, filmmakers are insistent that their film can only be a feature, but if that's the case it's probably not going to be (as widely sold or seen) on television. I'm an artist first, but I have to eat, and there are some things that the market simply demands from most of us.

"We don't have an American broadcaster yet, and distribution here is more important to me than elsewhere else on this project. Political discourse is just so awkward and limited in America, and I've known for a long time that US gatekeepers were probably going to wait as long as possible before committing. My sense is that they essentially need the film to be done before judging the film's tone, and some may even prefer waiting to gauge audience response at festivals. For these reasons, I've been focused on raising international money from the start, and we didn't spend too much time seeking US foundation funding either, although we approached a few funders unsuccessfully relatively early in the process. The film is now being seriously considered by a number of US broadcasters and outlets, from HBO to the prestigious POV series on PBS, as well as a few theatrical distributors. It's hard to predict what will happen next, and whether we will partner with a major US broadcaster or distributor, or have a more 'do-it-yourself' (or more appropriately 'do-it-with-others') release here.

"Overall, making *Follow the Leader* has had little in common with the experience that I was expecting when we set out on this project years ago. Apart from the film taking twice as long to make as expected, the industry is just a less forgiving place now than the harsh place it already was. The recession has been used by some forces in the industry to solidify their already strong positions and it can be an excuse for bad behavior. Documentary filmmakers not making reality television series product are constantly reminded of what small fish we are in the industry's ecosystem, and that can be demoralizing. I think people are reluctant to talk about difficulties because you don't want to jeopardize any potential funding or goodwill; and yet when I talked with other filmmakers while I was having some problems, I found that a lot of them had experienced similar things.

"The 'new normal' is often even the reverse of what it was. A friend sent me a contract the other day (for my advice before signing it) from one of the most respected distributors, and as part of the deal he actually has to advance them money—maybe a few thousand Euros—to cover their initial promotional costs. And this is for a film that premièred in IDFA's Joris Ivens Competition [now the VPRO IDFA Award for Best Feature-Length Documentary]. When we recently agreed TV distribution with DR International Sales for our film, we got a small advance because the distributor knew we needed it to deliver, but even that was a big deal in spite of the fact that multiple distributors wanted the film. It's just another indication of how rough the environment is for everyone, with more people fighting over less money. In many ways, it's just a very bleak time for financing; but even so, a lot of great work is getting made somehow."

Dan Chambers
Company Director, Blink Films, London
www.blinkfilmsuk.com

Blink Films has been one of the pioneers of brand-funded content in the UK. Here Dan Chambers explains how Chinese Food in Minutes *originated.*

"Chef Ching-He Huang had done a BBC series with Lion Television, but we were speaking to her agent and we developed a cookery format for her. Having done one cookery series with her and Lion, the BBC were unlikely to commission another from us, so we had to go for another channel. The only place we could see it working was Channel 5. I used to be Director of Programmes at Channel 5 so I know about their funding set-up, and what they can and can't spend money on in the 7.30 p.m. slot. That slot traditionally doesn't have much money because of how Channel 5 works: they are limited to the number of minutes of advertising they can put in primetime, so it makes more sense for them to put their commercials in the 8 p.m. and 9 p.m. and 10 p.m. slots. The 7.30 p.m. slot doesn't tend to carry commercials; therefore they don't like to spend a lot of money on that slot. I knew that they wouldn't be able to come in at a high enough level to be able to fully fund, so that pushed us into the AFP [advertiser funded program] route.

"We approached Channel 5, who said they really loved the idea and confirmed that they couldn't come in with very much money. So then we went to Krempelwood, a branded content agency, who pitched the idea to various different brands. Several months elapsed before they came back to us with two interested brands. There was an urgency for each of them to get their bid in as they knew that we were going to go with whoever came back first. Sharwoods, a cooking sauce brand, got their act together first and I think they put up about half the funding. A small amount came from Channel 5 and our distributor, ITV Global, came in at a fairly early stage with a chunk of money against future international sales. If no one wanted to buy the show they would be left holding the baby—it's a risky investment for them and so they got to recoup in first position. They made a big sale to Food Network Australia fairly early on and covered most or all of their deficit. I think that they've been pleased with how it's sold and it's in the black now.

"The distributor typically takes 30 percent of all the sales they make, which is a good return for them. They don't take any ownership, they just take a cut of all their sales, which works very well. They have much deeper pockets than an indie has, so they are able to bear some of the risk, but to offset the risk they recoup ahead of anyone else.

"We met with Sharwoods on two or three occasions to work out what it was that they needed. Ching-He met with them too and it was at that point they agreed to sign off on it. Sharwoods were very accepting of how TV works, and understood that they weren't able to influence the editorial but they could benefit from various other activities off screen—Ching-He did some special cookery for them at a supermarket opening; I think we gave them four separate videos of her cooking with Sharwoods products for her website; there was also a competition in the program that was sponsored by Sharwoods, which meant that they got further involved with the viewers. Sharwoods were very good partners, were very supportive; it worked for them, it worked for us and it worked for Channel 5—it was one of those all-round positive relationships.

"There would have been a debrief at Sharwoods, regarding whether their involvement with the program was worthwhile, but it didn't involve us, which is understandable because all of that data is commercially sensitive. What we get back is the viewing figures from Channel 5, which were good—the aggregate audience was almost 1 million a week. We are not in production with Series 2 yet, because there is a lengthy process where Sharwoods look at their spending priorities and decide if they want to put more money into AFP. In a way that is the proof of the pudding: whether it worked well enough for them to justify them coming in on the second series. We are hopeful!"

Francine Heywood
Independent Producer, England

Sons of Cuba is an award-winning feature-length documentary by first time-director Andrew Lang. Francine Heywood is a freelance producer who joined the production at the post-production stage. The budget for the TV version of the film was £220,000 with an additional £60,000, to turn it into a theatrical documentary plus at least another £100,000 of deferred salaries and services. She describes how financing a film is often about seeking out unconventional sources of funding, riding out the disappointments and keeping going even when everything seems lost.

"*Sons of Cuba* came about back in 2005. The director, Andrew Lang, wasn't a filmmaker, but he's always been very interested in, and inspired by, South American cinema. He was in his mid-twenties and teaching English as a foreign language, when he read a newspaper interview with double Olympic Boxing Champion Mario Kindelan. Andrew thought it would be interesting to look at a fight through the eyes of an eighteen- or nineteen-year-old boxer who was ready to break into the national team.

"Andrew managed to get himself into a film school in Havana (he was fluent in Spanish) with the aim of making a short film about someone breaking into the national boxing team. It was suggested that he should look at the younger boys and he was taken along to the world famous boxing school in Havana. He met the coach and was invited to stay overnight to watch the boys train in the morning. He got up at 4 a.m. and went out with these young boys of nine, ten and eleven who were training in the pitch black, and he thought 'that's my film.'

"He shot a ten-minute film in three days using his own money. As Andrew told Shooting People: "I was nearing the moment when I would have to fly to Mexico before boarding the same plane back to Havana, as my visa had expired … Just before leaving, my Cuban flatmate told me: 'If you really want to fund your film, buy some Puma T-shirts whilst you're in Mexico. I'll sell them for you on the streets. You can't buy designer labels in the stores here. We'll make some money.' I returned with 25 Puma t-shirts, we sold them, and the short was funded." This would become the trailer that was used to raise funds for the feature film.

"Andrew then decided that he wanted to try to make the short into a feature-length film. He approached Screen South*, a regional screen agency in the UK, to see if they would give him some money to finish the ten-minute piece. They weren't able to do that, but one of the Screen South board members, a man called Jack Gold, immediately rang his son Nick Gold, who owns the World Circuit record label, which is very big in Cuban music. Nick liked the project and put in the money to get the short finished. Then Andrew got some additional funding from CBA-DFID**, because the film would give UK audiences an idea of life in a developing country, which fulfils their remit.

"At the end of 2006, Andrew sent out a proposal to international commissioners using names from the EDN (European Documentary Network) handbook.

*Since restructured to be part of Creative England.
* *Since renamed WorldView Broadcast Media Scheme.

He got no response but he did manage to get himself involved in a pitch forum in Tenerife, where he pitched to ARTE, and they liked it. He then went to MeetMarket at Sheffield Doc/Fest and pitched it to Stephen Segaller at *Wide Angle* on WNET in the USA. Stephen thought it was about time to do something on Cuba, which was great because Andrew was just about to give up. The difficulty with *Wide Angle* is that they wanted to make sure that the rest of the budget was in place and they wanted a forty-five-minute narrated version of the film.

"Through personal contacts, Andrew knew David Dugan at Windfall Films and he also met another producer Mandy Chang; between them they started negotiating to try to get ARTE and *Wide Angle* to put the money together so Andrew could start shooting. ARTE had run out of money in their 2006 budget, so Andrew decided to use his own money to go back to Cuba. Windfall also gave him some money, so he was able to shoot a lot more footage. Stephen Segaller attended another pitching conference in the US and managed to get ITVS interested, so between them all they put together enough money to get a narrated forty-five-minute version delivered in 2007. One of the negotiation challenges was that Andrew was determined to keep the rights to the footage so he could make his feature film.

"Towards the end of 2007 Andrew met Simon Rose, a BAFTA-nominated editor who agreed to work on the film for a small weekly payment and to defer the rest of his fee. With Simon's help Andrew finished the rough-cut of the film and I was introduced to him just before Christmas 2008. My producing partner Laura Giles and I fell in love with the project and we were determined to work with Andrew to make it happen. We pulled together a budget for post-production, marketing the film at festivals and getting sales agents onboard, and set about raising funds.

"Molinaire [a post-production house in London] did all the post-production for free in return for an equity stake in the production, which was absolutely superb; I can't tell you how grateful we are to them.

"We also got money from private investors in the UK and a big loan from an individual in Hong Kong, which gave us enough to get all the marketing materials together. For the chap who gave us the loan, there were two motivating factors: he liked the project and wanted to be involved in the film business (he'd had a successful career in the world of technology). We had to pay back the loan with interest so there was a financial return for him too. Our other two investors put the money in because they believed in the project and wanted to support Andrew. They will recoup their money as the film makes money.

"With the help of Screen South we approached the UK Trade and Industry Council and they gave us two pots of money. One enabled us to attend the Full Frame Festival in the US in 2009, where *Sons of Cuba* was screened as the opening-night film. And the second pot of money was from the Passport to Export program, which is traditionally used for manufacturers looking to export goods abroad—because we were trying to sell the film internationally, we were able to qualify. We had to fill in an application form, so it's not a pitch per se, and the process helped us present our film as a 'product.'.

"The film was also accepted into the Havana Film Festival in 2009 and Andrew desperately wanted to go but we didn't have the money to pay for the flights so I approached Virgin Atlantic. I took an MBA at Cranfield School of Management, and the COO of Virgin was also an alumnus of Cranfield so I emailed him and basically begged and he put me in touch with the marketing department. The personal connection helped to get us noticed, but the important thing for Virgin was that the film was a positive film. After watching the film, Virgin gave us two flights so Andrew and Simon could go to the festival in Havana.

"After we launched the film at Full Frame we got two sales agents onboard, one handling North America and one handling the rest of the world. A sales agent will represent the film worldwide, looking to sell the film to distributors and broadcasters and they've got contacts with all the key players in the industry. ro*co Films in California have a strong track record and is one of the premier documentary sales agents so that was the reason that we went with them internationally. Because the film had already been broadcast on television in the US, ro*co weren't interested in taking the North American rights, so for those we worked with Cinetic Rights Management in New York who had been involved in the sales to ITVS and will handle DVD and download sales in the US for us.

"We've sold the film into the US, Italy, Japan, New Zealand, Poland, Brazil, the rest of South America, Spain, Lebanon, Ireland and the UK. In the majority of these countries it's either been sold to a terrestrial or satellite broadcaster, for example, in the UK it was broadcast by BBC as part of the *Storyville* strand and in the US, it was broadcast by ITVS World Compass. In the case of Italy, distributor Fandango took all of the rights in exchange for a Minimum Guarantee: they gave us some money upfront to buy the rights to sell the film in Italy and they recoup that money out of their sales. When they have recouped all the money they paid us upfront—the Minimum Guarantee—they start paying us royalties.

"When we set up the recoupment schedule there were already a number of contractual agreements in place because of the money we'd had from Screen South, ITVS and ARTE, plus deferments, salaries and making sure that Molinaire recouped their money. It was a challenging exercise because we had to build all that in and make sure that we serviced everybody in that process.

"We weren't able to find a UK distributor to do a theatrical launch so we did that ourselves, and that was a real learning curve—contacting the cinemas, getting everything booked in, doing the outreach. We were able to get a grant from the UK Film Council* to make a digital print of the film, which also helped with our cinema bookings. While all of this was going on Andrew wasn't earning money, so he was teaching English to kids. One kid's father owned a printing business and he did us a deal and printed all our posters. We did our theatrical launch and got a distributor onboard, Mr Bongo in Brighton, who took all the DVD rights in the UK.

Kat Mansoor

Producer/Director, Animal Monday, Brighton, West Sussex, England
www.animalmonday.co.uk
@AnimalMonday

Animal Monday is a multi-award-winning independent documentary production company that specializes in producing artistic documentaries that tackle important subjects. Their first feature film, Here's Johnny, *won two prestigious Grierson Awards. Kat Mansoor explains how, as a new independent production company, they raised money for the film and what she learned along the way.*

"I started Animal Monday with two university friends the year I finished my Masters degree in TV production at Bournemouth University. I am the producer of the company, Adam Lavis edits, Will Hood does sound and music, and we all direct too.

"We started making *Here's Johnny* in a very guerilla-style way very shortly after starting the company. Adam knew Johnny [Hicklenton] and thought he was a fantastic character. Johnny was a well-known graphic artist who was suffering

---

*The UK Film Council has been disbanded and its work taken up by the British Film Institute.

from multiple sclerosis. When we started filming with him he had an anarchistic way of dealing with the disease; he didn't want to take any of the drugs, he wanted to do everything his own way, and he was convinced that he would thwart the disease and be fine. Our first commission, a year earlier, was for a short film called *Retrograde* for ITV and we had got that commissioned really easily, so we thought it would be easy to get a TV commission for *Here's Johnny*.

"We pitched it at the Channel 4 Pitch at Sheffield Doc/Fest in 2004. It was my first public pitch and there were seven of us pitching to a panel that included Danny Cohen [then Head of Documentaries, Channel 4] and Jess Search [then Commissioning Editor, Channel 4]. It was very nerve-wracking: we were in a big auditorium and there were lots of people in the audience. The prize went to Lee Kern who did a very funny pitch. I think the power of comedy is really important in pitching. It would have been far better for us to go in via the comedy angle, as Johnny was so fantastic he would be able to deliver. Instead, we talked about the worthiness of what we were trying to do. We told people too much about multiple sclerosis rather than Johnny's character, the story, the person, the humor that was going to inspire the viewer. We read it all off a piece of paper and it just felt like an academic essay rather than showing people the passion we had in the project. We just didn't do a very good job of emphasizing that it wasn't going to be a depressing multiple sclerosis documentary, which is what's being pitched all the time. Johnny was taking us through the experience of living with multiple sclerosis, not telling us that multiple sclerosis is going to affect one in ten people in the UK. Whilst that's great background information, it's not what's going to make people interested in the story. We just didn't have a good handle on pitching and sexing up the story. If you are over-worthy as a filmmaker, people don't like it. We are not doing the most important work in the world, we are a conduit to it and so shouldn't be too preachy. However, Jess, who was at that time commissioning for a late-night slot Channel 4, said she liked it and offered us £8,000 for character piece on Johnny and his art for a thirty-minute late-night slot.

"At the same time, a documentary strand called BBC Fresh had just started and they were sniffing around the idea; they were interested in doing something with us for more money and more exposure. I wasn't a particularly experienced producer at the time so I got really excited and we said no to Jess at Channel 4. Things had begun to change with Johnny; he was getting worse and becoming more debilitated and we realized that he wasn't going to defy the disease and was going to go through something a lot more profound than we'd first thought.

"Then the BBC Fresh interest fell through: we just got an email, saying 'actually we don't want it,' like it had just been kicked to the curb. It was a big wake-up call for us—and especially for me in my role—as to how things work in commissioning. We went back to Jess with our tail between our legs, and she said the money had already been spent. So we had missed our chance with Jess and been thrown out by BBC Fresh, so we were left, three years into the project, feeling like we'd just messed up. We needed money to carry on filming, because it had become apparent that the film wasn't about Johnny overcoming his disease, but more about how he managed it, so it became very different and a much more serious film. We knew we could focus on the art and the science to engage younger people, but that was already a problem in commissioners' eyes, because they couldn't work out whether it was an arts program or a science program, when we wanted to combine both.

"Then we found out about the Wellcome Trust. They were looking for projects that could engage the public with science in different ways. It was perfect because we had an amazing comic book artist who was drawing images of his own disease. Whereas the TV commissioners were saying that combining two genres was difficult, the Wellcome Trust were saying the opposite. They saw that we were making an art program but bringing in science in an interesting way— we were proposing to put scientists in the film as though they were part of one of Johnny's comic books.

"I wrote the proposal, which took three months, and we got the go-ahead for about £26,100, which was the first big injection of cash that we'd ever had as a company. To us that was massive—and we now know that we could have spent that money far more wisely. We were so young and inexperienced and we'd never worked for anyone else so I didn't really understand how best to spend the money. We ended up overpaying for certain things, paying a commercial rate when we were making a low-budget film (even though we thought it was quite a big budget). If I'd known then what I know now, I would have got an executive producer onboard very early on to help me understand how to more wisely use the money that we had. Today I would always ask for a reduced rate on an independent film. We also didn't know how to structure the narrative so we spent a lot of time and money trying things that didn't work.

"By then Jess Search had left Channel 4 and had set up the Channel 4 BRITDOC Foundation, so we put in an application for funding. By this time we had a series of rushes, and a short film called *Drawing Is My Walking* that had a time-lapse of Johnny drawing an amazing picture as he talks about how he travels in his own mind rather than with his legs, because that was at the point where he had started to sit down rather than be able to walk on crutches. So we had this trailer and a series of rushes with Johnny just talking, because the film has a powerful confessional style, and that's what we showed BRITDOC. The feedback was that they loved his character; too often films like that are depressing, and although this was upsetting, there was a lot of joy too that you could get from his perspective on life. They gave us another £30,000 to do the post-production and put the film into comic book style. It wasn't just that they gave us money; there was a lot of support creatively too.

"Once we had finished the film, Johnny decided to go to Dignitas in Switzerland to end his own life. Channel 4 were interested in following him, so it could have turned into a primetime Channel 4 commission at that point. From Johnny's point of view—and from our point of view—we'd already done seven years together and were very close but it was just getting more and more difficult. Johnny had to make that decision—and he felt it would be too difficult for those around him that loved him—which included us. Working with a commissioner and then editing it afterwards would have been too personal.

"If I came across this film now, I would certainly look for a better budget, a better slot on TV. If you are going to make interesting films they are probably not going to get funded from one place, it's probably going to be a little bit from this fund and a little bit from that fund. You have to learn to squirrel your money away, do deals and get people involved in the spirit of your film rather than making money, because it's probably not going to make any.

"I don't want to keep having conversations with people about how hard it is because I don't actually think it needs to be as hard as we sometimes make it: you can find ways of getting things done. But as an independent filmmaker you do need to think laterally and work out how your concept can appeal to broader audiences; that's been part of my learning journey. Now, when people come to us with concepts I ask 'Who?' and 'What?' and 'Why?' so that concepts become real people with real stories and tangible journeys that commissioners or film funds will understand.

"With some projects you just have to admit that they are more commercially viable and go with it. While it's fun to go running round the world for a year of festival screenings, it's quite useful for me to say, 'OK we've got it funded let's just make a commercial project.' I used to see making a commercial film as a bad thing until BRITDOC ran a course called Creative Capital that was run by a load of creative New Yorkers. It was really good because it basically said that just because you're an artist it doesn't mean you shouldn't charge for your work. Actually it makes complete sense to monetize and commercialize when you need to, and you approach your pure art projects with a little more understanding of what you are actually worth. At the moment I'm making a film for nothing in a kids' home I used to work in but I've also got a commercial project on the go which feeds us, and I think that's brilliant. I enjoy getting money for projects now and I don't feel bad about it at all."

See Chapter 7 for a copy of the application form that secured Wellcome Trust funding for *Here's Johnny.*

Hugh Hartford
Independent Producer/Director, Banyak Films, London
www.banyak.co.uk
@banyakfilms

Hugh Hartford and his brother Anson are independent filmmakers. Their quest to fund an international documentary took them to pitch forums in London, Barcelona, Sheffield and Amsterdam. Hugh discovered that you need funding to attract funding and, if you know where to look, money can be found in the most unexpected of places.

"In summer 2009, I saw a picture in a magazine of the world's oldest competitive ping pong player; she was ninety-eight years old and was wearing the Australian national sports kit. I thought it was amazing for someone of that age to be representing their country. I found out that the European table tennis championships were being held in Croatia that year, so I went over for a week with my own camera and microphone kit and did it as cheaply as possible (flying with a budget airline), funding it through my company, Banyak Films.

"I met some of the UK and European characters in Croatia and that gave me enough footage to cut a rough trailer, which we pitched around to TV channels in the UK. We were focusing very much on the UK characters so the film was going to be about the UK team and their journey to the world championships. All the channels turned us down because although it was an interesting subject, it didn't fit their slot or remit.

"We knew it was a good subject, so we changed the subject slightly to follow players from around the world to make it international. We entered it into the Docs Barcelona forum, where it went down very well. We got interest from a lot of European TV channels, but no one committed any money. I think at the smaller forums like that the commissioners find out about projects and then track them—when a film is still at an early stage they are quite happy to wait. One of the hardest things is to get the first chunk of cash because that's the riskiest position to be in for whoever gives you that money—as no one else is involved there is no guarantee the film will be completed. So we got some good contacts but no money.

"We had a deadline as the world championships were coming up. We wanted to film with at least three of the characters before the competition, so we needed some money by April so we could start filming them before going out to China where the world championships were being held in June. We'd been in touch with BRITDOC right from the beginning, so they had been tracking our progress. After Docs Barcelona we let them know what had happened and that there were now channels interested, but still no funds committed. When it came up to the deadline, BRITDOC came up with a small amount of money to get us out to China so we didn't miss anything in terms of what we needed to shoot.

"In June 2010, Anson, my filmmaking partner, and I went to China and filmed for a month, which was the main body of the film. After that we could cut a really good trailer with the help of some money from the PUMA Catalyst Award (the first trailer was made from footage I'd shot on my own in Croatia, so it was very basic). We cut a five-minute version and a ten-minute version, which we then started sending out to people because we were applying for different funds.

"We attended a Films for Good workshop which is run by BRITDOC. They invite the heads of lots of trusts and foundations to come in and tell you what they are looking for, and part of the workshop involves pitching your project, so that's good practice. We were then accepted on to BRITDOC'S Good Pitch.* They give you two days of preparation and pitch practice so the build-up to the pitch was terrifying, but it was really good meeting the other filmmakers and everyone helps each

* The Channel 4 BRITDOC Foundation runs the Good Pitch several times a year in different locations. Its aim is to help independent filmmakers who are making socially conscious ("good") documentaries find funding, distribution and outreach support from brands, NGOs and charities.

other out. When we started pitching we were vague about what we needed the money for, but after going through the pitch workshop we realized that we had a deadline to hang the pitch on: we wanted to fly out to Australia to film the 100th birthday of one of our characters, which was three weeks after the pitch.

"The actual pitch format is pretty standard for all the pitch forums, such as IDFA and Meet Market at Sheffield Doc/Fest. We had seven minutes to pitch, including the trailer, which was three minutes; so our actual pitch was only four minutes. What often happens is that people pitch and nobody really understands what the film is about until you show the trailer, so the best thing is to say less and get to the trailer as quickly as possible. I don't enjoy public speaking at all, but we'd explained the film a lot of times by then, and actually doing the pitch was a lot of fun. In the end, I think we talked for about two minutes so all we really had to do was introduce ourselves and say and what the film was about. PUMA were at the Good Pitch and they awarded us a travel bursary, the Mobility Award, which paid for two flights to Australia to film the birthday celebrations.

"We knew that this film could have a use for foundations and NGOs and organizations, but we are not experts in doing outreach, so that was another reason for us pitching at the Good Pitch. Age UK were invited to the table and their response was brilliant, they were dead keen. The interesting thing is that I'd emailed Age UK six months earlier and they had written a one-line email saying, 'sorry we don't fund art projects.' Our pitch at the Good Pitch was not just to get funding but to get partnerships as well, and when we met after the pitch their response was, 'we can definitely find a use for this.' I think the theatre of these public pitches is brilliant, because the panel gauge and respond to the audience reaction. Age UK have kept in touch with us, and they'll be able to use the film in different ways, such as screenings.

"The financial advantage of partnering with organizations like Age UK, even though they can't give us any money, is that they are giving the film their stamp of approval, and that helps give our application more weight when we are applying for actual production money from grants and foundations. We went on to apply for a People Award from the Wellcome Trust, and part of their feedback on our application was that they were impressed that Age UK were interested, because it showed that the film had kudos or credibility, and that there were people who had an interest in screening the finished film.

"The English Table Tennis Association (ETTA) were also in the audience at the Good Pitch [the ETTA were specially invited by BRITDOC who wanted them to hear the pitch for *Ping Pong*]. They came up to us afterwards, and they said this is fantastic, we are really going to help you and they then pushed it forward to the International Table Tennis Association, who are the global body who look after all the national table tennis clubs and have about 2.5 million members. We sent our trailer to the head of the ITTA, and they loved it and gave us a generous grant for the production budget. I don't think that would have happened if it wasn't for the Good Pitch—we could have tracked down the right email address, but I don't think cold calling would have worked.

"Camden Council (a local London authority) were there too and it turns out that they were planning Active Ageing weeks for the Olympics in 2012, so we are talking to them about doing screenings in conjunction with Active Ageing around the time of the Olympics.

"After the Good Pitch we went to the Meet Market at Sheffield Doc/Fest in 2010. That was largely about pitching to TV channels; we met with many broadcasters and got a lot more interest: Mette Hoffmann Meyer from DRTV, Denmark; a couple of Canadian broadcasters; Jenny Westergård at YLE in Finland; RTÉ in Ireland; NHK in Japan; VPRO, Netherlands; Axel Arnö in Sweden; and HBO and PBS in the USA. So all of those people said to keep in touch

"We also made presales to two different channels, Yes in Israel and ETV2 in Estonia: presales are only a small amount of money, but it's useful in the early days to get things going. Channel 4 was onboard too, because it's a BRITDOC project [Channel 4 has a 'first look' deal on all the films funded by BRITDOC; if Channel 4 chooses to transmit the film they can do so for a nominal license fee of £1], so with letters of commitment (LOC) from those few broadcasters you start adding momentum.

"We also met with a couple of foundations, ITVS, Sundance, Tribeca and Fledging Funds and Cinereach, as they all go to these forums looking for good projects and then invite the filmmakers to apply to their various foundations. Sundance said it was probably not worth applying because it doesn't quite fit their remit—it's good to get a 'no' from people because that means we don't have to pursue that avenue.

"Then we went to the forum at IDFA (International Documentary Film Festival Amsterdam). All the channels we'd previously spoken to were there, so it was really good to meet up for a second or third meeting; it's slightly more friendly and you can talk in more depth about the project. So after IDFA we got commitment from Canada and PTS in Taiwan, and we concreted things a bit more with the others.

"Then the Wellcome Trust came onboard, so we had enough production money to make a rough-cut. After Spain, Sheffield and IDFA we've now got a list of maybe twenty-five commissioners from different countries who know about the project and are interested in tracking it and will definitely watch the first ten minutes of the rough-cut.

"At these forums you also meet distributors and we've had both theatrical and broadcast distributors who are really keen, which means we can go back to broadcasters and foundations to show them that there is interest in the film, and that we can help get finishing funds.

"Once the film is complete it's possible to raise marketing money from brands via their PR companies and advertising agencies. We've had interest from [PR firm] Edelman in New York City, who might be able to take it to their clients and see if they could find some money for the film's marketing budget.

"We've ended up getting money from some niche places like the European Table Tennis Association and Age UK, because they are a perfect fit with our film. So the trick is to find a good fit with potential funding partners. They will be different for every film, so for me that's where it gets really interesting."

Lindsey Dryden
Independent Filmmaker, London

Lindsey Dryden is a partially deaf filmmaker with a passion for music. When she wanted to make her film, Lost & Sound, which mixes art with science, she approached independent production company Animal Monday to help. She applied for a Broadcast Development Award from the Wellcome Trust and was awarded £10,000. Her story underlines the importance of forming alliances and partnering with the right people in order to qualify for different kinds of funding.

"Although I'm partially deaf I have a very satisfying relationship with music and the thing I am most concerned about, should my hearing deteriorate, is what would do I do without music? So my feature-length documentary asks: is it possible to access music even if you can't hear it ordinarily? And what is it about music that makes the brain so determined to welcome it in, even when it meets barriers like deafness?

"It's a character-led film that follows three deaf people who are all involved in music in different ways, alongside interviews with scientists who help contextualize how on earth they are able to do what they do. There is a little girl whose parents are both professional musicians. At the age of fourteen months she was left completely deaf from meningitis. Now aged twelve, she has cochlear implants and is a competition-winning pianist; she's learnt to hear in a very active, though mystifying way. There is Emily, who is a twenty-one-year-old profoundly deaf student at Laban dance school. She has a hearing aid and cochlear implant, but the way that she hears music is completely different from how most people can hear. She is filled with this need to dance—she feels she has some sort of internal 'switch' when music is playing that is quite mysterious to her and very interesting. And then there is Nick, a fifty-something music critic, who woke up one morning to find that one of his ears had suddenly stopped working. Since then, music makes no sense to him, it just sounds like noise and no longer has the power to move him. So for each of them I'm looking at what music has done for them and how they can have the musical futures they are hoping for.

"I'm working with Animal Monday who are a production company based in Brighton, England. I saw Kat Mansoor and Adam Lavis speaking about their film *Here's Johnny* at a screening event in London. Adam, who is their in-house editor, said he believed that disability can be a superpower because it gives you access to new and exciting worlds that you don't have if all your senses work in an ordinary way; disability is not just a negative thing. I believe that too, and it was really lovely to hear them say it. They'd previously made films that combined scientific information with a character going on an artistic journey, which is also what I wanted to do, although in a very different way, and so that's why I went to them.

"Initially, I wrote a very long email to Kat, saying this is what I want to do, this is who I am, and it's all quite early, but what do you think? They were interested and, after we had a meeting, Kat suggested we apply to the Wellcome Trust straight away. The deal was, if we get development money, we'd try and make it happen.

"So we filled in an application form via the Wellcome Trust website; they have four deadlines a year. The application form was based very much on what the story was, what we wanted to use the money for, and how we were going to be engaging a public audience with science. What was really important for them was having a really strong scientific team behind you, so you can deliver rigorous but also new and exciting science. The application is like a mini treatment but the award is for development so they were aware that there were lots of gaps to fill in. It was a very simple process and a few months later we got the funds.

"When I applied I knew the kind of story I wanted to tell, I knew the way I wanted to tell it, but I didn't have the main contributors and their stories, although I had a selection of possibilities. For me, the most important part of the entire process was really honing exactly what the story is, working out how to explain it to people in a couple of sentences. That's what the Broadcast Development Award allowed me to do, find my contributors and then find the best way to present the film to people. A major part of the award was to make a fundraising trailer so we spent time doing research and then made the trailer, and so the money mostly went on the screen.

"As part of the Wellcome Broadcast Development process they asked us to pitch the project back to them once we had developed the idea more fully and had made the trailer. There was a panel of twelve people, including the BBC head of science, John Lynch, and Steve Hewlett, who was the chairman of Sheffield Doc/Fest.

"The Wellcome Trust loved the first trailer and they gave us a small extra fund to pay for some animated footage because that was an important part of the production—you can't tell people you are going to do animation without showing them what it will look like. The animated trailer, which is a scene from the film, looks beautiful, and gives a hint of the characters and the stories.

"I'd pitched other projects at the Mini Meet Market at Sheffield twice before, and then we were selected for the main Meet Market in 2010. That is an online application process too—you have to take care to be more precise and use few words to pitch your idea. We uploaded the two-minute trailer and we were selected. I had to say who I wanted to meet out of the entire list of Meet Market attendees and the brilliant Meet Market team put together a selection of people on that list who wanted to meet us based on the trailer and what they'd read about the project. There were a few surprises in our final list so it helps you become aware of who is actually interested in your project as opposed to who you *want* to be interested in it.

"The meetings are about fifteen minutes long and are held in a busy room. As I'm partially deaf I struggled a little bit with the sound, but the Meet Market team kindly put us behind a screen so it was a bit quieter. It was a very hectic, very intense experience, because we had many meetings with broadcasters, commissioners and distributors. You pitch informally for about five minutes and then have ten minutes for discussion so although the meetings are short they are productive. Someone cried when they saw our trailer and said it was the best thing they'd seen, which was wonderful. So the Meet Market was fantastic because we spoke to a lot of commissioners and distributors and could then start to develop relationships with them. We also met a few people who were interested in executive producing the project; that's not something we were looking for, but it was an interesting avenue to explore. We got a good sense from the meetings who wanted to talk further so we followed up straight away and organized meetings with them.

"We are developing a multiplatform project alongside the film because there's a lot of potential to allow people to put themselves in the position of the people in the film and explore their own perception of sound scientifically in an online environment. We applied to Screen South for funding because Animal Monday are based in Brighton [which came under Screen South's jurisdiction]. That particular fund was tied to North Sea countries, so we were aiming to work with a Swedish production company who specialize in participatory media. Screen South awarded us £10,000 development funding to develop the interactive side of the project.

"In the meantime we are keeping the Wellcome Trust up to date with progress. We discussed that we were losing time because we'd not had a decision from the broadcasters we were waiting on since Doc/Fest, and that the dancer in the film was soon to finish dance college, which we couldn't afford to miss. They said, 'Come in and talk to us and we'll see if we can offer you any production funding so you don't lose key moments in the stories so far,' and they were able to award us £30,000 which was amazing.

"We still have to find top-up funds, because we're making the film on a much smaller budget than we were aiming for with a broadcaster, and we have some ambitious plans with music and animation. The difficulty with finding funding for this as an independent project is that it's not a big international documentary, it's not political, it's not about a big enough social issue, it's not about oil fields or rainforests. I struggled with that for a while because I think it *is* about a social issue, albeit with perhaps a gentle domestic way into the story. But the advantage of our position is that we can make an exciting creative documentary, independently, without any restrictions on the way we tell our story. That's a wonderful freedom to have, even though budget-wise it's a challenge.

"My background is TV but I prefer the independent route, even though my income is very meager in comparison; I'm happier, and I think I'm making more creative films. I prefer having time over money, I really appreciate that; it makes me more creative so it's really a lifestyle choice. I do several different things to support myself. Over the last few months I've made films for the Community Channel, the Royal Court, Accentuate, Creative Junction and Parliamentary Outreach, and I also do freelance proofreading work for publishers, which I love. I'm assistant producing a series of films part-time for the NSPCC [National Society for the Prevention of Cruelty to Children] and I will get a small salary from the film's budget.

"I think everyone gives their time generously when working on independent documentaries that are modestly funded but ambitious. Everyone's working for very reduced rates on this film; my Director of Photography has been very generous and given us lots of time for free, and the team at Animal Monday have contributed many more hours than the project has been able to pay them for.

"Personally, directing my first feature-length documentary has been a very hard process because I've been finding my way through it in a less structured way than if it was being made on a full budget, and I've had to do a lot of learning fast. But I have amazing support from my executive producer and producer, and I'm glad I didn't know how difficult it would be—because I might not have done it!"

Dan Edelstyn
Independent Filmmaker, Optimistic Productions, London
http://www.optimisticproductions.co.uk/
@danedelstyn

A historical film about the Bolshevik Revolution failed to find any funding even after three years of trying, but once Dan Edelstyn's personal family story took an unexpected turn it started attracting interest—and money.

"For me, the call to action to make the film came was when I was five years old. My mum, a great storyteller, told me the story of how my grandparents escaped from the Bolshevik Revolution and ended up in Belfast, Northern Ireland. My granny was depicted as a glamorous violin-playing aristocrat who owned thousands of acres in the Ukraine. Because my dad died when I was three, my mum mythologized him and my grandparents and the whole thing sounded enchanting, but also deeply melancholic because she was grieving for them; her way of dealing with it was to pass the story on to us.

"It instilled in me a feeling of pride about my heritage and it made me want to go back to the Ukraine. I imagined taking our family back there where we could live as we deserved to, as opposed to growing up in Northern Ireland in the early 1980s with bombs going off everywhere. So I always had a European gaze as I grew up, but as you become an adult, you become more rational and so you quash those dreams.

"Skip forward twenty years, and I was wondering what to do next after making a series of *3 Minute Wonders* for Channel 4. I really didn't want to start making normal TV documentaries. Having opened my own production company straight out of university with no experience and no contacts (and almost no hope), I was something of an outsider, so it was difficult. I started to think about my grandmother and her story again, and asked my mum to tell me more and she told me she had a suitcase that had belonged to my grandmother, Maroussia. In the suitcase I found a typed manuscript that was my granny's account of her life. It was full of glamour and romance: ballrooms with girls in white dresses swooning with officers sporting huge mustaches and big swords; there were chandeliers and crystal and gleaming diamond rings. It presented an amazing tableau of what life was like for a wealthy family in pre-revolutionary Ukraine. What I thought might have been family myth was substantiated. I reread the manuscript and there's a section at the end, which describes life after the revolution when my granny seems to have been raped by a Red Army officer. There were some nasty, dark stories in there but the sweep of it was fascinating stuff. As I became increasingly obsessed with the story, rereading the manuscript and dreaming about it, I stopped pitching other projects and so I had quite a hard time financially that year.

"At first the film was based on that 300-page manuscript—a documentary featuring my weird time-traveling alter ego. There's nothing on television like that, added to which there was no present-day jeopardy, as all the action takes place in the past, so it was a very hard sell. Nonetheless, I believed I could make a film that would engage a wider audience but I had a really hard job persuading anybody in television; even on new filmmaker strands like *First Cut*, or BBC *Fresh*, no one would give me the time of day. However, I always think everyone else is wrong.

"In 2005, I was at Sheffield Doc/Fest and spotted Ralph Lee, commissioner for History, Channel 4, so went over. There were two really drunken women aggressively flirting with him; it was definitely an inopportune moment, but I just went ahead anyway and said, 'What do you think about this project, *Bolshevism to Belfast*,' as it was then called. He said, 'You are pushing a large boulder up a hill,' and he escaped from me as soon as he could. And I thought, yes, but that's my job because I care about the story. I exhausted every bloody channel that I could find by going through the *Radio Times* [a TV listings magazine], targeting all those obscure channels that might have a history slot on them to tell the story of my granny and the Bolshevik Revolution. It's so hard to track down a living human being on those channels, but I did and I pitched and … they rejected me.

"I had to get money from television somehow. Whenever I met someone I'd try to find out if they knew someone I could speak to. A personal connection is always much better than a cold call or email, but I don't mind doing that if I have to. Although I'd gained a reputation as an up-and-coming director with my *3-Minute Wonder* films, I was now becoming 'oh, no it's him again, that guy doing his project about his granny, make sure no one sees you speaking to him.' But I stayed with it and kept sending the pitch round. I was probably becoming quite annoying but I just had to keep going. With no TV interest I was forced towards the barren wastelands of charity funding and Community Channel viewership, which was pretty traumatic, because I didn't want to make a film that's only going to be viewed by four members of a niche audience.

"In the meantime, I wanted to go to the Ukraine to find out more. So after three years of developing *Bolshevism to Belfast* and getting nowhere, I hired a researcher to send out hundreds of letters to the sponsors of the Jewish Film Festival and we managed to get £5,000 from a small Jewish charity. We'd had so many Jewish charities say they would help but nothing happened but luckily this foundation were interested in filmmaking. Then we got £1,000 from another Jewish foundation. Buoyed by that my brothers and one sister clubbed together and put another £5,000 in, so suddenly we had £11,000. It's not a huge amount, but it paid for me and my partner Hilary to go to the Ukraine for a month to film and edit some new material, and that was where the breakthrough happened.

"We spent three weeks traveling through Kiev and Odessa looking for traces of my grandmother, Maroussia, and the family. We did some interviews with people at the Jewish Museum who told us that there used to be 30,000 Jews in the Ukraine but only 100 remained after the revolution, which is tragic, but quite generic. Eventually, during the last week of our trip, we found a village where there was a sugar factory that Maroussia had written about. We found out that there was also a vodka distillery that had been owned by my great-grandfather. A 103-year-old woman remembered my granny; the director of the spirits factory told us about Zorokovich, my great-grandfather, who used to own the factory in 1917. An old man sold us an official Communist history book that said the evil capitalist Zorokovich was ousted for the good of the people. The village was so impoverished, and we met so many people who were just desperate, that when they heard that I was Zorokovich's descendant from the West, they immediately thought that I had been sent to save the village. The 103-year-old woman said that she'd dreamed that I would come. So the whole story started to come to life, and that's when the whole three years became worth it. I felt that this was the beginning of something rather than the end.

"At first I thought I should try to reclaim the distillery, but then I thought I should try to work with the village in a positive way and try to align that impoverished village with the global vodka market. It's got a real heritage and back-story—not one fabricated in an advertising agency. That spark of an idea turned the whole project on its head.

I'd applied to pitch *Bolshevism to Belfast* to the BRITDOC Festival and paid a £150 submission fee so was really annoyed when they said no. I went along anyway, and met Rosie Ellison from Interdoc. I told her the two different approaches to telling the story and she said I should go with the vodka one. So *Bolshevism to Belfast* died and a different story that could engage a wider audience began to rise from the ashes. By this time I've been working on the project for three years, there's family money invested in it and it was putting pressure on the relationships around me, so there was a lot riding on it.

"I took it to executive producer Rachel Wexler and she loved it and took us in to see Jo Lapping and Greg Sanderson at BBC *Storyville* and there was immediate interest, although they were nervous because I didn't really have a track record, so they wanted to see a rough-cut. The problem was, how was I going to be able to get it to a rough-cut without having a UK broadcaster onboard to start the funding ball rolling? I'd never tried to raise any money internationally before getting the UK commission—no one from outside your country is realistically going to fund you unless you can get your home broadcaster aboard.

"Rachel also took me in to see Tabitha Jackson at Channel 4. I always think it's so nice if people give me a present, so when I met Tabitha and the *Storyville* people, I took the suitcase containing all Maroussia's things, and really tried to get them involved with the material. It's like going round to see someone's parents—

you want to give them the best impression you can about you and the project. And this project is good because it is based on archival materials. It's very tactile. I also left them a bottle of vodka.

"Whilst we were waiting for Tabitha to pitch the idea up to her boss, Hamish Mykura, our other executive producer, Christo Hird, went to Sundance with another film he had exec produced, *The End of the Line*. He ended up sharing a ski lift with Hamish, and he pitched my vodka film and got him excited about it, so after a very long journey we got our TV commission.

"I think the key thing about funding is your passion and commitment to the project. Whatever it is that you are doing, whether it's making a film or launching a vodka business, you really want to do it because it means something to you."

Jilann Spitzmiller
Producer/Director, Philomath Films, Santa Fe, USA
www.documentaryhowto.com
@philomathfilms @DocuMentors

Jilann Spitzmiller is an award-winning filmmaker, has been a grant reader and has successfully applied for large grants in the USA. However, as she explains, it can still take several applications to the same grantor before securing funding.

"The first time we applied to ITVS for funding we didn't get anything except a nice rejection letter. I think there is a lot of very heavy lifting when you are a first-time filmmaker; you really have a lot to prove. Funders are going to wait and see how an idea is panning out and developing, because there is so much competition out there.

"The next time we applied for a grant we got more than $200,000 in funding on the first try for a film called *Homeland*. It takes place on the Pine Ridge Reservation and it follows four families over the course of three years. It's about contemporary Native American life essentially—the dreams and hopes of the families. By the time we applied for funding we were quite desperate and discouraged. Up to that point we'd gotten grants from Open Society Institute, and from another private foundation in Seattle that was interested in Native American issues. We'd also put a lot on our credit cards and had done a lot of fundraising events. We had also made a phenomenal eight-minute trailer because we had been filming the characters for two-and-a-half years. I think that our application was fine, but it was the trailer that ultimately got us the funding, which in the case of ITVS is actually a licensing fee, not traditional grant money.

"I'll never forget the day we heard about the ITVS funding. My birthday was coming up and the notification date was supposed to be one day before my birthday. My husband and partner Hank kept asking me what I wanted for my birthday and I just kept saying 'I want the ITVS funding.' We were really at the end of our rope financially and we had exhausted all of our resources. We really needed a much larger amount of money to bring the project home. My birthday came and went and there was no notification. The day after my birthday, I got a call from the production manager at ITVS and she said, 'Are you sitting down?,' and she said, 'We want you to stop fundraising and start creating.' I burst into tears, because we were still very new filmmakers, but I knew at that moment I was going to have a chance at a documentary career.

"Even though ITVS has funded us three times now, each time, it's taken a considerable amount of work on our part to get that funding. It's not like they call us up and say what do you guys want to do now? We have to apply like everyone else. Our application for our latest project didn't make it past the first round, but we're going to apply for the next round, because the third film that they funded for us, *Shakespeare Behind Bars*, we had to apply five times before we were successful. That's the most important tip that I would give people—don't give up, keep applying."

Go to Chapter 8 to read an extract from Jilann's grant application to ITVS Open Call for *Shakespeare Behind Bars*. The full ITVS application for *Shakespeare Behind Bars* and Jilann's ITVS application for *Homeland* are available to members of DocuMentors at www.documentaryhowto.com.

Samantha Farinella

Independent Filmmaker, One Angry Woman Productions, New York City
www.samanthafarinella.com

Samantha Farinella is an independent filmmaker who has supported her filmmaking by working in a series of TV producing jobs. Her current project, Hoonah's Heroes, is an independent feature-length documentary profiling the extraordinary stories of Tlingit Vietnam War veterans from the tiny village of Hoonah, Alaska. She successfully raised money through crowdfunding but is now trying to find completion funds.

"I spent some time working at The N network, tiny boutique off-the-radar network that did crazy things—I was hired to work on *South of Nowhere*, a show about two lesbian teenagers who fall in love in high school, so it was kind of cutting edge. I did that job for about four years and I loved it—flying to LA and shooting behind the scenes and little vignettes—it was a good day job to have.

"But the drawback of having a full-time job was that I was producing all the time so when I came home I didn't want to do more of that, so I was not really formulating my next film. In 2009, the bubble burst and I was laid off—about 1,000 people were laid off from Viacom that year.

"But then I thought, this could be my opportunity. I had severance pay and so I thought why don't I go back to filmmaking and do what I really want to do. Even though my job was good, I didn't really find it fulfilling, and making films is what I love. My friend, Danielle, who recently got a doctorate in anthropology and she was living in Hoonah, Alaska. I went out for a drink with her and her girlfriend, Sonya, who is native Tlingit from Hoonah, and they just told me this story, which was really fascinating.

"Hoonah is a really tiny native Tlingit fishing village in Alaska. During the Vietnam War, twenty-eight Tlingit men from Hoonah served in the US Armed Forces. Twenty-seven came back alive, making Hoonah the American town with the highest per capita enlistment rate as well as the highest survival rate. The same skills that enabled these men to survive the harsh nine-month Alaskan winters made the Tlingit soldiers expert snipers and infiltrators in Vietnam. But while the men were on their tours of duty, several changes to fishing law were enacted, ultimately robbing these vets of their livelihoods upon their return. These changes altered the political and economic dynamics of the community for years afterwards because there was no work for them to go to, so many of them are now unemployed, alcoholic and drug addicts. And of course, the United States couldn't really give a damn about them so I thought this could be really interesting.

"My good friend Christie was living in San Francisco with her partner Colin and I went out there to visit them. They told me about Kickstarter. I didn't know what that was, and they were like, 'It's a new thing, you go on there and you send this video out to your friends and you try and raise money for any cause you want, it could be a movie or whatever.' So I started learning about that and thought it was interesting and just did it.

"I sent Kickstarter my campaign proposal and they approved it really quickly. I made the trailer in a day; it was before I'd shot anything, so I had a TV producer friend videotape me. I had an editor who helped me by editing it for free, which took two or three days. I would say, within a week of Kickstarter greenlighting it I had something up on the site.

"Basically we offered a thanks in the credits and a postcard from me on production. If you went to $25 or more you got the same plus a copy of *Left Lane*, my previous film, and so on. The cost of doing the campaign was minimal. In terms of the pledges, that probably cost about $350 for the gifts and the postage.

"The way Kickstarter works, it is all or nothing. My goal was $15,000 and if you don't make that within however many days you choose—I chose forty-five days—you basically don't get the money. I had about $6,000 with a week to go and I thought, this is not going to happen. Then one of the veterans' sons just dropped $10,000 in there, so it was amazing, phenomenal. It was like a miracle. I would totally recommend it. It's amazing to see your friends, acquaintances and co-workers give you money. If you do it right, and get the word out, it works. But you need to know Kickstarter takes a percentage and Amazon [which processes the payments] takes a percentage, so I got around $14,000 out of $16,000 donations in the end.

"I also raised an additional $4,000 through my fiscal sponsor Women Make Movies, so I had about $20,000 going into production. I went up to Alaska with a small crew, myself, Christie and my ex-boss, who was also let go from Nickelodeon. We shot nineteen interviews and sixty hours of footage and got some amazing stories. There was one veteran that I wanted to interview but he was living in Hawaii. He was a thirty-year career man who was fluent in Vietnamese and he went to interrogate prisoners who were tortured, so he had a whole different angle, so I had to go to Hawaii to shoot him. So now the money is almost gone, I just have $2,000 left. I'm trying to save money by transcribing everything myself. It's a daunting experience.

"My friend Lance just got his masters in editing and he's helping me transfer the footage to a hard drive for free, which is awesome, but I would like Larilyn Sanchez, who edited *Left Lane*, to edit *Hoonah's Heroes* and she needs to be paid a living wage.

"I've applied to ten grants and have been denied by nine. A lot of the grants don't give feedback. The first grant I applied for was Alaska Humanities Forum and they have a pre-grant process where you send in an early stage of your grant application. That was interesting because they said it was written really well, but one of the vets I interviewed decided to make his own documentary, and so there were two people going after the same grant, so I think we basically canceled each other out.

"There's a grant coming up called NYSCA, which is New York State Council of the Arts. They want to see a twenty-five-minute piece, so that's pushing me to make a thirty-minute cut for that, which is good, because it's making me look at everything I have and then make something of it. I'm at this point right now, where I really can't depend on grants. The problem is that my film is historical. These men are older, they are going to be dying soon, and history will be erased. So it's not that conducive to getting money in this country, because it's not timely. I feel it's usually documentaries about current events, or dealing with a very famous person or event in history like the Holocaust would be more economically viable. If I was doing a piece on Afghanistan it would be easier to raise money; Vietnam's not that romantic and it's a sore spot for America.

"I'm at a crossroads now, I have to raise money, I can't keep spending my own money because I'm not independently wealthy, so I need to find a producer. I also have the angle of trying to find wealthy donors who want to give money to a personal cause in return for a credit as producer or executive producer. If they give through Women Make Movies it's a tax-refundable donation, which makes it more attractive.

"I could go back to Kickstarter, but I feel like I've tapped out my friends so I don't really want to do that again. I have a lot of great footage, and if people were to see it I'm sure they would be willing to back it. So I've just got to figure out a way around it. I'm having meetings with the woman who is in charge of film at the Native American Museum in New York City and I'm supposed to have a meeting with some of the producers of *Restrepo*, which was up for an Oscar. Part of me wants to hunker down somewhere and live at my parents' house and just do it all myself, but I do want to keep plugging away, because I do feel like there is money out there.

"It's a great process, I love filmmaking and I want to keep doing it but there isn't a blueprint, so you just have to keep making your own way. A lot of it is luck, who you meet, so you really have to put yourself out there and sell yourself in a way, and that's hard. A lot of people start films and don't finish them. A friend of mine gave me the best advice; you really need to finish this even if you don't think it's perfect, because it's so easy never to finish something and have it incomplete. And I see that with my previous film, *Left Lane*, it's not perfect, but it's out there and obviously people enjoyed it, so it's absolutely worth completing a flawed film and being amazed at how it affects people."

Ricki Stern

Producer/Director, Break Thru Films, New York City
www.breakthrufilms.org

Ricki Stern makes social issue documentaries and so is experienced in raising money from foundations. However, when she strayed from conventional social issues she found fundraising much more difficult.

"I was sitting in the office and was thinking what might be a good film to do next and I thought of Joan Rivers. I have a relationship with her through my mother, so I picked up the phone and called my mother, and she picked up the phone and called Joan, and Joan said, 'Sure, get her to call me.' I spoke to Joan five minutes later and I met with her for about an hour the next day, and she told me her story. My background is in theatre and in acting, so I was very interested in the performer's life and Joan is the quintessential performer. I had never seen anything that really chronicled what it's really like living the kind of life where you are constantly on the road, doing anything for your next gig. That alone I found pretty fascinating. Coupled with that was the fact that Joan had been a groundbreaking female comedian in a world that was originally much more male-oriented. I began to wonder who she really was, versus who I knew her to be, which was not this comedic persona.

"I quickly went on a two-day shoot with her to get some footage to cut together a teaser that we would use to raise funding. A lot of times you have to jump off the diving board, take a little bit of money, a camera and your friend who can shoot and get something in the can so that people can see what you are after. The teaser was really funny, and it was pretty good; people liked it. But a couple of things happened, either people just didn't like her comedy or didn't like her; they'd say 'she's too harsh for me,' or they would say 'I love her, but she's not the right demographic for my channel.' In the United States, I took it to

HBO, Showtime, IFC Television and in the UK, the BBC and Channel 4 too, I think. I spoke to Irish television and some other places who said, we love her but we can only give you $5,000.

"I had a friend at the BBC who offered to sponsor an event because she was doing something around women and aging, but she couldn't give me money for my film. So they threw a party for Joan and then I had her meet with Nick Fraser (Editor of *Storyville*). To see them talking for an hour was interesting; all of a sudden, he was like 'Oh, she's quite gracious'; and I think he was impressed. But again the money wasn't forthcoming.

"In the past, because most of our films have had some kind of social issue bent we've been able to get financing from social issue funds and grants. But Joan was just not a social issue. People will say, 'An aging woman comedian? we just don't have a big market for that.' I was having to say, she's got a huge gay following, she's got a much younger following than people expect, and she had a huge following on QVC shopping channel. Nobody wants to think of their project in terms of audience and the market, they just want to do their project, and do art and tell a good story; I had to really become the producer in terms of selling it.

"Cut to a year later, no place I went to would give us money upfront, so as a result we'd had to do it on the down and dirty. The two guys who shot the film were on deferred fees; we traveled as cheaply as we could in coach and Joan would bump us up to first-class on flights; Joan would be put up in an expensive hotel in Palm Beach and we'd be at the cheaper place around the corner. To me it was important just to get in the can, because once it's in the can, then I can breathe.

"And then we've got to get the edit done. Basically I took every last penny that I had from other films, borrowing from one to pay the other. So the major initial investment was the production with deferred fees and getting the editor onboard. It was hard, but once it got to rough-cut, I knew there was a good film there and I felt comfortable borrowing money, to actually finish it. The final costs of paying people back and replacing broken equipment and going to Sundance were all on the credit card. We were able to pay it back on the sale to IFC Films in the US and Channel 4 in the UK. I'm still not in the black on it—the budget expands as soon as the film starts to take off because all of a sudden you have traveling costs and Joan's travel costs then become part of the post-production part of the budget, along with press and distribution. So we are still not seeing a profit on it but we are hoping that there will be at some point."

The Final Word …

If the process of raising funds for your project feels daunting, Ricki Stern has some encouraging words. "Sometimes when it comes too easily—if you look some of the big-budget documentaries where the filmmaker was just handed the money to go out and make their film, I don't know that you feel the struggle of the filmmaking process in it. You get something from having to figure it out and having to make hard choices about what you can and can't film."

But the final word goes to Esther Robinson, author of *The Big Art/Little Debt Plan*: "There is no single way … No guru, no method—just what works. The way forward will be charted by your friends and colleagues. Bounce your ideas off others. Get new ideas. Keep talking and listening. Your way forward will be idiosyncratic, an amalgam of many people's plans." That excellent advice applies equally to all the funding information in this book. Some if it will be appropriate for you, much of it not; new funds will materialize, others will fold. What's important is that you keep an open mind, look out for opportunities and do everything you can to develop your project in a way that will maximize your funding options, be it by getting a well-known executive producer onboard or writing begging letters to oil barons.

Good luck!

Appendix

Festivals, Forums and Workshops

- AIDC (Australian International Documentary Conference) http://aidc.com.au/
- Archidoc—France http://www.lafemis.fr/
- Asia Television Forum Singapore http://www.asiatvforum.com/

- Baltic Sea Forum—Latvia http://www.mediadesklatvia.eu/archive-baltic-sea-forum/
- Banff World Media Festival—Canada http://www.banffmediafestival.com/

- CNEX Chinese Documentary Forum http://www.cnex.org.cn/
- COPRO—Israeli Documentary Screen Market—Israel http://www.copro.co.il/
- CPH:DOX—Denmark http://www.cphdox.dk/d/a1.lasso

- Doc Meeting Argentina http://www.docmeeting.com.ar/english.php
- DocedgeKolkata—India http://docresi.org/docedgeKolkat_about.html#
- Docs Barcelona—Spain http://www.docsbarcelona.com/
- Documentary Campus Masterschool—Germany http://www.documentary-campus.com/v2/
- Documentary Edge Festival—New Zealand http://www.docnz.org.nz/
- Dok Leipzig—Germany http://www.dok-leipzig.de/
- Dragon Forum—Poland http://www.dragonforum.pl/
- Durban FilmMart—South Africa http://www.durbanfilmmart.com/

- East European Forum—Czech Republic http://www.dokweb.net/en/east-european-forum/
- EAVE (European Audiovisual Entrepreneurs) European Producers Workshop—Luxembourg http://eave.org/
- ESoDoc (European Social Documentary)—Italy http://www.esodoc.eu/
- EURODOC—various locations in Europe http://www.eurodoc-net.com/en/

- Ex Oriente Film Workshop—Czech Republic http://www.dokweb.net/en/ex-oriente-film/

- Good Pitch—Various http://britdoc.org/real_good/pitch/

- HotDocs—Canada http://www.hotdocs.ca/

- IDFA—The Netherlands http://www.idfa.nl/industry.aspx

- Lisbon Docs—Portugal http://www.doclisboa.org/lisbondocs/en_home.php
- Lorcano Film Festival—Switzerland http://www.pardo.ch/jahia/Jahia/home/lang/en

- MIPCOM—France http://www.mipworld.com/mipcom/
- MIPDoc—France http://www.mipworld.com/mipdoc/
- MIPFormats—France http://www.mipworld.com/en/mipformats/
- MIPTV—France http://www.mipworld.com/en/miptv/
- Miradas Doc—Canary Islands http://miradasdoc.com/

- NATPE (National Association of Television Program Executives)—USA http://www.natpe.org/natpe/

- RealScreen Summit—USA http://summit.realscreen.com/

- Sheffield Doc/Fest—UK http://sheffdocfest.com/
- Sofia Meetings—Bulgaria http://www.siff.bg/sofiameetings/
- Sunnyside of the Doc—France http://www.sunnysideofthedoc.com/uk/

- Visions du Réel Pitching Forum—Switzerland http://www.visionsdureel.ch/en/market.html

- Westdoc—USA http://www.thewestdoc.com/
- Wildscreen Festival—UK http://www.wildscreenfestival.org/
- World Congress of Science & Factual Producers—Various http://www.wcsfp.com/

- Zagreb Dox—Croatia http://www.zagrebdox.net/en/

Sample Budget Template*

This template covers the main categories you might need to include in your budget. Budgets are referred to in terms of "per hou'" or "per 30" rather than total series budget. For example a 13x60' series that costs $1m in total will have a budget of approximately $77K per hour.

Schedule Item	Title	
	Programme Code	Episodes x Duration
	CORE PROJECT COSTS	0.00
1	Core Team Salaries	0.00
2	Contingencies	0.00
3	Production Fee	0.00
4	Completion Guarantees	0.00
	FILM PRODUCTION COSTS	0.00
5	Development —Rights/Options Payments —Writer's Fee —Research	0.00
6	Producer/Director —Executive Producer —Series Producer —Producer/Director 1 —Producer/Director 2 —Edit Producer —Assistant Producer	0.00
7	Artists —Artists —Overseas Artists/Extras etc. —Stand-ins, Doubles, Stuntmen —Footsteps and Effects —Tutor/Chaperones	0.00

*Based on a UK production budget.

8	**Presenters/Interviewees** —Presenters —Interviewees —Voiceover Artists	0.00
9	**Production Unit Salaries** —Production Executive —Production Manager —Production Co-ordinator 1 —Runner —Production Accountant —Accounts Assistant —Researcher —Loggers	0.00
11	**Crew—Camera** —Lighting Director —Lighting Cameraman —Camera Operator —Assistant Camera —Vision Mixer	0.00
12	**Crew—Sound** —Sound Recordist —Boom Operator —Sound Assitant —Sound Supervisor —Sound Engineer	0.00
13	**Crew—Lighting** —Gaffer —Electrician —Generator Operator	0.00
14	**Art Department** —Set Designer —Model Maker	0.00
15	**Crew—Wardrobe/Make-up/Hair**	0.00

16	**Crew—Editing** —Offline Editor —Online Editor —Dubbing Editor —Assistants	0.00
17	**Crew—Second Unit**	0.00
18	**Salary and Wage-Related Overheads** —Holiday Credits —Employers National Insurance—Crew —Employers National Insurance—Artists	0.00
19	**Materials—Art Department** —Sets —Construction Materials —Props—Hired —Props—Purchased —Action Props —Consumables	0.00
20	**Materials—Wardrobe/Make-up/Hair** —Wardrobe Costumes—Hired —Wardrobe Costumes—Purchased —Repair and Cleaning Costs —Wardrobe Storage —Make-up Materials —Hair Materials —Hair Consumables —Wigs	0.00
21	**Production Equipment** —Camera Equipment —Consumables —Grip Equipment —Sound Equipment —Lighting Equipment —Editing Equipment —Autocue	0.00

22	**Facility Package** —Camera Crew/Equipment —Sound Crew/Equipment —Lighting Crew/Equipment —Editing Facilities —Design Package	0.00
23	**Studios/Outside Broadcasts** —Studios Fee —Recording Studios —OB Unit —Sound Mobile —Portable Single Camera —Studio Crew Costs	0.00
24	**Other Production Facilities** —Rehearsal Room —Location Offices —Location Fees —Gratuities —Security and Police —Location Equipment	0.00
25	**Film/Tape Stock** —Film Stock —Shooting Tapes —Off-line Tapes —On-line Tapes —Viewing Copies —Sound Stock —Dubbing —Effects Stock —Masters—Vision —Masters—Sound —Safety/Delivery Copies	0.00
	Post-production-Tape —Tape transfers —Offline Editing	

27	—Online Editing —Caption Generator —Special Effects —Lay Off —Audio Dubbing incl. Sound Mix —Lay Back —Telecine —Autoconform	0.00
28	**Archive Material** —Viewing Costs —Search Fees —Processing and Transfer —Royalties—Film and Tape Archive —Stills Archive —Sound Archive	0.00
29	**Rostrum/Graphics** —Rostrum —Graphics —Titles and Credits	0.00
30	**Music (Copyright/Performance)** —Composer —Musicians —Musical Director —Hire of Music —Music Remixing and Editing	0.00
	OVERHEADS	**0.00**
31	**Travel/Transport** —Recce/Pre-production Costs —Production Costs —Artists —Equipment —Freight —Carnets and Agent Fees —Excess Baggage —Visas	

	—Inoculations —Petrol and Parking —Courier Bikes and Cabs —Set Storage/Disposal —Set Transport	0.00
32	**Hotel/Living** —Pre-production and Recce Costs —Crew Accommodation —Artists Accommodation —Location Catering —Living Allowances —Meal Allowances—Crew —Meal Allowances—Artists —Gratuities —Hospitality —Laundry	0.00
33	**Other Production Costs** —Transcription —Post-production Scripts —Publicity Stills	0.00
34	**Insurance/Finance/Legal**	0.00
35	**Production Overheads** —Office Rent —Rates —Power/ILighting/Heating —Printing and Stationery —Postage —Photocopying and Computers	0.00
Total		**0.00**

Don't forget to account for:

- 10 percent contingency fee (at least)
- Legal fees—for co-production agreements and private equity—"whatever you put in the budget, treble it," says Sue Bourne, director of Irish dance documentary, *Jig.*
- Financing costs—accountant, interest fees for loans, commissions for co-production executives etc.
- E&O insurance—errors and omissions insurance is taken out against libel, slander and copyright infringement, among other things, and is typically required by buyers or distributors on signing of contract.

End Notes

xii   "I don't care where the money comes from": Landis, John, 'Film Tree' [video] by filmtree1, April 11, 2011 Timecode: 4'46" http://www.youtube. com/watch?v=nS4UmzQs_dw&feature=player_embedded

Introduction

1   "Most documentary filmmakers are polygamous": VanDeCarr, Paul, 'The Prenups: What Filmmakers and Funders Should Talk About Before Tying the Knot', Active Voice Lab, 2009, p. 12 [PDF] www.theprenups.org

2   "funding shortfalls of 5–60 percent": Dams, Tim, 'Money', *Televisual*, April, 2011, p. 49

2   "and 85 percent of producers": Dams, Tim, 'Money', *Televisual*, April, 2011, pp. 49–50

PART I: The Idea

Getting Ready

9   "Not all stories are ready to be told": Clarke, Cheryl A., *Storytelling for Grant-seekers: A Guide to Creative Nonprofit Fundraising* (San Francisco: John Wiley & Sons, 2009), p. 8

11   "eco-documentaries ... are being made by impassioned experts": Maher, Kevin, "Is this the end of the line for documentary?," *The Times*, Saturday Review, September 18, 2010, p. 4

11   "At the end of the day, we the audience are coming for drama": Porath, Shlomo, "Jerusalem Film Festival: Bombay Beach," Midnight East, July 19, 2011, http://www.midnighteast.com/mag/?p=13711

11   "to find yourself at the Thessaloniki Documentary Festival": Moestrup, Steffen, "Bodily experience," *DOX*, Summer 2011, no. 90, p. 6

12   "wanted to do it now because those regions are changing very fast": "*Blue Planet*'s Alastair Fothergill talks to TBI," TBI Vision, April 26, 2011, http://www.tbivision.com/article.php?category=4&article=2112&page=1 retrieved April 26, 2011

13   "I've read grant applications that start off": Dean, Carole Lee, *The Art of Film Funding: Alternative Financing Concepts* (Studio City: Michael Wiese Productions, 2007), p. 1

13   "enhance the story": Ritchie, Kevin, "'Boomtown Babylon' uniting global filmmakers," RealScreen, December, 22 2010, http://www.realscreen.com/articles/news/20101222/boomtown.html retrieved January 31, 2010

14   "Every producer knows they've got a thing that everybody in the world needs to see": Hunt, Chris, "Show Me the Money: Making Up the Budget Shortfall—Deficit Financing for Beginners panel," Intelligent Factual Festival 2010

16   "ARTE (a Franco-German TV channel) opening up new documentary slots in 2012": "C21's Factual Week: Sunny Side update," C21, June 24, 2011, by email

16   "In France in 2010": quoted in Benzine, Adam, "Sunny Side looks for Eastern opportunities," Realscreen, June 20, 2011, http://realscreen.com/2011/06/20/sunny-side-looks-for-eastern-opportunities/

17   "I tried to get money for a year": quoted in Nord, Liz, "Tribeca: Q&A with Bombay Beach director Alma Har'el," The Film Panel Notemaker, April 28, 2011, http://thefilmpanelnotetaker.com/tribeca-q-a-with-bombay-beach-director-alma-harel

19   "They ran a story on a small kid from the slums of India": quoted in Ormes, Minjae, "A conversation with 2009 Gucci grantee Gemma Atwa'",

Tribeca Film Institute, November, 16 2010, http://www.tribecafilminstitute. org/filmmakers/gucci_documentary/news/108228719.html

21   "When Julia Redwood and Ed Punchard formed Prospero Productions": Hamilton, Peter, "Case study: *Dino Stampede*—an ABC commission triggers a cascade of tax benefits and international licenses, March 2, 2011 http:// documentarytelevision.com/sweet-spots/australian-case-study-dino-stampede-an-abc-commission-triggers-a-cascade-of-tax-benefits-and-international-licenses/, retrieved March 7, 2011

21   "the most creative thing about making docs today is building the business plan": Parker, Robin, "Funding issues cloud docs festival," *Broadcast,* July 3, 2009, p. 8

22   "there was a Harvard business book": Rossi, Fernanda, in Dean, Carole Lee, *The Art of Film Funding: Alternative Financing Concepts* (Studio City: Michael Wiese Productions, 2007), p. 108

The Pitch

24   "Joel Orosz, author of *The Insider's Guide to Grantmaking,* describes": Orosz, Joel, *The Insider's Guide to Grantmaking: How Foundations Find, Fund, and Manage Effective Programs* (San Francisco: Jossey-Bass Publishers, 2000) pp. 73–4

27   "a seven- to ten-minute audiovisual pitch of the film": Rossi, Fernanda, in Dean, Carole Lee, *The Art of Film Funding: Alternative Financing Concepts* (Studio City: Michael Wiese Productions, 2007), pp. 123–4

32   "music and archive clearance costs added another $400,000": Youngs, Ian, "Micro-budget film wows Cannes," BBC News, May 18, 2004, http://news. bbc.co.uk/1/hi/entertainment/3720455.stm

32   "*Oceans* (2010), which had a reported budget of $80 million": "*Oceans,* the numbers," http://www.the-numbers.com/movies/2010/OCENS.php, retrieved April 24, 2011

33   "*The Age of Stupid* cost £450,000 to make, and a further £400,000 to distribute":"Crowdfunding FAQ," Spanner Films, http://www.spannerfilms. net.node/1253/

33   "Leftfield Pictures made a seven-minute pitch reel for *Pawn Stars*": Hamilton, Peter, "History's Pawn Stars (part 2/4): Concept, talent, sizzle tape, pitch, green light, HIT!!," Documentary Television, March 16, 2011, http:// documentarytelevision.com/sweet-spots/historys-pawn-stars-part-24- concept-talent-sizzle-tape-pitch-green-light-hit/

34   "A lot of productions get caught out": Lapping, Jo, quoted in Search, Jess and McCarthy, Melissa, *Getting Your Documentary Funded and Distributed* (London: Shooting People, 2005), p. 140

34   "the same program in 3D would require a total budget of around $621,000": Hamilton, Peter, "What is the impact of 3D on factual budgets? 2/2—graphics, post, deliverables & takeaways," June 11, 2011, http:// documentarytelevision.com/3d-costs/how-does-3d-impact-factual- budgets-part-2-%E2%80%93- graphics-post-deliverables-and-takeaways/

35   "You've got to stay in business during that period": "Show me the money: courting international co production panel," Intelligent Factual Festival, 2010

36   *Oceans*: *Oceans*, The Numbers, http://www.the-numbers.com/movies/ 2010OCENS.php, retrieved April 24, 2011

36   *Jackass 3D*: *Jackass 3D*, The Numbers, http://www.the-numbers.com/ movie/Jackass-3D, retrieved August 28, 2011

36   *Persepolis*: IMDB http://www.imdb.com/title/tt0808417/

36   *Fahrenheit 9/11*: *Fahrenheit 9/11*, The Numbers, http://www.the-numbers. com/movies/2004/FH911.php, retrieved April 24, 2011

36   *Dolphins and Whales 3D: Tribes of the Ocean: Dolphins and Whales 3D: Tribes of the Ocean*, The Numbers, http://www.the-numbers.com/movies/2008/0DW3D.php, retrieved August 28, 2011

36   *Inside Job*: Box Office History for Documentary Movies, The Numbers, http://www.the-numbers.com/movies/series/Documentary.php, retrieved July 11, 2011

36   *Waltz with Bashir*: Box Office History for Documentary Movies, The Numbers, http://www.the-numbers.com/movies/series/Documentary.php, retrieved July 11, 2011

36   *In the Shadow of the Moon*: Box Office History for Documentary Movies, The Numbers, http://www.the-numbers.com/movies/series/Documentary.php, retrieved July 11, 2011

36   *End of the Line*: Levitt, Tom and Thomas, Ali, "*The End of the Line*: How a film changed the way we eat fish," *Guardian*, February 18, 2011, http://www.guardian.co.uk/environment/2011/feb/18/end-line-film-fish

37   *Jig*: Dams, Tim, "Dancing up a feature doc," *Televisual*, May 2011 p. 16

37   *Hoop Dreams*: Box Office History for Documentary Movies, The Numbers, http://www.the-numbers.com/movies/series/Documentary.php, retrieved July 11, 2011

37   *Murderball*: Box Office History for Documentary Movies, The Numbers, http://www.the-numbers.com/movies/series/Documentary.php, retrieved July 11, 2011

37   *Super Size Me*: Box Office History for Documentary Movies, The Numbers, http://www.the-numbers.com/movies/series/Documentary.php, retrieved July 11, 2011

37   *Tarnation*: Youngs, Ian, "Micro-budget film wows Cannes," BBC News, May 18, 2004, http://news.bbc.co.uk/1/hi/entertainment/3720455.stm

37   *Planet Earth*: Sherwin, Adam, "BBC ready to lead viewers into a vivid new world of television," *The Sunday Times*, December 10, 2005, http://www.timesonline.co.uk/tol/news/uk/article756783.ece

37   *Death of the Mega-beasts*: Hamilton, Peter, "Australian Case Study: *Dino Stampede*—An ABC commission triggers a cascade of tax benefits and international licenses," Documentary Television, March 2, 2011, http://documentarytelevision.com/sweet-spots/australian-case-study-dino-stampede-an-abc-commission-triggers-a-cascade-of-tax-benefits-and-international-licenses/

37   *Dino Stampede*: Hamilton, Peter, "Australian Case Study: *Dino Stampede*—An ABC commission triggers a cascade of tax benefits and international licenses," Documentary Television, March 2, 2011, http://documentarytelevision.com/sweet-spots/australian-case-study-dino-stampede-an-abc-commission-triggers-a-cascade-of-tax-benefits-and-international-licenses/, retrieved March 7, 2011

37   *One Born Every Minute*: Parker, Robin, "C4 takes back seat on co-pros to boost doc series budgets," *Broadcast*, October 30, 2009

37   *Globe Trekker*: Hamilton, Peter, "Case Study: *Globe Trekker* and how a deficit financed travel series became a winner for PBS and Pilot Productions," Documentary Television, February 19, 2011, http://documentarytelevision.com/distribution/case study-globe-trekker-and-how-a-deficit-financed-travel-series-became-a-winner-for-pbs-and-pilot-productions-12/

37   *Pawn Stars*: Hamilton, Peter, "History's *Pawn Stars* (part 2/4): Concept, talent, sizzle tape, pitch, green light, HIT!!," Documentary Television, March 16, 2011, http://documentarytelevision.com/sweet-spots/historys-pawn-stars-part-24-concept-talent-sizzle-tape-pitch-green-light-hit/

39   "Finance Plan Example: *Dino Stampede*": Hamilton, Peter, "Case Study: *Dino Stampede*—An ABC commission triggers a cascade of tax benefits and international licenses," March 2, 2011 http://documentarytelevision.

com/sweet-spots/australian-case-study-dino-stampede-an-abc-commission-triggers-a-cascade-of-tax-benefits-and-international-licenses/, retrieved March 7, 2011

43 "It also just gave me new friends and contacts": Smith, Geoffrey, EDN online masterclass, December 10, 2010

44 "We reached out to medical groups, people involved in caring in the community": Smith, Geoffrey, EDN online masterclass, December 10, 2010

PART II: The Funding

1: TV Channels—Ratings Addicts

60 "More recently, Channel 4 decided to pump more money": Parker, Robin, "C4 takes back seat on co-pros to boost doc series budgets," *Broadcast*, October 30, 2009

60 "There's no point in having the right idea and being unable to realize it": Parker, Robin, "C4 takes back seat on co-pros to boost doc series budgets," *Broadcast*, October 30, 2009

60 "A commissioner at TVOntario": Davidson, Sean, "Broadcaster, can you spare a dime?," C21 Media, May 5, 2011, http://www.c21media.net/features/detail.asp?area=24&article=60565

60 "KBS1 runs no commercials": "Korea Opportunities," C21's Factual Week: Feature, April 15, 2011 by email

61 "All other rights in the program are retained by the producer": "Terms of trade for independent producers finally arrive," Hartbottle & Lewis, http://www.harbottle.com/hnl/pages/article_view_hnl/679.php, retrieved July 14, 2011

61 "This provides independent producers with an important source of income": Dams, Tim, "Indies go global," *Televisual*, September, 2010, p. 22

61   "Now instead of knocking on broadcasters' doors": quoted in Anderson,
      Kelly, "Climate change: the global co-production update—France,"
      Realscreen, January–February, 2010, pp. 50–2

61   "at one point it was reported that the then RTL-owned Channel 5":
      Sweney, Mark, "Channel Five revenue drops for RTL," *Guardian*, August 26,
      2008, http://www.guardian.co.uk/media/2008/aug/26/rtl.channelfive

61   "Looking beyond TV, Netflix": "Netflix to build House of Cards," C21
      Media, March 16, 2011, http://www.c21media.net/news/detail.
      asp?area=1&article=59829

64   "It's been suggested that UK channels": Walsh Barry, "Climate change: the
      global co-production update—UK," *Realscreen*, January–February, 2010,
      pp. 55–6

64   "with channels in the USA, Canada, France, Germany and Spain the most
      likely to provide co-production funding": "The changing face of funding,"
      The Business Book 2010/11 Broadcast, December, 2010, p. 32

65   "Some channels, such as France Télévisions": Anderson, Kelly, "Climate
      change: the global co-production update—France", *Realscreen*, January–
      February, 2010, pp. 50–2

67   "When Darlow Smithson pitched *Concorde's Last Flight*": "Darlow Smithson
      lands Concord contract," http://www.darlowsmithson.com/About/
      News/2010/Concorde.html

68   "For example, when Indian producer/distributor Shemaroo": Natividad,
      Angela, "India's Shemaroo seals 3D coprod deal with South Africa's Astral
      Studios," Mipblog, October 7, 2010, http://blog.mipworld.com/2010/10/
      india%E2%80%99s-shemaroo-seals-3d-coprod-deal-with-south-
      africa%E2%80%99s-astral-studios/, retrieved April 6, 2011

68   "We did a show for ABC called *I Survived a Japanese Game Show*": quoted
      in Walsh, Barry, "Executive positions," *Realscreen*, May–June 2011, p. 45

70   "If the producer needs both a partner in Germany and an international distributor": quoted in Gibb, Lindsay, "Climate change: the global co-production update—Germany," *Realscreen*, January–February, 2010, pp. 53–4

71   "According to Thomas Dey, head of corporate finance at Grant Thornton": Wood, David, "The new British invasion," *Broadcast*, May 21, 2010, pp. 22–5

2: Distributors—Traveling Salesmen

87   "Rights are what allow you to make what you make.": "*Welcome*," http://rights.tv/

88   "According to Adam P. Davies and N. Wistreich": Davies, Adam P., and Wistreich, N., *The Film Finance Handbook—How to Fund Your Film* (London: Netribution, 2008) pp. 116–17

89   "Theatrical feature documentary *Inside Job*": "Company credits for *Inside Job*," IMDb, http://www.imdb.com/title/tt1645089/companycredits

90   "Fortunately, in the UK, at least 94 percent": Fry, Andy, "Distributors Survey 2010," Broadcast, September 23, 2010, http://www.broadcastnow.co.uk/news/international/distributors-survey-2010/5018611, article retrieved December 16, 2010

91   "In 2010, eight UK distributors spent £1million or more on development": Fry, Andy, "Distributors show resilience," Distributors 2010, Broadcast, September 24, 2010, p. 11

92   "pre-buying rather than commissioning": Wood, David, "Surviving the downturn," *Broadcast*, July 3, 2009, p. 30

92   "If a distributor is passionate about the show": "Show me the money: courting international co-production panel," Intelligent Factual Festival, 2010

93   "films that focus on social issues in need of a voice": "Cactus Three announces the establishment of a new film finishing fund," Cactus Three press release, October 13, 2010

93   "In a way, a process that starts out with a shortfall": "Show me the money: making up the budget shortfall—deficit financing for beginners panel," Intelligent Factual Festival, 2010

94   "eyes and ears into the international market": quoted in Dams, Tim, "Money," *Televisual*, April, 2011, p. 50

94   "You should be having monthly development meetings": "Show me the money: making up the budget shortfall—deficit financing for beginners panel," Intelligent Factual Festival, 2010

96   "It's been estimated that only 10–25 percent of UK TV programs": "Inside the distributors," Research Centre, 2005, p. 15

97   "Independent documentary distributor Dogwoof": Godas, Anna, "Going it alone" panel, University Centre, Hastings, February 19, 2011

98   "In the UK, Rights.TV, a legal and business affairs company": "New routes to funding," *The Business Book 2010/11 Broadcast*, December, 2010, pp. 34–5

99   "I know too many distributors who come to me": "Show me the money: courting international co-production panel," Intelligent Factual Festival, 2010

3: Brands—Dirty, Sexy Mad Men

104   "I've put myself in some pretty horrible situations": Spurlock, Morgan, "The greatest TED Talk ever sold," April, 2011 [Video file]. Retrieved from http://www.ted.com/talks/morgan_spurlock_the_greatest_ted_talk_ever_sold.html

104   "If you sit down to watch a reality TV show in the USA": Friedman, Wayne, "More than half viewing time devoted to ad messages in reality shows," TV Watch, September 14, 2010, http://www.mediapost.com/publications/?fa=Articles.showArticle&art_aid=135708&nid=118547, retrieved January 14, 2011

104   "For über reality producer Mark Burnett": Wenner, Lawrence, A., "On the ethics of product placement in media entertainment," in Galician, Mary-Lou (ed.), *Handbook of Product Placement in the Mass Media* (Binghamton, NY: 2006), p. 115

104   "*Survivor* is as much a marketing vehicle as a television show": "Burnett: *Survivor* is life," CBS News, February 11, 2011, http://www.cbsnews.com/ stories/2001/06/05/survivor/main294978.shtml

105   "My shows create an interest": Kern, T., "Commercial television," *Snack Food and Wholesale Bakery*, 90(6), June, 2001, quoted in Wenner, Lawrence, A., "On the ethics of product placement in media entertainment," in Galician, Mary-Lou (ed.), *Handbook of Product Placement in the Mass Media* (Binghamton, NY: 2006), p. 102

105   "Indeed, it's been noted that many of Burnett's shows": Lehu, Jean-Marc, *Branded Entertainment: Product Placement and Brand Strategy in the Entertainment Business*, (London: Kogan Page, 2007), p. 164

105   "The film was funded by twenty-two brands": Bernstein, Josh, "Morgan Spurlock punks Hollywood," The Daily Beast, April 19, 2011 http://www. thedailybeast.com/blogs-and-stories/2011-04-19/the-greatest-story-ever-sold-morgan-spurlock-punks-hollywood/#, retrieved April 22, 2011

105   "But he had to work hard": Sciretta, Peter, "Morgan Spurlock's *The Greatest Movie Ever Sold* might be the most meta movie ever made," Slash Film, January 24, 2011, http://www.slashfilm.com/morgan-spurlocks-the-greatest-movie-sold-sundance-review/, retrieved January 29, 2011

105   "burning money out of our own pockets": Anderson, Kelly, "Hot Docs preview: birth of a salesman," Realscreen, April 28, 2011, http://realscreen. com/2011/04/28/hot-docs-preview-birth-of-a-salesman/

105   "For example, POM Wonderful paid $500,000 upfront": Spurlock, Morgan, quoted in Blackman, Joshua, "Morgan Spurlock sells out in POM Wonderful presents *The Greatest Movie Ever Sold*," Atonal Film, August 11, 2011,

http://www.atonalfilm.com/headline/morgan-spurlock-sells-out-in-porn-wonderful-presents-the-greatest-movie-ever-sold/

105 "which it achieved at its Sundance première in 2011": Sauer, Abe, "Brandchannel presents: the greatest movie review ever told," Brandchannel, May 2, 2011, http://www.brandchannel.com/home/post/2011/05/02/Morgan-Spurlock-Movie-Review-Product-Placement.aspx

105 "as of August 24, 2011": "POM Wonderful presents: *The Greatest Movie Ever Sold*," Box Office Mojo, http://boxofficemojo.com/movies/?page=main &id=greatestmovieeversold.htm

106 "We were told our pitch was good": McMahon, Kate, "No AFP, no commission, frustrated indies claim," *Broadcast*, February 5, 2010, p. 5

106 "On 28th February 2011 product placement was made legal": Farber, Alex, "ITV signs first product placement deal," *Broadcast*, February 28, 2011

106 "By 1957, US advertisers were creating around 33 percent of TV programs": Turner, Kathleen, J., "The practice of product placement: insinuating the product into the message: an historical context for product placement," Galician, Mary-Lou (ed.), *Handbook of Product Placement in the Mass Media* (Binghamton, NY: 2006), p. 11

106 "*Firestone Orchestra, Kraft Television Theatre, United States Steel Hour, Colgate Comedy Hour*": Kretchner, Susan B., "Advertainment: the evolution of product placement as a mass media marketing strategy," Galician, Mary-Lou (ed.), *Handbook of Product Placement in the Mass Media* (Binghamton, NY: 2006), p. 41

106 "saying good night for Camel cigarettes": Turner, Kathleen, J., "The practice of product placement: insinuating the product into the message: an historical context for product placement," Galician, Mary-Lou (ed.), *Handbook of Product Placement in the Mass Media* (Binghamton, NY: 2006), p. 12

106 "To avoid any possible dilution": Kretchner, Susan B., "Advertainment: the
     evolution of product placement as a mass media marketing strategy,"
     Galician, Mary-Lou (ed.), *Handbook of Product Placement in the Mass
     Media* (Binghamton, NY: 2006), p. 43

107 "and which should be helped off air": Turner, Kathleen, J., "The practice of
     product placement: insinuating the product into the message: an historical
     context for product placement," Galician, Mary-Lou (ed.), *Handbook of
     Product Placement in the Mass Media* (Binghamton, NY: 2006), pp. 13–14

107 "Instead he invited a number of advertisers": Turner, Kathleen, J., "The
     practice of product placement: insinuating the product into the message:
     an historical context for product placement," Galician, Mary-Lou (ed.),
     Handbook of Product Placement in the Mass Media (Binghamton, NY:
     2006), pp. 12–13

107 "By 1968, advertisers were creating fewer than 3 percent of network tele-
     vision programs": Turner, Kathleen, J., "The practice of product placement:
     insinuating the product into the message: an historical context for product
     placement," Galician, Mary-Lou (ed.), *Handbook of Product Placement in
     the Mass Media* (Binghamton, NY: 2006), pp. 13–14

107 "Quiz show *Who Wants to Be a Millionaire*": Donaton, Scott, *Madison and
     Vine: Why the Entertainment and Advertising Industries Must Converge to
     Survive* (New York: McGraw Hill, 2005), p. 63

107 "so advertisers have got to find another way of funding television": "Show
     me the money: alternative funding—branded content panel," Intelligent
     Factual Festival 2010

107 "that's starting to happen now": Bashford, Suzy, "Making digital pay:
     AFP, archives and on-demand," Broadcast, August 26, 2010, http://www.
     broadcastnow.co.uk/news/analysis/making-digital-pay-afp-archives-and-
     on-demand/5017442, article retrieved January 14, 2011

107 "one of the key problems is no one's told the brands yet": "Show me the money: alternative funding—branded content panel," Intelligent Factual Festival 2010

108 "The actual involvement happens not on TV but online": Rose, Frank, *The Art of Immersion* (New York: W.W. Norton & Company, 2011), p. 235

108 "the MBAs who populate ad agencies": Rose, Frank, *The Art of Immersion* (New York: W.W. Norton & Company, 2011), p. 237

108 "sponsors take equity positions in shows, to become owners": Donaton, Scott, *Madison and Vine: Why the Entertainment and Advertising Industries Must Converge to Survive* (New York: McGraw Hill, 2005), p. 72

108 "For example, in the UK, Lime Pictures": Khalsa, Balihar, "Lime eyes TOWIE fashion line," *Broadcast*, June 24, 2011, p. 1

108 "In return they might get their brand's logo featured on 'bumpers'": *The Bulletin*, Brands on TV newsletter, February, 2011

109 "being seen on TV gives a brand credibility and means it is regarded by consumers as more trustworthy": Clay, Lindsey, "TV on a Shoestring" event, Thinkbox, London, February 17, 2011, http://www.thinkboxlive.tv/

109 "Consumers still tend to regard the internet with a certain mistrust": Clay, Lindsey, "TV on a Shoestring" event, Thinkbox, London, February 17, 2011, http://www.thinkboxlive.tv/

109 "Brands are drawn to TV for a range of reasons": Fuller, Zoe, "TV on a Shoestring" event, Thinkbox, London, February 17, 2011

109 "A brand that provides funding for a TV show": *The Bulletin*, Brands on TV newsletter, February, 2011

110 "It was suggested that several brands might want": *The Bulletin*, Brands on TV newsletter, April, 2011

110   "*Win a Dream Holiday* sought": *The Bulletin*, Brands on TV newsletter, April, 2011

110   "As Jean-Marc Lehu notes, '*The Contender*'": Lehu, Jean-Marc, *Branded Entertainment: Product Placement and Brand Strategy in the Entertainment Business* (London: Kogan Page, 2007), p. 99

110   "He was told by Lindsay Zaltman that": Spurlock, Morgan, "The greatest TED talk ever sold," April, 2011 [video file]. Retrieved from http://www.ted.com/talks/morgan_spurlock_the_greatest_ted_talk_ever_sold.html

111   "I have funded this entire film with money from some pretty strait-laced companies": Spurlock, Morgan, thegreatestmovieeversold.com website sign-up confirmation email, dated January 29, 2011

111   "For us, it's like we're in on the gag": quoted in Bernstein, Josh, "Morgan Spurlock punks Hollywood," The Daily Beast, April 19, 2011 http://www.thedailybeast.com/blogs-and-stories/2011-04-19/the-greatest-story-ever-sold-morgan-spurlock-punks-hollywood/# retrieved April 22, 2011

111   "studies even claim that this can lead to an improvement in morale and productivity": Lehu, Jean-Marc, *Branded Entertainment: Product Placement and Brand Strategy in the Entertainment Business* (London: Kogan Page, 2007), p. 99

111   "It is very difficult to get these things off the ground": "Show me the money: alternative funding—branded content panel," Intelligent Factual Festival 2010

111   "You are dealing with a trinity of brands": Booth, Emily and McMahon, Kate, "Brands on the box: what will it mean for the UK?," *Broadcast*, February 26, 2010, pp. 26–30

112   "The def[inition] of branded content": Kristen van Cott quoted by @_mip_ (MIP Markets) on Twitter, April 6, 2011

112   "Genius brand pairing this week": Carr, Jimmy (@jimmycarr), Twitter
      comment quoted in *Broadcast*, April 22, 2011, p. 40

112   "sold by the channel to whoever pays the highest price": Heys, Claire,
      "Ad-Funded Content and Product Placement" workshop run by Claire Heys,
      Indie Training Fund, January 27, 2011

113   "For example, *Chinese Food in Minutes* benefited": Buckley, Kate, "Plugging
      the funding gap," *Broadcast*, March 10, 2010, retrieved via http://
      krempelwood.com/rooney.html, January 13, 2011

113   "Another plus of sponsorship": Heys, Claire, "Ad-Funded Content and
      Product Placement" workshop run by Claire Heys, Indie Training Fund,
      January 27, 2011

113   "First of all, entertain. Second, advertise the entertainment": quoted in
      "Branded documentaries," *Marketing Week*, August 27, 2009, p. 18

113   "What sets AFP apart from sponsorship": Heys, Claire, "Ad-Funded Content
      and Product Placement" workshop run by Claire Heys, Indie Training Fund,
      January 27, 2011

114   "Association with TV can make the brand feel pioneering and noisy":
      Jordan, Julia, "TV on a Shoestring" event, Thinkbox, London, February 17,
      2011, http://www.thinkboxlive.tv/

114   "Containing reviews of hot new releases, interviews with celebrity cast":
      staff reporter, "Vue and C4 launch film show," Televisual, May 11, 2011,
      http://www.televisual.com/news-detail/Vue-and-C4-launch-film-show_nid-
      596.html

115   "We hope viewers will be inspired to get into their kitchens": "*The Lakes
      on a Plate* transmits on Channel 4," press release, Avalon, http://www.
      avalonuk.com/pressRelease/160

115 "Abercrombie & Fitch were reported": Lafayette, Jon, "A revenue generation 'Situation' for MTV?" Broacasting & Cable, August 17, 2011, http://www. broadcastingcable.com/blog/Currency/32631-A_Revenue_Generating_ Situation_for_MTV_.php

115 "It was soon rumbled as a ruse": Friedman, Wayne, "Abercrombie & Fitch, the 'Sitch,' and the misleading press release," *TV Watch*, Media Post, August 20, 2011

115 "Find out when your key agency and brand contacts are on holiday": Heys, Claire, "Ad-Funded Content and Product Placement" workshop run by Claire Heys, Indie Training Fund, January 27, 2011

115 "advertiser funded programming won't replace all channel funding": Heys, Claire, "Ad-Funded Content and Product Placement" workshop, Indie Training Fund, January 27, 2011

117 "Product placement is a contractual arrangement": Ganguzza, Patricia, in Dean, Carole Lee, *The Art of Film Funding: Alternative Financing Concepts* (Studio City: Michael Wiese Productions, 2007), pp. 139–40

117 "In the UK, product placement is signaled to viewers by a 'P' on the screen": Halliday, Josh, "Product placement: P logo stands for puzzled public," *Guardian*, June 20, 2011, http://www.guardian.co.uk/media/2011/ jun/20/product-placement-logo

117 "In the USA, the Federal Communications Commission (FCC) requires": Lewczak, Joseph, and DiGiovanni, Anne, "Enhanced FCC regulation of product placement would breach free speech rights," *Legal Backgrounder*, Washington Legal Foundation 25(11), April 9, 2010

117 "I worked with CBS Advertising Sales to design sponsorships": Burnett, Mark, *Jump In! Even if You Don't Know How to Swim* (New York: Ballantine Books, 2005), p. 86

118   "It far surpassed what you would get from a thirty-second spot": quoted in
       Donaton, Scott, *Madison and Vine: Why the Entertainment and Advertising
       Industries Must Converge to Survive* (New York: McGraw Hill, 2005), pp. 63–4

118   "brands are reaching out to us directly to feature their products in
       forthcoming programs": Bass, Larry, "Embrace product placement,"
       Broadcast, April 13, 2011, http://www.broadcastnow.co.uk/5026165.article,
       retrieved April 14, 2011

118   "The way that product placement has been shown to work": Steve
       Hewlett interview with Nick Price (MPG advertising agency) and Sally Quick
       (UKTV), *The Media Show*, BBC Radio 4, March 2, 2011

119   "However, this is a tricky area": "Ofcom Broadcast Bulletin," *Ofcom*, Issue
       169, November 8, 2010

119   "In the USA, Nielson Media Research recorded more than 100,000
       instances of product placement": Gutnik, Lilia, Huang, Tom, Lin, Jill Blue,
       Schmidt, Ted, "New trends in product placement," *Strategic Computing
       and Communications Technology*, Spring 2009, UC Berkley School of
       Information

119   "Nielson also logged a staggering 9,136 product placements": Castillo,
       David, "Product placements on *Top Chef*," Product Placement News,
       February 27, 2011, http://productplacement.biz/200902271277/news/
       televsion/product-placements-on-top-chef.html

119   "More shocking, perhaps": Allen, Ted, "Why America needs another
       cook-off show," December 29, 2008, http://www.tedallen.net/Blog/
       Entries/2008/12/29_Why_America_needs_another_cook-off_show.html,
       retrieved April 2, 2011

119   "Interestingly, one of *Top Chef*'s main product integrations": Schneider,
       Michael, "Leno leads in product placement," *Variety*, December 13 2009,
       http://www.variety.com/article/VR1118012672?refCatId=14, retrieved April 2,
       2011

120   "If all 300,000 voted for their colleague, that's an awful lot of votes":
      "Tesco checks out *X Factor*," *Evening Standard*, October 19, 2010, p. 44

120   "It's been estimated that the UK is five to ten years behind the US": Booth,
      Emily and McMahon, Kate, "Brands on the box: what will it mean for the
      UK?," *Broadcast*, February 26, 2010, pp. 26–30

120   "over [in the USA] you've got the Coke cups": quoted in Booth, Emily
      and McMahon, Kate, "Brands on the box: what will it mean for the UK?,"
      Broadcast, February 26, 2010, pp. 26–30

120   "PRODUCT PLACEMENT THIS SEGMENT: Ford": Tompkins, Paul F., "*American
      Idol* recap: Paul F. Tompkins on the double elimination," *New York
      Magazine*, April 1, 2011, http://nymag.com/daily/entertainment/2011/04/
      american_idol_paul_f_tompkins_7.html, retrieved April 2, 2011

120   "Fans of the show's choleric take-downs": Halpern, Ashlea, "*Project
      Runway* recap: the pageant problem," *New York Magazine*, September
      24, 2010, http://nymag.com/daily/fashion/2010/09/project_runway_4.html,
      retrieved April 2, 2011

121   "as the channel may have sold sponsorship which conflicts": Heys, Claire,
      "Ad-Funded Content and Product Placement" workshop run by Claire Heys,
      Indie Training Fund, January 27, 2011

121   "Digital product placement means": Wenner, Lawrence, A., "On the ethics
      of product placement in media entertainment," in Galician, Mary-Lou (ed.),
      Handbook of Product Placement in the Mass Media (Binghamton, NY:
      2006), pp. 119–20

121   "It has 'grown steadily'": "In words: Farewell Honey Nut Burst, welcomes
      product placement," *Perspectives on Television in Words and Numbers*,
      Deloitte LLP, 2010, p. 24

121   "There are a number of factors": Lehu, Jean-Marc, *Branded Entertainment: Product Placement and Brand Strategy in the Entertainment Business* (London: Kogan Page, 2007), pp. 71–5

122   "Whether the placement was valued": "Creating new producer–brand relationships through ad-funded programming, product placement and related licensing opportunities," BrandsonTV, http://www.bradsontv.com/product_placement_uk.html, retrieved April 23, 2011

122   "ITV uses a combined 'brand placement' score": Bulkley, Kate, "Putting a price on everything," Broadcast, March 24, 2011, http://www.broadcastnow.co.uk/news/finance/putting-a-price-on-everything/5025290.article, retrieved April 15, 2011

122   "None of these deals are going to be straightforward": quoted in Bulkley, Kate, "Putting a price on everything," Broadcast, March 24, 2011, http://www.broadcastnow.co.uk/news/finance/putting-a-price-on-everything/5025290.article, retrieved April 15, 2011

123   "Nick Price described a simpler model": Farber, Alex, "Setting the rules for product placement," *Broadcast*, February 11, 2011, p. 19

123   "don't believe that [it] will open the vaults to untold riches": Wood, Mark, "AFP: a practical reality," Broadcast, March 22, 2010, http://www.broadcastnow.co.uk/5012003, article retrieved January 14, 2010

123   "Contestants in *Britain's Next Top Model*": Brand Director, http://www.productplacement.co.uk/caseStudyDetail.cfm?caseStudyId=33

123   "85 percent of the time you see a Volkswagen": 1st Place, Volkswagen Case Study, http://www.productplacement.co.uk/caseStudyDetail.cfm?caseStudyId=13

123   "Olympus 770WSW compact digital": 1st Place, Olympus Case Study, http://www.productplacement.co.uk/caseStudyDetail.cfm?caseStudyId=15

123   "Products that are furnished as backdrops": Ong, Beng Soo, "A comparison of product placements in movies and television programs: an online research study," in Galician, Mary-Lou (ed.), *Handbook of Product Placement in the Mass Media* (Binghamton, NY: 2006), p. 128

124   "According to director of Seesaw Media, Darryl Collis": Booth, Emily and McMahon, Kate, "Brands on the box: what will it mean for the UK?," *Broadcast*, February 26, 2010, pp. 26–30

126   "It's better to go to the agency than to the brand": "The movie is the message," Williams, Phillip, *MovieMaker* 79(16), Winter 2009, pp. 40–1

126   "We're in the middle and you're talking two completely different languages ...": quoted in Donaton, Scott, *Madison and Vine: Why the Entertainment and Advertising Industries Must Converge to Survive* (New York: McGraw Hill, 2005), p. 171

126   "When they get to the point when": "Show me the money: alternative funding—branded content panel," Intelligent Factual Festival 2010

127   "We sit with a brand and we help them to understand": "Show me the money: alternative funding—branded content panel," Intelligent Factual Festival 2010

128   "Ben Devlin, executive producer at Brand Sponsor": Devlin, Ben, "Sponsorship FAQs," Brand Sponsor, http://www.brandsponsor.co.uk/live-event-sponsorship/

131   "According to Vicky Kell, Channel 4's business manager for sponsorship": Bulkley, Kate, "Putting a price on everything," Broadcast, March 24, 2011, http://www.broadcastnow.co.uk/news/finance/putting-a-price-on-everything/5025290.article, retrieved April 15, 2011

131   "In some cases, TV producers want millions of dollars": Donaton, Scott, *Madison and Vine: Why the Entertainment and Advertising Industries Must Converge to Survive* (New York: McGraw Hill, 2005), p. 174

131   "Every brand that funded Morgan Spurlock's *POM Wonderful Presents: The Greatest Movie Ever Sold*": Anderson, Kelly, "Hot Docs preview: birth of a salesman," Realscreen, April 28, 2011, http://www.realscreen. com/2011/04/28/hot-docs-preview-birth-of-a-salesman/#ixzz1KphuFqwZ

131   "Every advertiser I've ever worked with": "Show me the money: alternative funding—branded content panel," Intelligent Factual Festival 2010

132   "Producers, directors, writers, actors and other creative personnel": Wenner, Lawrence, A., "On the ethics of product placement in media entertainment," in Galician, Mary-Lou (ed.), *Handbook of Product Placement in the Mass Media* (Binghamton, NY: 2006), p. 113

132   "For example, in the eighth season of *Project Runway*": Ritchie, Kevin, "Fashion friendly," Realscreen, January 12, 2011, http://www.realscreen. com/articles/news/20110112/fashionweb.html, retrieved January 14, 2011

4: Banks and Private Equity Investors—Masters of the Funding Universe

136   "some banks will only finance films with budgets of at least $5 million": Shyjka, Michael, The role of the bank: Help or hindrance to the creative process?", Skillset, http://www.skillset.org/film/knowledge/article_5106_1. asp

137   "*Inside Job*: The film that cost over $20,000,000,000,000 to make": *Inside Job* website, http://www.sonyclassics.com/insidejob/

137   "*The Inside Job*, a feature documentary that exposed": Ferguson, Charles, quoted in Lashinsky, Adam, "*Inside Job* director on Geithner, Goldman, and criminal bankers," CNN Money, March 15, 2011, http://finance.fortune.cnn. com/2011/03/15/inside-job-director-on-geithner-goldman-and-criminal- bankers/

137   "The financial crash caused many individual investors": Steele, Jeff, "Seeking film finance? You get what you pay for," The Wrap, April 10, 2011, http://ht.ly/4yXjc, retrieved April 14, 2011

137 "For instance, *The Passion of Girls Aloud*": Dams, Tim, "Money," *Televisual*, April, 2011, p. 50

137 "Barclays Corporate also funded indie producer": Kanter, Jake, "C5 agrees financing deal with Barclays for Transparent show," *Broadcast*, June 24, 2011, p. 3

138 "A bank offering a gap finance deal": Davies, Adam P., and Wistreich, N., *The Film Finance Handbook—How to Fund Your Film* (London: Netribution, 2008), p. 127

138 "There are also private gap financiers who will recoup": Davies, Adam P., and Wistreich, N., *The Film Finance Handbook—How to Fund Your Film*, (London: Netribution, 2008), p. 128

138 "Simon Vyvyan, managing director of Industry Media": Dams, Tim, "Money," *Televisual*, April, 2011, p. 55

139 "Sometimes this type of funding is known as a bridging loan": Davies, Adam P., and Wistreich, N., *The Film Finance Handbook—How to Fund Your Film* (London: Netribution, 2008), pp. 136–7

139 "I will use all of my resources to check their credentials": Dams, Tim, "Money," *Televisual*, April, 2011, p. 50

139 "Banks offer a number of other services": Shyjka, Michael, "The role of the bank: help or hindrance to the creative process?," Skillset, http://www.skillset.org/film/knowledge/article_5106_1.asp

139 "Managing the exchange rate": "Barclays Corporate media specialist" advertorial, *Televisual*, April, 2011

140 "Return on investment can be most simply calculated": "Definition of return on investment," QFINANCE, Dictionaryhttp://www.qfinance.com/dictionary/return-on-investment

140 "In the UK, the James Grant Group": Parry, Caroline, "'Mould-breaking' TV format seeks funding," *Broadcast*, April 16, 2010, p. 5

141 "By financing a film": Allibhai, Shamir, in Search, Jess and McCarthy, Melissa, *Getting Your Documentary Funded and Distributed* (London: Shooting People, 2005), pp. 122–3

141 "The goal for the producer": Allibhai, Shamir, in Search, Jess and McCarthy, Melissa, *Getting Your Documentary Funded and Distributed* (London: Shooting People, 2005), pp. 122–3

142 "The people behind this are a private equity fund": "Show me the money: making up the budget shortfall—deficit financing for beginners panel," Intelligent Factual Festival 2010

142 "Benefits to the investor include income tax relief": "Quicksilver Films Information Memorandum" (London, Quicksilver Films, 2009), p. 3

142 "If someone invests the maximum £500,000 allowed": "Production Financing Using EIS" workshop with Harry Hicks and Charles Lévêque, Harbottle & Lewis, London, July 20, 2011

142 "There are strict rules governing EIS": "Quicksilver Films Information Memorandum" (London, Quicksilver Films, 2009), p. 13

142 "Sheryl Crown, managing director of the Documentary Company": Natividad, Angela, "Liveblog: MIPDoc: financing for new co-production," Mipblog, April 3, 2011, http://blog.mipworld.com/2011/04/liveblog-mipdoc-financing-for-new-co-production/, retrieved April 6, 2011

143 "In the USA, NYC-based Impact Partners": Impact Partners, http://www.impactpartnersfilm.com/bios.php

143 "There's a complicated set of rules": "New routes to funding," *The Business Book 2010/11 Broadcast*, December, 2010, p. 35

144 "It was even reported in an internet forum": Dave Gregory, comment on "Crowdfunding done legally" thread, Film TV Professionals Group, LinkedIn, retrieved January 19, 2011

146 "It is important," he says, "to remember the plot": Finch, Brian, *How to Write a Business Plan* (London: Kogan Page, 2007), pp. 5–6

148 *"End of the Line* table": Channel 4 BRITDOC Foundation, *"The End of the Line*: a social impact evaluation" (2010), p. 19

148 "Cinema (average audience for social issue theatrical documentaries)": Channel 4 BRITDOC Foundation, *"The End of the Line*: a social impact evaluation" (2010), p. 20

149 "experienced entertainment investors often completely disregard the business plans": Levitan, Peter, "Risk management in entertainment financing: do we know what we don't know?" Beverly Hills Bar Association Symposium on New Directions in Entertainment Financing, April 13, 2010

150 "There is an excellent section on handing negotiations": Davies, Adam P., and Wistreich, N., *The Film Finance Handbook—How to Fund Your Film* (London: Netribution, 2008), pp. 34–7

5: Government—Compliance-Driven Box Tickers

155 *"Nina's Heavenly Delights"*: Atkins, Chris, "Film council abolished!," *Starsuckers* blog, July 28, 2010 (reprinted from *The Times*), http://starsuckers3.blogspot.com/2010/07/film-council-abolished.html, retrieved January 16, 2011

156 "The advantage of soft money": Davies, Adam P., and Wistreich, N., *The Film Finance Handbook—How to Fund Your Film* (London: Netribution, 2008), p.113

156 "Soft money sources include": Davies, Adam P., and Wistreich, N., *The Film Finance Handbook—How to Fund Your Film* (London: Netribution, 2008), p. 104

157 "Canada has a well-established international co-production": Gibb, Lindsay, "Climate change: the global co-production update—Canada," *Realscreen*, January–February, 2010, pp. 48–50

157 "The European Convention on Cinematographic Co-Productions": Ritchie, Malcolm,"Introduction to independent film financing," Skillset, http://www.skillset.org/film/knowledge/article_5102_1.asp, retrieved August 28, 2011

158 "Australia": "Partner countries," Screen Australia, http://www.screenaustralia.gov.au/co-productions/treaties_mous.aspx, retrieved July 24, 2011

158 "Singapore": "Bilateral co-production agreements," Media Development Authority, http://www.mda.gov.sg/International/BilCoAgreement/Pages/agreements.aspx, retrieved July 24, 2011

158 "Spain": "Bilateral co-production treaties," Netribution, http://www.netribution.co.uk/funding/finance/co_production_treaties.html, retrieved July, 24 2011

158 "UK": "Co-production agreements," DCMS, http://www.culture.gov.uk/what_we_do/creative_industries/4112.aspx#agreements, retrieved July 23, 2011

158 "Like any marriage": Gibb, Lindsay, "Climate change: the global co-production update—Canada," *Realscreen*, January–February, 2010, pp. 48–50

159 "Most of these treaties require the 'junior'": Levitan, Peter, "Risk management in entertainment financing: do we know what we don't know?" Beverly Hills Bar Association Symposium on New Directions in Entertainment Financing, April 13, 2010, p. 11

159 "only worth the legal gymnastics": Walsh, Barry, "Climate change: the global co-production update—Australia," *Realscreen*, January–February, 2010, pp. 47–8

159 "Once production of the film or program has been finished": Davies, Adam P., and Wistreich, N., *The Film Finance Handbook—How to Fund Your Film* (London: Netribution, 2008), p. 103

161 "Brook Lapping is increasingly looking": "Percy warns of funding crisis for high-end docs," McMahon, Kate, *Broadcast*, April 10, 2009, p. 6

161 "For example, China Imagica": Benzine, Adam, "A taste for the Orient," C21's Factual Week: ATF 2010, December 10, 2010 [email]

162 "For example, in Germany, the Berlin-Brandenburg Film Commission": Gibb, Lindsay, "Climate change: the global co-production update—Germany," *Realscreen*, January–February, 2010, pp. 53–4

162 "Having said that, New South Wales": "Screen NSW news," June 16, 2009, http://screen.nsw.gov.au/index.php?page_id=44&news_id=507

163 "Every indie out there": McMahon, Kate, "Orion gets creative on funding for art-travel show," *Broadcast*, October 30, 2009, p. 10

163 "One night scene": "Manx on a mission," *Broadcast*, April 22, 2011, p. 40

163 "In 2011, a filmmaker was sentenced": Rood, Lee, "Filmmaker Wendy Weiner Runge sentenced to 10 years," *Des Moines Register*, May 17, 2011

6: Issue-Driven Funders—Guilt Trippers and Global Reformers

167 "The financial side of making documentary": Hampe, Barry, *Making Documentary Films and Videos*, Chapter 1, http://makingdocumentaryfilms.com/chapter1.html

168 "a tipping point in corporate policy": Channel 4 BRITDOC Foundation, '*The End of the Line*: A social impact evaluation" (2010), p. 4

168 "A little over one million people": Channel 4 BRITDOC Foundation, "*The End of the Line*: a social impact evaluation" (2010), p. 4

168   "The film's £1million budget was co-funded": Channel 4 BRITDOC
      Foundation, "*The End of the Line*: a social impact evaluation" (2010), p. 8

168   "However, the filmmakers only agreed": Channel 4 BRITDOC Foundation,
      "*The End of the Line*: a social impact evaluation" (2010), p. 8

168   "Waitrose's association with": Channel 4 BRITDOC Foundation, "*The End of
      the Line*: a social impact evaluation" (2010), p. 8

168   "40,000 people followed": "Keo hopeful for *Fish Fight* sequel after site
      success," Broadcast, February, 10 2011, http://www.broadcastnow.co.uk/
      news/multi-platform/keo-hopeful-for-fish-fight-sequel-after-site-success/
      5023476.article

169   "There are two ways to approach branded content": "Branded document-
      aries," *Marketing Week*, August 27, 2009, pp. 16–18

170   "It sponsored screenings of *Burma VJ*": "Branded documentaries,"
      Marketing Week, August 27, 2009, p. 17

170   "partly funded *The Vanishing of the Bees*": Langworthy, George, quoted
      in Papamichael, Stella, "*The Vanishing of the Bees*. George Langworthy
      interview," BBC Film Network, October 13, 2009 http://www.bbc.co.uk/dna/
      h2g2/A58334312

170   "works for us in a way that promotes": "Branded documentaries,"
      Marketing Week, August 27, 2009, p. 17

170   "The Puma Catalyst Fund": Mosses, Sarah, "Going It Alone" panel,
      University Centre, Hastings, February 19, 2011

170   "a world that is more peaceful": Maher, Kevin, "Is this the end of the line
      for documentary?," *The Times*, Saturday Review, September 18, 2010, p. 4

171   "Canada's CBC, for one": Hamilton, Peter, "Hot Docs adds a Hogwarts touch
      to the pitch session format. Oprah's OWN sent to the ER. Why Reality?,"

Documentary Television, May 8, 2011, http://documentarytelevision.com/
commissioning-process/hot-docs-adds-a-hogwarts-touch-to-the-pitch-
session-format-oprahs-own-sent-to-the-er-why-reality/

171 "can become an indirect editorial influence": Rehmann, Bettina, "Sustaining
credibility," *DOX*90, Summer, 2011, p. 10

171 "if you take your journalism seriously": Rushton, Katherine, "Nick Fraser,
Storyville," Broadcast, November 5, 2009, http://www.broadcastnow.co.uk/
news/interviews/nick-fraser-storyville/5007702, article retrieved January 15,
2011

172 *"Your Mommy Kills Animals"*: *Berman, R. and Flynn, M. vs. Johnson C.*,
Appeal from the United States District Court for the Eastern District of
Virginia, at Alexandria. T. S. Ellis, III, Senior District Judge (1:07-cv-00039-TSE-
TRJ) 2008, 072154.U.pdf http://pacer.ca4.uscourts.gov (unpublished), p. 5

172 "He 'was awarded $360,000 in damages'": *Berman, R. and Flynn,
M. vs. Johnson C.*, Appeal from the United States District Court for the
Eastern District of Virginia, at Alexandria. T. S. Ellis, III, Senior District Judge
(1:07-cv-00039-TSE-TRJ) 2008, 072154.U.pdf http://pacer.ca4.uscourts.gov
(unpublished), p. 6

177 "Active Voice and Participant Media": *"Food, Inc.* ingredients for change:
campaign overview," Active Voice, http://www.activevoice.net/ifc/index.html

178 *"Donor Unknown* is a challenging": Donor Unknown Press Pack, 2010

180 "In *Grant Seeking for Storytellers"*: Clarke, Cheryl A., *Storytelling for
Grantseekers: A Guide to Creative Nonprofit Fundraising* (San Francisco:
John Wiley & Sons, 2009), p. 25

181 "is not to be too aggressive": Clarke, Cheryl A., *Storytelling for Grantseekers:
A Guide to Creative Nonprofit Fundraising* (San Francisco: John Wiley &
Sons, 2009), p. 24

181 "It's reported that 5–10 percent of issue-driven grant": Clarke, Cheryl A., *Storytelling for Grantseekers: A Guide to Creative Nonprofit Fundraising* (San Francisco: John Wiley & Sons, 2009), p. 8

182 "a good proposal features 'heroes'": Phillips, Frances N., quoted in Clarke, Cheryl A., *Storytelling for Grantseekers: A Guide to Creative Nonprofit Fundraising* (San Francisco: John Wiley & Sons, 2009), p. xii

183 "to use the film as a strategic tool": Channel 4 BRITDOC Foundation, "*The End of the Line*: a social impact evaluation" (2010), p. 56

183 "The Fisheries Minister": Channel 4 BRITDOC Foundation, "*The End of the Line*: a social impact evaluation" (2010), p. 57

184 "give from their hearts.": Clarke, Cheryl A., *Storytelling for Grantseekers: A Guide to Creative Nonprofit Fundraising* (San Francisco: John Wiley & Sons, 2009), p. 77

7: Knowledge-Driven Funders—Scholars and Educators

191 "To talk about learning in Factual": Curtis, Adam, interview with author, April 2009

192 "dramatic reconstruction, computer graphics": "BBC One goes global with breathtaking journey through 20,000 years of human history," BBC press release, November 22, 2010 http://www.bbc.co.uk/pressoffice/pressreleases/stories/2010/11_november/22/history.shtml

192 "the significance of each key moment": "BBC One goes global with breathtaking journey throught 20,000 years of human history," BBC press release, November 22, 2010 http://www.bbc.co.uk/pressoffice/pressreleases/stories/2010/11_november/22/history.shtml

192 "students, insomniacs, night workers": "End of a cultural era—but OU on TV evolution continues," Open University, December 11, 2006, http://www3.open.ac.uk/media/fullstory.aspx?id=9898

192 "the BBC's reputation": "BBC One goes global with breathtaking journey through 20,000 years of human history," BBC press release, November 22, 2010 http://www.bbc.co.uk/pressoffice/pressreleases/stories/2010/11_ november/22/history.shtml

193 "Open Media Unit": Ogilvie, Caroline, "The Open University is now open for business," *Broadcast,* August 11, 2011, p. 15

194 "The Canadian Navy": Walsh, Barry, "Climate change: the global co-production update—UK," *Realscreen,* January–February, 2010, pp. 55–6

195 "When Professor Bekir Karlığa of Bahçeşehir University": "*River Flowing Westward* to tell story of global civilization," Hurriet Daily News and Economic Review, February 21, 2010 http://www.hurriyetdailynews.com/n. php?n=0220173125598-2010-02-21 retrieved January 16, 2011

195 "The Promotion Fund was set up": "Promotion Fund of the Prime Ministry," Republic of Turkey, Ministry of Foreign Affairs, http://www.mfa.gov.tr/ submitting-project-proposals-to-the-promotion-fund-of-the-turkish-prime-ministry.en.mfa

195 "Much government communication": "Future of COI-supplier information," COI, http://coi.gov.uk/suppliers.php?page=391, retrieved July 26, 2011

195 "With the availability of sponsorship": Seers, David, "Government departments and ad funded television programming: some notes for producers," Central Office of Information, article sent to author, March 3, 2011

195 "*Border Force*": Revoir, Paul, "Home Office funds Sky 'propaganda' show with £400,000 of taxpayers' money," MailOnline, May 21, 2008, http:// www.dailymail.co.uk/tvshowbiz/article-1020845/Home-Office-funds-Sky-propaganda-400-000-taxpayers-money.html

195 "*Beat: Life on the Street*": Pettie, Andrew, "Review: the television document-aries which aren't quite what they seem," *Telegraph,* August 2, 2008,

http://www.telegraph.co.uk/news/uknews/2489646/Review-The-television-documentaries-which-arent-quite-what-they-seem.html

195 "in 2009, Ofcom judged that": "Broadcast bulletin issue number 126," Ofcom, January 26, 2009

195 "Sky handed back £40,000": PC Plastic Fuzz, "Home Office in breach over PCSO programme," Planet Police, January 3, 2009 http://policecommunity supportofficer.blogspot.com/2009/02/home-office-in-breach-over-pcso.html

195 "The British government concluded": Seers, David, "Government departments and ad funded television programming: some notes for producers," Central Office of Information, article sent to author March 3, 2011

196 "where funding is available": Seers, David, "Government departments and ad funded television programming: some notes for producers," Central Office of Information, article sent to author March 3, 2011

196 "complicated science clear": "HHMI names Michael Rosenfeld to lead new documentary initiative," Howard Hughes Medical Institute press release, May 5, 2011

198 "we have our ear a little closer to the rail": "HHMI launches documentary film unit to create science features for television," Howard Hughes Medical Institute press release, February 4, 2011

8: Film Funds—Movie-Making Mentors

212 "Some filmmakers say they want to send a message": Dean, Carole Lee, quoted in"Funder FAQ: Roy W. Dean Film & Video Grants," *Independent Magazine*, April 24, 2009, http://www.independent-magazine.org/node/2577/print

213 "favor story over message, character over agenda": "Grants and awards: program guidelines," Cinereach, http://www.cinereach.org/grants/granting-program-guidelines

213   "The Gucci Tribeca Documentary Fund received": Harrington, Ryan, Gucci Tribeca Doccumentary Fund email, April 11, 2011

213   "Cinereach received more than 1,000 letters": Ladjevardi, Adella, Cinereach email, January 19, 2011

214   "Cinereach": "Cinereach announces wWinter 2011 grant recipients," Cinereach press release, April 5, 2011 http://www.cinereach.org/cinereach-announces-winter-2011-grant-recipients

214   "ITVS International Call $10,000–$150,000": Anderson, Kelly, "Climate change: the global co-production update—US," *Realscreen*, January–February, 2010, pp. 56–8

214   "ITVS Open Call 1–2 percent": "International call," ITVS, http://www.itvs.org/funding/international

214   "Sundance Post/Production": http://www.sundance.org/programs/documentary-fund/

214   "I really, really, hate these ITVS applications": Paglin, Laura Moire, post on "Developing stories and structures," D-Word forum, December 23, 2010, www.d-word.com

222   "a way of categorizing": Dean, Carole Lee, *The Art of Film Funding: Alternative Financing Concepts* (Studio City: Michael Wiese Productions, 2007), p. 31

223   "If you are not accumulating several rejections a month": Dean, Carole Lee, *The Art of Film Funding: Alternative Financing Concepts* (Studio City: Michael Wiese Productions, 2007), p. 47

9: Crowdfunding—Couch Producers and Micro-Patrons

242   "Learning the hard way": Proulx, Erik, Twitter, July 15, 2011

243   "Gary Huswit raised $118,505": Kaufman, Anthony, "Has Kickstarter reached

its goal of changing the way movies are made?," Indiewire, June 2, 2011, http://www.indiewire.com/article/has_kickstarter_reached_its_goal_of_ changing_the_way_movies_are_made/

243 "Internet Celebrities": "About," Internets Celebrities, http://internets celebrities.com/about/

244 "typical creatives now": quoted in Campbell, Lisa, "It takes all sorts to connect," *Broadcast*, December 3, 2010, p. 2

244 "When Nina Gilden Seavey": Dean, Carole Lee, *The Art of Film Funding: Alternative Financing Concepts* (Studio City: Michael Wiese Productions, 2007), pp. 4–5

244 "It's kind of boring": Hoyle, Ben, "The superdonors out to save the arts," *The Times: The Review*, April 2, 2011, p. 5

245 "Franny Armstrong raised": Lees, Nicola, *Greenlit: Developing Factual/ Reality TV Ideas from Concept to Pitch* (London: Methuen Drama, 2010), p. 258

245 "about 70 percent of people will give money at a fundraising party": Warsawski, Morrie, "The fundraising houseparty," The Crowdfunding Success Summit, December 5, 2010, www.crowdfundingsummit.com

246 "One filmmaker got chatting": Dean, Carole Lee, *The Art of Film Funding: Alternative Financing Concepts* (Studio City: Michael Wiese Productions, 2007), p. 26

246 "When you secure a donation": Dean, Carole Lee, *The Art of Film Funding: Alternative Financing Concepts* (Studio City: Michael Wiese Productions, 2007), p. 65

246 "In 1885 Joseph Pulitzer": "The story of the State of Liberty, told by Trust Art," Trust Art, http://trustart.org/statue

246 "In 2006, Robert Greenwald raised": Lees, Nicola, *Greenlit: Developing Factual/Reality TV Ideas from Concept to Pitch* (London: Methuen Drama, 2010), p. 275

246 "By August 2011, Nirvan Mullick's *1 Second Film*": "About the *1 Second Film*," http://www.the1secondfilmcom/about

247 "It's the most innovative film financing scheme": "How to crowdfund your film," http://www.spannerfilms.net/crowd_funding

247 "IndieGogo, for example, is in more than 159 countries": "Standing out from the crowd: Sheffield Doc/Fest partners with IndieGoGo," Sheffield Doc/Fest press release, April 6, 2011

248 "Hava Nagila (2nd campaign) ($10,000)": interview with Danae Ringelmann, April, 2011 (all other figures in the table from the respective websites)

249 "One report on Rockethub.org": Cohen, Jed, "Crowdfunding metrics: what we've learned that you need to know!," RocketHub.org, November 24, 2010, http://rockethub.org/profiles/blogs/crowdfunding-metrics-whatweve

249 "It's been reported that only 44 percent of Kickstarter projects receive funding": Walsh, Barry, "Silverdocs: talking transmedia and crowdfunding," *Realscreen*, June 24, 2011, http://realscreen.com/2011/06/24/silverdocs-talking-transmedia-and-crowdfunding

249 "If you do crowdfunding and you get no response": Broderick, Peter, "Crowdfunding and the indie landscape," The Crowdfunding Success Summit, December 5, 2010, www.crowdfundingsummit.com

249 "John Trigonis, who raised more than $6,000": Trigonis, John, "Filmmaker case study," The Crowdfunding Success Summit, December 5, 2010, www.crowdfundingsummit.com

250 "One filmmaker tackled this head on": www.virgoproductions.com.au/ws-content/.../Crowd_funding_FAQs_.pdf

251 "because people post projects then expect 'the internet' to take over": Cohen, Jed, "Crowdfunding metrics: what we've learned that you need to know!." RocketHub.org, November 24, 2010, http://rockethub.org/profiles/blogs/crowdfunding-metrics-whatweve

252 "First and foremost": Winter, Lewis, quoted in Marketos, Cassie, "Kickstarter Awards: By the Numbers," Kickstarter, January 10, 2011 http://www.kickstarter.com/blog/kickstarter-awards-by-the-numbers

253 "According to Danae Ringelmann": Ringelmann, Danae, "IndieGogo," The Crowdfunding Success Summit, December 5, 2010, www.crowdfundingsummit.com

253 "Aymar Jean Christian tracked 100 Kickstarter campaigns": Christian, Aymar Jean, "Kickstarter and crowdfunding: are web series successful raising money?," Televisual, October 9, 2010, http://blog.ajchristian.org/2010/10/09/kickstarter-and-crowdfunding-the-web-series-success-rate/

253 "Peter Broderick recommends choosing a conservative amount": Broderick, Peter, "Crowdfunding and the indie landscape," The Crowdfunding Success Summit, December 5, 2010, www.crowdfundingsummit.com

254 "On IndieGoGo, the optimum amount of time": Ringelmann, Danae, "IndieGogo," The Crowdfunding Success Summit, December 5, 2010, www.crowdfundingsummit.com

255 "very unique and specific to the project": "Follow the crowd," C21's Factual Week: Feature, emailed April 29, 2011

256 "a movie preview crossed with a public service announcement": Rossi, Fernanda, "IndieGogo," The Crowdfunding Success Summit, December 5, 2010, www.crowdfundingsummit.com

257 "tell us *who* you are, *why* you're doing": Sloan, Robin, in Strickler, Yancey, "Creator's Guide to Video," August 27, 2009, http://blog.kickstarter.com/post/173046259/creators-guide-to-video, retrieved January 19, 2011

257 "RocketHub have identified five things that make a video pitch successful": Crowdfunding Toolkit, Rockethub, http://rockethub.org/page/toolkit-tactics

257 "The producers of *Wish Me Away*": Danae Ringelmann interview, April 2011

258 "Similarly, a reader contacted maritime blog, gCaptain": Konrad, John, "Become a Hollywood producer—fund a documentary on piracy," gCaptain, March 30, 2011, http://gcaptain.com/hollywood-producer-fund-film-piracy?23430

260 "On IndieGoGo, the most successful campaigns": Ringelmann, Danae, "IndieGogo," The Crowdfunding Success Summit, December 5, 2010, www.crowdfundingsummit.com

260 "Producers of *The Bully Project*": Ringelmann, Danae, "IndieGogo," The Crowdfunding Success Summit, December 5, 2010, www.crowdfunding summit.com

261 "When JetBlue airline started": http://business.twitter.com/optimize/case-studies/jetblue

10: Beg, Borrow, and Negotiate—Local Heroes and Hopefuls

268 "We're living in a moment of tremendous change": quoted in Maher, Kevin, "Is this the end of the line for documentary?," *The Times*, Saturday Review, September 18, 2010, p. 4

269 "*Catfish* became a festival favorite, but it was shot for just $2,000": Schulman, Nev, quoted in Mapplebeck, Victoria, "Human catfish," *Dox*, no. 89, Spring 2011, p. 41

269 "and cost around $30,000 in total": French, Philip, "Catfish—review,"

Observer, December 19, 2010, http://www.guardian.co.uk/film/2010/dec/19/catfish-review-documentary-schulman-joost

270 "When I was asked to do the film the budget": Turner, Matthew, "Asif Kapadia Senna Interview," View Sheffield, http://www.viewsheffield.co.uk/cinemas/asif-kapadia-senna-interview-feature-interview-4064.html

271 "When Chris Atkins was making *Star Suckers*": "Fifty Ways to Get Funding Before You Die!," panel chaired by Steve Hewlett with Christo Hird (*End of the Line*) and Chris Atkins (*Starsuckers*), BECTU Freelancers' Fair, June 11, 2010

271 "I tried to get financing for the movie": Wilkinson, Amber, "*Bombay Beach dreams*," Eye for Film, http://www.eyeforfilm.co.uk/feature.php?id=905, retrieved July 5, 2011

272 "Chris Hedegus and D. A. Pennebaker couldn't get funding": Ritchie, Kevin, "Cooking up a classic," Realscreen, December 1, 2010, http://www.realscreen.com/articles/news/20101201/kingsofpastry.html

272 "Tim Hetherington and Sebastian Junger": McCarthy, James, "Oscar nod for war documentary *Restrepo*," Wales Online, February 11, 2011, http://www.walesonline.co.uk/showbiz-and-lifestyle/film-in-wales/2011/02/11/oscar-nod-for-war-documentary-restrepo-91466-28152053/#ixzz1NXVREBBw

273 "*Tarnation*, an award-winning documentary": Youngs, Ian, "Micro-budget film wows Cannes," BBC News Online, May 18, 2004 http://news.bbc.co.uk/1/hi/entertainment/3720455.stm

273 "It went on to make almost $600,000": "*Tarnation*," Box Office Mojo, http://www.boxofficemojo.com/movies/?page=int1&view=byweekend&id=tarnation.htm, retrieved July 31, 2011

275 "Epic Meal Time": "Innovators & start-ups," Cynopsis: Digital, April 27, 2011, http://www.cynopsis.com/index.php/editions/digital/042711/

275   "In July 2011, an episode of a cooking show, *Rick Stein's Spain*": "Weekly top 10 programmes," BBC2 w/e July 17, 2011, BARB, http://www.barb.co.uk/report/weeklyTopProgrammes?

275   "So, in this climate, I have decided": Bee, Sally, "Cooking up an internet show," Televisual Blog, January 24, 2011, http://www.televisual.com/blog-detail/Cooking-up-an-internet-show_bid-224.html, retrieved January 28, 2011

276   "If you don't have a big agent": Cynopsis: Digital email newsletter, June 13, 2011

276   "Emily Kim gave up her job": Sloane, Garett, "YouTube millionaires: Google paying big bucks for video sensations," February 25, 2011, http://www.nypost.com/p/news/business/youtube_millionaires_3h5V8I6FdnVLxQKbwOthoI#ixzz1JKPEFmTo, retrieved April 13, 2011

276   "When Luke Seomore and Joseph Bull": "Going It Alone'" panel, University Centre, Hastings, February 19, 2011

276   "When advertising executive Erik Proulx": Bosches, Edward, "This film brought to you by Twitter," creativity_unbound, August 18, 2009, http://edwardboches.com/this-film-brought-to-you-by-twitter

278   "The winner of a grant receives": "The Roy W. Dean LA June Grant closing 6/30 each year," From the Heart Productions, http://www.fromtheheartproductions.com/grant-lafilm.shtml

279   "When David Bond was making *Erasing David*": David Bond speaking at "Going It Alone" panel, University Centre, Hastings, February 19, 2011

280   "BECTU, the UK's film and TV union, tackled this issue": Coulter, Moray, "Freelancers look after each other—however you do it," *Broadcast*, June 4, 2010, p. 21

PART III: The Reality

Tales from the Frontlines of Film Finance: The Players and Producers

341 "£100,000 of deferred salaries and services": Cohn, Pamela, "*Sons of Cuba*—a conversation with Andrew Lang," Shooting People, February 18, 2010, http://shootingpeople.org/blog/page/4/

342 "the short was funded": Cohn, Pamela, "*Sons of Cuba*—a conversation with Andrew Lang," Shooting People, February 18, 2010, http://shootingpeople.org/blog/page/4/

345 "money to make a digital print": email from Francine Heywood, January 11, 2011

352 "nominal license fee of £1": Channel 4 BRITDOC Fund, http://britdoc.org/real_funds/britdoc_fund/

353 "Independent Filmmaker": combination of phone interview and email from Samantha Farinella

The Final Word ...

368 "There is no single way ...": Robinson, Esther, B., "Balancing risk and responsibility while making great films," Filmmaker, Winter 2010, http://www.filmmakermagazine.com/issues/winter2010/successful-filmmaker.php, retrieved January 23, 2011

Appendix

377 "whatever you put in the budget, treble it": Dams, Tim, "Dancing up a feature doc," Televisual, May 2011, p. 16

Bibliography

"1st draft guidelines for unpaid postings," Shooting People, March 21, 2010, http://shootingpeople.org/blog/category/minimum-wage-debate/

"50 Ways to Get Funding Before You Die!" panel chaired by Steve Hewlett with Christo Hird (*End of the Line*) and Chris Atkins (*Starsuckers*), BECTU Freelancers' Fair, June 11, 2010

"Ad-funded Content and Product Placement" workshop run by Claire Heys and Chantel Rickards), Indie Training Fund, January 27, 2011

Bazalgette, Peter, *Billion Dollar Game: How Three Men Risked it All and Changed the Face of Television* (London: Time Warner Books, 2005)

BBC Worldwide Catalogue, 2008

BBC Worldwide Catalogue: Science and History, 2007

Berman, R. and Flynn, M. vs. Johnson C, Appeal from the United States District Court for the Eastern District of Virginia, at Alexandria. T. S. Ellis, III, Senior District Judge (1:07-cv-00039-TSE-TRJ) 2008, 072154.U.pdf http://pacer.ca4.uscourts.gov (unpublished)

Browning, Beverly, *Perfect Phrases for Writing Grant Proposals* (New York: McGraw Hill, 2008)

Burnett, Mark, *Jump In! Even if You Don't Know How to Swim* (New York: Ballantine Books, 2005)

"Cactus Three announces the establishment of a new film finishing fund," Cactus Three press release, October 13, 2010

Channel 4 Britdoc Foundation, "*The End of the Line*: A social impact evaluation," 2011

Cinereach Grants and Awards: Fiscal Sponsors http://www.cinereach.org/grants/resources

Cinereach Grants and Awards: Funding and Support, http://www.cinereach.org/grants/resources/funding-support

Clarke, Cheryl A., *Storytelling for Grantseekers: A Guide to Creative Nonprofit Fundraising* (San Francisco: John Wiley & Sons, 2009)

Clarke, Cheryl A., and Fox, Susan P., *Grant Proposal Makeover: Transform Your Request From No to Yes* (San Francisco: John Wiley & Sons, 2007)

Davies, Adam P., and Wistreich, N., *The Film Finance Handbook—How to Fund Your Film* (London: Netribution, 2008)

Dean, Carole Lee, *The Art of Film Funding: Alternative Financing Concepts* (Studio City: Michael Wiese Productions, 2007)

Delves Broughton, Philip, "We're all killing off email," *Evening Standard*, January 17, 2011, p. 31

Donaton, Scott, *Madison and Vine: Why the Entertainment and Advertising Industries Must Converge to Survive* (New York: McGraw Hill, 2005)

Durman, Hilary, *Donor Unkown: Adventure in the Sperm Trade*, press pack, Redbird, 2010

Edelstyn, Dan, *How to Re-Establish a Vodka Empire*, proposal, Optimistic Productions, undated

—*How to Re-establish a Vodka Empire*, press pack, Optimistic Productions, 20011

EDN Financing Guide 2011: Documentaries, European Documentary Network, 2010

"Enterprise Investment Scheme," HM Revenue and Customs, http://www.hmrc.gov.uk/eis/index.htm

Fields, Jonathan, *Career Renegade: How to Make a Great Living Doing What You Love* (New York: Broadway Books, 2009)

Ferriss, Timothy, *The 4-Hour Work Week* (London: Vermilion, 2007)

"Fifty Ways of Funding" panel, BECTU, Freelancer's Fare, June 2010

Film Funding Club, http://magicmirror.com/

Film Tree Video by filmtree1, April 11, 2011, http://www.youtube.com/watch?v=nS4UmzQs_dw&feature=player_embedded

Finch, Brian, *How to Write a Business Plan* (London: Kogan Page, 2007)

"Funding your TV production in tougher times and making the most of your IP," Grant Thornton webinar, October, 2009, featuring Christine Corner, Peter Bazalgette, Louise Pederson and Justin Thomson-Glover, http://www.grant-thornton.co.uk/video/1_wmmulti.wmv, retrieved February 27, 2011

Galician, Mary-Lou (ed.), *Handbook of Product Placement in the Mass Media* (Binghamton, NY Best Business Books: 2006)

Glynne, Andy, *Documentaries ... And How to Make Them* (Hapenden: Kamera Books, 2008)

"Going It Alone" panel, University Centre, Hastings, February 19, 2011, featuring David Bond, Anna Godas, Chris Harris, Sarah Mosses, Luke Seomore and Joseph Bull

"Guidance for New Filmmakers—Make Your Film: Keep Your Friends" [PDF], BECTU, March 23, 2011, http://www.bectu.org.uk/advice-resources/library/955

Hayes, Floyd, "Floyd Hayes: How to Make a Viral Video," PSFK, December 15,

2010, http://www.psfk.com/2010/12/floyd-hayes-how-to-make-a-viral-video.html, retrieved March 6, 2011

How to Have a Successful Kickstarter Campaign workshop, Women Make Movies, New York, November 8, 2010, featuring Roddy Bogawa, Therese Shechter and Angela Tucker moderated by Tracie Holder

How to Re-establish a Vodka Empire press pack, Edelstyn, D., Powell, H., Optimistic Productions and Dartmouth Films, 2011

Inside CRM Editors, "The manager's cheat sheet: 101 common-sense rules for leaders," Inside CRM, http://www.insidecrm.com/features/Manager-Common-Sense-Rules-082207/, retrieved April 17, 2011

"Inside the Distributors," The Research Centre, 2005

"Jeremy tries to destroy a Toyota Hilux," part 1 (*Top Gear* series 3, episode 5), [video file], http://www.topgear.com/uk/videos/killing-a-toyota

Kapadia, Asif, "Asif Kapadia on *Senna*," uploaded by Empiremagazine, YouTube, June 6, 2011 [video], http://www.youtube.com/watch?v=dyKHNTwwsec

Lees, Nicola, *Greenlit: Developing Factual/Reality TV Ideas from Concept to Pitch* (London: Methuen Drama, 2010)

Lehu, Jean-Marc, *Branded Entertainment: Product Placement and Brand Strategy in the Entertainment Business* (London: Kogan Page, 2007)

Lemonade Movie, dir. Marc Colucci (Fighting Monk Inc., 2009)

Levison, Louise, *Filmmakers and Financing, Business Plans for Independents* (Focal Press, 2006)

Levitan, Peter, "Risk management in entertainment financing: do we know what we don't know?," Beverly Hills Bar Association Symposium on New Directions in Entertainment Financing, April 13, 2010

Maher, Kevin, "Is this the end of the line for documentary?," *The Times*, Saturday Review, September 18, 2010

Mansoor, Kat, *Here's Johnny* application to the Wellcome Trust, Animal Monday, November 26, 2005

MicroFilmmaker Magazine, http://microfilmmaker.com

Moore, Shuyler M., *The Biz: The Basic Business, Legal and Financial Aspects of the Film Industry*, 3rd edn (Los Angeles: Silman-James Press, 2007)

"Morgan Spurlock talks *The Greatest Movie Ever Sold*, Sundance, 2011," IndieWIRE, January 23, 2011, http://www.youtube.com/watch?v=ADt1hUITXKo, retrieved February 28, 2011

"Online Film Funding" seminar, Rio Cinema, Dalston, London, July 4, 2010, featuring Peter Broderick and Sandi DuBowski

Orosz, Joel, *The Insider's Guide to Grantmaking: How Foundations Find, Fund, and Manage Effective Programs* (San Francisco: Jossey-Bass Publishers, 2000)

"Production Financing Using EIS" workshop with Harry Hicks and Charles Lévêque, Harbottle & Lewis, London, July 20, 2011

"Quicksilver Films Information Memorandum," (London: Quicksilver Films, 2009)

"*River Flowing Westward* to tell story of global civilization," *Hurriet Daily News and Economic Review*, February 21, 2010 http://www.hurriyetdailynews.com/n.php?n=0220173125598-2010-02-21 retrieved January 16, 2011

Robinson, Esther, B., "Balancing risk and responsibility while making great films," *Filmmaker*, Winter 2010, http://www.filmmakermagazine.com/issues/winter2010/successful-filmmaker.php, retrieved January 23, 2011

Rose, Frank, *The Art of Immersion* (New York: W.W. Norton & Company, 2011)

—*Trailer Mechanics*, 2nd edn (New York: Magafilms, 2012)

—Trailer Mechanics Workshop, London, March 22, 2011

Search, Jess and McCarthy, Melissa, *Getting Your Documentary Funded and Distributed* (London: Shooting People, 2005)

Seers, David, "Government departments and ad funded programming," Central Office of Information, London, document received by email, March 3, 2011

"Show Me the Money: Alternative Funding—Branded Content" panel, Televisual Intelligent Factual Festival, London, June 30, 2010

"Show Me the Money: Courting International Co-production" panel, Televisual Intelligent Factual Festival, London, July 1, 2010

"Show Me the Money: Deficit Financing for Beginners" panel, Intelligent Factual Festival, London, July 1, 2010

Spitzmiller, Jilann, *Shakespeare Behind Bars* application to ITVS Open Call 2004, Philomath Films, April 30, 2004

Spurlock, Morgan, "The greatest TED Talk ever sold," April, 2011 [Video file], retrieved from http://www.ted.com/talks/morgan_spurlock_the_greatest_ted_talk_ever_sold.html

Square Eyes: Factual, BBC Worldwide, Issue 08, February, 2008

Stern, Caroline, "Women in Film and Television" masterclass, London, June 13, 2011

Steve Hewlett interview with Nick Price (MPG advertising agency) and Sally Quick (UKTV), *The Media Show*, BBC Radio 4, March 2, 2011

Televisual, Hard Cash: The Money and TV Issue, April, 2011

"The Crowdfunding Success Summit" online seminar, December 5, 2010, featuring Peter Broderick, Marc Rosenbush, Fernanda Rossi, Carole Dean, Danae Ringelmann, John Trigonis, Daphne Schmon, Robert Schmon, Jon Spira, Ingrid Kopp, Morris Warshawski, Greg Meyer, Emily James, www.crowdfundingsummit.com

"The Home Depot and Mark Burnett Productions Enter into Unique Broadcast Programming Partnership," Home Depot press release, February 1, 2005

"TV on a Shoestring" event, Thinkbox, London, February 17, 2011, featuring Lindsey Clay, Zoe Fuller, Nick Hurrell, Phil Springall, Julia Jordan, Ed Morris, Jeremy Rainbird, http://www.thinkboxlive.tv/

VanDeCarr, Paul, "The Prenups: What Filmmakers and Funders Should Talk About Before Tying the Knot," Active Voice Lab, 2009 [PDF], www.theprenups.org

Vehkalahti, Iikka, and Edkins, Don, *Steps by Steps* (Aukland Park, South Africa: Fanele, 2008)

Warren, Jarod, "Indie filmmaking guide: getting everything free!," The Movie Pool, February 23, 2011, http://www.themoviepool.com/on-filmmaking/item/809-indie-filmmaking-guide-getting-everything-free.html, retrieved February 23, 2011

Wynne, Paula, *Create a Successful Website: Easy Do It Yourself Steps to Online Success* (Lean Marketing Press, 2010)

Index